VRILOLOGY

VRILOGY

◆

THE SECRET SCIENCE OF THE ANCIENT ARYANS

Robert Blumetti

iUniverse, Inc.
New York Lincoln Shanghai

VRILOLOGY
THE SECRET SCIENCE OF THE ANCIENT ARYANS

Copyright © 2006, 2007 by Robert Blumetti

All rights reserved. No part of this book may be used or reproduced by any means, graphic, electronic, or mechanical, including photocopying, recording, taping or by any information storage retrieval system without the written permission of the publisher except in the case of brief quotations embodied in critical articles and reviews.

iUniverse books may be ordered through booksellers or by contacting:

iUniverse
2021 Pine Lake Road, Suite 100
Lincoln, NE 68512
www.iuniverse.com
1-800-Authors (1-800-288-4677)

Because of the dynamic nature of the Internet, any Web addresses or links contained in this book may have changed since publication and may no longer be valid.

The views expressed in this work are solely those of the author and do not necessarily reflect the views of the publisher, and the publisher hereby disclaims any responsibility for them.

ISBN: 978-0-595-38504-1 (pbk)
ISBN: 978-0-595-82885-2 (ebk)

Printed in the United States of America

I would like to dedicate this book to the following people, without whom I could not have been inspired to write it: Bill, Carol, Dave, Marek, Pattie, Phil, Steve, Lanquedoc and Victor.

I would like to extend a special thanks to Dr. Rand Waddingham and his lovely wife, Katherine, for all their hard work in editing and proofreading the manuscript.

Contents

INTRODUCTION REBIRTH: A JOYOUS JOURNEY 1

Part I   THE TURNING OF THE WHEEL

THE TURNING OF THE AGES. 7
OUR PLACE IN THE ORDER OF THINGS 9
RELIGION AND THE FOLK SOUL. 13
THE ODIN CONSCIOUSNESS 21
THE WYRD AND YOUR JOURNEY 23
BALDER'S RETURN 27

Part II   THE LOST HERITAGE

MADAME BLAVATSKY AND THE SECRET DOCTRINE 33
ULTIMA THULE 38
ATLANTIS. 43
THE ANCIENT ARYANS—THE TRUE ATLANTEANS 48
THE DESTRUCTION OF ARYAN ATLANTIS 55
THE GREAT BLACK SEA FLOOD 58
THE INDO-EUROPEANS: THE ATLANTEAN REFUGEES 65
ZOROASTER 71
MANICHAEISM. 76

DUALISM 78
THE TOCHARIANS 80
TIBET 85
THE DRUIDS 90
THE GNOSTICS 94
THE CATHARS 100
THE HOLY GRAIL IS THE HOLY BLOOD OF BALDER 109
THE PHOENIX AND THE ARYAN SUN GODS 114
JESUS CHRIST AND CHRISTIANITY 119
THE KABBALA 130

Part III   *VRILOGY—THE LOST SCIENCE OF THE VRIL*

USING THE RUNES TO HARNESS THE POWER OF THE
   VRIL 137
WHAT IS THE VRIL? 146
VRILOLOGY—THE SCIENCE OF THE FOLK FAITH 153
A QUICK LESSON ON HOW TO USE VRILOLOGY 167
THE VRIL IN THE HUMAN BODY 187
VRIL AND THE BIFROST GLAND 194
THE VRIL AND OUR SIXTH SENSE 198
THE VRIL AND YOUR HEALTH 201
THE PSYCHIC USE OF THE VRIL 216
GALDOR SCIENCE 220
SEITHER SCIENCE 227
THE VRIL SOCIETY AND FREE ENERGY 231

Part IV   THE FOLK FAITH

PRIESTLY ORDER OF THE FOLK FAITH 247
COMMUNICATING WITH THE GODS 256
LOVE AND HATE 259
SEVEN DEADLY SINS? 263
THE DEVIL AND HELL 268
LOVE LIFE! 271
THE NORNS AND OUR DESTINY 274
RECIPROCITY 280
THANKSGIVING 283
LIFE AFTER DEATH 285
THE INDIVIDUAL AND COLLECTIVE SOUL 288
THE LIFE YOU LEAD, WILL ECHOS IN ETERNITY! 293
WE ARE A LIGHT AGAINST THE APPROACHING
   DARKNESS 297
WORKING TOWARD THE NEW AGE OF GIMLI 301

INTRODUCTION
REBIRTH: A JOYOUS JOURNEY

Western Civilization has lost its spirituality, and Christianity has lost the European spiritual foundation upon which it was built. As it spread throughout the Third World during the 20th century, it has become a secular, hollow shield. This diversification of Christianity has caused the death of its soul, which was rooted in the old European pagan religions. Its European ethos has died, replaced by a movement seeking a universal creed of "social justice." As Christianity, both Protestant and Catholic, has become more multicultural and multiracial, it has incorporated the pagan religious beliefs and customs of the various races and nations of the Third World, causing a schism to appear that has resulted in the fractionalization and transformation of Christianity. The result so far, has been the decline of Christianity in Europe and North America. While small militant groups of Europeans and North Americans are returning to a highly traditional variation of Christianity, in an attempt to turn back the march of history toward a time when Christianity was a vibrant and aggressive expression of the will of European man, their numbers are insignificant. The election of Pope Benedict XVI is an attempt to turn back the tide of history and restore Christianity in Europe. Alas these attempts are futile, for European man has lost contact with the Gods who created their race, civilization and culture, and were incorporated into the essence of Christianity two thousand years ago.

The result of the loss of Europe's soul, has been a marked decrease in the birth rate. This decline in the birth rate has been accompanied by a loss of the will to resist the growing tide of foreign cultures that threatens to sweep over the West and drown its people in a tidal wave of alien humanity, alien culture, alien spirituality and alien civilization that will never tolerate European Civilization. A Militant and primitive manifestation of Islam threatens to destroy all civilization and plunged the world into another dark age. The Chinese are growing in strength. Their economy is being fed by the greed and misguidedness of the insatiable lust for quick profit by Western businessmen, who in the name of turning a fast buck are willing to sell out their country, civilization and race. The population of the United States is growing by leaps and bounds due to unrestricted immigration from the Third World. This irreversible surge of humanity has already transformed the Catholic Church in North America, and is doing the same to the Protestant churches. The infrastructures of North America have already begun a slow, but assured, collapse under the rapidly increasing pressure from the increase in population growth. Europe is now faced with a growing militant Muslim movement that seeks nothing less than the destruction of Western, Christian, European civilization and culture, and arrogantly boasts of its eventual triumph over Europe.

With the growing threat of Third World ascendency and the decline of the West, we can continue to look forward to a loss of spirituality, a gutting of the West's economic superiority, a continued invasion of the West by a flood of Third World humanity, and the growing racial and cultural diversity and Balkanization of Europe and North America. These conditions make manifest increasing violence, rivalry, conflicts and warfare among the many different religious and ethnic groups that are overwhelming Western Civilization, causing a collapse of its infrastructure, and making technology the reserve of a very small minority of a very wealthy and powerful few.

The twenty-first century will be a century of decline and collapse in the West, as immigration from the Third World continues unabated. The pressure from such a massive and dramatic increase in population unable to assimilate into the West will not only fractionalize the West, but the strains on its infrastructure will have other terrible affects as well. Systems of communication, transportation, housing, farming, health care, education, manufacturing, government, supply and distribution, and security will all suffer from corruption and disrepair. The inability of various populations to work together, cultural, religious and racial rivalries that will be imported from the Third World, and the lack of communication among a growing population speaking numerous languages, will all assure the growing unrest and chaos that are inevitable. The quality of humanity will decline and the most able and intelligent will cease to reproduce, while we will see huge families among those at the lowest end of the bell curve. The welfare system will grow until it cannot be supported, causing a crash in its services. The same crash will occur with the Social Security system.

Europe will face its greatest threat from the growing population of Muslims within their midst. The Islamic World is growing militantly aggressive, just as the West is suffering a spiritual and physical decline. Militant Muslims will try and forcibly convert Europe to Islam. In North America, the growing tide of Latinos, especially from Mexico, will cause the breakup of the United States. As the number of people belonging to the Third World cultures increases within the United States, its European population will rapidly decline to a small minority. By 2020 the influence of this Hispanic population alone will transform the government of the United States. Elected officials will depend on appealing to the growing Third World population, passing legislation favorable to their interest. Some time between 2020 and 2030, all restrictions on immigration will be eliminated. Within ten years after this become law, more than one hundred million people will flood into the United States from Latin America, Africa, the Middle East and Asia. By 2050 the population of the United States and Canada, will be more than 600 million. This is when the infrastructure will suffer a complete collapse, and the ecology of the continent will suffer from over population. Industry, communication, transportation, housing, medical care, agriculture and security will all disappear as North America descends into a new dark age of barbarism, interracial and intercultural wars and conflicts.

It is with this hard reality of a new dark age staring us in the face that we must bolster ourselves for the coming Fimbul, the Great Winter, that will herald a new Ragnarok. We will have to face and accept the reality that the world of "Father knows best" that we grew up in, no longer exists, and that the road ahead is to be one froth with conflict and struggle for survival. We will also have to accept the reality that democracy is dead. As the population continues to grow and diversify, the establishments in Europe and North America will grow more and more authoritarian in a vain attempt to maintain their control over their societies. But just as surely as the Roman Empire, fifteen hundred years ago, and the Soviet Union, a few decades ago, collapsed, so too will the governments of North America and Europe disintegrate. Unless some miracle occurs to halt the advance of history, we must prepare ourselves for the world that is awaiting us and our children.

But we can travel along the path that history has paved for the world with a faith that there is hope at the end of the journey. For the Gods that created us have not abandoned us, even if our people have abandoned them. For Odin has sacrificed his most beloved son, Balder, so that we as a people, can still survive, and will one day, rebuild a most glorious civilization, unlike anything that is known to us today. In my previous book, *The Book of Balder Rising*, I laid out the spiritual foundation for this new civilization. In this book, I hope to begin the process of building a fortress that will stand and survive the coming great deluge that will sweep over our world in the twenty-first century.

PART I
THE TURNING OF THE WHEEL

THE TURNING OF THE AGES

The old order is in advanced decay. The world as we know it is rapidly falling apart. The West is in a state of decline and the forces of darkness are rapidly spreading across the world.

We stand between two ages—the wheel turns. The previous age is fading into the past as Loki is rallying the forces of destruction to assault the old order, plunging the world into chaos. The darkness and oppression of the great winter, Fimbul, is quickly overtaking the ordered world of the previous age. We are entering a time of the Giants, when their chaos will rule over mankind, shattering the institutions, traditions and nations that gave meaning and hope to our people and ancestors. We are entering a new dark age—the Age of Fimbulvetr.

The previous age was one in which the Gods of our ancestors spoke to us through the facade of an alien creed. They existed in a semi-comatose state, because we had adopted a facade between us and them. That facade was the alien creed of Christianity. But now that Christianity is fading, and the old Gods are beginning to awaken once more, they are readying themselves to throw off the yoke of the foreign garb of a false identity, and speak to us once more in their true form. Our people have passed through two ages. In the first, they were born but were scattered and separated into different nations, ethnic groups and even civilizations. The Gods of our ancestors soon took on different names and were worshiped in various ways depending on the environment in which they chose to settle. Thus, the old Gods took on many different guises and names. Our ancestors tried to give order to the many different interpretations of their Gods, but eventually the confusion grew worse, until finally, a creed completely alien won out over this confusion of faiths. Because they were weakened and divided, they succumbed to the alien creed.

But the Life Force of the Gods that gave birth to our people could not be denied, and soon the alien creed was transformed by the spirit of the old Gods. The Gods that gave birth to us still spoke to us, but instead of speaking to us in a confused matter, through various identities, they now spoke to us through a single, but alien identity. But even this would not last, and that alien creed is now fading away. We are no longer divided into various nations and tribes. Within America, we have come together as one people. Even in Europe, there is a coming together of the many different nations and nationalities of our Folk. A time of unification is dawning and the opportunity for the Gods of our ancestors to speak to us once more in their true form, is upon us. And this time, they will speak with one voice to all our people.

But there are great dangers ahead. The turning of the ages, when one age dies and another is born, is always a dangerous time. Chaos rules and within the confusion, Loki has the opportunity to lead our people astray. If he is successful, his father, Sutur, will lay waste to everything, and fearfully, the devastation could be so great that we might never rise again. If that is so, the Gods will not return and there will be no rebirth, and hence the bright light of enlightened humanity will never again bless this world with the wonders capable of being manifested through the soul of our Folk. Darkness will rule and the gifts given to us in the beginning of time will be lost, and humanity will revert back to the level of the beast that roams the wilderness.

But hope still burns bright, and we have only to fan its flames to transform it into a beacon that will serve as a path to blaze through the darkness and unleash the regenerative powers of Balder. For in the Netherworld, Balder and his dear wife, Nanna, are preparing to return. They can see the light which has broken through the roof of Hel, like a translucent staircase for them to ascend back to the world of the living. All that awaits their return is our call—our call for them to return and give new life to the old Gods and Goddesses, so that we might re-forge those bonds that once united mortal with immortal, and thus, herald in the new Golden Age of Gimli.

OUR PLACE IN THE ORDER OF THINGS

The three monotheistic religions see God as someone with a master plan, who has laid down the law and demand that everyone obey this law, and if they don't, they will suffer the most excruciating pain for all eternity. Ironically, everyone who happens to be unfortunate enough to be born in a part of the world that has never heard his law is just as damned as those who heard it and rejected it. Thus, their God, who is suppose to be all-knowing and infallible, has deliberately created billions of people whom he has damned to Hell. He is all-knowing and infallible—so that means he knew that billions of people would never have the chance to be saved, and that billions more would choose to reject his law, and thus would be condemned after death. Why? Why would a God do such a thing? Well, the followers of monotheism like to say, "We can never know what God does, or why he does it, but we have got to have faith." This is poor comfort for those billions burning in Hell. Of course, that doesn't concern those who know that they are saved!

Pagans do not believe in a God who is concerned with suffering and pain. We don't see God as a great judge, passing judgement on everyone, condemning billions to eternal suffering. We don't fear a God or his wrath. We know that a God does not inflict pain and suffering on us. We know that the terrible things that happen to us are not the "Will of God." The monotheistic God is a God with a plan, and we are all suppose to be a part of his plan—whatever it may be? He is supposed to have created us so that he can torture us, and torment us with temptation. He created the Devil to tempt us away from him and make us weak so that the great majority of us will fall victim to the wily ways of Satan. He then deliberately makes our lives a living Hell by sending earthquakes, tornadoes, fires, floods, hurricanes, disease, and storms our way, to test our faith, all the while killing thousands, even millions in wars and plagues, and our clergy try to reassure us that it's all part of "God's will" and that the fallen are "in his hands." But if God is in complete control of the universe, why does he send such horror to torment us? Is this the behavior of a truly loving and merciful God?

For us, the Gods, by whatever name you refer to them as, are a balancing force in the universe. They represent the natural laws of science that act as a balancing factor in nature to counter the chaotic and destructive forces that are represented by the Giants. They are far too powerful a force to be concerned with the pain, suffering, and salvation, of every little individual on the face of the earth. But this does not mean we cannot tap into their power to help us in our lives. It does not mean that we are completely disconnected from the power that is the Gods, which maintains order in the universe, that can help us succeed in everything that we do.

We pagans, followers of the Folk Faith, realize that the universe is ruled by the physical laws of science, and that the actions and reactions of nature, are the opposing forces of chaos (the Giants) and order (the Gods). We were not created out of dirt to be tested and judged. We were created from the same Life Force that holds the universe together, the same Life Force that is the essence of the Gods. We are a part of the life-changing, evolutionary process that holds the universe together. This Life Force keeps the planets rotating around the sun, and the sun along with billions of other stars, rotating around the center of the galaxy, and propels the galaxy, and billions of other galaxies, through the vast, limitless void of space. This means we are part of nature and ruled by the same laws of nature that governs all living things on this planet, and on all other worlds. Because we are part of nature, the action-reaction of order and chaos that governs the universe, all our actions contribute to one or the other. By the way we live our lives, and the decisions we make every minute of the day, we either contribute to the chaotic, destructive forces that are the Giants, or, we contribute to the ordered forces that are the Gods. There is no sin or breaking of commandments, but the simple fact that the environment that surrounds us, the society we live in, the way people interact with each other and treat each other, are all determined by the way we act. If our actions are destructive, we will live within a chaotic destructive society, but if we live by the golden rule, we will live in a healthy, orderly and progressive society.

The Gods have set up the rules by which the universe works. If we adjust our lives according to those rules, we will benefit from them and eventually, we, both individually and collectively as a people, will become great. Over time, generations from now, our children will become Godlike.

This is a truth that we must understand. We are governed not by commandments, by which we will be judged. The only rule we should live by is the simple golden rule of treating people in the same way that we want them to treat us. At the same time, we must recognize that if others treat us badly, we will not tolerate it. Thus, we hate no one, and seek to do harm toward no one, but we are not pacifists, for pacifism is permitting others to dominate or harm you. We do not sit around praying for God to intervene for us, but we do seek to forge bonds with our Gods so that we can tap into the Life Force that we share with them to help us in our actions, and give us the power to succeed. We do not sit back and accept fate without doing anything about it. We know that we must act in a productive way if we are to be successful in life, in all things that we do. We know that we can only be successful by positive thinking, backed up by positive action.

We do not believe in sin, because we have no commandments to break. We understand that there are right and wrong actions, and when we make mistakes we don't pray for forgiveness. Instead, we accept the fact that we are not perfect and recognize that we did wrong and make a promise to ourselves and our loved ones to try not to do it again. We know that mistakes are part of life and we can learn from them and grow, becoming a better people by trying not to repeat them. Thus, while we should own up to our mistakes, and when necessary, make amends for the wrongs that we might do, we should not feel guilt or shame, especially if we truly recognize the wrong that we did. In fact, we should even talk about our mistakes as lessons, especially to our children and young people, as examples of what not to do if they want to lead happy and successful lives. We all know that it is often better to confess our mistakes than to keep them bottled up inside, permitting them to fester and eat away at our minds and souls with guilt and shame.

One problem with the monotheists is that they are intolerant of anyone who disagrees with them. Monotheists claim that anyone who disagrees with them is condemned. Even among themselves, they cannot agree and have a long history of hating each other, waging wars against each other and persecuting each other. Christians have always considered Jews the children of the Devil because they rejected Christ, and Jews consider anyone who does not belong to the chosen people, inferior. Even within Judaism and Christianity there is disagreement. Orthodox Jews disagree with Conservative Jews and both disagree with Reform Jews, and then of course, there are the Hasidic Jews and other sects which don't agree. The Christians are even more divided. Catholics, Protestants and Orthodox Christians all disagree. Catholics believe all Christians who do not belong to the Catholic Church are condemned to burn in Hell. Orthodox Christians believe the same about everyone who does not belong to the Orthodox Church. They are all condemned to burn in Hell. Protestants consider both Orthodox and Catholics to be heathens and "pagans." Then there are the Muslims, who are also divided and war among themselves. They consider everyone else heathens who can be killed, enslaved, raped, and tortured with impunity because they do not believe in Allah. Of course, all of this is insane.

As pagans we do not hate any other faith, even the monotheistic religions. We respect all religious beliefs. Even if we disagree with the interpretation, we respect the religiosity. Most of the people who practice these faiths are basically good, or seek to do good, but their faiths are damaging. Most people want to lead good lives. We respect anyone, no matter what they believe, who want to lead good lives. The ancient Romans made it a custom of trying to associate their Gods with the Gods worshiped by other people. There were certain practices that the Romans abhorred, such as human sacrifice and homosexuality, but as for the actual Gods that other people worshiped, the Romans tolerated and even adopted them into their own pantheon. As a pagan, I have no problem with saying a prayer to Jesus, because I know that the spiritual essence of the God, Jesus, that is worshiped, is essentially a God of peace, and I can associate Jesus with Balder or any other God of peace.

RELIGION AND THE FOLK SOUL

Religions flow from the soul of a particular people, like rivers from a spring. They are the expression of the soul of the race that gives birth to them. They are the expression of a particular people's spirituality, and flourish within the genetic landscape of that people, and kindred folk, who gave expression and form to the spirituality. Religions are manifestation of the way a people or race view the universe and the local environment they live within, and give birth to them as a nation. This is true of all the pagan religions as well as the universalist, monotheistic religions.

Christianity originated as a breakaway Jewish cult based on the teachings of the Essence-cult leader whom we call Jesus. He preached a heretical variation of Judaism that caused the Jewish leaders to goad the Roman leaders to condemn him to death for his heresy. But Christianity did not die with Jesus for several reasons. His followers claimed that Jesus was divine, the son of God and that he rose from the dead. They were able to do this by incorporating the spiritual beliefs of the many different pagan religions that existed in the Classical world. The idea of virgin birth through impregnation by a God was the foundation of both the Roman state and religion. Romulus, the founder of Rome, was born of a Vestal Virgin, who was impregnated by Mars, the God of War. There were many other religions during the classical period that claimed a demigod was born of a human female and fathered by a God. Hercules is just one example. Jesus was born of a God and rose from the dead, just like Balder and many others. The early followers of Jesus kept alive their movement, by incorporating pagan ideas and belief systems into their "Jewish cult," thus transforming their belief system into a non-Jewish religion. At first, the cult seemed destined to remain insignificant and obscure, existing within the peripheral lunatic-fringe of Jewish society, that is, until a Jew, who possessed Roman citizenship, converted to the new religion.

Saint Paul had converted after claiming he had a vision in which Jesus spoke to him and told him to go out and convert the pagans to Christianity. I will not go into the entire story of Paul's life and mission, but it is important to make the point that Paul tirelessly preached among the mostly Greek, Celtic, and Roman populations of the Roman Empire. During his lifetime and afterwards his followers began incorporating pagan ideals and belief systems into the Jesus cult, creating the image of Jesus that has come down to us today, and giving birth to a paganized version of Christianity. This was in opposition to the followers of Saint Peter, who wished to preserve the distinctively Jewish character of Christianity. One example is the issue of baptism verus circumcision. The latter custom was a common tradition among different Semitic peoples, but considered a barbaric and abhorrent practice by the Romans and Greeks. The Jewish followers of Saint Peters wanted to make circumcision a fundamental principle, just as it is within the Jewish religion, for anyone seeking to convert to Christianity. Paul knew that would sound the death-knell of Christianity. If Christianity was ever to spread among the non-Jewish population, he had to replace the custom with the common pagan practice of baptism, as a means of conversion. The entire story of John the Baptist was probably manufactured by Paul and his followers, to justify the practice and its replacement of circumcision.

As Christianity spread throughout the Roman Empire during the next, several hundred years, it continued to be transformed by paganism. Even the date of Jesus' birth, December 25, was borrowed from the religion that worshiped the pagan Indo-European God, Mithras, who was born in human form on that date. Many pagan ideas were incorporated into Christianity, including the idea of the Holy Trinity, and the Mother-Goddess worship of Mary, the image of Jehovah, which was taken from the face of the great statue of Zeus in his temple, to adopting the name of the head of the Roman pagan religion as the head of Christianity, *Ponteix Maximus*, which helped to transform Christianity into a religion palatable to the racial soul of the Roman people. By the time of Emperor Constantine, Christianity had become a religion that was more pagan than Semitic.

But as the Roman Empire divided politically and culturally, into two halves—the Latin West and the Greek East—so did the spirituality of Christianity. The western half of the Roman Empire was culturally and racially Roman/Celtic/Germanic, while the eastern half was culturally and racially Greek/Oriental/Egyptian. The former was more racially unified, as the Romans, Celts and Germans were all Indo-European peoples, sharing a similar spirituality and ancestry that once inhabited Europe thousands of years in the past. The religions they worshiped and the Gods they celebrated, were really the same Gods that their ancestors worshiped, and thus the spirituality they instilled within the new Christian religion was pure and vibrant and strong enough to survive the collapse of the political order when it came in 476 A.D. It was different in the east.

In the eastern half of the Roman Empire, there was a greater mixing of peoples, cultures and religions that were fundamentally different. The form of Christianity that evolved in eastern Europe is often referred to as Greek or Orthodox Christianity, was more Oriental, as opposed to the Occidental form of Christianity that appeared in the western half of the Roman Empire. Thus, its spirituality was not as strong and it never had the life-vibrance or expansion that Roman Christianity had. Even after the political collapse of the Western Roman Empire, Roman Christianity not only survived, but continued to expand into regions that were never under the control of Rome. Soon, Germany, Scotland and Ireland were all converted, and eventually, in the next five to six hundred years, Scandinavia, Poland, Hungary, the Baltic States, and parts of the Balkans were converted in turn. The story of Greek or Orthodox Christianity was very different.

Greek or Orthodox Christianity only survived because the political structure of the Eastern Roman Empire survived. Its political authority was more Oriental and Semitic, and thus, Orthodox Christianity never expanded, and in the next five hundred years it actually shrank as the political boundaries of the Eastern Roman Empire, or as it came to be referred to as, the Byzantine Empire shrank. Eventually, the Byzantine Empire was reduced to a third-rate power and Orthodox Christianity all but collapsed. It only survived because it was eventually adopted by the Russian Slavs to the north. After the last remnants of Constantinople fell to Islam in 1453, Orthodoxy was reborn as a purely Slavic or Russian religion, and thus was instilled within a new European racial spirituality.

The rise and growth in power and strength of Western Christianity, and the decline and withdrawal of Eastern Christianity before the rise and advancement of Islam, are reflected by the zeal and determination of Western Christianity, which was purely European. Thus it was Western Christianity which was able to halt the advancement of Islam and eventually turn back the Semitic tide, culminating in crusades in Spain, Sicily, in the Holy Lands and eventually the exploration and conversion of North and South America. In the east, Byzantium, which was a unified state, fell, and the Muslims burst into the Balkans and continued to threaten Europe right into the 17th century, but they were eventually halted and turned back by Western Christians. Orthodox Christianity survived because its center of spirituality was transferred from Greece to Moscow. The Russian/Slavic European soul gave it new life and prevented it from completely becoming extinct. The new Russian state prevented the Turks from extinguishing Orthodox Christianity within its empire by applying force and pressure. Unlike Western Christianity, which was totally European, both racially and spiritually, it never became a great expanding religion. Even after the Russians had crossed the length of Asia, the Orthodox Church never sent armies of missionaries to try and convert the peoples of China, India, or even those non-Christians within the Russian Empire.

Islam originated deep within the Arabian Peninsula. Its spirituality reflected the soul of the Semitic Arabic people. When it burst upon the stage of history, it swept aside the declining power of Orthodox Christianity, but was eventually stopped by Western Christianity, in Western Europe. Islam remained a powerful force, expanding into Central Asia and India, and eventually reaching as far east as present day Indonesia. But Islam soon reached its apex, as it overran the confines of its Semitic base. The Semitic Arabic people migrated and settled throughout North Africa and Central Asia, and even moved into Spain. But over the passing centuries, the Semitic population assimilated and disappeared within large sections of the Islamic world. In places like Indonesia, India, Central Asia, Iran and Spain, where the Semites either remained a tiny minority or disappeared entirely through intermarriage, Islam eventually retreated or was transformed. In Iran, where the mixed population was not Semitic, Shiite Islam was born and spread to other regions, while most of the Semitic world remained loyal to Sunni Islam. Other divisions also rose in India, in Lebanon and North Africa, reflecting the different ethnic divisions within the world that Islam conquered.

Islam remained vibrant and expansionist for centuries, but its height had passed. Unable to expand into China and Western Europe, it continued to expand against the declining power of Orthodox Christianity, until the center of Orthodox Christianity was transferred to the young, vibrant Russian nation. Islam eventually began a period of withdrawal and decline before the advancement of Western European Christianity.

From 1 A.D. to 500 A.D., Christianity split into Roman and Orthodox Christianity, reflecting the split between the Latin/Celtic/Germanic Western Roman Empire and the Greek/Oriental/Egyptian Eastern Roman Empire. Because the former was racially and spiritually more homogenous, Western Christianity evolved into a new and vibrant spirituality. This was due to the incorporation of European pagan spirituality that transformed Western Christianity. But Orthodox Christianity remained spiritually divided, a mixture between Greek/Hellenism and the more Semitic and Egyptian spiritualities, which prevented the Orthodox Church from becoming a stronger force than the political authority, and thus it remained subservient to the Emperor. In the West, the political authority declined and disintegrated, as the Western Church continued to grow stronger and outlived the Western Roman Empire's secular authority.

From 500 A.D. and 1000 A.D., the Western Church continued to grow stronger and was responsible for the resurrection of the secular authority of the Roman State. But the Church remained the dominate power until 1500 A.D., while in the East, the Orthodox Church remained subservient to the secular authority of the Byzantine state. Orthodox Christianity declined before the expansion of Islam and its only expansion was into the Russian Kiev Empire, which remained weak until after the decline and eventual fall, of the authority of the Orthodox Church (1000–1500 A.D.).

Between 1000 A.D. and 1500 A.D., Western Christianity became a powerful force, which continued to drive the Muslims back from the Iberian Peninsula, Sicily and the Holy Lands during the Crusades, and even challenged its hold over North Africa. The spirit of Western Christianity was purely European (Latin/Celtic/German/Slavic). It had incorporated the essence of European paganism into it, creating a new European religion, motivated by the soul of Europe. This culminated in the expansion of Western Christianity throughout the world.

It was during the decline and fall of the Orthodox Church that Orthodox Christianity was able to transplant its center of spirituality to the purely European Russian Empire and move its center from Constantinople to Moscow. Afterwards, Orthodox Christianity experienced a minor resurgence with the rise of the Russian Empire (1500 to 1900 A.D.). Though the Muslims conquered the Balkans, they could not completely wipe out Orthodox Christianity among the peoples of Greece and the Balkans, because of the transfer of the center of Orthodox spirituality outside of the authority of the Islamic World, to Russia.

Between 1500 A.D. and 2000 A.D., Western Europe began expanding beyond its borders, spreading Western Christianity throughout the world. North and South America was converted in the sixteenth and seventeenth centuries, followed by Africa and Asia in the eighteenth and nineteenth centuries. However, even as Western Christianity was spreading throughout the world, the seeds of its own destruction were taking root. This was initially heralded by the schism that resulted from the Protestant Reformation. The next blow was the conversion of non-Europeans to Christianity.

In the 16th century, the Protestant Reformation began with Martin Luther. In the next hundred and fifty years, Europe was rocked with one religious war after another, culminating in the disastrous Thirty Years' War that almost depopulated central Europe. The split in Western Christianity caused the Protestants to abandon the old Christianized pagan ceremonies, customs and traditions that had been incorporated into Christianity more than a thousand years earlier, and turn toward the Old Testament, thus becoming more Semitic and less European.

Since then, Christianity has become progressively more secularized. In the twentieth century, even Catholicism underwent a secularization after Vatican Two. The result has been a steady decline in Christianity throughout the Western World, and especially in the West's homeland, Europe. This trend was followed by a second—the "browning" of Christianity.

Beginning with the conquest of South and North America, Western Christianity began converting non-Europeans to their faith. Both Protestant and Catholic Churches have spent a great deal of time and resources in spreading the Christian faith to Africans, Asians and American aborigines. As a result, in the twenty-first century, about 80 percent of all Christians are of non-European ancestry. This has caused tremors throughout the Christian world. The European paganization that took place two thousand years ago, when Christianity was first brought to Europe, has been undone in the last five hundred years, beginning with the incorporation of customs, traditions and rituals of the pagan religions of the American aborigines, into the Christian Churches of South and Central America. This same process is now taking place in Africa and Asia, as hundreds of millions of Africans and Asians have converted to Christianity. The result is new spiritual chasms appearing in Christianity. Even within the "unified" or "universal" Catholic Church, there are divisions appearing, as the Church in Africa is becoming distinctively Africam, while the Church in India is becoming distinctively Indian. The same is true of the Catholic Church in every part of the world, and eventually they will have nothing in common with each other. The end result will be its collapse into separate churches, while in the European homeland of Christianity, both the Catholic and Protestant Churches have declined to the point that only about 20 percent of Europeans today, still consider themselves Christians, most of them are over fifty-years-old, and only about1 percent claim that they go to church every Sunday.

In the United States, the Christian Churches have both declined and resisted decline at the same time. If this seems confusing, let me explain. Among the European-American population in the United States, Christianity has been declining in importance for the last fifty years. But at the same time, the churches have been replacing their declining constituencies with immigrants from the Third World. Today, the membership of the Catholic Church in the United States in more than 50 percent non-White. The same is rapidly happening to the Protestant Churches. Even the Mormon Church, with its high birthrate among its original all-White membership, has become about 50 percent non-White, as it has conducted a rigorous campaign of conversion among Third World populations.

As the constituency of the Christian Churches become more and more diluted in a diversity of races, nationalities and cultures, the original Folk Soul of Europe has lost its spiritual hold over Christianity, thus weakening its spirituality. Our people have turned away from what has become an alien religion. They no longer find a spiritual solidarity within the Christian Churches. They have begun searching for a new spirituality, and many have turned to Eastern and other exotic cults. Still others have sought to try and resurrect the old spirituality, which once existed within the Christian Churches. Many Protestants have turned to an evangelical form of Christianity, in hope of recapturing that lost spirituality. The same has been true for Catholics. Many have turned to Churches that have resurrected pre-Vatican Two customs, rituals and the all-Latin Mass. But their efforts are too little, too late, and cannot reverse the tide of diversity and multicutluralism that is transforming every aspect of Western Civilization. The poison has seeped too deep into the institutions. Our people have lost contact with the Gods of their ancestors. Even though the bonds they shared with them were through a Christian filter, it was enough to ensure their spiritual vitality. Today those bonds have been cut and our people are adrift.

Today, Islam is experiencing a revival. It is partially due to the vacuum that has been created within the spiritual and moral decline of the West. Islam was born of the Semitic Folk Soul. It conquered a large section of the old world, passing beyond the ethnic and geographic boundaries of the Semitic homeland. Non-Semitic populations were conquered and many, though not all, were forced to convert to Islam. This diluted the spiritual power of Islam, which has begun a long decline. This decline was accelerated after another non-Semitic group of people, the Turks, invaded the Middle East and converted to Islam. They were a fierce, brave and determined race of nomadic warriors from the steppes of Asia. The Turks established a great empire that was centered in the territory of the old Byzantine Empire, and stretch west to include all of North Africa (except for Morocco), the Sudan, Arabia, parts of Persia, the Balkans right up to the gates of Vienna, the northern coast of the Black Sea and the Caucasus. But the Turks were not Semites and their soul was alien to the spirit of Islam. Thus, as soon as the Turks established their great empire, decay and decline rapidly set in, and the Ottoman Empire lingered on for four hundred years, only because of the rivalry of the European powers which actually fought to prevent any single nation from conquering the Turks, and thus upsetting the balance of power in Europe.

Turkish domination of the Islamic world helped to smother the spirit of Islam. The alien race and its alien Folk Soul caused the Islamic world to remain weak and divided. Eventually, the European powers carved up the Turkish

Empire and divided the Islamic world among themselves as part of their colonial empires. But with the decline and fall of Europe and the Turkish Empire, Islam has been able to reassert is spiritual identity. The Semitic Folk Soul has been unleashed and Islam is now a great force for change. Unfortunately that change is destructive. It has been unleashed by the Loki effect that has plunged the West into a state of helplessness, due to its domination by the Hodur effect—blind ignorance. Thus, the rise of Islam and especially Islamic terrorism and militancy, is part of the horde led by Loki in his assault on Asgard. The Loki effect caused weakness within the West, by striking the leaders of the West with ignorance about the true nature of the world, blinding them to the threats that the West face. Loki is now marshaling the forces of chaos and destruction to assault the gates of Asgard. We are now suffering through the great winter, the Age of Fimbul. Soon the forces of darkness will cancel out those of the light, and a new age of darkness and barbarism that will reign supreme. There is still hope that our people will survive the coming conflict and darkness, but to do so, we must turn to Balder. For only through Balder can we survive, and begin the task of rebuilding a new civilization, heralding in a new age—the Age of Gimli.

THE ODIN CONSCIOUSNESS

"In reality, only a change in the attitude of the individual can bring about a renewal in the spirit of the nations," so wrote Carl Gustav Jung. Jung understood that for a people to change, individuals must change first. I wrote the Book of Balder Rising because, if our people are to survive the coming collapse of the old order (Western Civilization) we have got to begin to change the spirit of our people. By changing the spirit of our people, I am referring to unleashing the essence of the Gods which lie dormant within each and every one of us. The Gods and Goddesses are asleep within our very DNA. They are waiting to be called back and once again forge a new bond between mortal and immortal. This process is known as Balder Rising. To accomplish, we must begin with the individual.

This sleeping essence of the Gods that lies dormant within each of us, is the Odin Consciousness. This Odin Consciousness manifest itself in the mythological symbols, folk tales and legends of our Folk. We can tap into these images, which resides deep within the subconscious, and release their power to transform us. They govern the religious, artistic, philosophical, heroic, and idealistic impulses that provide the traditional archetypes, with which we, as a race, nation or Folk, express ourselves as a people. These instruments build our culture and civilization. Some might refer to this as the racial memory, and we as both individuals and collectively as a people, can respond to these archetypes. These archetypes can initiate a revitalization of the soul and the will on both the individual and collective levels. Modern examples of this phenomenon are the *Star Wars* movies.

When the first *Star Wars* movie was released, millions of our people responded to the archetypical symbolism in the movie without thinking. The themes in the movie, which were Arthurian, Western, and Manichaean, acted like a key, unlocking a deep response to those heroic ideals that we all hold dear as a people. The average person did not consciously see the connection to Arthurian legends, or Western tales, or even the cosmic struggle between the forces of Light and Darkness that predominate much of our European metaphysical subconsciousness. But whether people understood it or not, they responded to it.

Jung wrote an essay entitled, *Wotan*. In it he explored the relevance that the power of the Gods has in our lives through our subconscious minds. He wrote, "We must go back to the age of myths, which did not explain everything in terms of man in his limited capacities, but sought the deeper cause in the psyche and its autonomous powers. Man's earliest institutions personified these powers as gods and described them in myths with great care and circumstantially according to their various characters. This could be done the more readily on account of the firmly established primordial types that exercise direct influence upon them."

What Jung is telling us, is that the Life Force of the Gods remained within our subconscious though it was suppressed by the intrusion of Christianity. This Life Force still manifested itself by transforming Christianity greatly. Now, with the decline of Christianity in the West, our people are once again freed from the oppressive imagery of an alien cult, and this will permit the opportunity for the rebirth of the Odin Consciousness. Jung, as many others who lived in the beginning of the twentieth century, understood that Christianity was failing and that this would permit a resurgence of the old Gods, especially Odin. With the decline and eventual collapse of the old order, the Odin Consciousness will have the opportunity to rise once more and come to dominate the will of our Folk, it will herald in a resurrection of our Folk-Ways. This process is Balder Rising. Balder Rising will permit the resurrection of the Odin Consciousness, to again govern the future course of our Folk.

THE WYRD AND YOUR JOURNEY

As each of us travel through life, we must make decisions that will change the course of our future—or so we think. This is the belief in free will. But nothing is free in the universe. Everything we do, say, and think has a price. Thus, every decision we make will have consequences. The Norns are believed to weave the threads of our destiny, and some interpret this as predestination. But what the Norns weave, are simply pathways that we may take. There are many crossroads in these pathways, and when we come to a crossroad we must make a decision concerning which path to take. There is a certain degree of free will involved, but at the same time we are at the mercy of the choices provided for us by the Norns. I consider these choices tests the All-Father presents to us to prove our worth. This process is referred to as Wyrd.

Wyrd is the process by which we are tested throughout our lives by the Gods, through the intervention of the Norns. What destiny lies in wait for us depends on the choices we make—which pathways we decide to travel. If we make the wrong decisions, then the Gods may choose another to fulfill their plans. Let me give you an example.

We have got to understand that the pathways that wait for us in our future are not carved in stone. We do have the power to create those pathways we wish to travel through Vrilology. The power to create the future we desire is within us and can be discovered and mastered through Vrilology. This is a fundamental principle that lies at the foundation of Vrilology. We will explore this possibility further in later chapters.

Let me give you an example how free will plays a role in the way we live. An individual might decide to abandon the traditional religion he was born into. In the West, this will most likely be Christianity. He might then begin to explore other alternative belief systems. If he is chosen by the Gods, they might offer him the opportunity to attend a study group or lecture on the old religions of our ancestors. He must decide if he will go, and then he must make the decision whether or not to begin the long journey back to the Gods. He might then spend twenty to thirty years of his life exploring the old religion and celebrating his reunion with the Gods. In the course of his life he might affect the lives of many others. Perhaps one individual will be convinced by him to join him on his journey back to the Gods. This individual might then prove to be one who can fulfill the plans of the Gods better then he. It is possible that the first person will even lose faith in the Gods and turn away from them, even turn back to his own faith, but he will have fulfilled his role in the Gods' plan. This process is called Wyrd.

Each individual is born into certain circumstances, possessing certain abilities and is presented with certain opportunities. His experiences and the way he deals with them can lead him to the Gods and fulfill their plans. But he must make that decision and then decide if he is to continue to serve the Gods, or turn away from them once he has fulfilled his great part. No one individual is indispensable to the Gods. There is no Moses or Mohammad within the Folk Faith. We are all the Gods' prophets, and we can all play great roles in the recreation of the bond between them and their children. That choice is one, which each individual must make on his own. There is within our individual Wyrd our own road to fulfillment, our individual role to inspiration that brings us closer to the Gods.

Every individual has his own Wyrd. He has the ability to serve and exercise his genius, to reap his rewards and live and work with the Gods. Within a man's Wyrd is his destiny and free will, as well as his rights and duties in which he can find happiness and peace. If we continue to think that we are entities that exist independent of the cosmic forces that govern and hold the universe together, then we will remain slaves to forces that are beyond our control. But we have it within us to direct our destinies, and this can be done by understanding the nature of the Vril and learning to harness this universal power. Existence is a battle if we are to heroically fight this battle, we must develop the power within us to control the Vril and use it to our advantage in this struggle for existence to evolve upward.

With the multidimensional aspect of the European soul is that part known as Orlog. It is within the Orlog that all our past experiences, thoughts and feelings are stored. Stored there are also those experienced that were passed down to us by our ancestors that Carl Jung referred to as the collective unconscious or the racial soul. Those things that are stored in your Orlog are constantly at play, affecting the way you think and feel, and in effect, causing you to react to whatever it is you face in the present. The interplay of what is stored in your Orlog (the past) on what is happening in the present, will help shape and form the pathways that will guide you toward a future of your own making. You might not be conscious of this process, but once you have discovered the methodology that is found within Vrilology, you will learn for yourself that you can cleanse your Orlog of those things stored there that will cause you to create pathways that will attract all the things you least desire to be part of your life. You can learn the process to create pathways with the power of your mind, which will be filled with all the things you desire to be part of your life.

There will always be a side to the Gods that is beyond our understanding and we must not concern ourselves about this. The Gods will choose to bestow upon us something of their essence, and each of us has the opportunity to learn something of it. The decision whether or not to partake of that offered lies with each of us. This is also part of Wyrd. Wyrd can be described as a form of fellowship between us and the Gods, and thus with the entire universe, along the path that we follow through life. In this way we can each play our individual part in the grand orchestra of time and space. Know that once you discover the methodology of using your mind to shape Vril into pathways you desire, you are in effect, sending the Gods blueprints that they will incorporate into their great plan for the universe.

If you seek the Gods, they will hear your call, but when and how they will answer one cannot say. But if you seek them, you can be assured that sometime during your journey through life, you will be confronted by them. You will have an experience in which you will meet one or more of the Gods (or Goddesses) face to face. You will then be given a choice. But what they will ask of you, we cannot foresee. When the time comes, you will have to decide.

Let me tell you of an experience I had. This happened twenty years ago when I was part of a study group, researching the old religion. I refer to it as a study group because those of us who belong to our little group were not believers in the Gods. Some of them attended with the intension of simply expanding their knowledge of the universe, others because they had an interest in mythology and still others because they believed in the occult. I personally fell into the second group. I always loved tales about the Gods, and heroes in general, and everything and anything that had to do with European folklore and mythology. After several years, we had progressed beyond just studying the legends and were deep into the practical end of forging new links with the Gods. One of the experiences I had was very profound and changed my life forever.

Through a process of Rune meditation and chanting, we were able to put ourselves into a trance-like state. We accomplished this many times and had many wonderful experiences. I discovered that I was psychically talented and could easily slip into a deep trance. At that time, we were concentrating on Freyja, and it was She who first spoke to me. You should concentrate on a God or Goddess of love and joy when forging your link or bond with the Gods, because the path you travel to them should be a joyful experience. On this occasion I found myself on a ship. I guess we can call it a Viking ship. I was at the bow of the ship and remember that the ship was made of gold and surrounded by a golden halo. It sailed in a sea of black waters, under a black sky. In the waters floated huge gold icebergs. Then, before me, appeared a woman who was beautiful, powerful, and surrounded by a halo. She told me that she was Freyja, and if I would dedicate my life to the Gods, and fulfill a task that would later be revealed to me, she would choose me to spend eternity with her in her hall, Sessrumnir, in the Folksvang. She also told me that those she and the Valkyries took back to Asgard weren't just heros who died in battle, but anyone who led a heroic life. It was the battle of life and the willingness to dedicate oneself to something higher than oneself that was truly the heroic deed. She said there were many ways one could live a life of heroism. One way was to remain faithful to the Gods throughout one's life, and perform deeds in their celebration. She told me that every person is a child of the Life-Force of the Gods, and that we each have a divine origin. We all have a divine mission to fulfill according to our individual abilities, but the choice to do so is up to each of us. She was now presenting me with my choice. She told me many things that day, but for now I will simply say that I had agreed to dedicate my life to the Gods. When I woke from my trance, I discovered that the room where we had held our meetings was filled with a strange and eerie ether. It seemed that the air in the room was charged with a living presence. We could all feel it and it was moving beyond words. All of us admitted to some form of experience while in our own individual trance-like state, and we knew that the Goddess Freyja had actually presented herself to us in that room. For me, it was a life-changing experience.

BALDER'S RETURN

We know that Balder will return, so we have to ask ourselves—how will he return? Many have asked me, after reading my book, *The Book of Balder Rising*, if Balder will appear on earth in human form and walk among us like some twenty-first century Christ. Is he a Norse messiah, who will appear and judge us? The question reflects a state of mind of someone who has read the *Book of Balder Rising* through a Christian mind-set. This is understandable. As one who had been raised Catholic, I found myself constantly having to check my own perception of things, which were constantly clouded by my traditional Christian upbringing. It is difficult to truly change the way one thinks and feels, when traveling along a road toward a new spirituality.

When I wrote that Balder will rise from Hel and that his resurrection will herald the return of the Gods, in *The Book of Balder Rising*, I believe I made it clear that I was not referring to some kind of "Jesus" prophecy—predicting that Balder will appear in human form, claiming he is some kind of messiah. Balder is not Christ, though elements of the Balder tale were borrowed and incorporated into the Jesus myth. When Christians, especially European Christians, pray to Christ, they are really praying to the God Balder without realizing it. I will later explore how Jesus was transformed from a heretical Jewish prophet into a neo-pagan deity by the early Christians, the followers of Paul, who had dedicated himself to converting the European pagans, which resulted in transforming Christianity from a Jewish heresy into a quasi-pagan religion. Other pagan Gods such as Adonis, who was born in human form in a place called Bethlehem, as well as Mithras, who was born on December 25, were also incorporated into the myth of Jesus Christ. Balder *is not* some kind of pagan Christ who will rise and judge us, condemn the sinful and sets up some kind of mythical paradise on earth, thus ending history for all time.

When I say that Balder will rise from Hel, I am not prophesying an actual, physical event that will take place on a certain date. I am speaking of the rebirth of the Balder-Force, which is the Life-Force of the Gods (Vril), which will restore us to a celestial state of existence. This Balder-Force will exist within each of us. It is symbolized by two Runes: Elhaz, the Rune of Balder rising, and Sowilo, the

Rune of Balder risen. This spiritual force has existed and will always exist within each person of every race, but will take on different characteristics depending on one's race and the pantheon of Gods that created them. Each race was given form and substance in the most ancient times by different pantheons of Gods. Within our Folk, the strength of the Life-Force of our ancient Gods decreased because our people turned to an alien religion, but that Life-Force did not die out. There is another way to look at what happened. Vril is an never-ending current of life energy that is always flowing into each of us. The archetypes, which inhabit our subconscious, give shape to our perceptions of the spiritual realm. After Christianity spread throughout Europe, the way we viewed the Gods was altered due to the new, alien archetypes that were laid over the pagan memories and images within our subconscious, thus weakening the bond we share with the Gods, causing a weakening of our Bifrost Gland, and thus causing the God-forces within us to weaken, or fall into a state of sleep. But now, as Christianity is declining, the Life-Force of the Gods that created us, has the opportunity to reassert itself among our people. This can only happen if we make an effort to restore the conscious bond with the Gods that created us. This is the essence of what we mean by *Balder Rising*.

The Life-Force of the Gods fills us, pulsates through every cell in our bodies, and for this reason, the Gods exist within us. Their influence has been warped, but now we have the opportunity, by turning to the Folk Faith, to awaken the Gods that sleep within us. We can do this by celebrating the Gods, and by creating new communities based on this celebration. These new communities must be filled with the joy of life, the love of ourselves and each other, our families and ancestors and the children that we bring into the world. By living this way, we will be living pure lives, physically and spiritually, and it is through this way of life that the Balder-Force will grow strong. It is with this Balder-Force that we will awaken the Gods once more, and together we will be able to face the dark ages that are approaching and threaten to engulf not only our people, but the entire world.

In the Semitic Bible, God created man from the dust of the earth, *from dirt*. But in the Folk Faith, the first man and woman were created from two trees—the ash and the elm. So are we claiming that we are actually living vegetables—like the creature in the movie—*The Thing*? No. No! Unlike the Semitic Bible, we don't interpret our tales literally. The tree is a living thing. In Indo-European mythology, it is often a symbol of the divine Life Force. Thus, the Gods created the first humans from the Life Force, from Vril. The myths are tales passed down to us by our ancestors, who lacked a fundamental knowledge of the physical laws of the universe. They understood the esoteric meaning of the universe, but could not explain it within its physical workings. We have to understand that when the Gods created man and woman from two trees, the tree is symbolic of the Life Force of the universe. The Life Force is symbolized by the World Tree, Yggdrasill. Yggdrasill is Vril, and Vril is natural law—the essence of the gods.

This leads us to an understanding of why the Gods created mankind, which is a very different understanding than what the followers of the Semitic Bible (Judaism, Christianity and Islam) believe. The God of the Semitic Bible is a tyrannical God who created man to be ruled over. Man is the plaything of this God. He gives them paradise and then creates Satan (evil) to tempt them from paradise, so they must suffer. They have to suffer to prove themselves worthy enough to spend eternity with him. He creates trials and tribulations, plagues, natural disasters, wars and oppressions that are inflicted upon mankind. Then, He chooses only those who know of Him and submit to Him, as the *Select,* who will be saved. The rest are condemned to suffer the greatest horrors in Hell for all eternity. Even if you did convert, you might be condemned to Hell if you broke even one of His laws. You could lead a virtuous life and then, in the end, you commit one sin, and Bam!—you are condemned to suffer for all eternity. These poor unfortunate victims are not restricted to those who rejected or turned from Him. They also include the billions of people who never heard of Him, and who never had to opportunity to convert to his religion. They also include those that submitted, but failed to prove themselves worthy of His laws! Think about it. Whether its Judaism, Christianity or Islam, why did God not send his messenger, whether it be Moses, Jesus or Mohammad, to earth in the very beginning, and travel across the entire face of the world, to permit the entire world to hear the word of salvation? But then again, who would want to spend eternity with such a cruel and sadistic being?

The Gods of the Folk Faith did not create mankind to torture them. Mankind was created as a part of the organic nature of the world. We evolved according to the laws that govern nature. If we want to be successful, we must live according to those laws. We can decide if we want to align ourselves with the Gods, and become part of their divine order, or submit to Chaos, and live a life of decay and destruction, at the mercy of the haphazard forces of the universe, personified by the Giants. Thus, we are part of the natural order of the universe, either contributing to the order that the Gods maintain, or contributing to the chaos that is the essence of the Giants. We are part of the universe, and part of the process, along with every other living thing. If we live by those natural laws, we will be successful and help maintain order, but if we don't, we won't. If we do, we will also be closer to the Gods. When we die, we will join the Gods in either Sessrumnir or Valhalla, or inhabit that section of the Netherworld known as Odainsaker, where Balder and his wife, Nanna dwell. If we inhabit the two former realms, we will continue to play a role in ordering the universe. When we enter Valhalla, we join the ranks of the Einherjar, who ride out with Odin to do battle with the giants. This process is part of the turning of the ages, the evolutionary process of becoming. Only those who are worthy join such ranks, but the rest are not condemned to suffering. There is no final judgement, no such thing as sin. You create the aftermath that you will inhabit by your actions in this life—the sum total of all your actions in this life.

The life you lead in Midgard will either support the Gods in ordering the universe or the Giants in trying to destroy that order. By returning to the Gods and joining the Folk Faith, you are joining the ranks of those who have dedicated their lives to helping the Gods hold back the destructive forces of the Giants. It is through this process of dedication to the Gods that will ensure the resurrection of Balder.

Part II
THE LOST HERITAGE

MADAME BLAVATSKY AND THE SECRET DOCTRINE

Madame Helena Petrovna Blavatsky was born in Ukraine in 1831. Her father was a German living in Russia by the name of Peter Alexeyeivich von Hahn, and her mother was Helena Andreyevna. Her father was a soldier who had little time for his family. Helena was taken to Astrakhan on the Caspian Sea by her mother to live. There, in that cosmopolitan city of people from all over Europe and Asia, she grew into womanhood. It was here that Helena first met Tibetans, and claimed that she was fascinated by them. Her great-grandfather was a Rosicrucian and Mason, and belonged to the German society, the "Rite of Strict Observance," which claimed it was in contact with "Unknown Superiors." He had built a huge library of occult books during his lifetime, which Helena spent long hours studying. Her grandfather was also involved in these secret societies and had become friends with many of the leaders of the Buddhist Kalmycks from Tibet. Helena Blavatsky later claimed that these "Unknown Superiors" had contacted her and gave her the knowledge that she used to write *The Secret Doctrine*.

In 1875 she created the Theosophical Society in New York City. Two years later she published *Isis Unveiled*, based on a mixture of Western mythology, Eastern religions, mysticism and Egyptian occultism. In 1888, her second book, *The Secret Doctrine,* was published. The thesis of Blavatsky's doctrine was an outline of evolution that exceeded anything Charles Darwin imagined. She claimed that there was a series of different races that devolved into the imperfect races of today, and that present-day state of the world was in the grip of a spiritual struggle between them. The Aryan race is fighting in the service of the Light. She told her followers that she based her *Secret Doctrine* on the "Stanzas of Dzyan," which she read during her travels in the Himalayas. She claimed that deep within the mountains, in caves and caverns, there existed monasteries in possession of huge libraries containing such manuscripts. Other centers of secret learning and knowledge were hidden in Agartha and Shamballah.

The Dalai Lama of Tibet claimed the city of Shamballah was hidden beneath the Himalayan Mountains. It was the capital of a subterranean kingdom and its inhabitants possessed superhuman powers, which included telepathy and telekinesis. The citizens of this kingdom referred to themselves as the Great White Brotherhood. They controlled a power source that was called the Vril or Fahot, and used this power to remain hidden from the rest of the world. They educated Blavatsky about the Vril, telling her that it was a reservoir of endless power that existed in the human organism, as well as throughout the universe. To tap into its power, one had to undergo initiation to learn how to harness this vital force.

The Theosophical Society believed that this Great White Brotherhood lived among us, but remained hidden, waiting for the West to prove itself worthy of their assistance. If this idea of a superior race of Thule supermen seems strange, is it any stranger than the Jewish belief of a Messiah who will appear to conquer and purify the world, afterwards setting up a millennium; or the Muslim notion of the "Hidden Iman," an Ismaili belief in the arrival of a great leader who will unite all of Islam and conquer the world in the name of Allah; or the Hindu belief in the Nine Unknown Men of India who are secret Masters guiding the progression of world history and the human race?

The Rosicrucian English author, Sir Edward Bulwer-Lytton wrote in his novel, *The Coming Race* (1871), of a subterranean race of supermen who were in possession of a secret source of power that he called Vril. According to Bulwer-Lytton, Vril is an unlimited source of energy that resides within the human organism and the entire cosmos. It lies dormant to all but those who have been initiated with the knowledge of how to master its power. Those few may make themselves masters over all nature, possessing powers of telepathy and telekinesis. Bulwer-Lytton referred to this mysterious race in his book as the Vril-ya.

Madame Blavatsky described how God created the universe through a cyclical process in her book, *The Secret Doctrine*. She outlined the regenerative process of cyclical rebirths of the universe that is in many ways similar to the theory of the origin of the universe, in which the universe is created in this Big Bang, then expands until it reaches an ultimate state of expansion, and then begins to retract until everything is compressed into its original form, only to repeat the process in another Big Bang. She describes a process of primary unity in the first part of her book entitled, *Cosmogenesis*. In it the divine being, still unmanifested, differentiates itself into multiple conscious beings. This can be considered the mysterious All-Father, evolving into first, the Divine Trinity of Odin, Vili and Ve, and then later into the multiple Gods and Goddesses, each being a separate and unique part of the universal divine. Madame Blavatsky claims that this divine being manifested itself into the three Logoi (Odin, Vili and Ve), which created time, space and matter. From this, seven evolutionary processions followed in which fire was created in the first, air in the second, water in the third, earth in the fourth and three other cycles which witnessed the creation of ether. The first four cycles collectively were an expanding process, followed by three contracting cycles that reflected the cyclical process in which everything contracted back into the primal unity, only to start the process all over again. She described the force behind this process as something called Fohat (Vril). It was the universal agent used by the "Sons of God" (the Gods) to create and uphold the universe. This is the story of how Odin, Vili and Ve slaughtered the original life-force entity of Ymir, giving it new form and order and creating the universe in the process. Blavatsky claimed that this force was a combination of some form of electricity and solar power (electromagnetism) combined with the will of the Gods which gave order to the universe. This overcame the negative chaotic force of the giants. This "electro-spiritual force" was the foundation of physical existence.

According to Blavatsky, in the beginning, the universe was a bipolar conduit representing the opposite forces of matter and spirit, male and female, fire and ice. The attraction of the opposites caused the Big Bang that formed the universe. This was the creation of life—the birth of Ymir—from whose chaotic essence the ordered universe was formed by the Gods. It is the attraction of sexual opposites that is the key to evolution, progress and advancement. All improvements and advancements are achieved by the union of the male and female, the bonding of opposites, which release the primal life energy that is the very cause of their polarity and thus generates improvements with each succeeding generation.

Blavatsky's four previous manifestations of can be identified with the realms of Muspellheim, Asgard, Vanaheim and Midgard, which can be respectfully associated with fire-dragons, the Gods, the Giants, and mankind. The previous root races can also be associated with Bergelmir, who survived the flooding of the world by Ymir's blood, in a ship. The ship is a structure that requires organized effort, thus symbolizing the orderly process of the Gods. As the Gods slaughtered Ymir, and began fashioning the ordered universe from his remains, Bergelmir tapped into their power to build the ship and thus survived. This myth is a memory of those who survived the flooding of the Black Sea in 5600 B.C., when the ancient Aryan civilization that existed on its shores, which has come down to us as the legend of Atlantis, was destroyed. Those who survived still possessed some memory of how to use Vril. They used this power to help them survive the great catastrophe.

We can also reckon that the third race, as the kinsmen of the Giant, Thrudgelmir, were the first to propagate themselves through sexual reproduction. Did the Aryan Atlanteans possess the technology of genetic engineering, and thus used this technology for reproduction? Could Blavastky's third race actually be those humans who did not possess this knowledge, and thus relied on the natural act of sexual reproduction? The first race she called the Astral Race and the second race she referred to as the Hyperboreans, corresponding nicely to the kinsmen of Ymir and Orgelmir, who were both androgynous.

In the second section entitled, *Anthropogenesis*, she explained the grandiose plan of the universe and man's place within it. She claimed that humanity was far older than thought during her time, and that humanity was an integral part of the spiritual and biological evolution of the universe. She felt that humankind was originally made up of purely spiritual beings which then devolved in stages to a material form of existence. There were four previous manifestations of man, the last being what has been described as the Atlanteans. They by psychic means, controlled great power (the Vril) and was a race of giants (six to seven feet tall). They had great beauty and grace and possessed a superior technology. Their civilization was destroyed in a great flood. The three previous races were proto-humans and more spiritual than physical in nature. The first she referred to as the Astral root-race, the second as the Hyperborean, which had dwelled in a vanished polar continent, and the third as the Lemurians, which lived on a vanished continent in the Pacific Ocean.

We should not take her claims literally, but interpret them as attempts to understand the evolutionary process of humanity. She was inspired spiritually, but without a corresponding understanding of the scientific knowledge interpretation of such inspiration can be distorted, and thus the forwarding of lost knowledge is distorted, but still no less valid. With the destruction of the Atlantean civilization, which was the ancient Aryan civilization that existed around the coast of the much smaller Black Sea, the survivors were scattered and dispersed across the face of the Eurasian continent. These were the Indo-European tribes that spread west into Europe, south into the Middle East and India, east, across Asia, into China.

Blavastky's *Secret Doctrine* can be summarized as belief in an omnipresent God-entity who is immutable and universal, and whose essence is the life force that she refers to as Fohat. This is an electro-spiritual force which gives order to the universe, is understood as the laws of nature, and has been called by the name Fohat or Vril. The All-Father created the universe by use of this primal fire (Fohat or Vril) as a source of energy, whisking it out of the chaos of fire and ice, the manifest and unmanifest forces. This set up the evolutionary laws of nature by which the universe and everything in it, macrocosm and microcosm, are ever growing and changing. This process describes the coming together of the ice of

Niflheim and the fire of Musspellheim, causing a reaction (the Big Bang) and thus initiating the creation of the chaotic force of Ymir. The Great Bovine, the nurturing force (the Fohat or Vril) caused the creation of the first Gods, who in turn, attacked, slaughtered, and then refashioned the universe (Ymir) giving it order and structure. The universe is not progressing toward an end, but is cyclical in nature, all creation is subject to the process of destruction and rebirth.

ULTIMA THULE

From Northern Europe to India, most cultures possess a memory of a once and lost Golden Age that existed in the primeval past, when men and women possessed superior powers of mind and body and lived in harmony with the natural environment. In the Middle East, the Garden of Eden of the Old Testament is an obvious reference to this lost Golden Age, when people lived side-by-side with God. The Egyptians of antiquity spoke of a time when they were ruled by a race of God-kings. In Babylonian mythology there is a reference to three ages, each lasting thousands of years. The first was a Golden Age that existed before the Great Flood. The ancient Iranians have a reference to a Golden Age in the Avesta texts. It describes a thousand-year reign of King Yima.

The most fully developed legend of a Golden Age is found in the Hindu text of *The Doctrine of the Four Yugas*. Each Yuga is a different age, referred to in Sanskrit as Krita or Satya Yuga, Tretu Yuga, Dvapara Yuga and Kali or Sitya Yuga. The first of these Yugas was a Golden Age, but things got progressively worse in the following ages, as the human race gradually lost its link with the Gods. Legends like this also existed in both the Greek and Norse mythologies, which speak of a Golden Age that was lost, when men and Gods lived in a harmonious union. The Greek farmer-poet of the eighth century B.C., Hesiod, wrote of four succeeding ages that he referred to as the Gold, Silver, Bronze and Iron. In the first of these ages, the Golden Age, man lived under the rule of Kronos and his life was free of hard work, pain and old age. He had mastery over his environment and was on good terms with the Gods. The Roman writer, Ovid, gave a more descriptive account of these ages. He said that the Golden Age was actually a pastoral paradise in which it was spring all year around, and mankind was free from labor or heavy work. War, famine and disease were unknown and man lived alongside the Gods. Plato wrote that during the Golden Age the Gods and mortals lived side-by-side, but that the Gods gradually departed, leaving mortals to deal with their existence, relying on their own abilities, thus succumbing to the laws of entropy. What he was trying to explain was how mankind gradually lost the knowledge of how to use Vril Science. Like many others telling of a lost Golden Age, Plato believed in a cycle of the ages. After an Iron Age, there would be a return to a Golden Age. Since we are presently living in an Iron Age, the next age will be another Golden Age—the Golden Age of Gimli.

The people of the Mediterranean and Northern Europe referred to the lost age as Thule, or Ultima Thule. Ultima Thule was believed to be the ancient homeland of the original Indo-European or Aryan Race. It was described as an entryway to a subterranean realm populated by superior giants possessing magical powers, located in the northern most point on the planet. This mythical land was also referred to as Hyperborea and thought to be a magical island that was located somewhere in the North Atlantic. Thule was sometimes thought to be the capital city on an island by the name of Hyperborea. It was described as an island surrounded by a great wall of mountains and covered with huge glaciers. Hyperborea means "beyond the poles." In the center of the island once lived a race of giant-men, or God-men. The Greeks and Romans believed this. Herodotus wrote that he believed it was "... a glacial island located in the Great North, where lived transparent men."

The legendary land of Thule or Hyperborea was thought to exist somewhere between Labrador and Iceland, and many people think it could have been the island of Greenland. The interior of the island was believed to be warm and mild, and filled with lush vegetation. The women were unbelievably beautiful and the men heroic and dynamic. This race of God-men possessed great powers of clairvoyance and extrasensory perception. They were reputed to be the descendants of "otherworldly" visitation—the Gods themselves who visited them and interbreed with them, creating a Divine Race. These Gods lived among them, and shared with them their ambrosia, served in a golden cup, which gave them great powers including eternal youth. This drink was actually the secret Science of the Vril. Its memory was transformed into the legend of a sacred cup and holy drink—the Holy Grail.

The Celtic and Germanic peoples thought Thule was a northern Garden of Eden, where a great and wondrous race of God-men lived. This great race of supermen held power over nature through their possession of secret knowledge. These theories were actually racial memories of the long forgotten homeland of the ancient Aryans, the ancestors of the Indo-Europeans. This Great North, a land of mountains and ice, was actually the shore of the ancient Black Sea. Around the southern, eastern and western coasts of the Black Sea, even today, there are mountains in the Balkans, in Asia Minor and in the Caucasus, while to the north, most of northern Europe, including the great Russian landscape, was once covered by a huge sheet of ice rising a mile high.

This ancient homeland of the original Indo-Europeans, or the ancient Aryans (not to be confused with the Nazi ideal of the Aryan race), was the wondrous civilization known as Atlantis. Around the now submerged coast of that ancient sea, which was much smaller than now and of fresh water, lived a race of tall, beautiful people possessing a civilization in many ways superior to our current civilization. They were in possession of a power that enabled them to construct a great civilization in harmony with the natural forces of the universe. They lost their civilization when a terrible deluge broke through what is now the Bosporus Straits, flooding the Black Sea coastal settlements and filling the sea with salt water.

The people living there were thrown into a state of chaos, with thousands dying. Hundreds of cities and settlements were lost under the resulting tidal waves and floods which raised the water levels of the Black Sea hundreds of feet. Those who survived were scattered, migrating north, south, east and west. This mighty race of golden-haired, blue-eyed giants, who once considered themselves the masters of nature, now wandered across Eurasia, mingling with other peoples, forgetting how to use the power that they commanded, which resulted in the weakening of their bond with their Gods.

Many believed Thule was in Iceland, while others thought it might even be Greenland, and still others felt it once existed in the Arctic, at the North Pole. The Nazis believed that it existed as an entryway into a subterranean domain inhabited by a race of blond-haired and blue-eyed giants at the North Pole. It was none of these mythological lands, but did exist. It was a prehistoric civilization—a pagan Eden—but not in a sweltering desert, or the marshlands of Mesopotamia, or in the Persian Gulf. We have to remember that Europe, twelve thousand years ago, was covered with a great sheet of ice and was much colder than today. The memory of Thule has been confused and mixed with other legends. Many eventually came to believe that it had existed at the North Pole because they did not consider the glacial environment that existed in Europe at that time. Thule was actually an advanced culture in the cool landscape of virgin woods and rich, black, earth that existed along the shores of the freshwater Black Sea. A land of uncompromising beauty and natural purity, this was the source for the legend of Atlantis.

The prehistoric golden age described this civilization by the Black Sea. The society was ruled by a gnostic priesthood who guarded knowledge on how to tap into the Vril's power. Their civilization utilized this source of power which was free, clean and limitless. This power was a common creative energy that was generated from a biological collective, and its source was the bond with the Gods that created them. This Life Force is the metaphysical quality that defines the original Aryan ancestors that all Indo-Europeans are descended from. Because of this, they were able to maintain a society that was pure and holy. Once they reached a level of technological sophistication which caused them to think of themselves as eternal. They eventually let their guard drop, and they grew careless. The natural state of the universe is chaos. If one does not maintain order, everything in nature will naturally succumb to the forces of decay and disintegration. Once the ancient Aryan Atlanteans ceased to be vigilant, the destructive powers of chaos took over and the environmental forces once again caused the ice sheets to melt, raising the sea levels of the world. This resulted in a disaster that destroyed the earthen wall that had held back the waters of the Mediterranean. The natural earth barrier collapsed and the salt waters flooded into the Black Sea, causing tidal waves and flooding that destroyed the communities along the shore. The waters turned brackish as they mixed with salt water. The sea-levels rose hundreds of feet, destroying towns, farmlands and cities, killing thousands and causing thousands more to flee. The old priestly order disappeared and the people lost their knowledge of the use of Vril. Only bits and pieces of this lost esoteric knowledge survived, and were carried across Eurasia and North Africa by those who had survived this terrible catastrophe.

The priesthood that ruled over the ancient Aryans was an elite within their society, adepts dedicated to maintaining the bonds that united the people with the Gods who created them. They were an advanced evolutionary guard dedicated to act as a conduit between their race and their Gods, imparting their wisdom and knowledge of the Vril to the rest of the people. After the great fall, due to the flooding of the Black Sea, most of what was left of this priestly order survived by fleeing east into what is today the Sinkiang province of western China. They built a new civilization there, imparting much of their knowledge to the Chinese and helped found Chinese civilization. Their mummified remains have been discovered and we refer to them as the Tocharians. In the first century B.C., they were driven west and south by the descendants of the Huns. Most of them eventually invaded India and founded the Kuchean Empire, which lasted for about one hundred years. A small group of them settled in Tibet and transformed that ancient land into a warrior society. They ruled Tibet for hundreds of years until they disappeared through intermarriage with the local population. Tibet was feared by its neighbors as a great military power, and after the Tocharians disappeared, the Tibetan people were forced to accept the pacifism of Buddhism, so that they would never again be a threat to their neighbors. What was left of their knowledge was passed down in a distorted and incomplete form among the Tibetan monks.

In its purest form, the name Thule represents the universal power of the universe. It is the spiritual home of the ancient "Elder Race" or Gods, who originally had intercourse genetically with the proto-humans and created the race of humans that we refer to today as the Europeans.

Our original Aryan ancestors worshiped Gods whose names have been lost through time. Our Indo-European descendants have given the original Gods different names as their original Aryan language splintered into Germanic, Latin, Celtic, Slavic, Baltic, Vedic, Iranian, and others. The original religion of the lost civilization that existed along the Black Sea, and their knowledge and ability to tap into and harness the Life Force of the Gods, known as the Vril, was passed down partially to the ancient Indo-Europeans in the form of gnostic religions, emphasizing the bonding of man with their Gods through the initiation into natural mysteries. Among the Norse, this religion was known as Odinism, named for the principal God of the Norse people. The Vril religion also survived among the Celtic, Roman, Vedic, Iranian and other Indo-European peoples. It has been passed down to us in a raw and natural form, though only partially, through many different sources that include the Riga-Veda, the Upanishads, the Gita, the Zend-Avesta, the Egyptian Book of the Dead, the Niebelungenlied, the Grail Legends, the Volsung, the Greek and Celtic myths and especially the Edda and the Runes.

ATLANTIS

There have been many legends about an ancient civilization that sank beneath the sea. Ancient scholars have told of such civilizations existing long before their time. One fifth century B.C. Greek, by the name of Herodotus, described such a civilization. The Egyptian Pharaoh by the name of Pepi I, who lived around 2800 B.C., also tells us of such a civilization. The most famous ancient writer who spoke of such a civilization was the Greek Philosopher, Plato. In his dialogues, *Critias* and the *Timaeus*, he claimed that a Greek traveler by the name of Solon, learned of a civilization named, Atlantis, which sank beneath the waves nine thousand years earlier and was located "beyond the Pillars of Hercules."

Plato was writing in 355 B.C. and relying on tales and legends handed down to him. The world of Plato was filled with legends and tales of civilizations sinking beneath the sea, being destroyed by a terrible catastrophe, of floods that covered the earth wiping out whole civilizations. The truth is, when Plato wrote his account of Atlantis, he was actually drawing on not one source, but many. Plato tried to give us a complete account of the Atlantis legend by combining bits and pieces of different tales into his legend. He probably confused many of the facts, so there are both truth and error in his account.

I would like to try and clear up many of the misconceptions surrounding the legend of Atlantis that we inherited from Plato. First, I will say that Atlantis did not exist in the Atlantic Ocean. Many will say that it had to because of two facts: it is named Atlantis after the Atlantic Ocean, and it is placed "beyond the Pillars of Hercules." As for the first, the Atlantic Ocean was named after Atlantis. That Ocean was never referred to as the Atlantic until *after* Plato's account of Atlantis. The ancient civilizations, including the Greeks, referred to the Atlantic Ocean, as the "Great Sea," the "Western Sea," the "Great Sea Beyond," and other such names. Plato tells us that "Atlantis" means "Daughter of Atlas." Atlas was the oldest son of the God Poseidon and his mortal wife Cleito. This is an important fact, because it means that Plato is telling us that the Gods mixed with mortals and produced a race of God-men! They created an advanced civilization known as Atlantis.

As for the second, which Plato claimed Atlantis was "beyond the Pillars of Hercules" (the Straits of Gibralter were referred to as the Pillars of Hercules). Here is a misunderstanding of the meaning of the term, "Pillars of Hercules." The Pillars of Hercules was not *the* name for the Straits of Gibraltar. The term, "the Pillars of Hercules," was not the name of a specific geographic landmark, but a geographic description, like "island," "peninsula," or "mountain." It was the name for all geographical landmarks that included a channel of water passing through two land points possessing some kind of tall mountain or hill. The Straits of Gibraltar had been referred to as the Pillars of Hercules, but so were the Straits of Messina between Sicily and Italy, the waterway between Attica and Argolis in Greece, the Dardanelles, and the Bosporus. Most straits in the Mediterranean Sea were referred to as the Pillars of Hercules. So Atlantis could have been located beyond Attica or beyond Sicily or beyond the Bosporus, just as much as it could have been located beyond Gibraltar.

The original name for Atlantis was probably Thule, but the Greek philosopher, Plato, Hellenized the name of this lost civilization, because he was writing for a Greek audience. One of the results of this has been the modern truth-seeker mistaking the location of ancient Atlantis. We have to remember that pagans changed the names of the Gods and their homelands, translating them into their own language, using their own names and terminology to explain tales of other people. This made it easier for them to relate to the tales. To them it was not the literal truth that was important, but the essence the tale. Plato and others saw nothing wrong with explaining the legend of Thule with Greek names and terms.

The Atlanteans that Plato wrote about were actually the original Aryans that existed along the shores of the Black Sea. Their civilization existed nine thousand years before his time. He spoke of their accomplishments and expansion and then described their fall and destruction. We must remember that Plato was relying on bits and pieces of information about Atlantis passed down through millennia, combined with other legends from many different cultures and civilizations.

Plato described for us a great civilization possessing highly advanced technology and a source of energy beyond anything that existed in his time, or our own. The Atlanteans harnessed this power and used it to transform themselves and the world around them. They had become masters of their environment, creating great cities and vehicles in which they could travel far beyond their homeland. They possessed a science that was very different from what we know today. This technology was the science of Vril, and it was given to them by the Gods. Vril, which the Atlanteans used to power their civilization, is an etheric organism, which exists everywhere in the universe.

The original language spoken by the Atlanteans was the mother tongue of all Indo-European languages, and was intimately linked to Vril. They used language as an instrument to help plants grow, to tame wild animals, and heal the sick. It could also unleash terrible forces of destruction. Their mental and spiritual abilities were far beyond what we possess today, and made them seem like Gods to other humans that existed in the world at the time. By mastering the power of the Vril, they had advanced their evolutionary development, altering their DNA and transforming themselves into semi-divine race of God-men. In their travels, they assisted other humans in establishing civilizations, instructed them in law and religion, and bestowed upon them science and techniques in tool-crafting, architecture and agriculture. Other humans venerated them as Gods, or God-men to whom they looked for advice and guidance, unquestioningly obeying their commands.

The Atlantean scientists broke the secret of the genetic code and discovered that this was the secret to Vril as a power source. They established both a religion and science based on this knowledge, and thus they were able to master the use of Vril. This permitted them to speed up their evolutionary process, transforming themselves into a race of supermen, or God-men. Their scientists had carefully cultivated new traits that enhanced their abilities mentally, psychically and physically. Through carefully cultivating mutations within themselves, they rapidly transformed themselves into a new species that caused them to stand out compared to the rest of humanity. This is true not just in technology, but in their appearance as well, making them seemed like a race of giants or God-men.

Besides appearing beautiful and radiant, their race possessed an average height between six and seven feet tall, with perfectly developed features and bodies that made them appear, superhuman. Their minds were also transformed, possessing the ability to pass on their memories to the next generation in a form of blood memory, or what science today calls racial memory. People could recall the events and achievements of their ancestors with the clarity of remembering things within their own lifetimes. Their minds also could photographically recall everything they saw, read or heard, and so we have accounts of people remembering thousands of lines of text verbally. The Greeks, Druids and others never wrote down their legend, and could recite thousands and even tens of thousands of lines of verse orally.

Though the descendants of the Atlanteans have fallen from the heights from which they had risen through the utilization of Vril Science, something of their extraordinary faculties, their capacity to harness the magical powers of Vril and the racial memory of a lost Golden Age, has lingered within the deepest recesses of our inner soul—our "id." This is manifest in the creation of the marvelous mythology of the Indo-Europeans, especially the Norse mythology and its cosmology.

We are discovering that these Atlanteans were not made up of crude and primitive tribes. Unlike the rest of humanity that existed at the time, the Atlantean civilization on the shores of the Black Sea had reached heights of technological perfection in science, the arts, social environment, education, scholarship and exploration that we still have not regained today. Since their science was based on the Vril, which did not exploit the natural world and its resources, there was no need for imperialistic expansion. They did not have to conquer other peoples and their lands, enslave their fellow humans, exploit them commercially, or seek to extract the natural resources of the earth, forest and seas to build their civilizations. The source of their power was the Vril, and it was an endless and clean reservoir of energy. Their buildings were not grandiose, but designed in an environmentally pleasing style. Their cities and communities were modestly designed, richly decorated, possessing the most modern devices and harmoniously blending in with their natural environment. They did not have to rip up the landscape to build roads, railroads or airports since their transportation crafts were powered by the power of Vril, and thus, utilized a form of anti-gravity propulsion, able to lift vertically, and fly effortlessly at great speeds everywhere, including over the sea and to the deepest depths of the ocean, and even leave the atmosphere of this planet and beyond.

It is hard for us today to envision a civilization built on a technology that was so different from what we have come to depend on for our entire existence. The Atlanteans relied on a technology that created conditions between themselves and the natural world totally different, from that which we are familiar with, in the twenty-first century.

The Vril and its powers transformed the Atlanteans themselves, not just in their appearance, but also by empowering them with abilities that we moderns no longer possess. This was done by using the Vril to expand their etheric organism which forced mutations within them, thus endowing them with great powers. Through the use of their voice, mobilizing the power of sound and vibration, they could stimulate the growth of vegetation and affect the course of weather. Their speech was constructed in such ways that they could communicate with their natural environment, including the wild beasts that roamed their world. They also possessed the power to assist in the healing of those who were afflicted with illnesses and diseases. This made them appear to be like Gods to the other tribes of humans who still dwelled in a primitive state of existence.

Though they were venerated by other humans, they refrained from inflicting harm on them, nor did they impose their ways on them, at least for most of their history. It was only later in the history of their civilization that they dared to think of interfering with the evolution of other peoples. These primitives, witnessing the powers they possessed, were all too ready to accept their guidance and bow down before them. The Atlanteans tried to educate them in the ways of science, law, religion and the arts, teaching them the rudimentary foundations of civilization. In time, these other humans discovered that they were not Gods, but rather, humans like them, and soon their admiration turned to contempt and eventually, jealousy and hate.

THE ANCIENT ARYANS—THE TRUE ATLANTEANS

I would like to make clear that my use of the term Aryan is a completely cultural-ethnic, and not a racial term, as used by the Nazis. The term Aryan has been much misused in the 20th century. In the 19th century, the term was used to refer to the original people that all Indo-Europeans are descended from. They were believed to be in possession of a "golden age." It is this golden age that all Indo-European myths refer to. The Nazis used this romanticization of legend of the original Aryan civilization as a justification of their racial policies. The Aryans began genetically the same as the other Whites or Caucasians, but they had initiated a transformation through a program of genetic engineering and breeding that gave them abilities superior to other humans. If they were a "master race" it was because of the mutations that they created within their own DNA. The differences among the races were, and still are, real. These differences are the result of different pantheons of Gods mixing with proto-homo sapiens. Thus, all humans are the sons and daughters of the Gods, just different pantheons of Gods. The ancient Aryans understood this and unlike other communities of humans, they sought to remove the differences between themselves and the Gods that created their race. They eventually created a great civilization. The memory of this civilization has survived its destruction in the legend of Atlantis.

All Indo-Europeans today share a common ancestry that is reflected in the languages they speak and the myths and legends that have been handed down through the ages. The truth is, the Atlanteans who survived the great destruction of their civilization became refugees who wandered throughout Eurasia. They became known as the ancient Aryans, from whom the many different Indo-European peoples are descended. They migrated east, west and south and mixed with other humans wherever they went. Many of the people these Indo-Europeans mixed with adopted their languages and cultures. Most of the people they came into contact, especially in Europe, were racially the same as they were before they underwent their transformation into God-men. But in other places, as in the Middle East, North Africa and southern Asia, they mixed with Semites, Hamites, and others belonging to non-Caucasian races. Their descendants today possess mixed souls. Still, many of them adopted the Indo-European language and culture. Being of mixed heritage, their descendants today need to explore their own individual identity, discover which heritage dominates their soul, and which path they must follow to return to the Gods of their ancestry. They will discover that they are torn and divided by their mixed heritage and are pulled in different directions, toward different pantheons of Gods. In this book, I am addressing those nations possessing blood or DNA that establishes them as direct descendants of the ancient civilization from which all Indo-Europeans are descended. Their ancestors, long ago, discovered the secret of Vril Science (Vrilology), and used it to build a civilization. Though it was more advanced, it was also very different, for it did not utilize a power source depended on fossil fuels or other destructive forms of energy. This civilization was ancient Atlantis, which is the mother civilization and culture of all Indo-European civilizations. It is the true Atlantis of legend described by Plato.

Around 12,000 to 10,000 B.C., the region extending from western Europe to central Asia was inhabited by modern humans. Humanity had already divided into the different races that we recognize today. These humans belonged to what we would refer to today, as the White, or Caucasian Race. We also know that a small portion of this White or Caucasian race spread out across the Eurasian continent and imposed their language and culture on those peoples they came into contact with. Most of the peoples they either conquered or settled among, were of the same genetically, while others were different. They have been referred to as the "Aryans," the original nation of all Indo-European speaking peoples. They also have been referred to as the Ur-people. "Ur" is another name for the Vril. Around this time, this small group of people, living along the shores of the Black Sea, was taught the secrets of Vril Science by the Gods. About 40,000 to 50,000 years ago, the Gods of our ancestors (still proto-humans), mixed their Life Force with ours and caused evolution to speed up, creating our distinct race of humans. Later, these same Gods once again spoke to our ancestors, appearing to a small group of them living around the shore of the Black Sea. They heard their call and answered. The Gods walked among them and educated them. The Greek, Hesiod, wrote, "At the time of the Golden Age, the Gods clothed in air moved among men."

These Gods came to Midgard and taught the Aryans the secrets of the Runes. With this secret knowledge, the Aryans were able to harness the power of the

Vril. Their shamans learned how to use the gift of the Gods—the Vril. They were able to use the Vril to build an advanced civilization, master their environment, and even escalate their own evolution. They refashioned their environment through the construction of beautiful cities and communities, free of pollution, and used Vril Science to cause mutations within their own DNA. They were able to remake themselves into a race of supermen, possessing superior physical, mental and psychic powers.

The society of the ancient Aryans was divided into three classes or degrees, according to the initiation into the knowledge of the Vril: the priestly class, the warrior class and the rest of society. The possession of Vril Science was a sacred legitimation of an individual's political authority. Thus, the priestly class held most of the political power, though the knowledge of Vril Science was accessible to all members of society. The determination of an individual's place in society was decided by his ability to comprehend the use the Vril on two levels, the exoteric and the esoteric. The exoteric understanding of Vril Science related to mechanical technology. This meant being able to utilize the Vril through the mundane use of machines, as in a flying, anti-gravity craft, or "flying saucer." The esoteric understanding of Vril Science was restricted to cadets who were trained to hold higher office. These individuals were people who possessed a natural ability to tap into the Vril by employing Runic meditation and chanting.

This priestly class was also divided into three grades, which were equivalent to the Free Masons' Entered Apprentice, Fellow Craft and Master Mason. A cadet entered each grade only after learning a certain degree of understanding of the use of Vril Science on a personal level. This was also true of the warrior class, though the warrior class learned to use the Vril to destroy their enemies, but, only in the defense of their civilization, never to engage in aggressive action of conquest. The priestly class learned to use the Vril to hold together their civilization. Thus, one class used the Vril to create, and the other class used it to destroy. Each class possessed only one half of the understanding of Vril Science, but together, they created a whole, and thus balanced society that was the foundation of the civilization of these ancient Atlantean Aryans. This layout of their society is the origin to the gnostic ideal behind the story of the union of the Aesir and the Vanir, in creating and maintaining order throughout the universe.

The priestly order spent their entire lives studying and mastering the use of the Vril. In this way, they developed the ability to listen to their inner voice, through which the Gods spoke to them and continued to convey the knowledge and technology to control and use the power of the Vril. They discovered the use of this new science, which helped them to control Nature, both the external nature of the world they lived within, and their own inner nature, or genetic make up. In a short time, they had succeeded in speeding up the process of evolution, transforming their people into a new race of superior humans.

By harnessing the Vril, they brought about a metamorphosis in their intelligence, physiognomy and psychic abilities. They used these newfound powers to transform their world. They bred their new race amidst the glacial environment of the world they live within. Over generations, they continued to make improvements to their genetic makeup, which included the development of their "Bifrost Gland," the etheric organism that permitted them to draw on the Vril's power effortlessly. Many have referred to this gland as the "Third Eye." With the development of their Bifrost Gland, they soon were in possession of powers that enabled them to defend their civilization against other tribes of humans that might threaten them, and they also used their newfound powers to drive away the great beasts of the ice age world. The development of their Bifrost Gland gave them a greater awareness of their relationships to the world they lived in, both the Microcosm (Midgard), and with the Macrocosm (Asgard) realms.

The Aryans discovered the fundamental truth about mankind—that the different races were created through unions between different pantheons of Gods and with different proto-humans. After several generations, they appeared like the sons and daughters of the Gods to the other humans in their world.

Using the Vril, they obtained the ability to transform themselves, causing mutations, and transforming themselves into a superior race of humans. They selected among themselves the best individuals. These were individuals possessing special gifts. They served as soldiers, high priests, leaders in government and the sciences. They were schooled in the use of the Vril in great academies, isolated in the mountains that surrounded their Black Sea homeland. There the cadets were trained with the most rigorous, uncompromising discipline. In this way, they were made to understand, the importance of the responsibility of bestowing upon them the mastery of the Vril and its use to maintain and advance their civilization. They were instructed to understand the relationship between the physical world they lived in and unseen forces, manifested in the Vril, that controlled and directed the evolution of the world and universe they were a part of. Instilled with this sense of always placing the good of their Folk before their own self-interests, they dedicated themselves to serve their people. In this way, they were taught to respect and protect the purity of their Folk, both physical and spiritual. Realizing that their ability to master the power of the Vril was rooted in their own genetic composition, they fostered a strong will to put aside all cravings and desires of their selfish nature that might cause them to act in any way that could cause harm to their Folk. In this way, those individuals possessing the best qualities of intellect, altruism and cooperation in the pursuit of refining and advancing the progressive development of their people, were given leadership positions.

After graduating from these universities they were trained to develop their powers for specific purposes. Many served in the military, some became leaders who governed their people, while others joined professions, becoming scientists, doctors, professors, engineers, technicians or judges. But no matter what their profession, they were all given a sense of belonging to a special community. They would eventually become the leaders of their civilization, maintaining its integrity under the symbol of the Sun Wheel, becoming intermediaries between their people and their Gods. This was the class known as Vril Lord and Vril Ladies. They not only were given the right to rule, but were burdened with the responsibility to serve the entire community. With the knowledge of the Vril, these Lord and Ladies came to understand the true nature of their relationship with the Gods, and taught this knowledge to all citizens. This became the foundation of their religion.

This sense of belonging to a special community was strengthened by their ability to inherit the racial memories of their ancestors. This ability to pass down from generation to generation a kind of blood memory enabled each generation to recall the deeds, rationale and causes for events that took place in their history. It allowed the people to retain a deep sense of connection with their community and its history. It prevented unscrupulous people from rewriting their history. People lived with their history within them. It was as natural a part of their life as the day-to-day events that took place in one's personal life. Racial memory was a cornerstone of their civilization. It helped to forge a strong sense of community and sacrifice among the ancient Aryans.

They developed a form of transportation that was beyond anything we have today, outside of science fiction. Their control of the Vril provided them with endless free energy that did not pollute the environment. It gave them the ability to construct aircraft powered by anti-gravity. The aircraft they built was saucer shape, like the flying saucers that are alleged to exist today. These aircraft gave them the ability to travel across the face of the earth and into space. There are many accounts of images carved in stones that look like pilots or astronauts—men wearing suits and helmets very much like those worn by our contemporary jet pilots and astronauts. There is evidence of their existence, and of how the ancient Aryans explored and traveled across the earth by the many prehistoric rock carvings that can be found throughout the world of what looks like flying saucers and men wearing suits similar to those worn by modern-day jet pilots. Some people like to imagine they are proof of extraterrestrials having visited earth in the past. With the knowledge of whom the Atlanteans were, and the powers and technology they possessed, this is an unnecessary assumption.

When the Aryans first appeared among the less developed humans, they were venerated as either God-men or the Gods themselves. They possessed superhuman abilities that made them appear like Gods to their fellow humans, even to other Caucasians who resembled them. Because the Aryans had used the Vril to cause mutations, making themselves genetically closer to the Gods that created them, other humans, especially other Caucasians, used their appearance to imagine and visualize what the Gods actually looked like. This caused the Aryans to eventually think of themselves as Gods, and eventually, they dared to play God. This caused them to develop a misplaced altruism toward the other races. Because of this, the Aryans began instructing other humans in developing the ability to harness the Vril, much in the way modern Europeans tried to bring the benefits of Western technology to the Third World people in the nineteenth and twentieth centuries. The ancient Aryans also tried to introduce their science, law, education, religious beliefs, arts and technology to those who were too genetically and culturally different to understand or comprehend the way they were able to tap into the Vril.

Because the genetic and cultural gulf between the Aryans and most of the tribes they came into contact was so great, many of the leaders of these peoples betrayed the trust placed in them. Unable to properly use the technology of the Vril because of the genetic differences, they formed dark cults that engaged in dark rights. They wished to use the power of the Vril to set themselves up as masters of their neighbors. These attempts to conquer their neighbors through the use of the Vril by people who lacked a fundamental understanding of the way the Aryans harnessed the Vril's power, manifested itself by releasing ominous forces that would lead to a disruption in the natural order of the environment of the world. The eventual result was the destruction of the ancient Aryan civilization.

The alien races were able to use what little understanding of the Vril that was given to them by the Aryans, to try and imitate what the Aryans had accomplished. They also sought to cause transmutations within their own genetic composition, but with disastrous effects. The rulers of the alien races united and made war against the Aryans. The Aryan warriors were confronted with hordes of deformed and misshapen monsters, possessing magical abilities similar to those powers they possessed. The titanic struggle raged on and off for centuries. These wars are remembered in the legends and folk tales of the Indo-Europeans, who are the direct descendants of the Aryans. The diminished racial memories that they possessed in their fallen state, were recorded in myths about wars between the Gods and Giants by the Norse, the Greeks, the Celts and the Aryans who settled in India. There is a moral to learn here. Each people or race has the innate ability to accomplish what the Aryans did, but they each have to discover their own individual means, based on their own unique genetic link with their own particular pantheon of Gods. The result of this misplaced altruistic attempt to bestow their knowledge of the Vril to other humans resulted in the same disastrous consequences as the present-day attempts by the West to Westernize the rest of the world.

THE DESTRUCTION OF ARYAN ATLANTIS

There is an old saying: "What goes around, comes around." In an attempt to share their advanced Vril technology with other races, the Aryans planted the seeds of their own destruction. In an altruistic attempt to share their superior abilities and science with all of humanity, they taught them the fundamentals of Vrilology, in an attempt to enhance the evolutionary process of the rest of humanity. It was not enough that they tried and failed to teach other races the use of the Vril through the means given to them by their Gods, they thought they could rectify this by transforming their genetic make up. Mutations were generated in the other races, in the hope of giving them the understanding of how to use Vril technology. Each race is genetically unique and thus needs to discover, for itself, through its individual genetic composition, its own individual pathway to the Gods that created them. Only by establishing their individual bridge to their own Gods could the different races forge links with them, and thus tap into and harness the power of the Vril, in a way appropriate to their unique genetic makeup. By trying to teach and educate other races in the use and knowledge of the Vril, the Aryans caused the creation of a corrupt form of Vril Science among the other races. Thus, the other races that tried to utilize the Vril inadvertently drew on the destructive nature of the Life Force of the universal power, not on its ordering nature. These other races became unwilling agents for the Giants, not the Gods. They did not, like the Aryans, master Nature in a way that was harmonious with the disciplined and orderly nature of the Gods.

One particular race known to us through historical records is the Turanians. They employed the Vril for their own purposes. But because their racial soul (rooted in their DNA), was alien to the process they were taught by the Aryans to harness its power, they could only tap into the destructive side of this force, and thus, without realizing it, they served the chaotic forces of the Giants. It was this abuse of the Vril science by the Turanians, who were spiritually and genetically incompatible to comprehend and understand its power, that led to their misuse of the Vril. The abuse of Vril Science, which included rituals that involved the perversion of human reproduction and genetics, unleashed horrific and ominous forces that led to terrible disruptions in the world climate. These destructive forces upset the natural order of the world climate, thus causing chaotic transformations that had catastrophic results on the environment of the world in the sixth millennium BC. Changes caused in both evolution of living organisms, and the transformation of the planetary environment over the billions of year, are the result of different levels of Vril energy currents that bathe the planet from time to time. The misuse of Vril technology by the different races, caused a disruption in ordering of the evolution of the planet by the Gods, and strengthened the influence of the chaotic powers of the Giants, resulting in the acceleration of the melting of the ice caps. This in turn, caused the ocean levels to rise at a faster rate, resulting in the destruction of the Bosporus land bridge, causing the great flooding of the Black Sea, and the destruction of the Aryan Atlantis.

From the time when our Gods first walked among our most-distant ancestors and created our unique race, they have been guiding our development through the millenniums. But the Gods are only one half of opposing hierarchies of the cosmos. They represent order and evolution, and the Giants, representing chaos and destruction, are in opposition to the Gods. Both sides are in competition for the possession of the collective soul of our race, and all races. The Giant forces are collectively under the guidance of Loki, whom the myths describe as leading the Giants, the forces of destruction, against the Gods in the days of Ragnarok. Loki seeks to encourage the spread and proliferation of anarchy and nihilism among our Folk, encouraging wrong activities and lifestyles that would hasten the decline and death of our Folk. Rather than working toward the improvement of our Folk, seeking to reestablish the rainbow bridge between us in Midgard, and the Gods in Asgard, Loki would encourage us to act and live in ways that would ensure the destruction and collapse of our rainbow bridge, thus forever establishing a gulf between us and the Gods that created us.

This happened long ago in Atlantis. Remember the nature of Loki? He is the trickster, who whispers falsehoods in our ears, convincing us that wrong action is really right action. He uses Hoder, the God of darkness, to blind us to the light that is Balder, and thus make us ignorant of the eternal truths established by the Gods. Loki seeks to make us think we can be the equals of the Gods without knowing the Gods. He flatters us and inflates our egos by making us believe we know more than the Gods that we are above their natural laws. The Aryans permitted Loki to expand their egos, causing them to think of themselves as Gods, and eventually believe that it was not necessary to maintain their bond with the Gods. Once they had severed their union with the Gods, the orderly essence of the Gods no longer guided and regulated the cravings and urges of the Atlantean Aryans, and so they began to upset the order of the universe, affecting the etherical body of the Earth, and initiating the transformation of the world environment. The result was the destruction of their civilization.

Loki and Balder are the two great adversaries in the Indo-European cosmology, affecting the course of the evolution and progression in the development of our Folk. Balder is the light and truth. Only by reestablishing our links to the Gods that created us can we, as a people, survive and grow in an orderly fashion. Loki, through the use of Hoder, by plunging our Folk into a state of ignorance, causes chaos to govern the affairs of our people by leading them toward nihilism, which will cause our own self-destruction. Eight thousand years ago, Loki brought about the destruction of the Aryan civilization, and is attempting to repeat his mischief once more.

Even the training and discipline in the use of the Vril by the Aryans was not sufficient to prevent their destruction once they started down the path of cultural and spiritual nihilism, and all our technology today will not halt the inevitable progression toward the Ragnarok that we face in the twenty-first century. Once the Aryan civilization was destroyed, the memory of the great civilization that once spanned the shores of the ancient Black Sea gave rise to the many different legends of lost civilizations.

THE GREAT BLACK SEA FLOOD

One hundred and twenty thousand years ago, the sea level was about where it is today, but things were about to change radically. During the next 100,000 years, the climate of the planet cooled rapidly. Large regions of the world's oceans froze. Great ice sheets formed when water evaporated, and fell as snow, in the Arctic region. The ice sheets grew into monstrous glaciers, in some place up to two miles thick, as if great Ymir reached out his hand to claim the world as his domain. By twenty thousand years ago, so much of the world's water was trapped in these sheets of ice that the water levels had declined tremendously. The sea level was about several hundred feet lower than it is today. The Frost Giants terrorized the world, holding it in their icy gripe. They caused great sheets of ice to cover large regions of North America, Europe, Russia, Asia and South America. Most of the mountains of the world were covered in the ice. This was the Age of the Frost Giants.

Modern man was around to witness the Age of the Frost Giants. Having emerged from Africa more than 100,000 years ago, the human race spread out across Eurasia and soon evolved into both the White and Yellow races. Our ancestors appeared in Europe about 35,000 years ago, and they displaced the Neanderthals that inhabited the region. Our ancestors possessed remarkable powers, permitting them to adapt and adjust to the climate they found in this region of the world. They possessed a unique ability to understand their surroundings and invent new technologies that permitted them to survive in the harsh environment. Their ability to innovate served them well.

The ice sheets began melting about 20,000 years ago. There were ebbs and flow of ice that gradually changed the climate of the world. As the glacial meltdown intensified, frigid waters filled rivers that flooded the lands and emptied into lakes, seas and the ocean, causing the water levels of the world to gradually rise. In northern Russia and Siberia, huge lakes, like those that exist in North America, were formed by the melting ice. These lakes no longer exist because the waters that poured south across the great steppes of Russia and Central Asia, feeding lakes further to the south, eventually dried up. This process began around 12,500 B.C., and peaked about 9,400 B.C. and created many great fresh water lakes in central Eurasia. Across Russia, the icy melt continued to flow down rivers into what were then the fresh waters of the Black Sea, the Caspian Sea and the Aral Sea. Both the Caspian and Aral seas were much larger than they are today, but the Black Sea was actually much smaller, and its water level much lower. Between 10,000 and 5600 B.C., the sea level of the Black Sea was about 350 feet below where it is today, and the rest of the world's ocean levels were about 50 feet below its present levels. Prior to that, the ocean's waters were prevented from flooding into the Black Sea by a natural damn that was formed by a land bridge that existed where the Straits of the Dardanelles and the Bosporus presently exist, isolating the Black Sea from the Mediterranean Sea and the oceans beyond.

Our ancestors found the coastal regions around this ancient Black Sea to be rich with black earth that could produce lush vegetation. They quickly settled down and developed farming communities that eventually grew into an advanced civilization. Today, the Black Sea is really a huge lake surrounded by land, with its only outlet through the Bosporus and Dardanelles to the Mediterranean. It is more than six thousand feet deep and fed by numerous rivers including the Danube, Don and Dnieper. More fresh water runs into the sea from the rivers and rainfall, than is lost through evaporation, but the excessive freshwater are lost through the runoff to the Mediterranean Sea. Thousands of years ago, the Black Sea was very different. Enough water evaporated into the air to maintain the water levels. This was true throughout the world. The ice caps melted and sea levels rose, but gradually.

In Roman and Greek times, the Black Sea was known as the Euxine Sea because of the deposits of light gray clay. In 12,500 B.C. the sea, much smaller than now, was fed by runoff water from the great ice sheet that covered northern Europe and Russia. The climate began to grow warmer and the amount of fresh water flowing into the lake became enormous. There were once many great lakes in northern Russia, and combined with the Caspian and Aral Seas, there was five times as much water trapped in them as there was in the Black Sea. Eventually, the lakes grew larger until they could no longer contain the water that was stored within them, and one by one, their crest burst through the natural land damns that contained them. Their freed discharge flowed down rivers, filling the Black Sea. But still, the environment was able to adjust to these changes. The Black Sea remained a fresh water lake, far below the present sea levels of today. Changes took place gradually, permitting people who lived along its shorelines to adjust to the rise and fall of the water levels.

The climate once again grew colder, and by 9,400 B.C., the melting waters of the ice caps had changed direction, flowing westward across Poland and Germany to what is now the North Sea. The Black Sea once again shrank until, around 5600 B.C., it reached its smallest size, its surface level being about 350 feet below the Bosporus dam. But again, it is important to note that these changes happened gradually, over many years, permitting the communities living there to adjust with terrible consequences. At this time, the sea level of the global oceans had risen, and was only about 50 feet below its present level.

But the climate rapidly changed and sea levels suddenly rose very quickly in the sixth millennium B.C., until the waters from the Mediterranean Sea finally burst through into the Black Sea with such force that the land bridge across the Bosporus, which had served as a natural dam, collapsed, making it impossible for anyone to cross from Europe into Asia Minor for many years. This happened around 5600 B.C. according to geological records. The people living along the Black Sea were forced to flee before the rapidly rising water levels. Since the Caucasus Mountains at the eastern end of the lake, were covered with huge glaciers, it would have been almost impossible for people to move south when the Black Sea finally flooded. Those living on the northern coast, would have fled north and west, while those living in the smaller communities on the southern coast, would have fled south into the Middle East and Egypt. Few would have fled east for a while because of the huge barrier formed by the much larger Caspian Sea, but in time, many refugees would make their way east into Central Asia and beyond. In the west, many traveled along the natural arteries formed by the Danube, Dniester, Dnieper and Don Rivers. They traveled into the rich landscapes of Russia and Europe, discovering that the inhabitants already living there were racially related to them. They would have appeared like Gods, or God-men because of their superior physical, mental and psychic abilities, but in appearance the European would have realized that they were related to them in some way.

These refugees probably lost most of their possessions, being forced to flee their homes rather suddenly. Several great migration routes have been discovered by modern archeologists. One migration route was taken by a group of tribes known today as the Linear Pottery Farmers. They traveled along the Dnieper River, north of the Carpathian Mountains, through Bohemia and southern Germany into France. Recent discoveries have shown that their movement was more like an invasion that swept across northern Europe. Another group of refugees came to be known as the Vincas. They traveled up the Danube and into Hungary. Still another group, much smaller, settled in what is now Bulgaria and is known as the Hamangians. This group of refugees seems to be the only group that was willing to settle along the coast. Others perhaps feared that there might be a repeat of the great flood and stayed inland. Another group eventually crossed the Bosporus and traveled by sea through the Aegean and into the Adriatic. This migration became known as the Danilo-Hvar migration. All these refugees brought with them knowledge of the Vril, but were unable to reconstruct their lost civilization. Their appearance helped to spur a cultural revolution in technology among the people they encountered.

Civilizations built on highly advanced technology are very fragile. The more advance and complex the technology, the greater is the threat for total collapse. Think what would happen if our civilization today was suddenly wrenched apart from a worldwide catastrophe? How many of us would be able to reconstruct the technological contrivances that we use daily, and take for granted? We all know how to drive cars, use electric shavers, use televisions, but who among us knows how to build or even repair such devices? Very few, indeed. These devices that we take for granted would simply disappear overnight. The great majority of people surviving such a catastrophe would be plunged back to the stone age. The same was true of the ancient Aryans. Those who survived or were forced to flee before the rapidly rising waters were able to take with them something of their knowledge of Vril and how to use it, especially those adept in the arts of personally being able to harness its powers. But the ability to harness it mechanically would have been lost.

The Aryan refugees possessed a technological understanding superior to those among whom they settled. Despite being refugees, they still possessed great powers bestowed upon them by their personal knowledge on how to use the power of Vril. In many cases they conquered the indigenous Europeans, and with their superior abilities, they soon established themselves as a ruling aristocracy. In some places they displaced them entirely, but in most places they mixed with the native Europeans. Since they were of the same race, though the Aryans were the product of their eugenics program, the assimilation process was rapid. Modern archeologists and linguists have confirmed that these newcomers brought with them new ideas, skills, and language. This raised the level of culture in Europe to new heights, giving birth to a completely new civilization. Only now are we discovering the remains of vast cities in central Europe dating to 4,000 B.C., buried beneath the present communities. Huge pyramids are being discovered in different parts of Europe, as well as evidence of the oldest written language.

Because the newcomers had been engaged in commerce for centuries, their presence in Europe helped to create a rapid expansion in trade. New techniques in mining and smelting metal were introduced, which stimulated the production of all sorts of new goods including tools, weapons, jewelry and other items. This new revolution in production generated a wide exchange of manufactured goods.

The migration of refugees southward was a very different event. Because the southern coast of the Black Sea was much more mountainous, there were fewer settlements by the Atlantean Aryans established in Asia Minor. The number of refugees was smaller. The exodus south had to cross the wild mountainous region of the Anatolian plateau, and the region was already populated. Many of those there probably had contact with the Atlantean Aryans before the terrible flood. There is evidence that this region experienced an influx of people right after the flooding of the Black Sea. This was especially true of the Lebanese coast. In the sixth millennium B.C., there was a massive influx of farming peoples, who were refugees from the Black Sea flood. Egypt also experienced a rise in its cultural levels at this time, its economy expanding as well. Everything from the introduction of new cereals and domesticated animals to new agricultural methods and irrigation planing, were introduced during this period.

Transcaucasia, the region between the Black and Caspian Seas, experienced a sudden appearance of advanced farming technology around this time. As if the knowledge materialized out of thin air, the people of this region abruptly began constructing buildings and planning towns surrounded by planted fields and farms. Archaeologists agree that the transformation was so sudden that it had to be the result of an invasion by outsiders with superior technology. Carbon 14 dating has shown that the transformation taking place throughout the Middle East, in Egypt, and in Transcaucasia, all dates from right after the Black Sea was flooded.

In the hot and arid ancient land known as Mesopotamia, saddled between the Tigris and Euphrates Rivers, grew one of the first civilizations often recognized as the cradle of the Western and Semitic civilizations. It was here that the first great cities recorded in history appeared. Suddenly, as if they leapt out of the desert sands, communities appeared and very rapidly grew into city-states. The region experienced an invasion by refugees of the Black Sea flood driven out of the mountainous north. They followed the two great rivers until they could go no farther, because they had come to the Gulf of Persia. Here they mixed with the local people, who far outnumbered them. With the assistance of the displaced Aryans, the native people began to irrigate the desert, transforming the hot, burning landscape into lush gardens and fields rich with green vegetation. They next began to construct great cities. Trade and commerce soon appeared between the city-states. The newcomers were Atlantean Aryans and they brought with them what they were able to salvage of the Vril Science. They used the power of the

Vril to transform the deserts into breadbaskets. The civilization that grew up is known to us as Sumeria, and the Sumerian people recorded the arrival of the Atlantean Aryans out of the north, in their myths and religions, referring to them as God-men, possessing great powers and superior knowledge and technology.

The Sumerian language escapes definition, but most linguists agree it is not native to the region. Genetically, the people are similar to the most ancient and original Egyptians, who was a small, Mediterranean White race. In the Sumerian *Poem of the Supersage*, they speak of their own origin beginning with the arrival of a race of God-men from the north, dating back to a time right after the great flooding of the Black Sea. In the tale of *Gilgamesh* there were seven sages or wise men, appearing from the sea wearing fish skins. They are credited with the construction of the walls of the city Uruk, and bring civilization to the Sumerians, which included irrigation, farming, construction, the smelting and use of metals, and the art of writing. Before their arrival, for seven millenniums, the native people of this region lived among the foot hills of the Taurus and Zagros mountains, never venturing down to the desert banks of the Tigris and Euphrates rivers. It was not until the Atlantean Aryans arrived that they followed them and did their bidding. Under their leadership, they built the great city-states.

The colonization of the desert was achieved under the leadership of the God-men from the north. Only with the new farming and irrigation technologies that they brought with them, based on Vril Science, could they transform this most harsh desert region into a garden. Using Vril Science, they were able to master the waters of the Tigris and Euphrates rivers. They built great estates for themselves, as well as public temples and walls around their cities. The native people were not slaves, and they benefitted and grew rich under the rule of these God-men. The God-men were depicted in Sumerian art as tall and possessing long, narrow heads with Caucasian or European features.

Even in such far away places as South and North America, refugees from the Black sea flooding settled among the natives. Their numbers were small, perhaps only hundreds, but they escaped in what few surviving anti-gravity flying machines that escaped the destruction of the Atlantean Aryan civilization. They settled among the natives and soon became the ruling classes. There are many legends in the American aboriginal legends of White Gods descending from the heavens or arriving from the east and building the aboriginal civilizations, using Vril Science. We can see the proud of this in such ancient cities as Tiahunanaco in Bolivia, and Machu Picchu in Peru. The huge blocks that were cut and moved into place, couldd only have been done, by using a form of anti-gravity technology that has been lost to modern man. These cities are clearly a great deal older than modern archeologists' claim. We can see evidence of Vril science in the construction of Stonehenge, the pyramids and huge buildings that have been discovered below the surface of the ocean off the coasts of India and Japan.

The Aryans ruled over the more numerous natives, yet in time, through intermarriage, they disappeared into the population. Traces of their existence were left behind in the Sumerian language. The Sumerian language is described as monosyllabic. But there are exceptions to this rule. Those words dealing with agriculture and crafts are not monosyllabic, but actually polysyllabic and thus foreign. This is especially true for words describing farmer, herdsmen, shepherds, fishermen, plows, metal smith, blacksmith, carpenter, weaver, leather-worker, mason, brick-maker, potter, merchant, and a banker. These words were not native to the Sumerian language, but were introduced by the northern invaders—the Godmen from the north.

The language or languages of the original Atlantean Aryans are no longer spoken, but linguists have been able to reconstruct the dead languages, and with the use of sometimes like a tree diagram, they can show how the languages spoken to day are related to one another. Traces of the language spoken by the ancient Atlantean Aryans can be found in many of the ancient languages, and in those languages spoken at the present time in Europe and Asia, those territories to which the Atlantean Aryans fled after the flood.

Genetic studies have also shown the relationship among the present day peoples of these regions. Genes related to the ancient Atlantean Aryans can be detected in the populations throughout Europe, the Middle East, India, Central Asia and North Africa. Those who fled from the flood migrated throughout these regions and have left their genetic traces, in varying degrees in the gene pools of the populations, leaving behind proof of their one-time presence.

THE INDO-EUROPEANS: THE ATLANTEAN REFUGEES

Genetic evidence has shown that a great wave of people migrated through Europe, possessing superior technology. As they met people already living in Europe, who were racially related to them though lacking their superior technology and genetic modifications, they interbred with one another. Geneticists have been able to construct a genetic family tree showing the relationship of all European peoples to each other. Each ethnic group on the branches of the tree, signifies the magnitude of the genetic variation that developed throughout these millenniums. Since the branches reflect a genetic drift, the geneticists were able to trace the ancestry of the Europeans backward to their original primeval homeland.

The Human Genome Project has shown that modern humans, *homo sapiens sapiens,* originated in Africa. About 100,000 years ago the first humans left Africa and settled in the Middle East. From here, one branch set out east across the Asian subcontinent and eventually crossed the Indonesian channel and settled in Australia. Another branch moved into eastern Asia, while still another branch moved north and eventually crossed the Bering land bridge into North and South America. Still, another branch crossed the Bosporus land bridge into Europe. As these different branches of the original proto-humans spread out across Eurasia, different pantheons of Gods then descended to earth and mixed their Life Forces (Vril energies) with different populations of the proto-humans, thus stimulating the evolutionary process and dividing mankind into the different races that we are familiar with today. All pagan religions, not just the Indo-European religions, have "origin stories" describing how their pantheon of Gods once walked the surface of the earth and mixed their essence with their ancestors, creating their own particular race. In *The Secret Doctrine*, Blavatsky explains how the evolution of mankind was affected by the intervention of superior beings—Gods.

This racial memory is typical of all humans and has survived thousands of years, usually somewhat distorted. A good example of this is the *Hymns of the Rigveda*, which has been passed down for twenty-five centuries in two versions: one written and the other oral. Amazingly, both versions have remained consistent through the centuries, the oral eventually written down by monks who no longer spoke the language in which it was told. The monks who eventually put it to the pen, probably no longer understood most of what they were writing, but still they kept it unchanged. The reason for the survival of these myths and legends is simple—they are racial memories that find nourishment from the well of knowledge, the Mimir Well, that is located deep within the brain of each person.

Throughout Eurasia there are many myths about fantastic civilizations now lost in prehistory, and extinct Golden Ages when humans lived in a semi-divine state with the Gods and possessed superior intelligence, physical powers and psychic abilities. The memories of these lost civilizations, or civilization—the mother civilization—remains alive within each of us. All these tales end in the same way—with the terrible fall of man. Numerous myths and religious traditions speak of a race of men who were equal to the Gods, or born of the Gods. Most of them include some terrible natural calamity involving a flood or of a land sinking beneath the sea thousands of years in the past. It is told that those who survived made their way to the great plateaus or mountains of central Asia, Tibet, Ethiopia, Asia Minor or Iran. Those survivors eventually spread out across Europe, Asia, the Middle East and North Africa, mixing with the native peoples already living in these regions. As they did, they brought with them great knowledge from which they taught the native populations to build great new civilizations. As a result, the refugees were often looked upon as Gods, or as a race of God-men.

The refugees divided into tribes speaking languages descended from the original language that they once spoke in their homeland along the shores of the Black Sea. They were the Aryans. Also, referred to as Atlanteans by later scholars. They possessed the secrets of Vril Science, and though most took only part of this lost science with them, it was enough to make them appear as if they possessed supernatural powers. These Indo-Europeans migrated east into China and India, south into Iran, Sumeria and Egypt, west into Europe and the Mediterranean, and even settled on the Canary islands in the Atlantic Ocean. In most cases, they mixed with the native people they found living in these regions. In those regions where the natives were of an alien race, such as in India, the Middle East or Egypt, they set themselves up as a ruling class, separate and distinct from those they ruled. But, in time they too assimilated and disappeared into the mix. In other places, where there were no native populations, such as Sinkiang, in western China, they created new and superior civilizations that lasted thousands of years in isolation. In places like Europe, where the native population was of the same race as the Indo-Europeans, but in a pre-Vril state, they quickly assimilated into the population, losing their superior powers.

Plato claims that another Greek by the name of Solon, transmitted to him information about Atlantis. He also claimed that Solon learned of Atlantis directly from the Egyptians. They explained to Solon that the descendants of the Atlanteans, who settled in Egypt, told the Egyptians how their original homeland was destroyed in a great flood. They were among the many Indo-Europeans who moved south into the Middle East, settling in Sumeria, Palestine and eventually making their way into Egypt. They brought with them bits and pieces of their Vril Science. They set themselves up as God-men and rulers over the Semitic, Hamitic and other peoples that lived in these regions. They are remembered in the Old Testament as giants. In Egypt, they were worshiped as the "Sons of the Gods," and ruled over Egypt as pharaohs. These pharaohs used the anti-gravity powers of the Vril to move great stones, hundreds of miles, and set them in place in the construction of the great pyramids, cities and other monuments.

The Egyptians believed that these God-men were descended from a land they called Pount, located far from Egypt. The Egyptians venerated this distant land that they claimed sank beneath the sea. According to Egyptian belief, two of the members of this race of Gods or God-men, Min and Hothor, were said to have journeyed to Egypt from this Divine Land, and they instructed them in the use of Vril Science. They were distinctively different in appearance from the smaller, copper-colored Egyptians, who were primarily of Caucasian-Mediterranean types. The God-men were tall, almost giant like. Their eyes sparkled with the color of the sea and their hair shined yellow, like the sun. They were fair and beautiful to look upon and they set themselves up as an aristocracy among the Egyptians. In time, they mixed with the native population and eventually degenerated, losing their genetically enhanced powers. As they continued to intermarry with the native population, the genetic mutations that gave them their great powers disappeared, and by the Eighteenth Dynasty, these God-men had disappeared completely into the gene pool of the native Egyptians.

When the Spaniards first discovered and explored the chain of islands off the northwest coast of Africa, known as the Canary Islands, in 1409, they found an unspoiled race of beautiful people living there. The natives of the Canaries claimed they were the direct and unpolluted descendants of Atlantis. Their height was imposing, averaging seven feet tall, which is similar to ancient mummies found on the islands, as well as in northwestern China. They had a cranial capacity of 1,900 cubic centimeters, the largest known brain size ever recorded among humans anywhere. The cephalic index of the male skulls was 77.77. They had blond hair, as did the mummies which were thousands of years old.

The refugees of the Black Sea flood split into two groups. The first were the majority of citizens, who had lived on the northern, eastern and western coasts of the Black Sea. The remainder lived along the narrow southern coast. When the Black Sea was flooded, the two groups were separated because the collapse of the Bosporus land bridge in the west and the natural barrier that the glacier-covered Caucasian Mountains formed in the east. The southern group of survivors fled south into Asia Minor, the Middle East and eventually North Africa, mixing with the peoples they found there. Many of the people living in Asia Minor had been influenced by the Aryans long before the flood. As far back as 7,000 B.C., people living there had been smelting copper into hooks, pins, knives and other tools and instruments. Those that remained there after the flood eventually became the Indo-European nations of Anatolian Group: the Hittites, Phrygians and Lydians. Others would continue their journey south into Mesopotamia, Palestine and eventually into Egypt. Their numbers were small and though they introduced civilization to these lands, their language never replaced those spoken by the local people.

While the original Aryans survived for a time in Asia Minor, evolving into the speakers of the Anatolian Group, those in the north eventually broke up into several additional groups. One moved west, into the interior of Europe and evolved into the speakers of Germanic, Celtic and Italic languages. Another group traveled into the Mediterranean, evolving into the speakers of Greek, Thracian and Illyrian. Other groups ventured east across the northern coast of the Caspian Sea and into Central Asia. This last migration also broke up into several groups. One branch settled along the shores of a lake that once existed in the Tarim Basin, in western China, and there founded what is known as the Tocharian civilization. The rest of this group moved southeast into Iran, Afghanistan and India. These were the speakers of the Iranian and Vedic languages. According the both linguistic and genetic researchers, the divisions took place in the early fifth millennium B.C., about six hundred years after the flooding of the Black Sea.

As early as the eighteenth century, Sir William Jones in India, who was interested in philology, noticed the similarities of Sanskrit and the European languages. Soon a new discipline developed studying what became known as the family of Indo-European languages. Philologists began speculating about the original language of the Indo-Europeans and the location of its original home-

THE INDO-EUROPEANS: THE ATLANTEAN REFUGEES   69

land. They referred to this language as the Ur-language, the people who spoke it as the Ur-people, and their original homeland as the Ur-homeland. "Ur" stood for "proto" or "original."

In Europe, the Indo-Europeans spread across the continent in several waves, mixing with those Caucasians already living there. Research into DNA has revealed genetic evidence that reveals only about 20 percent of the DNA of modern Europeans is actually descended from the invading Indo-Europeans. The Indo-European tribes that spread across Europe settled among the non-Indo-Europeans, ruling over them, and eventually assimilating with them. In most cases they were a minority, but because of their superior abilities and science, they quickly became the ruling aristocracy. In time, most Europeans adopted their language, religion and customs, though much of the original European culture survived. In some cases, as with the Basques, the original culture and language survived in a much purer form.

The first wave of Indo-Europeans began in the sixth millennium B.C. Mentioned earlier, the remains of huge cities and great pyramids have been discovered throughout central Europe, dating back to the fifth and sixth millenniums B.C. This lost civilization eventually declined and a second semi-stone age culture rose up, that we are discovering was much more sophisticated than previous thought. This second culture and civilization in Europe left evidence of its existence in large timber temple complexes recently discovered, and in the many megalithic stone structures scattered across Europe. These monuments can be found as far south as the islands of Malta and Sicily, to Spain in the west, in the British Islands, and in Scandinavia in the north. It was incorrectly thought at one time that they were evidence of explorers from the Mediterranean—the Phoenicians, the Egyptians or Cretans—sailing through the Straits of Gibraltar and settling along the coast of southern, western and northern Europe. However, carbon dating has revealed that these megalithic monuments and structures were built long before these people developed sea travel. Even as late as the first millennium B.C., none of the Mediterranean civilizations had developed a ship that could sail successfully in the rough waters of the northern Atlantic. But we do have evidence that Europeans once possessed such a ship. Rock-paintings found in Bohuslan, in southern Sweden, dating as far back as 1800 B.C., show a long, low, streamlined ship that looks remarkably like a primitive Viking ship that would be seaworthy in the northern Atlantic waters. The Phoenicians did not develop such a ship until around 1100 B.C.

Most of the megalith structures predate the Phoenicians by thousands of years. We now know that the 1,168 menhirs which stand in endless rows at Menec near the Bretan resort of Carnac, were erected between 3500 and 2500 B.C. In Ireland, the oldest stone structure in the world, New Grange, dates back to around 3500 B.C., and work on Stonehenge began before 1400 B.C.

A new image of prehistoric Western Europe is emerging from recent evidence, not that of a dark, primitive and barbaric region existing in the shadow of the more civilized Middle East, but as that of an advanced civilization. This civilization used bits and pieces of a lost science—Vril Science—to construct great stone structures and communities close to Nature, building dolmens, erecting menhirs, constructing stone tombs and houses, even studying the motion of the sun, the moon and the stars. The climate around 5000 B.C. was warmer than in 2000 B.C.. Vines grew as far north as southern Norway and deciduous forests covered most of Scandinavia.

To illustrate where Atlantis was located in the Black Sea, see the illustrations from the book, *Atlantis Motherland,* by Flying Eagle and Whispering Wind.

To sum-up what happened between the destruction of Atlantis and the rise of recorded history, the survivors of the lost civilization of Atlantis, which existed not in the Atlantic Ocean, but on the shores of the ancient Black Sea, built two very different types of civilizations. In the Middle East, India and North Africa, where they were a tiny minority among alien races, and where the land was often arid and dry, they ruled over the majority of people and eventually disappeared through intermarriage. The civilizations they founded were highly urbanized because of the shortage of fertile land. In the more fertile and lush landscapes of Europe, they found people who were racially the same as they were and an environment that could support large agrarian communities. The civilization they built in Europe was more agricultural and existed in greater harmony with its natural surroundings. The Aryans quickly assimilated into the people there, becoming one race, which adopted the Aryan customs, language and religion. Thus, after 5000 B.C., there were at least two poles of civilization—one in western Europe and another in the Middle East.

ZOROASTER

Whether it is the Greek Myths, the Germanic *Eddas*, or the Hindu *Vedas* and *Bhagavad-Gita*, the cosmology described is basically the same—the world exists within the middle of a great conflict between opposing forces, and we mortals are caught right in the middle of this titanic struggle. If we don't learn how to transmute the struggle, we will be consumed by it and destroyed. It was in ancient Persia that the first serious attempt to codify this cosmology among the Indo-Europeans took place with the Mazdaist or Zoroastrian religion of Light. The emphasis on forming an allegiance with the Light of the Sun deity, within the light-dark struggle of Zoroastrianism, is common to all Indo-European religions.

Of all the major religions, Zoroastrianism is the oldest, reaching back to 4500 B.C., and has been a source for the spiritual foundation of many of the other major religions. For this reason, its theological foundation has become the bases for what we know as Gnosticism. Gnosticism is derived from the Greek word *gnosis* and means "knowledge." The purpose of Gnostic intellectual and spiritual thought is the quest to achieve an integral understanding of the material and spiritual essence of the universe. This goal of obtaining a deeper understanding of reality has never been for the masses. It has always been an elite that has tried to penetrate these deeper mysteries of the universe. To achieve this end, one has to undergo stages of initiation and move onto higher planes of existence. Without committing oneself to this quest, one cannot hope to discover the deeper meaning of existence. The masses, or common *Pistis*, are unable to devote the time and energy necessary to achieve this goal. For them it is enough to possess "faith." It was once the function of the religious elite to convey this knowledge to the masses. Eventually, these elites, especially within the major religions of today, held it from the masses, guarding it as their private sources of power and used it to rule over the masses. Because of its elitist nature, the state of illumination for the Gnostics derives from the discovery of the secret science of superhuman origin. This science is the science of the Vril—the Holy Grail.

Though there are Christian and Jewish Gnostic traditions, Gnosticism is a movement that has roots running back to prehistory—to the ancient Aryan civilization that was destroyed with the great flooding of the Black Sea. Its foundation is the aspiration of man to achieve a state of God-like existence. Its spirituality has found its way into Greek philosophy, Egyptian mysteries, Zoroastrianism, the sacred books of the *Vedas* and *Bhagavid-Gita,* Christian and Cabalistic philosophy, and pagan spiritualism, but all of these traditions have their origins in the Vril Science of the ancient Aryan civilization that we refer to as Atlantis, and its fundamental principal is simple—the achievement of exaltation through knowledge of Vril Science.

The Brahman religion of ancient India represents one of the earliest attempts by the descendants of those who survived the destruction of Aryan Atlantis to preserve and pass on the primordial wisdom in the post-Atlantis world. The civilizations that were founded by the refugees of Aryan Atlantis—India, Persia, Chaldea, Egypt, Greece, Rome, the Celts and the Germans—all represented different stages in the spiritual advancement of the White race. Following the fall of Aryan Atlantis, knowledge and awareness of the ancient science of the Vril declined and was forgotten as speculative philosophy increased its hold on the spirituality of the Indo-Europeans in the following millenniums. The rational mind and the type of thinking that evolved from observation, analysis, reason and logic fed the need for personal freedom to express oneself in nihilistic and self-destructive ways. This increasingly corrupt way of living caused the majority of the people to lose contact with their inner spirituality, and thus become deaf and blind to the call of their ancestral Gods. But the responsibility for maintaining those ties with the Gods of our ancestors, who created our Folk, fell onto the shoulders of a small elite of initiates, who could guard the secret of Vril Science from the corrupting influence of the mundane existence. This is the reason why there is the need for the select few who are initiated into the secrets of the Vril. It is their responsibility to maintain the spirituality of the Folk, and prevent it from dissipating, thus diluting its power.

Around 4500 B.C., at the foot of the Pamir and Hundu Kush Mountains in the heartland of central Asia, the religion of Zoroastrianism was born. This is the heartland of ancient Iran and central Asia. For more than one thousand years, the Indo-European refugees of the Black Sea flood had been settling throughout this part of Asia. They eventually became known as the Iranian branch of the family of Indo-Europeans. The land is saddled between the Mediterranean Sea, the Persian Gulf, and the Black Sea. It forms immense stairways, progressively rising as one travels eastward. The entire region is dotted with enormous mountain peaks that encircle the great plateau that stretches to the western regions of China and the banks of the Indus River. These includes the Taurus, Caucasus, the Shiraz and Ispahan, the Gordyen, and the Laristan Mountains, and the entire land is thick with mystery and an immenseness that seems timeless and eternal. It was in this wild and mysterious world that Zoroaster was born over six thousand years ago.

The Indo-Europeans who lived there had settled down to raising wheat and herding cattle, spoke a primitive form of Iranian. They worshiped fire as the symbol of the lost knowledge (the Light) of the Vril. From the east, the Turanians, who were of the Yellow Race, began attacking the Indo-European people of central Asia. They descended upon the agricultural settlements of the Indo-Europeans, pillaging and burning their communities. They too worshiped fire (Vril), but in a crude and demoniacal form. They possessed a corrupt form of Vril Science that was given to their ancestors by the ancient Aryans, but because they were not Caucasian, they could not fully understand how to use its power properly. The Aryan science and traditions were alien to their understanding, so they were turned away from the Gods that the Vril drew its power from, and served the forces of chaos—the Giants. Their practices included human sacrifice, killing their human victims in the name of two flying monsters that the Turanian priests had made symbols of their cult. The beasts are represented in their carvings, and descriptions of them have been handed down to us. They have been described as terrible pterodactyls (dragons?). Eventually the Indo-European Iranians were driven out of their homes and were forced to seek refuge in the mountains.

It was during this period of the Indo-European diaspora that a child was born to the Iranians. He was born of the Elbrus clan, which was of royal heritage. His parents named him Ardjap. He grew into brave and courageous young man, hunting the wild buffalo and attacking and ambushing the Turanians whenever he could. One day he was given a vision by the Gods, and claimed that they told him he would someday be a great king, but a king without a crown, and that he would be more powerful than all the kings and chieftains of the world. His crown would be the Sun.

The leader of the priestly order of the Iranians, Vohumano, recognized that Ardjap was the chosen of the Gods, and convinced him to withdraw to their mountain order, where he was educated and initiated into the secrets of the Vril. Upon his initiation, he was reborn and took the name of Zarathustra, or Zoroaster, which translates as "Star of Gold" or "Splendor of the Sun." He belonged to an aristocratic family named Spitama, which translates as "white" or "pure." The name is also a Celtic word, which means "whites" or as "of a pure race." Universally, every race or people on earth, has always associated whiteness with purity and light. Zoroaster was now a disciple of Ahura Mazda, the God of Light and the Sun (Balder).

Upon his initiation, Zoroaster experienced a revelation after spending several years in isolation, with only a rock eagle as a companion. He lived the life of a hermit, and experienced frightening visions, in which Ormazd, (Hermod) representing the power of the Light (Balder), visited him and revealed to him that the universe was an arena in which two forces, the Light and Darkness, were in eternal conflict. Ahura Mazda was the embodiment of the Light or Order, and Ahriman was his opponent, representing the Darkness or Chaos. It was Ahriman that the Turanians served in their raids of destruction and death, and the Iranians, as descendants of the Aryan Atlanteans, served Ahura Mazda.

Zoroaster returned to his people and began preaching among them. Quickly, they converted to his teachings. The three pillars of his new faith were: purification of the body and soul, work on building a new ordered community upon their purification, and of course battle—the willingness to defend their new civilization against the chaotic forces of darkness and destruction. It was a blueprint for the resurrection of the Golden Age of the ancient Aryans, the new Age of Gimli.

The Iranians were roused by his preaching, and converted to their new "folk faith." Through his teachings, they rediscovered their lost heritage of the ancient Aryan Atlanteans. They were now motivated by a new idealism and discipline that set their determination to drive the Turanians from their homeland. After forty years of struggle and warfare, they finally succeeded in driving the last of the Turanians back to the east. Before his death, Zoroaster claimed to have had a vision of the future. He witnessed Nineveh in the form of a white buffalo crushing underfoot the alien races who tried to exterminate the pure Aryans. He saw a great serpent that he referred to as Babylon, breathing fire and driving back the attacks of the eagle that served Ormazd. This was followed by a vision of the Persians and Medes as a winged lion marching triumphantly, leading a huge army of countless soldiers. The lion eventually mutated into a ferocious tiger that began devouring its young, spreading death and chaos everywhere, including ancient Egypt and the sanctuary of the Sun in that sacred land.

The sacred book of Zoroastrianism is the *Avesta*, and is comparable to the Bible. It contains a series of religious precepts, moral lessons, magical spells, rituals and chanting, mythological tales and a series of prophecies. The foundations of this religion are the eternal struggles between Light and Darkness, fire and ice, good and evil, personified in the deities Ahura-Mazda and Ahriman. The former represented Order and the latter Chaos. All humans are in service of one of these two deities. The totality of every individual's actions either supports the maintenance of order throughout the universe, or contributes to chaos and thus destruction. The two forces would eventually cancel each other out, but Ahura-Mazda would be triumphant for no other reason than that reality did not end but began anew in the cycle of existence. This is the evolutionary process of birth-growth-aging-death-rebirth that exists on every level, from the infinite Macrocosm of the universe to the Microcosm of cells that exist within every living thing. The conflict between the two deities is necessary for the evolutionary process and without it there would be no existence.

Zoroastrianism advocates that we serve Ahura-Mazda and contribute to the process of maintaining an orderly universe governed by the physical laws of science. We can contribute to this process in three simple ways: by thinking good thoughts, speaking good words and doing good deeds. These three simple principles correspond to three more complex principles. Good thoughts belong to the realm of the mind, good words belong to the realm of the soul and good deeds belong to the realm of the physical body. Here we have the triad of the spirit, the soul and the material (body). There is a contradiction here for those who prescribe to the Christian concept of doing good deeds even toward your enemies. The three ways, of good thoughts, good words, and good deeds, are not to be applied on a universal basis. We must recognize that not everyone is in the service of the Gods, contributing to maintain order. Those who serve the Giants and contribute to chaos, are the enemy. Now there is no reason to attack or seek their destruction, but we must not think good, speak good or perform good deeds in their name, for to do so, is to assist such people in their quest to strengthen the forces of chaos. We must refrain from assisting them in all ways, and so long as they do not attack us, we can avoid them, and work to assist the Gods. This is the basis for that old saying, "The best revenge is to live a good life." By being happy and successful we strengthen ourselves, our families and kin, and thus work toward supporting the Gods. This will ensure our success in this world and ensure the same qualities in the afterlife.

MANICHAEISM

Zoroastrianism served as the foundation for much of the cosmology of other religions, including Judaism and Christianity, and especially Manichaeism. In 216 A.D., in Babylon, was born Manes, later known as the "Apostle of Light." He was descended from the Parthian aristocracy through his mother, and his existence has been recorded in the writings of *Acts of Achelaus*, the bishop of Kashkar. Manes, or Mani, was of Iranian blood and looked to Zoroaster as his spiritual mentor. He belonged to a cult known as Mandeanism, but at the age of twenty-four, he received a great revelation in which he claimed Zoroaster, Buddha and Jesus spoke to him. They instructed him to journey to India, where he studied and eventually was initiated into the priestly order of the Brahmans. He then returned to Iran, where he spent the remainder of his life teaching his new doctrine to the masses.

In Iran, he found a benefactor in King Shapur I, who belonged to the Arsacid dynasty, and thus was related to Manes' family. After the death of his benefactor, Manes and his followers, now called Manichaeans, soon suffered great persecution by the new ruler, Bahram I, of the Sassanian dynasty. Manes was thrown into jail, where he died in 277, after suffering greatly at the hands of his tormentors. After Manes' death, his religion took on a life of its own, spreading as far east as China and as far west as North Africa, and eventually reached the Bogomils in present-day Bulgaria.

Manichaeism and Christianity share certain theological beliefs, but the former is closer to Zoroastrianism, and thus, contains many of the secret mysteries (the knowledge of the lost science of the Vril) in its belief system. Though Manes taught that good and evil was in conflict with each other, and equated this struggle with the theology of the Christians, he claimed that the struggle went back to the very beginning of things and was not the result of God's creation of Satan. He claimed that the universe was not created from nothing, but from eternal matter, given form by the Gods (Christ), the good principle. He also taught that the Giants, the evil principle, jealously wished to possess it. In the end, good would triumph over evil. Manes was not a Christian, but he recognized Christ as a "God of Light," who never took human form. Theodore of Mopsuestia, the Greek theologian in the fourth century A.D., wrote that, "the Manichaeans called Christ, the Sun of this world, and that for them, Christ was not the body of the Sun, but that he was in the Sun as father of the inaccessible light." Saint Augustus, who was a Manichaean before converting to Christianity, wrote the same thing about Christ.

The Manichaeans were in agreement with the Zoroastrian cosmology, and rejected the Old Testament of the Jews. Manes felt that Jehovah was a cruel and tyrannical God. He believed that man should seek escape from the materialist world through purity, knowledge and liberty. He and his followers, considered themselves members of the race of the chosen, of superior resolute beings who would one day rise again to the heights that their race had fallen from long ago, in the dark, primordial past of their ancestors.

DUALISM

Zoroaster's dualism spoke of a conflict between opposing powers in the universe. The Life Force, or Vril, of the Universe was created out of this conflict when the fires of Musspellheim and the ice of Niflheim met violently, resulting in the creation of the first life form—Ymir. Though Ymir, the destructive, unorganized power of the Vril, was slaughtered and refashioned by the Gods into a more orderly universe, the destructive nature of Ymir lived on in the guise of the Giants. The Norse tales tell of how two Giants, male and female, survived the death of Ymir in a ship that floated on the waves of blood that flooded the universe after the Gods killed him. This destructive force was latter personified by Loki. His influence on the universe has continued on both the level of the Gods in Asgard, and of man in Midgard. Loki, the representation of the destructive chaotic power, seeks to influence man and causes him to engage in activities that will strengthen the power of the Giants. This *Loki Factor* desires to seduce man into the service of chaos.

Loki's intervention in the affairs of mankind is through the initiation of a process by which mankind becomes his own master of his affairs, thus abandoning the guidance of the Gods. This is accomplished by the shattering of the bonds shared between the Gods and their Children. Once these bonds have been broken, man is led into an existence where his proclivity for destruction and chaos take over his actions. His inner "I" or ego soon becomes dependant upon the lower elements in his nature. Just as the Gods have the essence of the destructive nature of the Giants within them, which they mastered and used for their own purposes, so to does man. This essence of the Giants was passed onto us by the intervention of the Gods in the evolution of proto-humans. Just as the Gods gave us the ability to transcend this earthly existence by learning to master the Vril and transform ourselves into a race of God-men, so to did they give us the ability to turn toward the Giants. Once we have made the decision to abandon the Gods, we become slaves to our ego, to our unbridled passions and cravings, and thus may mankind become servants to the chaotic nature of the Giants. By submitting to the chaotic impulses of the Giants, we become absorbed by the purely material existence of this world, and thus become Midgard bound. Once we become Midgard bound, we fall prey to the danger of descending into the lower realms.

This is the purpose of Loki—to shatter the bonds that unite us with the Gods. He seeks to destroy the rainbow bridge that joins Midgard with Asgard, and thus, condemn us to the three-dimensional existence of Niflheim, Musspellheim, Svartalfheim and Jotunheim. Let me just briefly describe these realms. Niflheim is the realm of contraction. Nothing can survive here. It is like a Black Hole. Musspellheim is the realm of fire. Surtur and his giant demons live there and they consume everything that dares to entire Musspellheim. Jotunheim is a barren wasteland of rocky mountains and freezing winds. Svartalfheim is the realm of the dark elves or dwarves. It is neither positive nor negative. There the dwarves display their skills of creativity, but what they create serves neither the Gods nor the Giants. Their creative impulse is neutral, to be used by either the Gods or the Giants. It represents the creative urge in all of us, but how this urge is used is dependent on our individual nature. This nature is in turn, determined by the conscious decision on whether to serve the Gods in maintaining order, or aligning with the Giants in contributing to the chaotic forces.

It is the nature of Loki (Ahriman) to lead man away from the Gods and down into this material existence so that we might serve the destructive nature of the Giants. Loki is the great adversary of the evolution of mankind and especially our Folk. He seeks nothing less than the destruction of the Gods, and to accomplish this, he must first destroy Balder (Ahura Mazda), the regenerative power of the Gods (Vril). He seeks to accomplish this by severing the link between the Gods and their children. by causing our Folk to become blind of the reality of the universe. This blindness makes us ignorant of our heritage, who we are, and of the essence we share with the Gods who created us.

THE TOCHARIANS

From 3000 to 2000 B.C., the Tocharians lived in the Tarim Basin and possessed an advanced civilization. At this time, Egypt was still young. The Sumerians ruled over most of Mesopotamia and the Greeks and Romans were still two among the many different Indo-European tribes slowly moving across central Europe, and had not yet settled in Greece and Italy. Europe was still in the Bronze Age and the Chinese had not learned how to use metal. All that is left of the Tocharians today are the mummified remains that are being excavated in Sinkiang. But there are genetic traces of the Tocharians within the gene pool of the present population of that region of China. The people of Sinkiang are mixed, mostly Turkic, Mongolian and Chinese. But among these people, there are many who possess light brown and blond hair, as well as blue and green eyes. Many are tall and have fair complexions. All these traits are alien to these people, but they were common among the ancient Tocharians. The Tocharian mummies have verified this fact.

Many anthropologists have been amazed at the discoveries being made every day in northwestern China. They had assumed that this region was always inhabited by Asians—that is, Mongoloids—since the end of the last major ice age forty thousand years ago. Chinese historical records clearly state that the Chinese did not begin to move into this region until around 120 B.C., yet the anthropologists had convinced themselves that this region had always been the homeland of Asians, who are the ancestors of the present-day Altaic speaking nations, those who speak Mongolian and the various Turkic and Tungusic languages.

The Tocharians buried their dead, but did not erect stone tombs. Instead, they posted thousands of wooden stakes in the earth over the graves. The posts served as markers for the sites, but what is most impressive about these simple posts is how they are arranged. The posts are set deeply into the ground in the form of seven tightly packed huge concentric circles, with radiating lines of posts stretching straight out in all directions, giving the entire burial site the image of a radiating sun. This clearly shows that the Tocharians remembered their ancestral religion based on the Sun God, (Balder) and the Vril. One thing that amazes the anthropologists is that these sights are located in the middle of the desert. There are no forests or other wooded regions around for hundreds of miles. So where did the wood come from? The answer is simple. This region was heavily forested thousands of years ago. This means, the Tocharians had to be living there before 3000 B.C. In fact, there was still a large, shallow lake located at the eastern end of the Tarim Basin three thousand years ago. Today, this lake has shrunk into two smaller lakes.

The Egyptians first developed their civilization about the second millennium B.C., and learned to weave and use metals from the Indo-Europeans who migrated to Egypt from the north. The same was true of the Sumerians in the Middle East. In China, it was not until about 1500 B.C. that the Chinese rose out of the stone age and began to learn the use of metal. But the use of metals and other traits that mark the beginning of civilization was common in the Tarim Basin as far back as 4000 B.C. This was about the time when the Tarim Basin was first settled by Indo-European refugees from the lost Aryan-Atlantean civilization.

When the Tocharians first settled in Sinkiang, the Tarim Basin was a large lake fed by melting ice in the mountains surrounding it. On the shores of this lake, the Tocharians tried to resurrect their lost civilization that had once existed on the shores of the Black Sea, destroyed fifteen hundred years before. They were able to preserve some of the lost Vril Science after they fled eastward, and used it to build a thriving civilization in Sinkiang. But in time, the lake dried up and their civilization began to decline.

Chinese records from as far back as 200 B.C. describe the Tocharians as tall, well over six feet in height, possessing fair complexions, blond hair and deep-set, blue-green eyes, pronounced noses, and an abundance of facial and body hair, which the Chinese and other Asians lack. The Tocharians taught the Chinese the use of metals, how to weave cloth, how to tame and ride horses and other skills that are common when a people begin the long march toward civilization. Proof of the influence of the Tocharians in the creation of Chinese civilization can be found in the three hundred or more Tocharian words that are still part of the Chinese language today. Words for such devices as saddle, axle, chariot, and wheel are all of Indo-European origin. Names for such mountains as the Qilian and Kunlun are also Tocharian words, which mean "Holy" and "Heavenly."

The Tocharian civilization was first discovered by a Hungarian-born German explorer by the name of Mark Auel Stein. He had crossed central Asia on foot through some of the most hostile and difficult terrain in the world. He left India and traveled up the Oxus River until he reached the snowy peaks of the Pamir Mountains. From here he traveled through the Mingtepe Pass and crossed over the "Roof of the World," moving north of the glacial-fed rivers and passing through the Takla Makan Desert, in western China. It was in the spring of 1907 when he reached his destination, which was an oasis in the middle of the barren wastelands of northwestern China. This was known as the Cave of the Thousand Buddhas, and considered the Mecca of Buddhism.

The Cave of the Thousand Buddhas is located west of the Great Wall of China, and situated along the famous Silk Road that was traveled by Marco Polo one thousand years ago. The region is honeycombed with countless caves carved out of the cliff walls and transformed into Buddhist temples. The walls of these temples are carved and painted with frescos and sculptures of marvelous beauty. Taoist and Buddhist monks from across Asia once came to these caves to pay homage and tend to the ruins of these holy sites.

Stein discovered the treasure he was looking for. It was not gold or jewels, but a collection of ancient manuscripts hidden behind a wall for hundreds of years, written in a language that seemed unknown and mysterious. Some of the manuscripts were written in two languages. One was an Indo-European language. All Indo-European languages can trace their origin back to the proto-Indo-European language once spoken by the Atlantean Aryans. The language they spoke eventually evolved into separate dialects, which continued to evolve into different languages. This breakup of the original language began around 4000 to 3000 B.C., until it eventually atomized into Celtic, Italic/Latin, Germanic, Albanian, Greek, Phrygian, Hittite, Armenian, Baltic, Slavic, Indo-Iranian and Tocharian. The language of the manuscripts could be broken down into two dialects known as Tocharian A and B (Turfanian and Kuchean). With his knowledge of Sanskrit, Stein was able to penetrate the mystery of the manuscripts and translate them. The language was given the name Tocharian, after an ancient tribe of Indo-Europeans living in Central Asia two thousand years ago.

The historical events played out this way. The scattered refugees from the destruction of the Aryan Atlantis in 5600 B.C. included those who moved eastward until they settled around the large lake that existed in what is now the Takla Makan Desert. In the next several thousand years, they constructed a civilization similar to that which existed on the shores of the Black Sea, but not as advanced technologically. Their knowledge of Vril Science was limited and spotty. The ancestors of the Tocharians remained racially pure, mixing with other people, Caucasian or Asian, almost not at all. Then, by around 3000 to 2000 B.C., their civilization began to decline as a result of the changing climate in central Asia. The lush landscape began to dry up as the melt water from the glaciers ceased. The rivers that fed their lake disappeared, and the lake began to shrink, as its waters evaporated from the heat. By 200 B.C., the Tocharians had declined to the semi-barbarous tribes living around a small lake at the eastern edge of what had been a great lake, and was now the Takla Makan Desert. The mummies that date back to 2000 B.C. indicate that the Tocharians were still a pure and superior race, possessing the physical traits endowed by their ancestors when they still lived on the shores of the Black Sea. They were tall, well over six feet, including the women, possessing beautiful Caucasian features, unsoiled by mixture with other races. This is proven by the frescoes that the Tocharians drew of themselves, as well as the records of the Chinese, who first made contact with them in around 200 B.C., which depict them as tall, possessing blond hair and blue or green eyes, and sporting heavy beards and handlebar mustaches. They referred to them by the Chinese word *Hu*, which is used for anyone who possesses deeply set eyes (Caucasian eyes), prominent noses, and beards. This is why they were eventually referred to by the Chinese as the Yue-zhi or Yue-chi.

Today, the Chinese name for this region of China is Xinjiang, which has replaced the older form that I have used, Sinkiang. Both words mean "New Territory" in Chinese. This is an indication that the Chinese had settled this region in the last two thousand years. Most of the names of geographical landmarks in this region bear out this historical fact. The names are either Indo-European or Turkic, (another people who settled this region between 500 B.C. and 500 A.D. and eventually mixed with and then drove out the Tocharians). When the Tocharian language was eventually examined by philologists, they discovered that Tocharian belongs to a branch of the Indo-European language that includes the Celtic languages, sharing more linguistic features with Celtic than with any other known language. Most likely, a group of Indo-Europeans speaking a branch of the mother Aryan tongue lingered in the region of what is now Ukraine and southern Russia and eventually separated, some moving east, and some west. What is interesting is the clothing that was discovered on the mummies found in the Tarim Basin. They were similar to the tartans that the Celts wore. We know that the Celtic peoples in the British Islands, Gaul, Spain, northern Italy, the Balkans and Asia Minor all wore some form of clothing with plaid designs. The Celts did not originate in the British Islands, but settled there about 400 B.C., migrating north from Europe. The original inhabitants of the British islands were a short, dark-haired, white-skinned people associated with those whites who inhabited the Mediterranean coastal regions. But the Celts were a huge, blond-haired and blue-green eyed people who traveled across Europe between 2000 and 1000 B.C., and settled in that region of Europe north of the Alps, extending from eastern France, across southern Germany, into Hungary and Czechoslovakia, and were the creators of what we refer to today as the Hallstatt culture.

TIBET

Egypt has always been a land of sacred knowledge and occult mysteries, but it has shared this reputation with another mysterious and exotic realm situated in the heart of Asia, known as the "Roof of the World." This land is Tibet. There have been innumerous books about the mysterious land of Tibet, and the belief of hidden domains and cities there inhabited by superior beings possessing superhuman powers. In the last few centuries, a tiny number of Westerners claimed to have been initiated by secret brotherhoods, who are alleged to live in these hidden abodes, in the mountains of Tibet. They claim that secret knowledge of the history of mankind and the source of great power has been conveyed to them. Many claims include the belief that those who live hidden within these secret domains in Tibet, are descended from a lost civilization. Some say that this mysterious race has been manipulating the course of human history from their hidden domain. It is reputed that huge libraries that possess records of human history going back ten and twelve thousand years, possibly, hundreds of thousands of years, are maintained within these mountains.

The truth is that the descendants of the ancient Aryans had settled in Tibet, but they came to this land, not five, seven or ten thousand years ago, but less than two thousand years ago. Today Tibet is ruled by Communist China, but for the last one thousand years that mountainous kingdom, dotted with hundreds of monasteries, was ruled by Buddhist monks, whose leader was the Dali Lama. This was a mysterious land in which one third of the men became monks, and it is told, possess mysterious powers. But Tibet was not always a land of lamas and deep religious convictions. Long ago Tibet was a nation of warriors.

A group of people from northwestern China conquered Tibet about two thousand years ago, and founded an empire ruled by an aristocracy of warrior knights. They were known as the Kucheans, and they established a glorious imperial heritage for Tibet. The oldest building in Tibet is the Yumbu Lagang, and it was from this huge palace that the Kucheans ruled over their empire. This "race of giants" was descended from the Tarim Basin Tocharians who had built a civilization thousands of years earlier.

The ancestors of the Kucheans, the Tocharians, were referred to as the Yue-zhi or Yue-chi, by the Chinese. They lived near the western edge of the Great Wall of China, in the Sinkiang Province. But as this region slowly turned into a desert, their civilization declined. For centuries they had been settling central Asia in search of new, more fertile lands to inhabit. They were known by Plato as the Thaguri. Then, in 165 B.C., they were driven out of Sinkiang by the westward movement of the Hsiung-nu (the Huns). One branch of the Kucheans climbed the plateau of northeast Tibet, and was known as the Lesser Yue-chi, or Lesser Kucheans. But the majority of the Kucheans remained for several centuries in central Asia until they finally moved south into India. They were known as the Kuei-shang, from which the name Kucheans was eventually derived. One tribe finally gained supremacy over the others and united them into a great power. In 120 A.D., under the rule of King Kuyula Kadphises, they conquered most of what is now Afghanistan. His son and successor, King Vima Kadphises defeated the Sakas and Parthians and conquered the Indus River Valley.

The Lesser Kucheans eventually settled down and formed knightly orders. These knights eventually united under a king and forged a powerful empire in the mountains and plateaus of Tibet. With their knightly customs and warriors' tradition, they were able to expand the borders of their kingdom, conquering the surrounding lands. By the seventh century, A.D., Tibet had established itself as the foremost military power in central Asia. Their armies invaded all the lands in every direction, as far west as Persia and the Caspian Sea, and as far east as China.

The ruling order of knights and their king practiced a religion that was descended from their ancestral homeland. It was called Bon. This religion was based on the central idea of the Vril, the Life Force of the Gods. It was believed that the knights could tap into the power of the Vril, or the Bon, because of the Life Force that was rooted in their bloodlines, which they claimed ran true and pure, back thousands of years to their ancestral homeland of Atlantis on the shores of the Black Sea. The religion claimed that its founder was Shenrab, who was also thought to be the God, Mithras, a Sun God, and the same deity as Balder. He was supposed to have descended from heaven to give the Bon religion to the Kucheans. Shenrab taught that the universe was controlled by the Wheel of Time, which represented a sacred knowledge of the structure of the universe. Time is structured in cycles and described as a "Vortex of Time." Since Balder is associated with the cycles of time—birth, death and rebirth—he can be viewed as a fountainhead of creation. Balder's wife is Nanna, who is a fertility Goddess, and from her emanates the universal power of creation. In the Hindu teachings, which is a corruption of this ancient Aryan doctrine, we discover Kali, the Hindu

Goddess of Time, from whose vagina flows sexual magic. This magic is the same principle by which magicians try to harness the powers of the Vril. Thus, the Kucheans arrived in Tibet with an incomplete knowledge of the Vril, but the king and the knights eventually abandoned their ancestral religion for a new religion—Buddhism. This happened as a result of the contamination of their bloodline through intermarriage with the native Asia races.

The first of the kings to adopt Buddhism was King Srongtsan Gampo. In the Sixth century A.D., under his leadership the knights of Tibet invaded and conquered the Yarlung Valley, east of the capital city of Lhasa. This brought Tibet into contact with the Chinese. The King wanted to form an alliance with China and other surrounding kingdoms that were strong military powers. He eventually married princesses from both neighboring countries of China and Nepal, and formed alliances with those lands. The princesses practiced Buddhism and convinced the King to adopt the religion as his own. His influence by his Asian wives was total. He soon began encouraging his knights to convert to the new religion, and eventually depleted the treasury of the kingdom in the construction of hundreds of Buddhist monasteries and temples. He then invited Buddhist monks from India to settle in Tibet, and began the process of converting the entire population to his new religion. In 767 A.D., King Trisong Detsen built the Sanye Monastery, which sealed the fate of Tibet. Buddhism now became the official religion of Tibet and dominated every aspect of Tibetan life.

The Bon religion continued to be practiced as a shadowy cult, reserved for the elite. Many Tibetan nationalists today like to claim that Bon is still practiced, and is the true and secret religion of Tibet. The Buddhists adopted the Bon religion and corrupted it, altered it and absorbed it into their teachings. In its most pure form, the Bon Religion was centered around a Sun God (Balder), and the Vril or Black Sun, as the Life Force of the Gods. The Life Force or Vril, represented the power of the Gods, which created all and gave order to the universe. The memory of their Atlantean Aryan ancestors was kept alive, but their knowledge of Vril Science and their ability to use it declined, and thus the Bon religion slowly gave way before the tide of Buddhism. Buddhism as the world knows it today, is a far cry from the original Buddhism that was practiced before the arrival of Siddhartha Guatama (Buddha). The decline of Bon and the rise of Buddhism, spelled the death knell for the ruling class of knights descended from the Kucheans.

Tibet as a military power quickly declined, as more and more men every year abandoned their warrior tradition and became monks, joining the growing orders of lamas, swearing an oath of chastity (at least heterosexual chastity) and adopting a pacifist philosophy. In time, the Kucheans disappeared, either through self-imposed genocide by refusing to reproduce, or through intermarriage with the native Asian population.

Lamaism acted like a cancer that sapped the vigor out of the ruling class, extinguishing forever Tibet's heroic age. The triumph of Lamaism transformed the people and character of Tibet, forever changing the racial and spiritual composition of the land. Because of the influence of the new religion, the once great race of knights eventually declined into a race of sheep, mixing with the native people they had long ago conquered, eventually disappearing. These lamas, who eventually came to rule over Tibet, claimed to be in possession of great magical powers, based on sacred knowledge passed down to them through the ages. In reality, they were a cult of monks who practice freakish rites and sinister ceremonies that spread terror and fear throughout the mongrelized population of that unhappy land. The people, who had been reduced to a bedraggled and motley horde, were oppressed by this cult of monks who lived in huge and ornate monasteries, where they collected young boys and forced them to submit to their perverted sexual practices, in bizarre religious initiations into their order. They threatened to call down an army of demons and devils on the population, if the people, who were oppressively taxed and forced to live in poverty, did not submit to their tyranny.

As much as one third of the male children was kidnaped in this way every year. The result was a depletion of the work force. The most talented and intelligent men were forced to belong to this disgusting cult, thus preventing the best men from reproducing, eliminating the best genes from the gene pool of the Tibetan population. This practice eventually sucked the life force and vitality from Tibet, transforming this once race of knightly giants, descended from a race of God-men, into a degenerate race of cattle.

The Kucheans had also conquered India and ruled over most of the subcontinent for one hundred years. Like their countrymen who conquered Tibet, they also set themselves up as a ruling aristocracy, but the class barriers quickly disappeared. They too mixed with the native population and disappeared through intermarriage. Long after they lost their hold on India, the Indian people continued to tell tales about the Kucheans, who they claimed ruled the subcontinent from the "Mouth of the Himalayas." They described these mountains as "the abode of the Gods." They referred to the Kucheans as *Vidyard hara*, a race of God-men or giant supermen, who possessed sacred knowledge that endowed them with superhuman powers. They were referring to the tall, Caucasian Kucheans who still maintained the Bon religion, which was the remnant of the lost Vril Science that they practiced through the millenniums in their homeland of Sinkiang, until they were forced out around 100 B.C. They fled to central Asia, and later invaded India.

For centuries the Indians retained distorted memories of the Kucheans in the form of tales and legends, and passed them down from generation to generation. These tales eventually turned into the legend of Shambhala, or Shangri-La. The Indians claimed that the Kucheans still lived in the Himalayas in a secret kingdom known as Shambhala. This land was in the shape of a giant lotus flower and possessed sandalwood forests and beautiful lakes. The entire land was supposed to be hidden within a valley ringed and protected by a wall of huge, towering mountains, impassable unless given knowledge of a secret passageway. They claimed that the land was inhabited by "960 million" villages ruled over by an elite race of God-men who lived in a palace made of gold and silver. The inhabitants were said to have lived for two hundred years and their kings ruled for one hundred years each, carrying the title of the "Holders of the Caste." The people were alleged to be a race of beautiful giants, virtuous and noble, living a life of purity, discipline and honor. A priestly order of "35 million" members governed the land and maintained a huge library possessing sacred knowledge, from the scriptures of the Veda. The Indians claimed that this race was transformed into this race of supermen only after they had converted to Buddhism. This legend is a corruption of the historical memories of the time when India was ruled by the Kucheans.

THE DRUIDS

When the Celts and other Indo-European tribes moved into Europe, they carried with them a partial memory of Vril Science. Over thousands of years, a priestly class grew up among the Celts, that is known to us today as the Druids. There has been a great deal of confusion about whom and what the Druids were. Besides acting as judges, priests, doctors and educators, the Druids were also religious leaders representing one of the highest points of spirituality ever achieved among the Indo-European peoples, and perhaps among any group of people anywhere in the world. Even Pythagoras sought their wisdom, by living with them, so that he could learn the sacred knowledge they possessed.

From their center, on the Isle of Man, the Druids spread out across Europe, from Spain and Ireland in the west to as far east as Asia Minor. They won great esteem and respect, helping the common people and Celtic leaders alike, worshiping the Celtic Gods of Taranis, Esus, Teutates, Lugh, and Dagda. Those who became Druids were expected to memorize a whole library of knowledge and text. They were reputed to possess great powers, and served as guardians of sacred knowledge passed down to them from the beginning of time. Much of what they knew and guarded has been lost because they never wrote it down. They lived ascetic lives like Tibetan or Christian monks, choosing to make their homes in the forests and mountains, so they could be close to nature. It was claimed that they could speak with birds, animals and even communicate with trees and stones. Wherever they congregated soon became a site known for its learning and spirituality. They did not eat meat for fear of harming animals, and lived in stone homes or huts, and made fires only from wood that had already fallen to the ground, wishing not to harm any living tree.

The Druids rejected gold and all wealth, detesting materialism. They were the high priests of the Celtic people, living simple lives, studying and helping the common people and great leaders alike. The Celts spoke a language that was closely related to Italic, from which Latin originated. Celtic is also very closely related to the language of the Tocharians, who lived in western China. The Tocharians shared many cultural similarities with the Celts, obvious from their clothing, jewelry and art.

As a religious class among the Celts, the Druids shared a status within Celtic society similar to that of the Brahmins within the Indo-European society of ancient India. Both the Druids and Brahmins preformed the same function within their societies—they were responsible for religious services, studying science, teaching and preserving knowledge, poetry, law and healing. Like the Brahmins, the Druids were political leaders, who held a higher position than both military leaders and tribal chieftains.

Druids met in sacred droves, and once a year they would come from across Europe to meet in the most sacred—the "Navel of Gaul." This site was located where the present-day Benedictine abbey of St. Benoit is located near Orleans, in France. There they discussed affairs of political and religious importance, and exchanged new knowledge and information acquired throughout the year. The leader of the meeting was the Arch-Druid, known as Chartres, named after one of the Celtic tribes, and now the name of a world-famous cathedral. Two thousand years before the invention of the post office, Druids were able to maintain communication among their tribes which were spread across Europe from Spain to the British Isles, and to Asia Minor. Many believe this was done through a form of telepathy or astral communication.

Julius Caesar has described the role of the Druids in Celtic society in his accounts of his campaigns in Gaul. "They officiate at the worship of the Gods, regulate public and private sacrifices, and give rulings on all religious questions. Large numbers of young men flock to them for instruction, and they are held in great honor by the people. They act as judges in practically all disputes, whether between tribes or between individuals." Cicero tells us that they were the guardians of scientific knowledge, especially dealing with astronomy and physics. Pliny explained that the Druids dealt with matters concerning medical knowledge, served as teachers, healers, judges, poets, and were augurs of Celtic society, possessing the ability to foretell the future. Diodorus called them philosophers and theologians, claimed they possessed a superior moral philosophy, and were great scholars of natural science.

The only eyewitness account of a Druid ceremony was recorded by Pliny the Elder (23–79 A.D.). He described a ceremony taking place in a grove beneath a sacred oak. The Druids, dressed in white robes, harvested mistletoe on the sixth day of the waxing moon, and used it in their sacrifice of two white bulls to a God. Prayers were offered to ask the God to make the mistletoe an effectively potent medicine. They believed that mistletoe growing on oak was a sacred plant that possessed the power to harness the Vril, and were calling on the God to fill the mistletoe with that power. In the Norse tales it was mistletoe that was used to kill

Balder. Since the Vril is the regenerative power of Balder, mistletoe was used to master the Vril's power by the Druids.

It is possible that the God they worshiped at this ceremony was Lug. Lug was one of the greatest of the sixty-nine major deities of the Celtic religion. He is often described as a noble warrior, who possessed a golden breast plate and helmet, a green cloak and on his white skin he wore a shirt of silk, and on his feet, sandals made of gold. His primary weapon was a spear. He was accompanied by ravens who flew over the world every day and returned to tell Lug of everything that happened. When the city of Lyon, France, was founded (the city was named after Lug), it was claimed that swarms of ravens descended from the sky. Lug was believed to walk with a limp and had lost an eye somehow. He has been identified with Odin, who also was accompanied by ravens, possessed a spear and had one eye. Both Odin and Lug fought the Giants. The two Gods also had something else in common—they were both great shamans. Zeus was also related to both Gods. He too had slain a Giant, Chronos, his father, so that he could come to power. Like Odin, Lug also dies and is reborn. Unlike Odin, who death is a sacrifice to himself, Lug is suppose to die in a war and then rises from the Netherworld. Upon his resurrection, he is transformed as the leader of a divine hierarchy. Since Balder is Odin's son, it would seem that the Celts merged the tale of the father (Odin) with the son (Balder). On August 1, Lugnasad (Lug's Day), the God enters into a marriage with an Earth Goddess. Remember, both Odin and Balder are married to earth Goddesses, Frigg (Odin) and Nanna (Balder).

Like most Indo-Europeans, the Celts held certain trees sacred, especially the oak. The region of Europe they inhabited was covered with great oak forests. Lightning often struck the oak tree and they considered this a mark of favor by the Gods. They believed that the oak tree possessed sacred qualities and through the oak, one could communicate with the Gods. In fact, the word, "druid," was derived from the word for oak. In Sanskrit, *druh* is the word for oak. The Greek word for oak was *drus*. The word "druid" was probably derived from two words. The first syllable, *dru*, clearly means oak, but the second syllable is probably derived from the word *wid* (which is related to *wyrd)*. It is an Indo-European root word that means "to know." Thus, the two words mean "knowledge of the oak." This is a reference to the Druids as an order of holy men possessing a sacred knowledge rooted in the Vril, which is represented by the world tree, Yggdrasill. They clearly were in possession of what knowledge had been passed down to them through the millenniums—the lost Science of the Vril.

This knowledge was passed down through oral tradition. The Druids never wrote down their sacred knowledge, and those who became Druids had to possess exceptional memory. When a student became a Druid, he was expected to commit to memory, the entire teachings of the Druids' sacred knowledge. Though they did not develop a written language for their native Celtic, most Druids could read and write Latin and Greek.

Anyone could become a Druid, provided he had the fortitude to survive the rigorous training. Once a young man of exceptional intelligence and memory passed the training, he had to dedicate his life to serving his people. A candidate could be from any class within Celtic society. They were expected to memorize tens of thousands of lines of text, which were put to verse to make them easier to memorize. Because of these requirements, the best and most intelligent Celts often became Druids. Druids could marry and have families, so that their genes could be passed on to the next generation.

The Druids held an exceptionally sacred place in Celtic society. If anyone refused to accept a decision made by a Druid, he was excommunicated from participating in any sacrifices, which was the worst punishment short of death that could be passed in Celtic society. When they passed judgement in a dispute, the decision was considered final, and it was accepted not just by the community in which the Druid resided, but by all Celtic tribes. Even opposing Celtic armies stopped fighting when a Druid made his appearance on the battlefield. The Druid was the center of the Celtic community, thus maintaining a sacredness that can still inspire us today.

The Druids resisted Roman conquest. Their order was destroyed by the Romans, not for their beliefs, but for their political resistance. Most of their sacred knowledge was lost with their destruction because they never wrote down this storehouse of knowledge. How much of what had survived the destruction of that ancient civilization on the Black Sea long ago will never be known. But from the legends, we can surmised that the Druids did possess a large part of what the ancient Aryan had learn of the use and nature of Vril.

THE GNOSTICS

The major religions of antiquity can be divided into two categories, each based on a different fundamental view of the universe and God. The first theory is based on the notion that there is only one true God, who is all good. He created the universe, and the world, and since he is all-good, his creation must also be all-good. This God is omnipotent and all-knowing, and thus, is in control of everything that happens. He created the world, including the evil forces, usually known as Satan or the Devil, for a reason. That reason is to test man and see if he is worthy of a reward of everlasting bliss in the afterlife. In this cosmology, the world is "progressing" toward the "City of God." This theory is the foundation of the Jewish-Christian-Islamic tradition. God is all-good and has given us his Law, which we must accept faithfully and blindly, without questioning his divine plan. Everything else is irrelevant. This tradition is based on faith and absolute obedience.

The idea of an omnipotent God ruling us, and making all decisions for us, and promising everlasting bliss in the next life, is very reassuring to the common people, who must suffer and struggle to survive from day-to-day. But this theory has never been satisfying to the elites of the world, for it ignores the dilemma of conflict, which is at the foundation of all human activity. It is this struggle for life that is at the foundation of the second theory. Whether between good and evil, light and darkness, order and chaos, or fire and ice, we have only to look about us to realize that our existence is one of continuing conflict between opposing forces. If we are to succeed in this life, we must learn to transmute the world in which we live by tapping into the God-force, and rise above this struggle. The way to accomplish this is by discovering the scared knowledge that is hidden from us, but is obtainable.

This second theology is based on dualism, and interprets life as one of an endless struggle between opposing forces. We inhabit a world, which is part of the Macrocosm of the universe, that is constantly changing and in a state of evolution, and not congealed or static. We are not "progressing" but evolving. This second theology is often referred to as Gnosticism.

Gnosticism is nothing more than the desire to acquire *higher knowledge*, and use this knowledge to achieve a higher state of existence or awareness. What interest us is this knowledge that is sought after by the Gnostic tradition. Classical Gnosticism is actually a product of Greek pagan thought. This Gnostic tradition penetrated Christianity, along with other pagan ideas. Christianity never tired of incorporating and digesting pagan ideals. The traditional Christian leadership would never publically admit this fact, for the churches have maintained two doctrines: one for public consumption, and another to be kept secret and taught only among the elite of the church hierarchy.

The father of Greek Gnosticism was Pythagoras. He actually disguised his doctrine in an elaborate system of symbolism, so we can learn more about his doctrine from Plato. *Timaeus* is in a sense a condensed rendition of the cosmology that Pythagoras taught. What he preached was the principle of a great power that could transform both the physical and spiritual essence of the individual—the Vril. We can find much in common between Pythagoras' teachings and the secret knowledge of the Sun, the solar religion taught by the high priest of Ammon-Ra of the ancient Egyptians.

Christian Gnosticism can be divided into two main branches: Syrian and Alexandrian. Christian Gnosticism does not deny the divinity of Christ, but rejects his earthly form, considering him perfect in every way and associating him with the Indo-European Sun Gods. Syrian Gnosticism is heavily influenced by Hebrew and Eastern spirituality, while Alexandrian Gnosticism looks to Greek pagan philosophy and even ancient Egyptian learning, both of which includes remnants of Vril Science. This reflects the dual nature of Christian spirituality—its Semitic roots and its later paganization at the hands of Paul and his followers.

Within the Syrian tradition, we discover all sorts of orientalism that can be traced to the spirituality of Hebraic tradition common among most Semitic esoteric spiritualism. There is much here in common with the Jewish Kabbala. All Gnostic traditions are based on the belief that humanity once enjoyed a golden age built upon this knowledge, but has been plunged into chaos through its loss. Memory of this golden age is part of the racial memory of the great flood of the Black Sea that caused the destruction of the ancient Aryan civilization. This memory has continued to haunt the descendants of the refugees of that cataclysm and has survived in different Gnostic traditions. We find an example of this in the Biblical tale of the serpent trying to give Adam and Eve the opportunity to recover this lost primordial knowledge for themselves. Both the Jewish and Christian hierarchies guard this secret knowledge from the masses, and so the serpent has become a symbol of evil. Adam and Eve are told that if they eat the fruit from the Tree of Knowledge, they will become like God. Is not the Tree of Knowledge Yggdrasill, and the fruit that grows on it Vril science? By eating from it, humanity will become Godlike by ingesting the Life Force of the Gods. Thus, the serpent should not be associated with the Christian Satan, who is often referred to as Lucifer. Lucifer is actually the name of the Roman God of Light, who has been demonized by Christianity. Christian Gnostics did not consider Lucifer the devil, but the *bringer of enlightenment*, who would bestow upon man the secret of Vril science. They actually believe that Jehovah is the devil, for he has reduced man to a state of ignorance and servitude to his tyrannical will.

In the Jewish Torah, the serpent is not Satan, but rather a symbol for the desire in every human to become Godlike. The Jews refer to this inner evil nature as *yetzen*. The Gnostics also knew that the serpent was not Satan, but the need for man to seek higher knowledge. The serpent can slither into hidden places no accessible to others because of its slick form. In the Norse tales, Odin transforms himself into a serpent so he can slither through a small hole in a wall and enter a chamber where the Mead of Knowledge is held by a Giant. He then seduces the Giant's daughter and escapes with the Mead. It is through the union of the male and female that we can discover this hidden knowledge, which is linked to the synchronicity of the male/female nature of humanity—the organic nature of human society. We do not have the space to fully explore the implications its symbolism, and it relevancy of the symbolism of the Adam and Eve's tale, and how she seduced him (reversal of Odin and the Giant's daughter), how they ate from the tree of knowledge, and were thus expelled from paradise (translated as, being free from living under the tyranny of Jehovah).

Unlike the Hebrew tradition, the Aryan or Indo-European tradition encouraged man to seek spiritual elevation, and rejected the Semitic message of accepting the *Law of God* through faith, instead of through knowledge. The symbol of the serpent has always been one of evil or danger or poison, and was used by the Jewish and later the Christian and Islamic hierarchies, to discourage the masses from seeking the key to knowledge—the Vril Science. Like Odin, we must seek this hidden knowledge in the darkness of the past. Darkness is not the symbol of evil, but for what is lost to us. Once humanity begins the journey of becoming God-men, they no longer need the tyrannical hierarchies that govern the three monotheist religions. What the Gnostics did believe is that man can and should discover for himself, the intimate secret of Vril Science, which will illuminate his soul and cause transmutations of body, mind and the spirit.

In the second century A.D., one of the most influential Gnostics was Basilides who believed that the Great Flood was caused by the Forces of Chaos, personified as the demiurage (Jormungand, the Midgard Serpent) a creature who pretends to be God. He is a Giant who can cause the animation of matter, resulting in earthquakes, terrible storms, tornadoes and other destructive phenomena. Jormungand is the knowledge of Vril that is lost to us (hidden at the bottom of the ocean—a dark realm). There is a tale of Thor who tries to catch Jormungand, but fails to do so because of the cowardice of a Giant). Man has fallen under the domination of the Giants, abandoning the sacred knowledge (Vril Science) of the ancient Aryans, and has adopted the science of destruction. But he has it within him the Life Force of the Gods, and so can rediscover that lost knowledge. He must abandon a life of chaos, and seek the courage of Thor.

Basilides viewed existence as a realm where Matter (the Giants) is not separated from the Spirit (the Gods) and the world is organized in a hierarchical stratum. Within the Gods is the essence of both the Gods and the Giants. Odin's father took a Giantess as a bride, and so Odin is part Giant. The tale of Odin, Vile and Ve killing Ymir and refashioning his body to construct the universe is a dual tale of the Gods conquering Chaos and creating an orderly universe, as well as conquering their own inner destructive nature. According to Basilides, the higher plane of existence is the Spirit (Asgard) represented by the Light or Logos (Balder—the secret of Vril Science) and the lower, the realm of the unconsciousness (Jotunheim—the Realm of the Giants). Christianity gave Vril a new name—the Holy Spirit.

We, as the Children of the Gods, can, by the illumination of our souls through Vril Science, which is the process of reestablishing the lost bonds with those Gods who created us, transform ourselves, our physical forms, our mental capacities and our very souls. If we are to do so, we must overcome the temptation to succumb to the easier path of material degeneration, becoming servants of the forces of Chaos and corrupting the blood, and the domination of the principle of quantity over the principle of the evolution of the God-man.

In the scale of all living things, mankind is the furthest removed from Chaos and the unorganized. Within mankind, different groups of people are closer to one of the two opposing forces—Order or Chaos, the Gods or the Giants. The different races (genetic groups) of mankind were created through the union between proto-humans and different Life Forces of the various pantheons of Gods. It is even possible that some races owe their existence not to a union with Gods, but with Giants. This is also true of individuals within all races. Since the Gods have within them, the destructiveness of the Giants, they have imparted this aspect of their Life Force to us as well. This trait is recessive but it can rise to the surface in all of us, like any recessive inherited trait. The gene is there, hidden and unseen, but can rise to the surface at any time. So to is the destructive nature of the Giants.

Because of this recessive trait within us all, many humans forged bonds with the Giants and thus serve Chaos, while others serve that of the ordering principle of the Gods. Just as individuals may make a conscious decision, or in most cases, an unconscious decision, to serve Chaos, so to may whole groups of people, races and nations. For such Gnostics like Basilides, "… evolution consists of a differentiation and a separation, a sorting out of material substances originally mixed together." I personally that today, the ruling elite of Western civilization has aligned itself with the Giants, which is leading the world toward another Ragnarok.

The Gods were created through the union of the first Gods and Giants. Borr, the father of Odin, took a Giantess as his wife. Thus, Odin and all the Gods are part Giant. They have within them the capacity for destruction, but that capacity is controlled by the orderly vital force of their Godly ancestor, Buri. This is why Odin, Vili and Ve had to kill Ymir, for he represented the Giant-Chaotic forces within themselves. When they killed him, they were mastering their own destructive nature. Thus, all humans have both the capacity for order and chaos within them. Which type of life they will lead will be determined by which innate nature they will follow.

For those of us who belong to the Folk Faith, the Gnostic belief that Gods will only intervene in the progression of the evolution of the universe (Macrocosm) from without, and in the affairs of man (Microcosm) from within, by transmitting the thoughts of Gods, which is the Logos (Balder), who will bestow the sacred knowledge (Vril Science), is fundamental. We do not accept the notion of a tyrannical God sitting in judgement of us, as to whether or not we have lived by his Laws. We can draw on the Life Force of the Gods, the Vril, and use it to transform ourselves and the world we live in, but we must make a conscious effort to achieve this end. This is possible because we mortals possess the same Life Force as the Gods. Like the Gods, we possess the essence of the Giants and the Gods, and through our conscious efforts, we can raise ourselves beyond this earthly existence that is Midgard, and move closer to the higher realm of Asgard. But the great danger for us is that we have the capacity to drop down below Midgard, to the lower realms of Yggdrasill. The three monotheistic religions feared that the masses would make such decisions on their own, and they believe that only they, the hierarchies of their religions, are wise enough to decide how to use Vril Science in affecting the "progression" or evolution of the universe.

Just as it was the mission of the Gnostic movement to strive for the creation of a superior human race of men and women who would resist the corruption of the hierarchies of the Monotheistic religions and follow the teachings of Christ the Savior, so too, we of the Folk Faith believe that we can, through the use of Vril Science, create a superior species of man, who will be the instrument of the return of the Gods through the essence of Balder the Pure.

THE CATHARS

The Sun played a primal role in the cosmology of the ancient Aryans, and for all Indo-Europeans descended from the Aryans, the Sun was an important element in their religious beliefs. This was also true with the Cathars of the Middle Ages. To the Cathars, the Sun represented the spiritual Jesus. They had rejected the notion that Jesus was born in human form, and thought of Jesus as the embodiment of a pagan God of Peace, similar to Balder. Encompassing this interpretation, they held to a school of pagan thought known as Gnosticism that was directly linked to the ancient Indo-European religious tradition of Manichaeism. This tradition in turn, was descended from Iranian Zoroastrianism. For this reason, all three monotheistic religions considered the Cathars a threat. Islam rejected them and crushed any attempt by the Cathars to spread into Muslim-dominated Iberia. The Jews opposed them because they wanted to use the Gnostic mysteries for their own use, which they encoded in their Kabbala. The Catholic Church saw it as a direct threat to their authority in Europe.

During the Middle Ages, many questioned the fundamental principles upon which Christian doctrine was based. They questioned the story of Jesus born in human form, dying on the cross, and his resurrection. Philosophers, writers and prophets appeared in Europe claiming that Jesus was never possessed a physical body, and that he was a purely spiritual entity, similar to the pagan Gods their ancestors worshiped. Turning away from the material world that Christianity had created in Europe, many sought wisdom and spiritual fulfillment within the primordial tradition that existed among Indo-Europeans for thousands of years. They turned to the teachings of the ancient Iranian prophet, Zoroaster. He had received initiation from a Solar entity whom he called Ahura-Mazda. Millenniums later, another Iranian by the name of Mani founded another religion based on Zoroastrianism, and his teachings, though suppressed by the Muslims, continued to spread, and eventually made their way into Europe.

In the seventh century, Gnosticism offered its believers a cosmology that was spiritually closer to the paganism of their ancestors, transcending Christianity and its explanation of the universe. Its spiritual center was in Asia Minor and the movement was known as Manichaeism. They possessed a fountain of esoteric knowledge that offered a contrast to the "Pistis" (blind faith) that the Catholic Church demanded of the common people. Thus, many scholars turned toward the Gnosticism, seeking an intellectual satisfaction that the Gospels lacked. The movement became primarily an elitist movement, and its members were expected to possess a deep understanding of the Gnostic principles, as opposed to the simple message that the Church spread among the common people.

The Church relentlessly worked to stamp out this movement, and almost succeeded. But it continued to survive in secret, within the Byzantium Empire, mainly in the regions of the Balkans known today as Bulgaria. In the next several centuries, it spread to Italy and took on new form. By the twelfth century, it had turned into the movement known today as the Cathars, and spread throughout western Europe. In southern France it grew particularly strong, especially in Languedoc. The nobility of the Aquitaine region of France traced their ancestry to the Visigoths, and maintained a tradition of support for Manichaeism. Soon they turned to the new movement of the Cathars (which is a word derived from the Greek *catharos*, and means "pure"). They received this name from the incorruptible principles by which they lived their lives, and provided a contrast to the clergy of the Catholic Church of the time. The Church had grown rich and its clergy had indulged in the pleasures of the material world with abandonment, while most people had to spend long hours working hard in the fields, or fighting as knights to defend the realm, putting their lives at risk. Because of the simple life that the Cathars led, they were also called by other names that included the *Albigensians*, or the *Bons hommes* (Virtuous Ones), or *Parfaits* (Perfect Ones). Their lives and the spiritualism they preached, were based on a more sophisticated doctrine that had as its foundation, rooted in the pagan traditions of the Sun (Balder). They claimed that their doctrine was based on all great Sun worshiping traditions of the past that included the doctrines taught by the Egyptian Pharaoh Akhnaton, Plato and his tale of Atlantis and Pythagorus and his symbol of the Sun, (the Pentagon).

In the eleventh century, the Cathars were burned alive in Orleans, France (1017). The same thing happened to a group of Cathars in Toulouse in 1022. In the next decade, Cathars were discovered in the northern Italian town of Asti, and were massacred to the last man, woman and child. The Church continued to hunt down the heretics and persecute them, but the Cathar movement continued to spread, establishing itself in Germany, Italy, and Hungary. The north Italian city of Milan was considered a major center of Cathar activity. Pope Innocent II succeeded in containing the Cathar movement in Italy, only after dealing with them by the most brutal and ruthless methods. Elsewhere, the Cathar movement continued to spread. By the end of the twelfth century and the beginning of the thirteenth century, the Cathar movement made rapid gains, especially in southern France and the Languedoc region.

Like most pagan societies, the Cathars had three orders of believers. They corresponded with different degrees of initiation. Also, like old pagan traditions, the sacred bath played an important role in the initiation ritual. It is from this ancient, pagan tradition that baptism replaced circumcision among the early Christians. (Yes Virginia, there was *no* John the Baptist). It is no small coincidence that one thousand years earlier, the Languedoc region of France had been a stronghold of the Druids. Much pagan spiritualism was incorporated into the Cathar tradition through the Arian Christian heresy of earlier centuries that flourished in Languedoc, which also borrowed extensively from the old pagan religions.

The Cathars believed that man had three natures: the flesh, the spirit and the soul. Though the soul resided within the body, it served as the abode of the spirit. The Cathars rejected the sacraments of the Church, the Cross and many of the Church's rituals. The Old Testament was completely rejected. Besides their rejection of Jesus's human form, and considering him a purely spiritual entity, they also considered Jehovah the Dark Lord, synonymous with the devil. After all, he created the material world, and they considered everything associated with the material world as evil. They felt that the dead would not be resurrected at the end of time, because the material body was evil. They also accepted the dualism that is typical of most Indo-European pagan religions, believing there was two forces in the universes, one good and another evil.

The Cathars considered the Gospel of John as the only authentic Gospel, because it underscores the conflict between good and evil. They saw the universe in terms of equal and opposing forces of good and evil, light and darkness, spiritualism and materialism, and saw Satan as the Lord of the Earth (the material world). This is why they considered Jehovah and the Devil to be one and the same, because Jehovah created the material world and entrapped man into this earthly existence, so that Jehovah could rule over them. This world was a prison in which humanity suffered under the rule of Jehovah. Humanity's only escape was through the cosmic Christ, and through his light, the soul could obtain perfection. This meant it had to be cleansed of defilement and purified. It was through this initiation that included the most severe self-discipline, that the individual could find salvation from the tyranny of Jehovah.

The Cathars realized that the masses could never accept this life of chastity and self-discipline, so it was up to a small elite of Perfects to receive the illumination of the Secret Knowledge, and use it to save the world. They wore black robes (as a protection against evil), and they kept their rituals simple. They would often hold services outdoors, in the forests and fields, in communion with nature, just as their pagan ancestors did. Their sermons were based on the books of Mani and other Gnostic works.

Two ceremonies were most important to the Cathars. The first was the *Apparellamentum*, which was a public confession, but their principal ceremony was the *Consolamentum*. The Consolamentum was administered either to an aspiring cadet who sought entrance into the elite order of the Perfects, or to the ordinary person who was dying. A member of the Perfects would lay his hands on the head of the one to be consoled. We don't know what words were said, as they have been lost through time and the Inquisition, but it is believed that they were designed to transmit a life force that would enlighten and transform the soul. This force was the Vril, the Life Force of the Gods. By drawing on Vril, the Perfects hoped that the soul would be transformed, and thus reborn within the Kingdom of God, through the shared Life Force. The Cathars sought nothing less than the transmutation of man into a purely spiritual being. They believed they were in possession of a secret knowledge (Vril Science), and could use it to initiate an evolution of mankind into a higher state of being.

Their belief in two Gods—one good and another evil—was rooted in the tale of the Balder/Hoder twins. Balder being good and beautiful, representing the Light, and his twin brother Hoder, who was blind and represented Darkness, and was the instrument of Balder's death, was at the center of the Indo-European belief in the dual nature of the universe. This most ancient Aryan pagan belief, the root of Zoroastrian dualism, was held by the Cathars.

The Cathars lived exemplary lives among the common people, administrating assistance, healing the sick, offering services to the needy, and spreading the Good Word. People were converting to the Cathar movement throughout western Europe in large numbers. It was only a matter of time before the Church took some kind of action to destroy this heretical movement.

Dante was heavily influenced by the Cathars and their Gnostic paganism. He felt that the Church had been corrupted by the priestly orders, and that the Emperor of the Holy Roman Empire should replace the Pope as the head of the Church, purifying it and himself. In his *Divine Comedy,* he incorporated a great many elements of pagan lore. In fact, he describes the innermost circle of Hell as a realm of ice, much like Nifleheim. The *Divine Comedy* was a commentary on the corruption within the Church, and a criticism of the Church's persecution of the Cathars.

Pope Alexander II issued a decree at the Council of Tours in 1163, condemning the Cathar heresy. He was supported by the prelates of northern France. This was followed by the excommunication of the Count of Toulouse, the Count of Foix, the Viscount of Beziers and most of the Barons and Lords of the Holy Roman Empire in 1173, by Alexander III at the Third Lateran Council. These degrees were establishing the groundwork for a crusade to be directed, for the first time, against fellow Christians. The Pope finally took action against the growing heresy in 1207.

From northern France, an army of 20,000 knights and 200,000 foot soldiers, descended on the Cathars. From Loire, they invaded southern France through the Rhone Valley on July 24, 1209. They were led by the Abbot of Citeaux, and a smaller army of archbishops, bishops, monks, priests and other members of the Catholic Clergy. It was when they surrounded the town of Beziers, a town that was part Catholic and part Cathar, that the abbot shouted his infamous order, "Kill everyone, God will know his own!" Like a hot knife slicing through butter, the invading army laid town after town to the ground, killing everyone, Cathar and Catholic alike. No one was spared. Men, women, children and the elderly were all put to the sword or burned to death. Such towns as Carassome, Lavaur, and Minerve were destroyed. More than a million people were eventually killed before the crusade was completed.

The Church had dealt with heresy in the past without resorting to mass murder, so why was the Cathars dealt within such a brutal way? The truth is they had discovered the secret knowledge of Vril Science (symbolized in the legend of the Holy Grail) which the major religious organizations of the thirteenth century had guarded as their own property. This Vril Science was jealously guard by Christian, Jewish and Islamic leadership, keeping it, the property of the elites of their own communities. They could not allow a heretic movement to spread this knowledge among the common people, which is exactly what the Cathars were willing to do. If the average people had learned about this hidden science, the religious authorities of the day would have lost power over their followers. The Cathars had to be destroyed.

The last holdouts of the Cathars retreated to their fortress, built in the shape of the Pentagon (the symbol of the Sun God, Balder), Mount Monsegur, in 1243. For six months the Catholic forces laid siege to this mountain fortress. It was reputed that they were in possession of the Holy Grail, and it was in Monswgur. The mountain redoubt was eventually breached and the Catholic forces were able to reach the top of the mountain. It was only a matter of time before the fortress fell. There was just a little more than two hundred Cathars trapped within the fortress, and they still refused to surrender. On March 1, 1244, a truce was signed, and on March 16, the citadel surrendered. The Cathars, which included fifty Perfects, surrendered, but refused to recant their beliefs and accepted the sentence of death by burning. They were brought down from the mountain and tied to stakes on what became known as *The Field of the Burned.*

But what happened to the Grail? Church documents reveal that the night before the surrender, four Cathar Perfects climbed down ropes over the vertical side of the mountain cliffs. Their names were Aicart, Poitevin, Hugh and Alfaro, and they managed to make good their escape. With them they took the Cather treasure that they were holding in the fortress—the Holy Grail. They had disappeared into the wild countryside, but right before the fortress was surrendered by the Cathar, there appeared on the top of neighboring mountain of Biaorta, a flame, announcing that the Cathars had made good their escape with the Holy Grail.

The Cathars had represented a purer form of Christianity, which was closer to its pagan origins. Jesus was a Jewish rebel, a member of the heretical Essences, who had rejected traditional Jewish teachings. He was not the Son of God, and did not rise from the dead. After his death, his brother, James, joined with Peter, the leader of those who followed Jesus, and together they preached among the Jews. They considered Christianity the fulfillment of Jewish Law, and a Jewish religion, for Jews only. If non-Jews wanted to convert, they could, but they had to be circumcised and accept Mosaic Law. Not very many Romans, Greeks or Celts were willing to undergo such an abhorrent ritual. It was only after Paul converted, and began preaching among the gentiles, that Christianity began to take on a more familiar form. As Paul traveled among the Romans, Greeks or Celts, he began incorporating elements of their pagan religious beliefs into Christianity. He eventually transformed Jesus from a Jewish prophetic rebel, into a semi-divine "Son of God," whose father was God, and his mother a mortal virgin. This was not an uncommon belief among the pagans. Romulus, the founder of Rome, had a divine father and a mortal virgin for a mother. So did Hercules and Adonis. Many other tales were invented and incorporated into Christian belief by Paul, such as John the Baptist, to make Christianity acceptable to the pagans. As more and more Romans, Greeks and other pagans converted to Christianity, the Jewish Christians dwindled in both numbers and importance, until Christianity was eventually made the official religion of the Roman Empire, under Constantine, in the fourth century.

It was a time when the Catholic Church had become corrupted by the decadent influences of Loki. This had weakened the hold that the Church had over the spirituality of Europe. It caused the Gods to partly awaken and call to the Cathars, speaking to them through their blood. The Cathars were seeking a return to their Indo-European pagan roots within Christianity. They were not conscious of what they were doing, only that the spirituality of their ancient Gods was calling to them through the blood. The Gods were making an attempt to throw off the Middle Eastern facade of Christianity, and once again speak to their children directly. But it was not yet time for Balder to rise from Hel and initiate the return of the Gods.

Though the Cathars were influenced by ideas that are descended from the Mediterranean and Middle Eastern cultures, we should not overlook the influence from Germanic sources. The truth is that the Cathars were essentially born out of northern Italy and Occitania. The theology it shared with Persia and the Middle East was Aryan spiritualism that was descended from those Indo-Europeans who not only settled in Persia and the Middle East, but also Europe. Northern Italy in the Middle Age was a cosmopolitan region made up of people from the north: the Gauls and Celts, the Germanic Lombards and Ostrogoths, Venitians, Illyrians, and even Slavs from the Balkans, as well as contemporary Germans from the German kingdoms that were part of the Holy Roman Empire of Germany. The region of Occitania, which was a hotbed of Cathar activity, was primarily a Germanic region where the Visigoths had settled. These Germanic people, who originated in Scandinavia, had mixed with the Roman-Celtic population of this region. So while Catharism was considered a Christian heresy, it is incorrect to view it in this way. The truth is, Catharism was a separate pagan religion that incorporated elements of Christian spiritualism. Its fundamental principle was a dualism that traced its origins back to the most ancient pre-Christian religions of the Indo-Europeans and the ancient Atlantean Aryans. It is true that this dualism had been diluted somewhat in the Celtic and Roman religions, but its spiritualism still resonated with the struggle between the Gods and the Titans of Greek pagan religious belief, and remained central core of the Germanic and Scandinavian religions. A great deal of the old religion has been lost because it was never written down. Fortunately, Christian Scandinavian scholars around 1000 A.D., decided to put what was left to paper, or it too would have been lost.

It is because of these scholars that the Norse tradition has been passed down to us and that there is a revivalism of Odinism today. The Greek religion had been transformed by the incorporation of alien ideas, though most of it still remained intact, and present-day scholars are doing an excellent job in reconstructing it. The original Roman religion was lost, or at least many of its mythological tales had disappeared. The Roman religion was transformed into a state-religion, closely identified with the Roman state, which was probably the most religious state ever to exist, second only to ancient Israel. By the time the Roman Empire fell, the Romans had assimilated the Greek tales and then other religious beliefs, some of Aryan origin, but others from alien religions. Much of the Celtic religion was lost because no one wrote it down. This is even more true of the Slavic and Baltic religions. Bit and pieces of the old religions were recorded by ancient scholars, such as the Roman Tacitus, who described the ancient Germans and their religious beliefs in detail. For instance, he described the God Wutanas, who most certainly was Odin.

The description of a titanic struggle between opposing forces to dominate the universe is part of the racial memory passed down from generation to generation by our ancestors. Its origins lie in the memory of the encroaching and receding ice caps of the last ice age that were the result of the misuse of the Vril by the Atlantean Aryans. They understood that the climatic transformations were the result of the struggle between the Gods (representing Order) and the Giants (representing Chaos), for control of the world. This cosmology of a perpetual struggle between the cosmic forces of heat and cold, is at the root of Aryan religion, and its memory survived among the Indo-Europeans of central Asia and Europe, and eventually was reinterpreted by Zoroastrianism, Manichaeism, and eventually influenced Christianity. Among the Iranians, Ahura-Mazda represented by light and fire while Ahriman was personified by cold and darkness. We find this idea of opposing forces of light and darkness, or fire and ice, surviving even among the Indo-European Scythians.

The Scythians told a story about a God-man by the name of Batraz, whose mother dies before his birth, but he survives because his father placed his embryo under the skin of his back. Batraz is born and grows into a man clad in iron and covered with flames. The incredible heat that he generates is a weapon that he uses in his struggle to protect the Scythians from the forces of ice and darkness that constantly threaten to overwhelm them. In Celtic mythology Batraz appears as the warrior God-man known as Cuchulainn, whose armor radiates with such heat that it must be constantly cooled in a vat of cold water. In the Germanic religion, he is represented by the Einherjar, who are the souls of the fallen heroes, who are transformed into warriors as hard as iron and who burn like fire. They are destined to ride with the Gods under Odin's command, and do battle with the Giants, the forces of darkness and destruction. The Giants are led by Loki, who tries to assault Asgard, the domain of spirituality and purity. The Gods of Asgard are the Perfecti, the Pure Ones, and the Einheirjar are those mortals who have transcended their earthly existence through the power of the Vril, which transformed them into God-men. Their ride into battle with the Gods represents their contribution to the Gods' power to maintain order throughout the universe.

The difference between the Cathars and the Indo-European cosmology of the Germanic people can be seen in the Cathar belief that in the end, Satan and his dark legions will be destroyed in a lake of fire, while the Germanic people believed both the Gods and the Giants will be destroyed by fire. But they understood that this was not the end of time, for Odin/Wotan had a son, Balder/Baldur, who was his instrument for resurrection. Balder was the divine force of the Gods (the Vril) that would ensure the turning of the ages and the rise of a new age, one in which the Gods are reborn. Here we can see the difference between the Cathars and the Indo-European cosmology. The Cathars' perception of the end was influenced by the Hebraic-Semitic idea of a God who would sit in judgement at the end of time. The Indo-European idea of the end that has survived among the Germanic/Norse tradition was not really the end, but a turning of the ages. It was the passing of one age and the birth of a new age, from the seeds of the previous. This is what we would today refer to as evolution.

The reason why the Cathars failed and were eventually destroyed was due to this difference in perception of the end of the world. But we should not forget that the idea of an undying struggle between the Gods, representing light, fire, purity and order, and the Giants, representing darkness, ice, corruption and chaos, was shared by both the Norse and the Cathars. Those individuals who surrender to the darkness are numbed and lost to an icy fate, and their Life Force is forever lost to the Gods. But those who work and struggle for the survival of the Gods, energize the Life Force of the Gods, and are filled with the power of the Vril, and will one day ride with the Gods in their struggle to maintain the order that supports the universe. In this titanic conflagration, our Folk will die, but be reborn in a new and better form through the power of Vril, and this process is known as *Balder Rising!* Like the Cathar doctrine of purification, absolute purification can only be achieved through fire or light, which represent the Vril. The key word is *purification*. This purification is becoming one with the Vril or Balder. Balder, the personification of the Vril (the fire) is the same figure as Batraz, who will be reborn from the heat like the phoenix.

THE HOLY GRAIL IS THE HOLY BLOOD OF BALDER

The Holy Grail has a pagan origin that transcends the Christian legends. Plato refers to it in his *Timeaus*, where he talks about the high priests of ancient Atlantis, who would sacrifice a young bull to the ten Gods they worshiped. The blood of the bull was collected in a cup and considered a symbol of the Life Force of the Gods and a source of renewal and rebirth. This symbolism was based on their knowledge that the power that they command (Vril), was tied to their blood or DNA. This idea that the Life Force or Vril, which is the essence of the Gods, was related to their DNA or blood, was passed down from the earliest Indo-European tradition. It survived through the ages and eventually evolved into the Arthurian Legend, the Grail Legend, and other manifestations of myths about a "Vessel of Knowledge," the "Cup of the Pure Blood," and in modern times, the idea of the "Holy Bloodline of Jesus Christ."

Throughout the centuries, the Grail Legend has spoken of an extraordinary object endowed with power capable of spiritually transforming both the individual and all of society. These legends go back thousands of years, long before the birth of Christianity and long before the birth of the Greco-Roman Civilization. During the Christianized period in Europe's history, the Grail Legend was transformed with Christian symbolism, along with all other pagan traditions. In the Middle Ages, the Grail was associated with the chalice from which Jesus drank wine at the Last Supper. He told his followers that the wine in the chalice was his blood. It was also claimed that Jesus' uncle, Joseph of Arimathaea, collected Christ's blood in the cup, as it ran down from the wound that was made by the lance plunged into his side by the Roman soldier, Longinus, while Christ hung on the cross. How this cup was transformed into a magical talisman has never been explained, but it eventually was loss after Joseph sailed from the Middle East, and settled either in the British Isles or in Gaul (France).

There are disagreements as to the true meaning of the word "Grail." One interpretation is that the term *Sangraal* or *San Graal* (Holy Grail) is a play on the word *Sang Real* or Royal Blood. A whole industry of thought has spread during the last two decades of the twentieth century that the Holy Grail is actually metaphor for the bloodline of Jesus Christ and his descendants. This line of thinking claims that Jesus Christ married Mary Magdalen and they produced a child, a daughter. This child fled to France and through the protection of a secret organization known as Priory de Sion, her bloodline it has been supported and maintained against the tyranny of the Catholic Church. But this is just a distortion of the truth behind the Grail, which is the knowledge that through the Blood or DNA, one can become Godlike by harnessing and shaping the power of the Vril.

The Grail also took on other manifestations during the centuries that followed, and has been described as a sacred vessel of knowledge or a magical stone, sometimes referred to as an alchemist stone, or a stone that once was embedded on a crown that was fashioned by Lucifer during his rebellion against the Heavenly Realm, that fell to earth after Lucifer was defeated by God. In pre-Christian times, it was sometimes referred to as a chalice filled with water. If one drank from it, one would be filled with secret knowledge, much in the same way as Odin discovered secret knowledge after drinking from Mimir's Well. In another pagan tradition, the Grail was said to be a stone, or a stone tablet. On the stone was cut Runes, containing the secret of ultimate power.

One of the most famous Grail Romances to appear on the continent of Europe was composed in the Middle Age by Wolfram von Eschenbach. Von Eschenbach described the Grail in his *Parzival*, as a precious stone. He thought the word, Grail, originated with the Manichaeans, who derived the word from the Iranian words *Gorr*, which means precious stone, and the word for splinter or cut, *Al*. Thus, we have the word *Graal*, which can be interpreted as meaning a precious stone engraved or cut with symbols or words. In von Eschenbach's *Parzival*, the Grail is described as a number of tablets made from stone. They are engraved with ancient Runic writing that the Cathars could not translate:

Guyot, the master of high renown,
Found, in confused pagan writing,
The legend which reaches back to the prime source of all legends.

In *Parzival*, von Eschenbach explained that the Grail was actually the lost science of Vril, engraved on stone tablets, that could trace its origin back through Persia, to the realm of the ancient Aryans and their civilization. The science was lost, but parts of it survived and were carried across Eurasia by the scattered Indo-Europeans, who were descended from the Aryans.

Von Eschenbach was right about the Grail. The Holy Grail is actually the lost science of the ancient Aryans, whose civilization was destroyed when the Black Sea flooded. It is the knowledge of how to control the power of the Vril, by forging spiritual bonds with the Gods who dwell within our DNA or blood. Through this spiritual knowledge, the ancient Aryans were able to master a science that is mostly unknown to us moderns. They had discovered how to harness and use a source of free and limitless energy, which was implosive, and thus in harmony with nature and the natural world. Thus, the Grail is the understanding of a science, as well as a spirituality, which is unknown to us today, and the two are rooted in the methodology of mastering this limitless power that fills the universe. This power is often referred to today as some mysterious force that accounts for 95 percent of the universe, and is called Dark Matter, Dark Energy, magnetism, electromagnetism, vital energy, the Force or the Life Force. It is in actuality, the ordering power of the Gods that prevents the universe from wheeling off into the chaotic abyss—it is Vril!

As Christianity spread across Europe, pagan beliefs were Christianized and assimilated into Christian doctrine and lore. This was also true of the Grail Legend. If there was ever an actual object that was the Grail, it probably was a stone or stones with secret knowledge carved in Runes. It symbolized the lost Vril Science—the knowledge that the Gods dwell with us, within our DNA, within our blood, and the methodology of how to harness this power. The knowledge that the Gods dwelled within us and spoke to us through our DNA (blood) was rewritten by the Christian scholars. In this way, the Grail came to be described as a chalice or cup, carved from a jewel that once was part of the crown that Lucifer wore, but fell to earth after he was defeated. This cup was in the possession of the Essences (of which Jesus was a member) and used by Jesus at the Last Supper. Jesus poured wine into it and told his followers that it represented his blood, and through it, he would communicate and transform those who drank from it. This story was created by Paul, or his followers, and taken from pagan lore. The Jesus that the early Christians created was actually Balder, who was slain and resurrected like many other pagan Gods.

The Grail was thus the sacred knowledge of the ancient Aryans (Vril Science), lost and forgotten for millenniums until it was once more discovered. It was guarded by the Cathars, but they failed to decipher its Runic script. Having failed to translate the Grail, the Cathars took it with them when they fled from the Crusaders. They held out in the pentagon-shaped fortress of Monsegur, in the Pyrenees for months, until finally, four monks escaped over the cliffs and took the Grail with them. It is reputed that they hid it somewhere in the wild countryside of that region of France. Some believe they hid it in a cave known as the Grotto of Hercules. Hercules had a mortal mother, while his father was a God, just like Jesus. Otto Rahn, who wrote *The Crusade Against the Grail*, claims to have discovered the lost Grail in the Grotto of Hercules and brought it to Germany, where Heinrich Himmler placed it in the castle of Wewelsburg, the SS headquarters and spiritual center. In his book, Rahn describes the Grotto:

In a time out of mind, in an epoch whose remoteness has been barely touched by modern historical science, it was used as a temple consecrated to the Iberian god Iihomber, god of the sun (Hercules and Balder) ... Between two monoliths, one of which has crumbled, the steep path leads into the gigantic vestibule of the cathedral of Lombrives ... Between stalactites of white limestone, between walls of deep brown color and brilliant rock crystal, the path leads down into the bowels of the mountain. A hall 260 feet in height served as a cathedral for the heretics.

The Grail was never fully deciphered by the Cathars because they lacked the ability to translate the Runes. To them they must have seemed like a confused pagan language, mysterious and puzzling. But they did understand enough to realize that the object of life on earth was to transform the human body through this lost and sacred knowledge. They used the Vril to try and transform the physical body into a vehicle to house the sacred spirit of the Gods (the Holy Spirit—love—Balder—Jesus). This was done through Jesus' revelation at the Last Supper, that the wine was his blood, which was symbolic of the secret of the Vril Science. The meaning of what Jesus revealed was nothing less than a eugenics program—genetic engineering. This is why the Cathars rejected Jesus the man and believed him to be a purely spiritual entity—the Sun God, Balder.

The Cathars claimed that Jesus preached in the pre-Flood language, which they also claimed was the language or dialect of Languedoc—Oc. To them, the root *Oc* was the root of *octo* or the number 8, which was the root for the world, *ocular*, which means the eye. The Egyptian word, *Ak*, which is closely related to *Oc*, means light, and *aker* refers to a being of the light. *Ak-hu* is the ideal archetypical ideal for a perfect race of humans that would be the "Men of the Light." Once again, the light is the same as the Vril—the secret knowledge of the ancient Aryans, brought to Egypt after the Atlantean civilization on the shores of the ancient Black Sea which was destroyed. Thus, *Oc* is symbolic for the secret path of 8, or the Vril. This is why Jesus' number is 888. If we add 8+8+8 we get the number 24. Remember. There are twenty-four Runes in the Elder Futhark. Then, when we add 2+4, we get 6, and 666 is the number of Lucifer, the "Bringer of Light." In the eyes of the Cathars, Lucifer and Satan were different entities. The Cathars considered the true devil (Satan) to be Jehovah, not Lucifer, for Jehovah created the materialistic world of war, death and suffering, while Lucifer tried to reveal to Adam and Eve the Knowledge of Life, (Vril Science), which would liberate them from their enslavement to Jehovah, who kept them in a state of blind ignorance (Hoder).

THE PHOENIX AND THE ARYAN SUN GODS

A very ancient fable that is told in Egypt and reported by Herodotus, is that of the Phoenix. The Phoenix can be found in the Norse Edda and many other mythological traditions. The Phoenix is a great bird that dies and is reborn. It is described as having feathers on its head and breast, the color of fire. Its wings and tail are sky blue. It has a life span of 300 days, after which it flies off to Ethiopia and there makes a nest. It then burns itself along with its eggs. From the ashes there emerges a red worm which rapidly grows into another bird—an exact duplicate of its former self. It then takes flight and heads north.

The Phoenix is a Sun symbol, and its death and rebirth represents the eternal return of the sun. Its flight north to the Arctic is representative of the annual disappearance of the sun, dipping below the Arctic circle. At the latitude of 71 degrees, the very north of Norway, the sun shines for 300 days and then does not appear for the next 65 days. We can compare this to the Roman God, Janus, who looks both ways, forward and backward, at once. In one hand he holds the number 300 and in the other the number 65. This could only make us believe that Janus was a very ancient God, known to the Italic Indo-Europeans, whom the Romans are descended from, and who once lived farther north. In the Norse Edda, there is a story of golden Freyja, and her Husband Oda (Odin), who refuses to spend 65 days out of the year with her, as punishment for her transgression for sleeping with four dwarfs, as her payment for possession of a necklace. Thus, we see once more the division of the year into 300 and 65 days. Of course, Balder is the Phoenix, the symbol of the Sun. His death and resurrection are reflected in the death and rebirth of the Phoenix, representing the regenerative powers of the Vril.

There is also another tale similar to the Phoenix. It is that of Adonis. His father was Zeus, and his mother was a virgin mortal woman. So beautiful he was to look upon—like the light of the sun—that it was agreed that he would spend four months with Zeus, four months with Venus and four months with Pluto in Hades. Of course, this would relate to the 79 degrees latitude, much farther north of the Arctic Circle, but this tale is also another version of the Balder tale. Adonis, like Balder, dies and goes to the Netherworld, only to be resurrected. What is interesting about this tale is that the remaining eight months of his stay in the world of the living is divided between Zeus (Odin) and Venus (Freyja). Odin is the master of Galdor Science and Freyja is the Mistress of Seither Science, and they divide the dead, whom the Valkyries bring to Asgard. Thus, Balder spends half of his time in Asgard studying Galdor and the other half studying Seither, permitting his return from the realm of the dead.

The Phoenix is clearly a symbol of a Sun deity that constantly dies and is reborn, just as the sun is reborn each morning when it rises in the east. Like the Phoenix rising out of flames, so to our ancestors envision the sun rising out of the fiery red morning sky, its first rays bathing them in its warmth. There could be no life without the sun each day driving back the cold and darkness of night, nourishing the world with its life-giving rays. To them the sun was not just the sun, but the life-giver and light-giver. The sun was *the* Sun, the product of the union between the Sky Father and the Mother Earth. In driving back the cold darkness of the night, and giving nourishment to the world, the Sun became both creator and preserver of all things. It was the Savior of mankind. But the Sun could also destroy when it grew too hot. So it was also the destroyer. In this way, our ancestors saw the Sun as a Great Trinity—Creator, Preserver and Destroyer (Odin, Vili and Ve). They destroyed Ymir and created the universe from him, and work constantly to preserve the order of the universe.

The ancient Aryans looked into the sky and saw that it produced the rain that nourished the Earth, which in turn brought forth vegetation and supported life. They called the sky Dyaus, which is the ancient Aryan word "to shine," and referred to it as the All-Father, who fertilized the Great Mother, who was the Earth. The union between the two gave birth to the Sun, who gave light to the world and was reborn every morning. From this cosmic process they recognized a universal truth that the secret of rebirth and resurrection is the foundation for the physical laws of science. These laws are the property of the Gods, who gave order to the universe. When the Gods descended to the surface of the world and walked among the Aryans, they taught them their sacred knowledge and how to use it to make themselves God-men. They told them how Odin and Frigga gave birth to their beloved son, Balder, who served as the instrument of their rebirth, and the force that is known as evolution.

The Aryans came to see the Sun as the symbol of Balder, the Resurrector, and celebrated his birth on December 25, the day when the Sun begins its annual northward journey. On December 22, the sun enters the sign of Capricorn, or the Goat. It appears to remain there for three days and then begins to ascend. From this date the days grew longer and with each lengthening day, Balder's power increases. This is a time of great celebration and rejoicing. Hence, we have the Virgin, giving birth to a son, and thus, Virgo, is one of the signs of the Zodiac. She was depicted sitting in a chair or throne, holding two ears of corn, suckled by an infant, the anointed one, who ensures the rebirth of the Gods and Goddesses, and thus, maintains the universal order of cyclical growth.

The spring or vernal equinox, is governed by the lamb or ram, and this is representative of Balder. Before his birth each day, his approach is heralded by the morning star, Venus or Freyja, the Goddess of Love and Fertility, and is followed at dusk by the evening star, her twin brother, Frey, the God of Love and Fertility. With him travel his twelve companions, the signs of the Zodiac. The days grow longer until Balder ascends from Hel, the Netherworld. As Balder crosses the sky, he is cheered by Day, his brother, but as he descends beyond the western horizon, Night tries to seduce him to remain with her. Failing that, he is threatened as he continues his nightly journey through the Netherworld, surviving all attempts made to prevent his resurrection. But Balder is invincible. Though he can die of the poisonous mistletoe, he cannot be destroyed. The essences of Balder, the Vril, will ensure his resurrection. The symbolism of this process was explained to our ancestors by the Gods. They were never to forget the regenerative powers of the Vril that Balder personifies. Only through the Vril can they become God-men. But if they forget, falling under the spell of Balder's twin brother, Hodur, blind ignorance, they will suffer a fall which they might never recover from, severing their ties with the Gods, and causing all mankind to suffer and descend back toward the barbarism of the beastly savage, thus ensuring the triumph of the Giants.

The descendants of the Atlantean Aryans settled in India thousands of years ago. There, they retold the tale of Balder, calling him Krishna or Chrishna. There have been more than sixteen Sun Gods throughout the world that parallels the life of Christ. The case of Krishna or Chrishna is just one that we can quickly examine. Approximately fifteen hundred years before the birth of Christ, the Vedic hymns claim a Divine Being or Savior, was born. His name was Krishna and he was the incarnation of the God, Vishnu. He was born in human form, of a virgin, on December 25, to relieve the world of its sins and suffering. His birth was heralded in the heavens. "The spirits and nymphs of heaven danced and sang, and at midnight, when the 'Support of All' was born, the clouds emitted low, pleasing sounds, and poured down rain of flowers."

He was born of the house of Yadava, the oldest and most noble family in India. His mother and foster-father were on a journey to pay taxes to their king when he was born, forcing them to seek shelter in a cave. His birth was recognized by cow-herders and he was presented with gifts by wise men. The holy sage, Nared, examined the stars at the time of his birth and announced the divinity of Krishna's birth. Shortly after his birth, a heavenly voice warned Krishna's foster-father that the king, Kansa, sought his destruction and told him to flee across the River Jumna, and hide him in the land of Gokul. They escaped just as King Kansa ordered the murder of all newborn baby boys in an attempt to kill Krishna.

As a child, Krishna astonished his teachers with his wisdom and knowledge. He is reputed to have performed various miracles similar to those performed by Jesus in the Apocrypha of the New Testament. Among the miracles credited to Krishna is the healing of a leper, making the deaf hear, giving sight to the blind, healing the sick and raising the dead. The sacred books of the Hindu faith are filled with miracles contributed to Krishna.

As he traveled and preached, he was supported by twelve followers who accompanied him on his journeys. He declared his divinity to one of his disciples, Arjuna. "What ever thou dost perform, what ever thou eat, what ever thou give to the poor, what ever thou offer in sacrifice, do all these thing as if to me, Oh Arjuna. I am the great Sage, without beginning; I am the Ruler and the *All-sustainer.*" (The Vril). He also said, "Then be not sorrowful: from all thy sins I will deliver thee. Think thou on me, have faith in me, adore and worship me, and join thyself in meditation to me; thus shalt thou come to me, Oh Arjuna; thus shalt thou rise to my supreme abode, where neither sun nor moon hath need to shine, for know that all the luster they possess is mine.... I am the cause of the whole universe; through me it is created and dissolved; on me all things within it hang and suspend, like pearls upon a string.... I am the light in the sun and moon, far, far beyond the darkness. I am brilliancy in flame, the radiance in all that's radiant, and the light of lights.... I am the sustainer of the world, its friend and Lord; I am its way and refuge.... I am the Goodness of the good; I am Beginning, Middle, End, Eternal Time, the Birth, the Death of All."

Krishna came to a similar end as Christ. Both were crucified. His image is also similar to Christ. He is usually depicted as nailed to a cross with arms extended and nails in his palms and feet. His side was even pierced by a spear. One account has a hunter shooting him in the foot in an attempt to end his suffering on the cross. Krishna tells the hunter, "Fear not thou in the least. Go, hunter, with my favor, to heaven, the abode of the Gods."

After his death, Krishna descends to Hell and on the third day rises from the dead and then ascends bodily to heaven. Krishna returns to heaven and reunites with his fatherly form of Vishnu, but it is foretold that he will return to earth, but in this second coming, he will reappear as a warrior, riding a winged horse. When he does return, it will be at the end of time, and he will return to pass judgement on the dead.

JESUS CHRIST AND CHRISTIANITY

There were two different Jesus Christs—one was the "Son of Man" and the other was the "Son of God." They were not one and the same. When Christians pray to Jesus, they are praying to Jesus Christ, the Son of God, but he is not the Jesus Christ, the Son of Man, who appears in the New Testament. Let me first describe Jesus Christ, the Son of Man. Jesus Christ was born around 6 B.C., not 1 A.D. This error was due to a miscalculation by the Church in the third century. Not only the year of Christ's birth is wrong, but also the month and day. Most early Christians believed Jesus was born in the spring. We will discuss later why the Church decided to place his birth on December 25. The date of Christ's birth is wrong, as is the location. The truth is, Jesus was not born in Bethlehem, but in the small village of Nazareth. Nazareth is located in a hollow in the hills of Galilee, about twelve miles southwest from the Sea of Galilee. Jesus' father was Joseph, whose family claimed descent from King David. He has been described as a carpenter, but in reality, Joseph's family was wealthy and the Hebrew and Aramaic word for carpenter is also the word for "builder" and "architect." His mother, Mary, was a great deal younger than Joseph and it was believed that she was pregnant before she married Joseph. There is a question about who was Jesus' father, and that it was arranged for Joseph, a much older man and well-to-do, to marry Mary, a much younger girl.

Very little is known about Jesus' life when he was growing up, but there is the story of him teaching the priests and scholars The Law. He apparently was well educated. We find him engaged in a public ministry at the age of thirty, tending to the sick and poor. He abandon's his wealth and background and takes up a life of accepting gifts from wealthy patrons, especially women. There are tales of Jesus preforming miracles, healing the sick, making the crippled walk, curing the blind, walking on water and even raising the dead. He began to preach that the Kingdom of God was upon them and that its appearance on earth was imminent. He attacked the traditional Jewish establishment, who considered him a heretic and threat to both Judaism and their authority. They eventually had him arrested and found him guilty of heresy and convinced the Roman authorities to crucify him. His followers claimed that he rose from the dead three days later and that he ascended to heaven. This is where the second Jesus Christ—the Son of God—was born, or should we say—created.

As soon as Jesus died on the cross, his disciples began weaving tales that transformed him into a deity. To understand how and why this was done, we have to examine the state of Judaism at this time. At this time, Judaism was divided into several different groups. The first was the Pharisees. They were the spiritual leaders and controlled the synagogues. The next important group was the Sadducees. This group directed worship in the Temple of Jerusalem and collaborated with the Roman authorities. Next were the Scribes, who were the Doctors of The Law, experts on the Jewish religion and sided with either the Pharisees or Sadducees, though mostly with the former. Another group was the Essenes.

The Essenes were Jewish heretics who had rejected the Second Temple after the Maccabean revolt (167–160 B.C.). They disappeared after the destruction of the Second Temple in 70 A.D., which was a symbol of their victory. They followed a group of priests who had rejected the Second Temple, but after its destruction, they were no longer able to maintain their movement and identity. They merged with the Pharisees, and out of this merger rose the tradition of Rabbinical Judaism. But at the time of Christ, they lived in a community at Qumran, where the Dead Sea Scrolls were discovered, two thousand years later. It is believed that the Essenes wrote and hid the scrolls. Qumran was once the home to 4,000 Essenes, who abandoned urban existence to found a new civilization. One of their accomplishments was the transformation of this desert region into a garden. Their community disappeared after three hundred years, and the desert reclaimed the region. Jesus Christ, the Son of Man, was a member of the Essenes, and from their movement evolved Christianity as a sect of Judaism, which incorporated many of its practices, ideals and symbols. This is why it is important to examine these practices, ideals and symbols, even if only briefly.

The name Essenes is either derived from the Greek word for Holy, or various Semitic or Aramaic words that mean "pious." They worshiped the one God of the Old Testament, who they considered the Creator and Ruler of the universe. He was omnipotent and all-knowing. But the Essenes also retain many pagan beliefs. They held the sun in such reverence that they considered it the sources of enlightenment. This reverence for the sun can be traced back to a time long before the establishment of Judaism and its monotheism. Portions of their tradition can be found in the Dead Sea Scrolls and is clearly Gnostic, dating back to 4,000 B.C., to the lost Vril Science that the survivors of the lost civilization of the

Atlantean Aryans brought to the Middle East after the Black Sea flooded. These practices, ideals, symbols, and traditions were incorporated into the Kabbala in its earliest form before it was written down. Among their beliefs and practices was the establishment of a community of peace for themselves and the world, a community living in harmony with nature and the cosmic forces of the universe (the Vril), a deep love of the earth and an agricultural lifestyle, the recognition of both the masculine and feminine nature of the Divine, which is a recognition of the Gods and Goddesses, developing the ability to heal both the flesh and the inner self, and the expansion of one's psychic abilities. All this could be accomplished through mastering the science of the Vril.

Dr. Edmond Bordeaux Szekely, one of the major contributors to the translation of the Dead Sea Schrolls, described the Essenes:

"The Essenes lived on the shores of lakes and rivers, away from cities and towns, and practiced a communal way of life, sharing equally in everything. They were mainly agriculturalists and arbor culturists, having a vast knowledge of crops, soil and climatic conditions which enabled them to grow a great variety of fruits and vegetables in comparatively desert areas and with minimum of labor.

They had no servants or slaves and were said to have been the first people to condemn slavery both in theory and practice. There were no rich and no poor amongst them.

They spent much time in study, both of ancient writings and special branches of learning, such as education, healing and astronomy.

In the use of plants and herbs for healing man and beast they were likewise proficient.

They lived a simple regular life, rising each day before sunrise to study and commune with the forces of nature, bathing in cold water as a ritual and donning white garments. After their daily labor in the fields and vineyards they partook of their meals in silence, preceding and ending it with prayer.... Their evenings were devoted to study and communion with the heavenly forces.

Their way of life enabled them to live to advanced ages of 120 years or more and they were said to have marvelous strength and endurance. In all their activities they expressed creative love."

These passages are filled with references to the Essenes' study of Vril Science and their use of the power of Vril to transform themselves and their way of life. It is obvious that they have incorporated other traditions in their knowledge of mastering and use of Vril, but such passages from Dr. Szekely's description, such as "... having a vast knowledge of crops, soil and climatic conditions which enable them to grow a variety of fruits and vegetables in comparatively desert areas and with a minimum of labor," is descriptive of what the ancient Aryans accomplished, but on a much smaller scale. They were studying and communing with the forces of nature and heavenly forces (the Gods and their Life Force—the Vril), are all evidence that the Essenes possessed a secret science which undoubtedly was Vrilology. Dr. Szekely explanation that: "Their way of life enabled them to live to advanced ages of 120 years or more and they were said to have marvelous strength and endurance," can be nothing else but a reference to the Vril. This is why many Roman and Jewish scholars considered the Essenes to have been a race of God-men, separate and apart from the rest of humanity. It was of this community of unique people that Jesus Christ, the Son of Man, belonged.

Now we come to Jesus Christ, the Son of God. During this time, between 100 B.C. and 100 A.D., the orthodox Jewish establishment collapsed. Confidence in the promise of the Scriptures declined. Jerusalem was destroyed along with the Second Temple. Most Jews living in Judea fled to other parts of the Roman Empire. Many leading intellectuals abandoned the traditional priestly orders and joined the schools of the Jewish Gnosticism and Secret Mysteries. They were introduced to the Kabbala and other secret knowledge of the Ancients. Many of these Gnostic Jews joined the small Jewish sect that followed the teachings of the crucified Essene leader, Jesus Christ.

The leaders of this small sect were Peter, one of the Apostles, and Jesus' younger brother, James. They intended their new movement to be the fulfillment of the Jewish religion. They were joined by many other Jews who began creating a new image of their fallen leader. But the Christ they were creating was not to be taken literally, not at least by the initiated. He was presented as an ideal and model to be followed. But it was Paul, a Jew by the name of Saul, who was a Roman citizen and an enemy of the followers of Christ, who eventually changed the direction in which the new religion would grow. Paul hated the "Christians" because he considered them heretics. But one day, while traveling Damascus, he experienced a visitation by Christ, who asked him why he was persecuting him, and instructed him to go out and convert the Gentiles. Paul changed his name and became a devoted follower of Christ. He began traveling throughout the Roman Empire, speaking to the Gentiles about Christ and his message. This put him into conflict with Peter and James, who considered their new religion the fulfillment of Jewish Law and objected to Paul's activities among the Gentiles, especially because he began to transform the memory of Christ from a Jewish heretic to that of an Aryan Sun God.

The Christ that Christians worship today is not a unique deity in history. His virgin birth, miracles, death and resurrection are the stories of at least sixteen different Sun deities in history. They were all variations of the tale of one great God.

As Paul began preaching among the pagans of the Roman Empire, he began comparing Jesus to pagan deities. Like Romulus among the Romans and Hercules among the Greeks, Paul told the people that Jesus too was born of a virgin mortal woman and his father was a God. Like the Greek Soter and Alcmene, who were born of a virgin and had a God for a father, Jesus was referred to as their "Savior," and the "good shepherd." Many of these God-men died and journeyed to the Netherworld and then ascended to heaven or the realm of the Gods. They would rise again and their resurrection would herald the salvation of both mankind and the Gods. Most pagans found this tale of Jesus' virgin birth, death and resurrection a familiar tale that conformed to their own religious beliefs. The Pauline Christians, who agreed with his version of the Jesus myth, continued to create tales about Jesus and incorporated elements of what would eventually become the New Testament, into the telling of the story of the life and death of Jesus Christ from the pagan religious beliefs of the Gentiles.

Since most non-Jews hated and despised the custom of circumcision, Paul and his followers created the tale of John the Baptist as justification to replace circumcision with the ceremony of baptism. Baptism was a custom common among pagans for thousands of years. Peter and James opposed this change, and felt that anyone who desired to become a follower of Christ had to be circumcised. Paul could hardly expect thousands of people to seek conversion to Peter's variation of Christianity if they had to submit to circumcision, and he was right. Within three or four hundred years, "Jewish" Christianity disappeared in favor of Paul's "pagan" Christianity.

The Pauline Christians decided to place Jesus' birth at Bethlehem, because Adonis (another pagan Christ figure) was born there. December 25 was chosen as the date of Jesus' birth because it was the birthday of still another pagan Christ figure, Mithras, who was very popular with the Romans, especially within the ranks of the Roman Army. In fact, Jesus' birth at Nazareth may not even be the literal truth. Jesus the Nazarene may not refer to where Jesus originated, but to such words as *Nazarnenos* and *Nazoraios,* which are Semitic words for "Keeper of Observances" or "Guardian" or "Savior." In fact, the Essenes were often referred to as the Nazirites, because Nazareth was a stronghold of the Essenes. The term, Nazirite, meant "one who had separated from this worldly existence and dedicated himself to God." They were concerned with the creation of a better, Godly world in this life. In fact, the word *Nazoraios* could be from the Greek word *nester*, which means a "shoot" or "branch. This is probably a reference to the giant grape branch (the sacred knowledge of Vril Science) that Joshua and his men took from the sons of Anak

Of the many different Sun God myths that the early Pauline Christians were familiar with was that of Krishna from India, which has been explored in an earlier chapter. Krishna is sometimes spelled Christna, from the Greek word, Christus, from which the name Christ is derived. Around 38 to 40 B.C., a merchant from Antioch, by the name of Apollonius, traveled to Singapore in eastern Asia. There he heard of the story of Krishna and wrote it down in his native language of Samaritan. Thirty years later, an early follower of Christ by the name of Marcion found his tale and copied it, making several changes and bringing it to Rome, where it was translated into Greek and Latin. It was adopted by the Pauline Christians there, and Apollonus' name was changed to Apollo and Maricon's name was changed to Mark, and Christna's name was changed to Christ.

Among the miracles attributed to the story of Jesus was the immaculate conception of his mother, Mary, (Immaculate conception does not mean virgin birth as so many Christians think, but born without original sin). This was adopted from the pagan belief in the immaculate conception of the world or Mother Earth. The Great Mother Earth, who was created in a state of purity, is impregnated in most pagan religious beliefs by the Great Sky Father, and from this union is born the Sun. The Sun rises each day in the east, where the sky touches the earth. The Sun then travels across the sky and sinks in the west, only to be reborn again in the morning. Mary, the mother of Christ, is the virgin space, and her son is the future Sun. It is interesting that in many pagan religions, the mother of their Sun God is named Mary or a variation of that name: Maia is the mother of Buddha, Maia is the mother of Hermes, Maya is the mother of Agni, Myrrha is the mother of Adonis, Myrrha is the mother of Bacchus, Maya Maria is the mother of Sommona Cadom, and Mariana is the mother of Krishna. But the early Christians could not accept a Mary who was typical of the symbolism of the Great Mother Earth, and thus a second Mary was created—Mary Magdalene. Mary Magdalene is sometimes, and incorrectly, referred to as a prostitute. She is the symbol of fertility and fecundity, while Mary, the mother of Jesus, represents the pure and holy side of the Mother of God. Like Frigga and Freyja, they both are fertility and Earth Goddesses, but one is pure and represents traditional marriage and the other is more lustful and represents fecundity and sexuality.

Another Sun God, who is connected to the Vril, is the Aryan God, Mithras. Mithras worship had spread throughout the Roman Empire and was especially popular with the Roman soldiers. It was so popular that it could have easily supplanted Christianity as the religion adopted by the Emperor to unite the Empire. Mithras was actually a member of a sacred couple that included his wife, Varuna. Her name is very similar to the name for Balder's wife, Nanna. The two Gods represented two faces of one reality, much like the Roman God, Janus, who had two faces. But by the second century A.D., Mithras had more in common with Dionysius and Orpheus. The followers of the cult of Mithras sought to harness the power of the Vril and this is seen in the rituals of the Mithras cult. Mithras represented the physical and spiritual regeneration through the power of blood spilled in the sacrificial ceremonies, through the regenerative powers of the sun, and finally through the divine energy rays of the Vril. The need to seek regeneration meant that the followers of Mithras believed in a Golden Age that was lost, and that this loss resulted in the "fall" of mankind. It was part of Mithraian belief that the cosmos was the battle ground between the Light and the Darkness, between the forces of creation and destruction, between order and chaos.

Mithras was held up as the giver of this divine power or vital energy that is the Vril. He was the protector of the purity that is necessary for one to harness this power and use it to transform himself. He was referred to as *sol invictus*, the "unvanquished sun." Like the sun, he would die and be reborn. He was viewed as a hero who slaughtered the Bull, presenting the uncontrolled force of the cosmos (Ymir, who is nourished by the great bovine), and through his spilling of the Bull's blood, he reveals the secret of how to harness the power of that Life Force, the Vril. He was said to have been born on December 25, and considered a Herculean figure.

There were many pagan Gods who fit the description of the story of Jesus Christ. Here is a list of some of them:
1. Thulis of Egypt (about 1700 B.C.)
2. Crite of Chaldea (about 1200 B.C.)
3. Atys of Phrygis (about 1170 B.C.)
4. Thammus of Assyria (1160 B.C.)
5. Krishna of India (about 1100 B.C.)
6. Hesus of the Celts (834 B.C.)
7. Indra of Tibet (725 B.C.)
8. Bali of Orrisa (725 B.C.)
9. Heracles or Hercules of Thebes (about 700 B.C.)
10. Iao of Nepal (622 B.C.)
11. Buddha Sakia of India (about 600 B.C.)
12. Alcestos of Euripides (about 600 B.C.)
13. Mithras of Persia (about 600 B.C.)

14. Wittoba of Teligonese (522 B.C.)
15. Prometheus of Greece (547 B.C.)
16. Romulus of Rome (506 B.C.)

And all these Gods had the following characteristics in common:

1. Their birth was forewarned by a star of light in the sky.
2. Their father was a God.
3. They were born of a virgin mother.
4. Their birth took place at the Winter Solstice (about December 25).
5. They were born in a cave, barn or other place out of the ordinary.
6. They were born as the vehicle of mankind's redemption, the God's salvation or to build a better world.
7. Their birth was praised or celebrated by angels, the Gods or elves.
8. At their birth, they were visited by wise men.
9. There were attempts on their lives, or they were in danger of dying, when they were infants.
10. They spent their youths in obscurity.
11. They resisted the temptation to be seduced by evil forces.
12. They were crucified or suffered terrible deaths and then descended to Netherworld (Hell or Hel).
13. They rose from the dead and ascended into heaven on or near the Vernal Equinox.
14. They were the herald for a new golden age.

A schism soon developed between the Pauline and Peterine Christians, of which the latter group was made up of Christians who were Jews by race. They felt that it was necessary to observe The Law that was handed down to them by Moses. They were circumcised, refused to eat pork and kept the Sabbath on Saturday. Most of them were found in Palestine and Syria. But as Paul continued to travel throughout the Roman Empire, converting Greeks, Celts and Romans in great numbers, the Peterine Christians soon discovered that they were a minority and isolated. Their fellow Jews considered them traitors and heretics, while the growing majority of Gentiles who had converted to Pauline Christianity, did not share any sense of comradeship with them. These new Christians did not consider themselves Jews, and did not see the new faith that Paul had founded as a form of Judaism, or as the fulfillment of Jewish Law.

The wealthy pagans, who Paul and his followers had converted to the new faith, brought with them their ideas concerning ritual, tradition, spirituality and ceremony that had nothing in common with Judaism. They began to create a natural religion from their new ideas. One of these new ideas was that of dualism, which saw the universe as a battleground between two opposing forces—between two Gods, one good and one evil. Some felt that many of the rites and ceremonies of their pagan religions had merit and should be assimilated into the new faith. Paul was not as concerned with things such as ritual and ceremony, as were the Jewish followers of Peter. He was more concerned about the revelation of Christ. He felt that it was important to know Christ and be moved by his message (as he was), while the Jewish Christians believed that it was more important to adhere to The Law and observe the rituals and rites as laid down by Moses. Remember, the Jewish followers knew Christ personally and did not believe he was the Son of God, while Paul only knew Christ from a supernatural experience he claimed he had, and thus considered Christ to be divine. To Paul and his followers, Christ, the Son of God was more important then Christ, the Son of Man. Thus, many ideas and rituals of the new, growing Christianity did not originate with the Jews, but rather with older, pagan religions.

One ritual that was accepted and expanded on was that of the communion. It is alleged that this sacrament was based on the Lord's Last Supper, but the idea of a sacred meal was common in many pagan religions. If one was a follower of Mithras, the sacred meal was an accepted ritual to celebrate life. Pagans, like those who worshiped Mithras, celebrated everything to do with life—the Life Force, fertility, reproduction and the miracle of life itself. The symbols of their religion represented such things as birth, death, blood, food, drink, motherhood and everything necessary to support life. They would eat together in great feasts and devour food and drink in an atmosphere of joy, happiness and comradeship, all in the celebration of life, birth and rebirth. Pagan feasts usually began with the sacrifice of an animal, which was then butchered and cooked. A certain part of the meat was reserved for the Gods, and the rest of the animal was then cooked and distributed among those who were present. In this way, the participants joined in a feast with the Gods. These feasts were common among pagan religions, and permitted people to reaffirm their relationship to the Gods and give thanks for their support and assistance. These gatherings were often referred to as "feasts of love." The Pauline Christians soon adopted this custom, and referred to it as their "eucharist," from the Greek word *eucharista*, which means "thanksgiving."

Another symbol soon adopted by the Pauline Christians was that of the "Madonna." The image of the Blessed Virgin Mary holding the baby Christ on her knee is now a fundamental symbol among all Christian faiths that Christians take for granted, but the image originated from pagan religions. In the Egyptian religion, the image of the Goddess Isis was the chief symbol of motherhood. She was depicted as a mother holding the infant Horus on her knee, suckling one of her breasts. The symbol of the Earth Mother nursing a Sun God-infant was common throughout the ancient world. Most pagans who converted to the new Christian faith naturally would have associated the image of the Earth Mother and Sun God infant with Mary and the infant Jesus. Many of the pagans who converted to the new faith could not abandon their pagan imagery, and soon depicted Mary holding the baby Jesus on her lap.

The Jewish faith found the practice of idolizing their God through imagery heretical. Idolatry was considered a grave sin, but the pagans naturally created images of their Gods and Goddesses, and fashioned statues or paintings of them that they kept and maintained in their temples. One of the most renowned examples of pagan idolatry was the great statue of Zeus in his temple. It was considered, and still is, one of the seven great wonders of the ancient world. After Christianity was adopted by the pagan citizens of the Roman Empire, as the "one true faith," Christians adopted the image of Zeus, as he was depicted in the temple, for the face of their God. Even today, Christians depict, God the Father of the Old Testament, as an older man with a white or gray beard and long hair. Though he is old, he possesses the vigor and power of youth. This image of the old Indo-European pagan religions, was typical of how people imagined how Zeus, Jupiter, Odin, Wotan, and other All-Fathers, looked. When millions of Christians go to church and look at paintings and statues of God the Father, they are not looking into the face of the Hebrew God of the Old Testament, but of the pagan All-Father that their heathen ancestors once worshiped.

This is also true of the image of Jesus Christ. If Jesus was born to Jewish parents, he probably had dark hair and Semitic features. But wherever we go in the pre-twentieth century Christian world, we look upon a face that is considered the image of Jesus that is not only Aryan, but Nordic. He usually has blond hair and blue eyes and a fair complexion, and radiates a holy light. He is tall with features similar to those of a Greek statue. The image of Jesus is that of the Sun God. It is the same image of Apollo, Frey, Mithras or Balder.

These Pauline Christians adopted one of the most important pagan principles that was alien to the Jewish religion, and that was the symbolism of the Sun and the light that it emanated. The sun was a source of life. Its rays gave warmth to the world. It gave the world light that drove away the darkness and cold of the night. Without it there would be no time. The Cult of the Sun was common among all pagan religions, especially in Europe. The Romans would stand at dawn, praying to the Sun God, and welcome the rebirth of the Sun each morning, letting the warmth of its rays bathe their faces as it rose over the horizon.

They celebrated the winter and summer solstices, and other important events through the year dealing with the rebirth of the Sun. Christians adopted this pagan custom and began saying their prayers while facing east. As they built their churches (usually on holy pagan sites) they would always face them east, so that the congregation would face in the direction in which the sun would rise. This was not because Jerusalem, where Christ was crucified, was to the east. If churches were meant to face Jerusalem, then Christians located north of Jerusalem, should have faced their churches south.

In celebration of the Sun, Christians changed the Sabbath from Saturday to Sunday. Christians referred to this day as *dies dominica*, the Lord's Day. This term was adopted into the Romance languages of Europe (Italian *domenica*, French *dimanche*). The term, "Sunday," that is used in the English languages comes from the Germanic tradition of referring to that day as Balder's day. Balder is the Sun God who is resurrected and was referred to as the "White Christ."

The final triumph of the Pauline Christian came about in 325 A.D., when the Roman Emperor Constantine the Great, who was a supporter of the Sun God cult, called the Council of Nicaea. At this council, the conflicting aspects of Christian doctrine were debated until finally, they voted on the form and substance of their new religion, including the divinity of Christ. Up to this time, Jesus was considered a great prophet, but still mortal, though many had come to associate him with the many different Sun Gods. It was only after the council voted, and it was a very close vote, that it was agreed upon that Jesus Christ was the Son of God, and associated with the God of Peace and Love. Thus was born, Jesus Christ, the Son of God, or Jesus Christ, the Sun God.

THE KABBALA

During the Hebrews' exodus in search of the promised Land, there is a tale in the *Book of Numbers* 13, in which Yahweh appeared in his "pillar of light" and ordered Moses to send out a search party before entering the land of Canaan. In reality, he was ordering them to steal the secrets of the Anunnaki. Moses sends one of his most loyal followers, Joshua, the Son of Nun. Nun means fish and in the Hebrew alphabet glyphs, the letter nun is represented as a serpent. In one Norse myth, Odin transforms himself into a serpent to steal the Mead of Knowledge from Giants. The Hebrew alphabet glyphs, like the Runes, have magical symbolism associated with them. Nun means eternal regenerative life force, because the serpent sheds its skin over and over, each time taking on new life, and regenerating itself symbolically. Interestingly, Jesus is the Greek form of the Hebrew name Yeshua (Joshua). And, of course, Jesus is a Sun God—Balder—and represented by the fish, which is Nun.

In the Bible tale, Joshua and a companion enter the valley of *Eschol* (the valley of grape clusters). In the valley they discover a race of God-men—giants who were descendants of the Gods. They were known as the *Anak* or *A-nun* (the fish/serpent). The Sumerians referred to the race of giants as the *A-nun-naki*. Joshua steals into the valley and leaves the vineyard of the giants with a stolen branch, heavy with giant grapes. The grapes were so large, the story tells us, it took two men to carry each one.

We have to look at the tale and understand the symbolism of the story. From grapes we make wine and wine has always been symbolic for blood. Did Jesus not say that the wine was his blood, at the Last Supper? Blood (or DNA) is the basis for the secret of the Vril Science. Vril is the Life Force of the Gods, and the Gods reside within our DNA. Once again we have to understand the symbolism in the story. Blood has always referred to that inherited essence that we now understand to be DNA. Thus, when Joshua and his friends stole the grapes, they were actually taking away from the *Anak* their knowledge of the Vril—Vril Science or Vrilology. This secret knowledge was eventually codified by the Hebrew priests, and eventually transformed into the secret tradition known as the Kabbala.

The Kabbala, which is also spelled Kabalah, Qabala, Qabalah, Kabala, Cabbala, etc., is a form of Jewish mysticism based on Vril Science, codified in Jewish tradition, symbolism and language, which are based on Semitic pagan beliefs that predate the establishment of Judaism, and has existed alongside the Jewish religion for three thousand years. Because it is a form of Jewish Vril Science, it shares certain religious elements of Egypt, India and other ancient civilizations that were influenced by refugees from the great Black Sea Flood. The similarities between the Kabbala, and Vril Science that has been handed down to us from the ancient Aryans, are obvious, and these similarities are strikingly familiar with the Norse tradition. For instance, the words "Kabbala" and "Runa" both mean "secret" or "hidden." Then there is the Kabbalistic Tree of Life, which is similar to the World Tree called Yggdrasill. Yggdrasill contains nine worlds, while the Kabbala's Tree of Life contains ten realms or Sephiroth. Still another similarity, both the Kabbala and the Runic tradition were originally oral traditions handed down to those who studied them.

Connecting the ten circles of the Kabbala's Tree of Life is twenty-two paths. This fits nicely with the twenty-four paths (corresponding to the twenty-four Runes) between the nine worlds of Yggdrasill. In both cases, the paths and worlds, or Sephiroh, represent the Macrocosm (the universe) and the Microcosm (the individual human being), and the relationship between the two. This would be the Life Force of the Gods, or the Vril.

This is not the place for an in depth study of the Kabbala, but I touch on the subject to demonstrate that other people and nations have known of the Vril and its power for thousands of years, and have used it with much success. The Roman Catholic Church has practiced a form of Vril Science. Every Mass is an attempt to harness its power. The Anglo-Saxon establishment, in both the United States and Great Britain, is rooted in Free Masonry, has also sought to harness this power. Even the Soviet Union was conducting very effective experiments in Vril Science. The CIA got wind of these experiments in the 1950s and started its own program of trying to harness the power of the Vril.

The Kabbala deals with the explanation of how God created the universe. According the Kabbala, God created the universe through the use of thirty-two secret paths of wisdom, which are the ten Sephiroth and the twenty-two paths of wisdom connecting them. These paths also correspond to the twenty-two letters of the Hebrew alphabet. This is another similarity with the twenty-four paths connecting the nine worlds of the Yggdrasill, which corresponds to the twenty-four Runes of the Futhark. Like the different worlds of the Yggdrasill, each Sephiroth represents a different level of knowledge or inspiration. This knowledge can be obtained by traveling about the worlds of either tree. There are differences in the two trees. In the Kabbala's Tree of Life, Earth is at the bottom, but in the Yggdrasill, it is in the center, but despite such differences, meditation on the Tree of Life and the Yggdrasill are very similar, and in both cases its goal is to harness the Vril's power, and use it to discover the scared knowledge that is at the root of understanding the universe and existence.

According to the Kabbala, God created the universe by speaking the twenty-two letters of the Hebrew alphabet, combining their sounds to fashioning everything in it. Of course we now understanding something of the quantum nature of the universe and the relationship of vibrations or waves on particles. Through meditation, the Kabbalhist can transcend this world and pass through a series of gates leading to heaven. Each gate is guarded by an angel. To get pass the angel, one has to recite the correct name of each angel several time. The Kabbalhist does not believe that Gods drove Adam and Eve from the Garden of Paradise, but that man drove God from the garden. He did this by discovering the secret of the Kabbala that is referred to as the Tree of Knowledge in the Bible. By achieving this knowledge, man can know God and discover his true nature. Interesting enough, God's nature is androgynous—part male and female. When one studies the Kabbala's Tree of Life, one discovers that the diagram is actually a blueprint of God's body. Within it is not only the true nature of God's body, but the structure of the universe.

This is all very interesting because the Kabbala's Tree of Life is very similar to the Norse Yggdrasill. The Yggdrasill was fashioned from the body parts of the Ymir, who is androgynous. And while God fashioned the universe by speaking the twenty-two letters in the Hebrew alphabet, Odin did the same by chanting the twenty-four Runes of the Futhark.

Like the nine worlds of the Yggdrasill, the ten Sephiroth of the Tree of Life have different meanings that are basic to understanding the entire tree. Each realm offers insights into a different aspect of the universe and the Gods. This is true of both traditions. In the Tree of Life, the ten Sephiroth are:

1) Kether—crown
2) Chokmah—wisdom
3) Binah—understanding
4) Chesed—mercy
5) Geburah—severity
6) Tiphareth—beauty
7) Netzach—victory
8) Hod—glory

9) Yesod—foundation

10) Malkuth—kingdom

In studying the Kabbala, the student concentrates on one of the Sephiroth at a time. Once the student has established a connection with a particular Sepirath, its force and power fills him and transforms him. The student then has access to a great source of power and energy. This is the same method that is used by a student studying the use of the Runes in conjunction with the nine worlds of the Yggdrasill, and harnessing the power of the Vril. The energy that is harnessed in both traditions is the power of the Vril. The word, Kabbala, is derived from the Hebrew word meaning "to receive in secret." Other meanings for the word are "The Law," and "Secret Wisdom or Knowledge."

Kabbalists claim that the Kabbala was given to Moses on Mount Sinai by God, but others claim it was given to Adam by the angels. Though both claims are unlikely, there is some truth in both claims that the Kabbala is knowledge originally given to man by a superior force (the Gods) by way of Joshua stealing it from the *Anak*. The secret knowledge of the Kabbala is a blueprint on how to harness the "Godly" power behind it, and use this power to initiate a transformation of the inner self and thus, literately create God-men. This is done through meditation on the Sepiroth of the Tree of Life, and learning how to manifest changes in the personality of the practitioner of the Kabbala, for the purpose of causing a spiritual transformation. This is done by traveling the different paths within the Tree of Life. This forces the practitioner to reexamine himself and thus, know himself, so that he can begin the work of transforming himself into a superior being. Once the practitioner has transformed his inner self (the Microcosm), he can then use the Tree of Life to understand and clarify just what goal he seeks to manifest in the objective world (the Macrocosm). He will discover and unravel the secret of the Tree of Life to learn just what paths he must travel, and the order in which he must travel them, arranging his ideas in the proper order, so that he can draw on the power (the Vril) to cause his ideas to be manifested in the objective world. The process is done in the same way anyone would use the Runes to fashion the power of the Vril into directing its power to create their desired goals—through meditation, chanting, visualization and astral projection. And as with all variations of Vril Science, this can be done on both an individual and a collective level.

PART III
VRILOLOGY—THE LOST SCIENCE OF THE VRIL

USING THE RUNES TO HARNESS THE POWER OF THE VRIL

Humans have invented signs to communicate with each other for thousands of years. In the caves of Europe, we have discovered such symbols that date back to the 12,000 and 17,000 years ago. Though the meaning of the symbols is unknown to us, they have an uncanny resemblance to later alphabets, and is certainly the earliest form of writing ever discovered. A mammoth skull was discovered with such symbols painted on it dating back 14,000 years ago, in Mezhirich, Ukraine. These symbols belong to Old Europe, which was in the earliest stage of development, leading to the development of the Atlantean Aryan civilization that was to appear on the shores of the Black Sea between 10,000 and 5600 B.C. It was from this culture that the Runes were born and eventually, under the tutelage of the Gods, used by the Aryans to master the Vril. The Runes have survived the flooding of the Black Sea and destruction of the Aryan civilization. Rune writing has been discovered in various locations throughout Old Europe, which included such Runic symbols as the sun wheel, the swastika, and various forms of crosses, which all represent the Sun God, Balder.

The earliest Runes used by the original Indo-European people, evolved into the present-day Elder Futhark. Early Europeans retained memory of the Runes, though that memory was often distorted by time, and evolved into various types of writing. Archeologists have found traces of Runic script that predate both Latin and Greek, and both alphabets can trace their origins to the Runes. Runic writing has been found throughout Europe dating back to the time between the great Black Sea Flood and the rise of Greek and Roman civilizations. In the past, some anthropologists thought the Runes evolved from Greek or Roman alphabets, but Runic writing has been found predating both alphabets. Examples of North Italic and Etruscan writing have been discovered that are clearly examples of Runic writing. Knowledge of the Runes was carried throughout Eurasia by the surviving Indo-Europeans. Their knowledge of the Runes may have been only partial due to the destruction of their civilization, and the Elder Futhark that we use today may not be the exact Runic row that was used by the ancient Aryans. Our knowledge of the secret code of the Runes has evolved with time, and various forms of Rune rows have been used over the millenniums that include the Younger Futhark and the Anglo-Saxon Futhark. It was from the surviving Aryans that settled in the Middle East that the Semitic Phoenicians developed their alphabet. And by examining various forms of early writing throughout Eurasia that includes Phoenician, Greek, Roman, Etruscan, and Sumerian scripts, we find traces of this lost knowledge that was spread across the ancient world by the surviving Aryans.

The Futhark is truly a gift from the Gods to their children. The Aryans received the Runes and the knowledge of how to use them, from their Gods. The Futhark has been described as an alphabet, but that is not exactly correct. Like the Greek alphabet, the Elder Futhark has twenty-four Runes that always appear in the same order with few exceptions, but true alphabets always begin with the letters *alpha* and *beta*. The Runes are referred to as Futhark, which is made up of the first six Runes (F, U, Th, A, R, K). Though the Futhark has been used as a form of writing, it is more than just an alphabet. Its symbols possess secret powers, and can be used like a printed circuitry. If decoded, they can be used to establish a link between mortals and the Gods. Once deciphered, they can be used to transform the individual body into a magical machine, with powers of telepathic abilities to forecast the future or peer into the past, restoring the innate abilities that our ancestral Folk once possessed, but lost over time due to interbreeding, neglect, ruthless suppression by the Christian authority and modern-day secularism. These lost powers can be restored by ritual use of the Runes (Galdor Science) in conjunction with a well-thought-out scientific program of up-breeding. This cannot happen within one generation, but will take many—the end results will enable our descendants to once again walk with Odin, Thor, Freyja and Balder, in a future age—the Age of Gimli.

Madam Blavatsky wrote of the hidden science of the Runes and claimed that they could be found throughout the world in different forms. This was proof that other races also tried to tap into the power of the Vril. Though they had undergone transformation throughout the millenniums, they have come down to us in a form, the Elder Futhark, that possesses great potential as a tool to harness the Vril. If used properly, the Runes can be used to forge a connection, a bridge, between Midgard and Asgard. Like an electric circuit, they can connect the user with the Gods, because within their design there is a hidden secret formula that will permit us to acquire telepathic powers, foresee the future, and look back into history. If we learn to unlock the hidden science of the Vril that is within the Runes, we can even transform ourselves into a race of God-men, and once again walk with Odin, Freyja, Balder and the other Gods and Goddesses. It might take several generations, but it is possible through mastering the power of the Vril, through the use of the Runes, to cause biological mutations within our DNA, and thus recreate the lost civilization of the ancient Aryans.

The Hagalaz Rune, which is the H-rune and sometimes is written as an asterisk, is the mother of all Runes. This is the Rune of creation, the icy egg or seed of primal cosmic life. From it flows crystalized power and cosmic patterns. These cosmic patterns are the ordering force of the universe—the God-force. This God-force is Vril, the eternal cosmic harmony. It is the ninth Rune in the Futhark, and nine is a powerful number. There are nine worlds in the Yggdrasill, which represent the complete cosmic forces. Hagalaz is the first Rune of the second aett of the Rune row, and represents Heimdall, who governs this aett. He was born of nine mothers, one from each world. He is the creator of the races of humanity—the genetic code and laws of genetic truth.

The Runes and the coded knowledge that lie within them, hold the secret to the structure of the universe, its order and physical laws. The inner nature of existence is encoded within the Runes, and through the study and use of the Futhark we have the potential to unlock these secrets, just as the ancient Aryans did thousands of years in the past.

Each individual Rune is a storehouse of knowledge waiting to be discovered. The limitless power of the Life Force of the Gods, the Vril, that is the inner essence of existence and holds the universe together, can be harnessed and mastered through the use and understanding of the Runes. Each Rune is an expression of a specific aspect of reality and within their totality lies the secret to reality. We have to think of the Futhark as a code to be examined and experimented with if we are to unlock its secrets.

To discover the code of the Runes, Odin underwent a self-inflicted ordeal. This ordeal caused a transformation within his inner self, a metamorphosis, that endowed him with an understanding of existence. He wrote down this code of existence in the form of the Futhark. This tale of Odin, sacrificing himself to himself, is not to be taken literally, but examined and understood as a process by which we can also undergo such an inner transformation, endowing ourselves with the ability to comprehend the meaning of existence and learning how to read its code and use it in the methodology known as Galdor Science.

As Odin underwent his ordeal, he envisioned certain symbols. The nature of existence appeared in his mind in the form of these symbols. The symbols appeared as geometric forms that we refer to as Runes. By undergoing a similar process, we too can unleash this secret knowledge of the universe. This is done through many hours of meditation, chanting and visualization. The methodology of Galdor Science triggers a neurological process that is an ingrained part of the way the brain functions that involves phosphenes. Phosphenes is an integral way the brain functions. In the brain's visual cortex, geometrical shapes and images are processed. Every brain possesses phosphenes, naturally transforming the electrical currents into these geometric shapes. When we shut our eyes, we can see evidence of phosphenes by the appearance of geometric shapes and images that appear on the insides of our eyelids. They also can appear to us while we are in a trance-like state. This natural process is at the heart of the creation of the Runes, and how the Gods communicate with us, bestowing upon us the encoded knowledge and understanding of the Vril. One of the fundamental shapes that we see is the form of the Rune, Hagalaz.

As was stated before, the Hagalaz, which is the "H" Rune, can be visualized as an asterisk, combining the Runes, Gebo and Isa. It is the symbol for the divine spark and creation (the Big Bang). Gebo represents the union of opposites. The joining of the female and male is the reproductive force of evolution and thus, outward expansion or growth. Isa is the center point and Eternal Ice, and the Rune of contraction. Gebo, which is actually two Kenaz Runes facing away from each other, representing expanding power. When joined together like this they are light and power being emanated in all directions from a central point. Isa is the center point, and the Rune of attraction—a Black Hole. Thus, we have attraction and emanation. This is the great pulsating force that powers the birth, death and rebirth of the universe. Now, if we combine this with Wunjo, the Rune of harmonic union, joy and happiness, we actually have the symbol that the Catholic Church uses to represent Christ. The Church adopted this sign for Christ because it understood the cosmic symbolism of this Runic sign—which represents Balder, the Resurrection.

Another Rune representing Balder used by the Folk Faith, is the Elhaz. This is the symbol of life and resurrection. As the Hagalaz Rune is the Rune of creation, the Elhaz Rune is the Rune of resurrection. It is the Rune of Balder, the son of the All-Father, who is "Born-Again." It is the Rune of Balder Rising. He overcomes the winter-like force of darkness and death and ascends from the Netherworld. He draws new life into the dead, and as he rises with arms raised up, he brings with him the light of the sun to a universe that has been plunged into the darkness of chaos. This is represented by the Elhaz Rune, with arms stretched upright. It is the Rune of Returning Light.

A third Rune that is associated with Balder is Sowilo, the "S" Rune. It is the Rune of the Sun, light and victory. It is the light that has returned with Balder's resurrection, and the Rune of Balder Risen. It is the lightning that strikes the earth and causes creation and destruction. We now know that the sun in the center of our solar system is not just a nuclear plant but an electromagnetic powerhouse, and the Vril is an electromagnetic force. In the defensive form it is the sun wheel, the shield, and in the offensive form, it is the striking lightening.

The Edda, which has been passed down to us, probably incomplete and slightly distorted because it was written down by Christians, is a record of the myths of the ancient Germanic peoples. Of the old European pagan religions, the Norse variation seems to still hold a fascination that speaks directly to our souls. This is probably due to the fact that it was still a living religion just nine hundred years ago. We also find a revival of the old Baltic religion in present day Lithuania. This is due to the fact that the Lithuanians were still practicing their old religion in the 13th century, and had actually reconverted back to it for a time, after being forced to adopt Christianity.

In the Edda, Odin is the God of War, Lord of the Dead, All-Father of the Gods and a magician and necromancer who mastered the magical art of Galdor Science and learned Seither Science from Freyja. In the *Havamal* poems he is described as performing a sacrifice of himself to himself by hanging on the Yggdrasill. For nine days and nights he remained hanging on the World Tree, without food or drink and finally ending the ordeal by impaling himself on his spear. This is a form of ritual suffering, in which he was imparted with the secret knowledge of the Runes. Odin's ritual sacrifice was a means by which he formalized the process of learning the Runic powers, so that we mortals could discover that power for ourselves. This science could give us the power to heal the sick, reveal to us the secret of immortality, defend ourselves from our enemies and crush them in battle, make us successful in love, give us the power to control the elements, and much more. In the *Voluspa*, we read that Odin gave one of his eyes as payment for a drink from Mimir's Well, the Well of Knowledge. The waters of this well gave him knowledge of all future events. This gave him the wisdom to use the Runes, and that wisdom is available for us to use and transform ourselves into a new race of God-men.

The wisdom of the Runes is simple but profound.

I am providing a brief description of each Rune, with its proper pronunciation, symbolic meaning and how they can be used to empower your thoughts and feelings in your quest to control and shape Vril into future pathways.

Fehu (fayhoo)—Money, Fire—Used to increase your personal Luck and charisma, to increase your intake of Vril, and then send it outward.

Uruz (oorooze)—Wild Auroch—It possess great healing powers, can harness the raw, untamed forces of the universe, especially those of the Earth, and strengthen the power of other Runes, as well as your thoughts and feelings.

Thurisaz (thoorrisasz)—The God Thor, and the Giants—Possess active, aggressive power used for defense, breaking down resistance, the projection of power the crush, but also possesses secondary healing powers.

Ansuz (ahnssoosz)—The Gods, Odin—The primary Rune of communication, wisdom, knowledge, speech, creativity, and psychic abilities.

Raidho (rraydhoh)—Wagon, Riding—The Rune of divine, or correct order. It can be used to channel power onto the right road, or direction. Use on journeys, treks, or quests.

Kenaz (kehnahsz)—Torch or Light—The Rune of technology, harnessed fire, controlled energy used for creation and transformation.

Gebo (gayboe)—Gifts, Exchange—Representing the law of compensation, the exchange of powers, gifts, and the union of polarities to create balance.

Wunjo (woonyoh)—Joy, Fellowship, Harmony—The Rune of harmony, joy and happiness. Helps to create harmony among people. The fulfiller of wishes. Strengthens and breaks bonds. Helps to maintain order.

Hagalaz (hahgahlahsz)—Hail—The force of devolution and evolution. Has the power to destroy what needs to be removed so that new life can grow, and helps one to start over. Can destroy what stands in your way of forward movement.

Nauthiz (nowthese)—Necessity, Need Fire—The force that drives you forward. "Necessity is the Mother of Invention." The force that is the drive behind determination. Primary counter-force to negative Orlog.

Isa (eesa)—Ice—The power of concentration, contraction, stability, containment and confinement. Cause the cessation of all movement.

Jera (yeerrah)—The Harvest—The fulfillment of good deeds planted. It represents the natural growth and development of the yearly and seasonal cycles of growth and turning. Powerful Fertility Rune.

Eihwaz (eyewahsz)—Yggdrasill (World Tree)—Connections among the nine realms of Norse cosmology. Its powers, helps one to travel astrally among the Nine Worlds of the Yggdrasill. It represents the Vril-ordered universe in the form of the World Tree, the Axis of Life.

Perthro (peerrthrow)—Lot Cup—It is the Rune representing the Law of Cause and Effect. One can use it to cleanse one's Orlog of negative influences. Can control your evolutionary development and growth. The Rune of Chance. Use to help you to learn to think runically.

Elhaz (ehlhahsz)—Elk—represents the Life Force or Vril energy. You can use it to forge a link with the Valkyries, who communicate directly with the Gods. The Rune of Resurrection, representing Balder rising from the Netherworld. You can stand in this position when communicating with the Gods. Rune of Protection. Represents Bifrost, the rainbow bridge linking Midgard (the realm of humans) and Asgard (the realm of the Gods).

Sowilo (sohweeloh)—The Sun, the Lightning Bolt—The Rune of Balder, the Son of Odin reborn. The Rune of Success. It can be use to increase your psychic powers. Use it to help you become an enlightened and illuminated Being. The God-man.

Tiwaz (teewahsz)—Tyr—It personifies the God, Tyr, the God of Law, Government, Order and War. World Order. Helps to obtain Victory, justice and maintain social order. Can increase the powers of self-discipline, loyalty and honor.

Berkano (beerkahnoh)—Birch Tree—Represents the Earth Mother, Frigga, the wife of Odin. This Rune deals with all affairs concerning birth, children, family, traditional marriage and traditional love. Use it to help with the creation of new ideas, and concepts. Used with all matter dealing with female sexual potency.

Ehwaz (aywahsz)—Horse—This Rune represents the harmonious team between horse and man, representing trust and loyalty. Can increase harmony in partnerships, marriage and all types of team work. Used to help with spiritual growth, development and journey. Use this Rune when dealing with all matters concerning the Fetch.

Mannaz (mahnnahsz)—Mankind—The Rune of the God-man. Use to help with the evolution of superior of divine human. Used to open one's Bifrost Gland or Third Eye. Works toward the creation of an union of mortal and immortal. Deals with all affairs concerning marriage and love, traditional union between man and woman.

Laguz (lahgooze)—Lake or Water—The Rune of the Life Force or Vril. Helps to explore the unconscious mind-states, as well as the unseen etheric patterns and fold of Vril energy fields. Development of your psychic abilities and Emotions.

Ingwaz (eengwahsz)—The God Ing—Personifies the Earth God, Frey or Ing. Rune of male fertility, and sexual potency. Used to manifest a sudden release of power or energy, as well as the transformation of power.

Dagaz (dhahgahsz)—Day, Light—Used to create a union or cooperation between the right and left sides of the brain for the purpose of divine evolution and the development of your psychic powers. The Rune of Enlightenment and inspiration growth and development. Spiritual awakening.

Othala (ohtahlah)—Homeland, land, property—This Rune deals with all matters concerning ancestral wealth, inheritance, genetics, DNA, blood and race, homeland, kind and nation. It is the Rune of Odin. Increase prosperity for the nation and family and all growths connected through blood and genetics. The Rune of the Erulians (the Wizards of Wotan).

By meditating on and chanting the Runes, both individually and collectively, we can tap into the power that resides within them. The knowledge is basic but profound, emphasizing the power that resides within the human spirit and its identity with the Gods.

When meditating with Runes, there are several Norse magical terms you should know and use. The first is "Alu." It is reference to the magical power that lies within something. The second term is "Lathu." Lathu translates into "I summon," or "I invite." You can combine the two terms into "Lathu Alu." Then, you should add the name of a Rune or Runes, such as, "Lathu Alu Uruz." This would mean, "I summon the magical healing powers of Uruz." Lastly, is the term, "Gibu." Gibu means, "I send." You can also combine it with Alu and the name of a Rune, such as, "Gibu Alu Uruz." This means, "I send the healing powers of Uruz."

Know yourself first and everything else will become obvious!

If you learn to embrace the universe in yourself, you can master the universe you dwell within!

Fear not death, for death cannot harm you!

Your destiny is laid out before you and death cannot cause you to deviate from it once you have mastered the Runes!

Your destiny lies within the web of life that has been woven by the Norns!

Work hard and be successful!

Go forth and multiply and you will live forever in your genes!

Man is one with God!

The fundamental belief of the Folk Faith is the mystical and spiritual union of man and the universe through the development of the magical powers that reside within us. The universe is constantly being transformed through birth, death and rebirth. Everywhere in the vast endlessness of the universe, stars and worlds are constantly being formed, aging and dying, and again being reborn. This ceaseless process of birth, death and rebirth, is powered by the Life Force—the same Life Force that is the essence of the Gods and man—the Vril. It is the fundamental force behind the simple cyclical cosmology of the universe and the primal laws of nature, representing the inherent nature of the Gods. All things in the universe spring from this Life Force of the Gods, including man. We are all part of this unifying cosmic force and thus, if we are to be successful in all things we do, we must adhere to the ethical process of living according to the Laws of Nature. The best way to achieve this end is to forge a spiritual bond with the Gods who created you, and the best way to achieve this is to immerse your self in the mystical union of the individual with the race or folk from which you were born. In this way, your soul is united with the collective souls from whence you sprang, and your spiritual essence is at home with the collective spiritual essence of the folk. This is done by achieving a degree of harmony with the natural world around you and the universe.

We seek nothing less that to recreate the lost science of the Runes that was commonly used by the ancient Aryans living along the coast of the Black Sea. The Runes are the conductors of the divine power that animates the universe, produces endless free energy, and influences the material world and human events. The Runes are the unifying conduits between the macrocosm of the Gods and the microcosm of man. They were passed on to our ancestors by the Gods, when they created our Folk, who was a race of God-men, but the knowledge was partially lost after the destructive forces of the Giants caused the great flooding of the Black Sea, which destroyed that ancient civilization.

WHAT IS THE VRIL?

Vril is an ancient word. In the Tibetan language it means chi or life force, but it can simply mean vibration. In ancient Sumeria, the word *Vri* means "God," and *Il* means "to be like." Thus, Vril means, "to be Godlike." Lord Bulwer-Lytton popularized the word in his novel *The Coming Race*, and portrayed it as a mysterious power used by a race of superior beings living in a subterranean civilization. In the novel, according to the *Vril-ya*, the name of the subterranean race, Vril is the "unity in natural energy agencies which has been conjectured by many philosophers above ground." Bulwer-Lytton goes on to describe the Vril in the novel in this way. "I have long held an opinion, almost amounting to a conviction, in common, I believe, with many other lovers of natural knowledge, that the various forms of which the forces of matter are made manifest have one common origin; or, in other words, are so directly related and naturally dependent, that they are convertible, as it were, into one another, and possess equivalence of power in their action." Of course, this is just another way of explaining the unified field from which all creation proceeds forth.

In *The Coming Race*, we are told that the Vril-ya speaks an "original language." They are described as descended from the ancient Aryans. The author of the novel was an initiate of the most sacred occult learning, so I find the word *Vril*, an interesting occult name. The V, which is an inverted hieroglyph for a pyramid, is the symbol of the supreme being. We see this symbolism on the American dollar bill. But if we take the word *Vril* and break it down further, we have *ri* and *l*. The *ri* refers to the ruling principle that can be found in such words as *regal*, the *l* is symbolic of the word *El*, which means God. So the word *Vril*, is actually symbolic of the power source of God, or the Gods. Madame Helena Blavatsky referred to the Vril as *Fahot*, and claimed that the Atlanteans called it *Mash-Mak*.

The Vril is a universal force difficult to describe. Philosophers and occultists have known of its existence for millenniums, and today scientists have rediscovered it, but still do not know exactly what to make of it and are unaware of its true power. They refer to it by many different names: Dark Matter, Dark Energy, the Black Sun, I Ching, the Ur, the Force, the Life Force, the Universalist Spirit, or Electromagnetic Force. Einstein's law of $e=mc2$ claims that there must be a certain amount of matter to produce a given amount of energy, but scientists have discovered that this law no longer is valid. The energy emanated from exploding black holes produce gamma rays equivalent to thousands of times their mass. In fact, the physical laws of Einsteinian science are unable to explain the existence of black holes. Scientists realize that 95 percent of the universe is made up of some substance other than matter and energy, but cannot explain what that substance is. We call it the Vril.

Vril represents an endless source of power that is neither true energy nor matter. This power can be tapped into and harnessed on both a personal and mechanical level. Mechanically, we can produce devices and engines that can harness it as a source of free energy, and provide an unlimited supply of power, free of pollution, that could serve all our needs. On a personal level, both as individuals and collectively as a group, we can tap into this power source and use it for our own personal needs.

The Chinese knew something of the power of the Vril from their contact with the Tocharians. They referred to it as *Feng Shui*, which means "wind and water." It is also known as *Chi*, which means "breath of life." *Chi* is the force of the universe, filling the air, landscape, buildings, mountains. It exists everywhere in space—between the planets and stars. It cris-crosses the landscape as energy lines or *ley* lines. The Chinese believe they must be permitted to flow naturally, and any interruption causes "bad luck." If one where to construct a wall or building that disrupted its flow, it would cause terrible disruptions in the lives of those who lived in the structure or nearby. The ancient Celts of the British Isles knew of these energy lines, and referred to them as "elf or faire trails." There are many in British Isles today that believe it would bring misfortune if one was to construct a house across one of these elf lines. The Chinese have developed a whole system of rules for the design of buildings and homes, both the interior design and the exterior design, which must conform to certain esthetic guidelines, so that the structure would be in harmony with *Chi*. This system that the Chinese have developed is an attempt to utilize the power of the Vril to assist in the construction of buildings and help people live a harmonious life.

The Romans believed in the existence of the Vril and referred to it as *Rhea Kybele*, which is probably derived from the Phrygian Goddess, Cybele. The Romans referred to women who had the power to see the future and discover the will of the Gods, as Cybeles, who practiced a form of Seither Science. *Rhea Kybele* means "the rolling astral light," which was a divine source of universal fire or "the creative spirit." It was thought to be a vibrating source of power that vibrated everywhere in the universe and the breath of creative power. The Romans saw it as the ether which cements and holds existence together, existing between the invisible and the visible, spirit and matter, light and darkness, order and chaos, mortals and Gods. It is the substance that feeds the soul, being a source of astral light. It was fluid, and could be harnessed to magnify the souls' spiritual power. Such heros as Hercules and Romulus were thought to possess a natural ability to harness its power and gave them great powers, which resulted in their divinity after their deaths.

A nineteenth century writer, Baron Karl von Reichenbach, thought that the *Rhea Kybele* was the Odic Force in his work entitled, *Researches on Magnetism, Electricity, Heat, Light, Crystalization and Chemical Attraction* (1850).

Bulwer-Lytton was a member of the Rosicrucians and claimed to be in possession of sacred knowledge concerning Vril. His understanding of this knowledge is revealed in his novels, especially *The Coming Race*. But one must read between the lines. As with all who possess such knowledge, they often write fanciful tales, while impregnating their books with hidden understanding of this knowledge encoded within the story. We should not take these novels literally. An example is the belief that there is a race of supermen living in a subterranean civilization. Anyone who has studied myths and legends knows that the journey into a subterranean world, which is usually associated with darkness, is usually a parable of one who is seeking occult knowledge and must undergo the ritual of death and rebirth. The seeker has to journey into the realm of darkness, seeking the sacred knowledge, which, once is in his possession, will cause a metamorphosis, transforming him in body, mind and soul. Thus, the Vril-ya, in Bulwer-Lytton's book, is living in their hidden realm, which is a metaphor for existing on a higher plane of existence, hidden from the normal world occupied by the rest of mankind. Thus, the hero in *The Coming Race*, Faraday, is an initiate who is on a quest for this hidden knowledge.

Lord Lytton has Faraday ask Zee, of the Vril-ya, the question:
What is the Vril?
Therewith Zee began to enter into an explanation of which I understood very little, for there is no word in any language I know which is an exact synonym for Vril. I should call it electricity, except that it comprehends in its manifold branches other forces of nature, to which, in our scientific nomenclature, differing names are assigned, such as magnetism, galvanism, etc. These people consider that in Vril they have arrived at the unity in natural energic agencies, which has been conjectured by many philosophers above ground, and which Faraday thus intimates under the more cautious term of correlation:

"I have long held an opinion," says that illustrious experimentalist, *"almost amounting to a conviction, in common, I believe, with many other lovers of natural knowledge, that the various forms under which the forces of matter are man manifest have one common origin; or, in other words, are so directly related, and mutually dependent, that they are convertible, as it were into one another, and possess equivalents of power in their actions."*

The subterranean philosophers assert that, by one operation of Vril, which Faraday would perhaps call 'atmospheric magnetism', they can influence the variations of temperature—in plain words, the weather; that by other operations, akin to those ascribed to mesmerism, electro-biology, odic force, etc., but applied scientifically through Vril conductors, they can exercise influence over minds, and bodies, animal and vegetable, to an extent not surpassed in the romances of our mystics. To all such agencies they give the common name of Vril.

Bulwer-Lytton believed in the Vril as a source of power that existed and was used by ancient civilizations that included Atlantis. As a member of the Rosicrucians, he claimed that knowledge of this source of power was given to him from somewhere "below." By "below" he did not mean that he actually journeyed into a subterranean world, but that he had been initiated into the realm of greater *hidden* knowledge, transmitted to him from power above (the Gods) through his ritualistic journey into the realm of darkness. This is the same as that claimed by shamans who transcend this material world through meditation and chanting, and thus journey astrally to the other worlds of the Yggdrasill. Even Odin had to discover knowledge of the past from the Giants, the possessors of all ancient knowledge, and then drink from Mimir's Well, to discover that which has not yet happened.

Bulwer-Lytton explains that the Vril-ya had learned to harness the power of the Vril by "the gradual discovery of the latent powers stored in the all-permeating fluid, which they denominate Vril." He refers to the Vril as a "fluid." This is understandable because we know that the Vril fills the entire universe like water that fills an ocean. The Vril-ya learned to use the Vril to create their superior civilization, giving them great powers and making them appear like Gods to their fellow humans.

According to the account I received from Zee ... this fluid is capable of being raised and disciplined into the mightiest agency over all forms of matter, animated and inanimate. It can destroy like the flash of lightning; yet, differently applied, it can replenish or invigorate life, heal, and preserve, and on it they chiefly reply for the cure of disease, or rather for enabling the physical organization to reestablish the due equilibrium of its natural powers, and thereby to cure itself. By this agency they rend their way through the most solid substances, and open valleys for culture through the rocks of their subterranean wilderness. From it they extract the light which supplies their lamps, finding it steadier, softer, and healthier than the other inflammable materials they had formerly used.

The Vril-ya took regular "baths" in the Vril as a means of reinvigorating them. It is a means of restoring life and health, preserving one's youth and youthful appearance.

Bulwer-Lytton was a believer in the power of the pentacle or pentagram. This magical instrument is a device used to communicate with the other realms or worlds of the World Tree. In the Folk Faith, we use the Rune Circle, which is the same as the pentagram or pentacle. In one of his books, *A Strange Story*, published in 1861, he writes: "The pentacle itself has an intelligible meaning, it belongs to the only universal language of symbols, in which all races that think—around, and above and below us—can establish communion of thought."

The Vril-ya reveals that they once lived on the surface of the world, but were forced to seek refuge beneath the surface: "A band of the ill-fated race, thus invaded by the Flood had, during the march of the waters, taken refuge in caverns and, wandering through these hollows, they lost sight of the upper world for ever." This is a description of the destruction of the Atlantean Aryan civilization that was destroyed by the flooding of the Black Sea and the refugees that were plunged into a state of semi-barbarism as a result. Notice that he does not refer to the "sinking of Atlantis," but to its being destroyed by "invading Flood." This is reference to Atlantis being destroyed by rising waters and not by the submergence. The description of being forced to take refuge in caverns is a metaphor for the loss of the sacred knowledge of the Vril. Bulwer-Lytton believed they were the descendants of the ancient Atlantean Aryans.

I arrived at the conclusion that this people—though originally not only of our human race, but, as it seems to me clear by the roots of their language, descended from the same ancestors as the great Aryan family, from which in varied streams has flowed the dominant civilization of the world; and having, according to their myths and their history passed through phases of society familiar to ourselves—had yet now developed into a distinct species with which it was impossible that any community in the upper world could amalgamate.

It is clear from this passage of the novel that they were descended from the ancient Aryans. Bulwer-Lytton used the term, "Aryan," for Indo-European, which was commonly used during the nineteenth century. He also reveals to us in this passage that through the use of the Vril, the Vril-ya had stimulated mutations, thus transforming themselves into a superior species of humans. Then he claimed, "... that if they ever emerged from these nether recesses into the light of day, they would, according to their own traditional persuasions of their ultimate destiny, destroy and replace our extant varieties of man."

Bulwer-Lytton claims that through the use of Vril, people can communicate with each other through mental telepathy—speaking directly to each other by the transmission of thoughts from one mind to another. His hero claims, "It was through the agency of Vril, while I had been placed in the state of trance, that I had been made acquainted with the rudiments of the Vril-ya's language." He goes on to claim that the Vril-ya used the Vril to master disease, control the weather, generate energy to power machines, including robots, to drill through solid rock, to propel of both land vehicles and aircraft, to supply light for all their subterranean cities (which number more than one million), and grow all their food. He makes it clear that the Vril is an endless reservoir of power in the universe that can be drawn on both a personal level and through the use of machinery.

The fact that Bulwer-Lytton was a Rosicrucian should not be forgotten, because we must remember that Helena Blavatsky's grandfather was also a member of the same organization. She too was aware of the Vril and read *The Coming Race*. She mentions it in her first book, *Iris Unveiled*, published after Bulwer-Lytton's book, in 1877. She speaks of it in the chapter entitled, *The Force that Moves Atoms*.

There is a force in existence whose secret powers were thoroughly familiar to the ancient theurgists but which is denied by modern sceptics. The antediluvian children—who perhaps played with it, using it as the boys in Bulwer-Lytton's The Coming Race use the tremendous Vril—called in the "Water of Phtha"; their descendants named it the Anima Mundi, the soul of the universe; and still later the mediaeval hermetists termed it "sidereal light", or the "Milk of the Celestial Virgin", the "Magnes", and man other names. But our modern learned men will neither accept nor recognize it under such appellations; for it pertains to magic, and magic is, in their conception, a disgraceful superstition.

She then refers to the Vril again-

There has been an infinite confusion of names to express one and the same thing. The chaos of the ancients; the Zoroastrian sacred fire, or the Antusbyrum of the Parsees; the Elmes-fire of the ancient Germans; the lightning of Cybele; the burning torch of Apollo; the flame on the altar of Pan; the inextinguishable fire in the temple on the Acropolis, and in that of Vesta; the fire-flame of Pluto's helm; the brilliant sparks on the hats of the Dioscrui, on the Gorgon's head, the helm of Pallas, and the staff of Mercury; the Egyptian Phtha, or Ra; the Grecian Zeus Cataibates (the descending);

the pentecostal fire-tongues; the burning bush of Moses; the pillar of fire of the Exodus, and the "burning lamp" of Abram; the eternal fire of the "bottomless pit", the Delphic oracular vapors; the Sidereal light of the Rosicrucians; the Akasa of the Hindu adepts; the Astral light of Eliphas Levi; the nerve-aura and the fluid of the magnetists; the od of Reichenbach; the ectenic force of Thury; the atmospheric magnetism of some naturalists; galvanism; and finally, electricity, are but various names for many different manifestations, or effects of the same mysterious, all-pervading causes—the Greek Archeus. Sir E. Bulwer-Lytton, in his The Coming Race, describes it as the Vril, used by the subterranean populations, and allowed his reader to take it for a fiction. "These people," he says, "consider that in the Vril they had arrived at the unity in natural energetic agencies"; and proceeds to show that Faraday intimated them "under the more cautious term of correlation".

She returned to the subject of the Vril and its power in her second book, *The secret Doctrine* (1888), in the chapter entitled, *The Coming Force*.

There is a terrible sidereal Force known to, and named by the Atlanteans Mash-Mak, and by the Aryan Rishis in their Ashtar Vidya by a name that we do not like to give. It is the Vril of Bulwer-Lytton's "Coming Race", and of the coming race of mankind. The name Vril may be fiction; the Force itself is a fact doubted as little in India as the existence itself of their Rishis, since it is mentioned in all the secret works.

It is this vibratory Force, which, when aimed at an army from an Agni Rath fixed on a flying vessel, a balloon, according to the instructions found in Ashtar Vidya, reduced to ashes 100,000 men and elephants, as easily as it would a dead rat. It is allegorised in the Vishnu Purana, in the Ramayana and other works, in the fable about the sage Kapilla whose glance made a mountain of ashes of King Sagara's 60,000 sons, and which is explained in the esoteric works, and referred to as the Kapilaksha—"Kapila Eye".

VRILOLOGY—THE SCIENCE OF THE FOLK FAITH

The ancient religion of our pagan ancestors was a spirituality based on the mysteries of Nature. This included the power of the Vril, which is the Life Force of the Gods. What the Folk Faith seeks to accomplish is a return by the Children of the Gods to that religious tradition, and reforging the old bonds that were shattered, or at best, weakened by the introduction of Christianity into Europe. To help us accomplish this we seek to unlock the mysteries of Vril Science through the study of the Runes or Galdor Science, as well as Seither Science. Collectively, this includes visualization, chanting, meditation, controlled breathing, and Rune exercises, as well as studying the *Eddas*, and other pagan texts.

In the *Eddas*, Odin is identified as the principle God, who sacrificed himself to himself so that he could unlock the secret powers of the Runes, and thus, learn to master the power of the Vril. Odin is the chief magician, who engaged in rituals to enhance his own powers and learn the secret science of the Vril. The pain and suffering that Odin experienced was symbolic of the suffering involved in spending long hours in meditation, chanting and studying Vril Science or Vrilology. Nothing in life is achieved without effort, even if the effort is just a euphemism for spending long tedious hours studying. But it must be done if we are to achieve the same magical powers as Odin. This is of course, a fairly typical shamanistic death-rebirth ritual.

In the *Havamal*, Odin pierced himself with his spear, permitting his divine blood to flow as he hung himself on Yggdrasill, the World Tree (Vrilic power of Life Force), which is the pillar that holds the universe in place. His blood thus flows and mixes with Yggdrasill, the Vril, the Life Force of the universe. At the conclusion of his ordeal, after spending nine days and nights without food or drink, the secrets of the Runes were revealed to him. This is another way of saying that Odin immersed himself in the ritual of becoming one with the Vril, denying himself distractions and spending the entire time concentrating on the Vril. The secrets included that of immortality, the ability to heal oneself and others, domination and courage in battle, mastery over Nature and success in love.

In the *Voluspa*, Odin gives one of his eyes, flinging it into the Well of Knowledge, Mimir's Well, so that he might drink its waters and possess knowledge of the future.

The Folk Faith stresses the mystical union of man with the universe, by mastering Vril Science or Vrilology, which is the process of drawing on the Life Force of the Gods to enhance our mental, physical and psychic powers. As the substance that holds the universe together, Vril is the force that ensures the evolution of the universe through birth, being, death and rebirth. This process is taking place everywhere in the universe, and by tapping into the Vril and drawing on it to transform ourselves into conduits for this power, we can influence the course of history, the lives of nations, and even speed-up evolution by initiating mutations in our Folk to transform us into a race of God-men. The entire evolution of the universe, the process of planets rotating around their stars, comets flying through space, the rotation of the galaxies, the power of black holes, the destruction of stars in super novas, the continuous creation of new stars and star systems as well as the creation and evolution of living organisms on Earth and other worlds, are all part of the process of the Gods giving order to the universe through the manipulation of Vril. We have not yet unlocked all of Vrilology's secrets, but its laws represent the inherent laws of the Gods.

All things are an emanation of the Vril and its spiritual force, and we mortals are part of this unified cosmic process. Thus, if we want to be happy and successful in our lives, we must learn to live according to the Laws of Nature. This means, we must align ourselves with the Gods. We can do this by studying the nature of the Vril, hoping to achieve, in time, a mystical union with the Gods. To do so, we must recognize that it is necessary to forge new bonds, first with our Folk, and then, by drawing on the collective soul of our Folk, we can reforge the bonds that unite us with the Gods who created us.

Whether we are performing a ritual, meditating or chanting, or calling on the Gods for their assistance, we are working toward reestablishing the old bonds anew with our Creators. How do we do this, and just who are the Gods? Well, first of all, the Gods are real intelligent beings, but not the way we have been brought up to conceive of them. Our ancestors envisioned the Gods as forces of Nature who can be contacted through ritual and ceremony, and asked to intervene in the affairs of man. They have the power to influence every aspect of our lives, including the affairs of whole nations, but we must call on them to do so. Unlike the monotheist concept of God, which is tyrannical and dominating, who enacts laws demanding that we follow them to the letter or be damned for all eternity, our Gods are not judgmental. The Gods are collectively a universal force which we call the Vril, which can be tapped into on a personal level. We can call this process, Vril Science or Vrilology.

This universal force, the Vril, represents a source of power that is neither energy nor matter, as we understand these concepts. This power can be tapped into and harnessed on both a personal level and on a mechanical level. Mechanically, it can be harnessed as a source of free energy, providing unlimited power at almost no cost, and free of pollution. On a personal level, we, as both individuals and collectively as a group, can tap into this power for our own use through the power of our mind.

The power of your mind is limitless. You have only to discover how to use it correctly and you will be able to harness the power of Vril and use it to shape pathways into your future, creating the life you most desire. You are alive because Vril is constantly flowing into you, powering every cell in your body. Every atom in your body is mostly Vril energy. Every cell in you body is made up of these atoms. It is this force, Vril, which gives you life. As you age, your body's ability to tap into the currents of Vril energy decreases, and thus, the amount of Vril decreases. But you can reverse this trend. Through Vrilology, you can maintain and even increase the flow of Vril flowing into you. This is done through the way you think. It is done by learning to use the Runes to draw on Vril energy, transforming it into whatever it is you desire. In this way, you are shaping it into pathways (Wyrd) that will create a future filled with those things you most desire.

By thinking correctly, you are sending blueprints to the Gods. The Gods are constantly working to maintain order throughout the universe. As you meditate, you are mentally sending them your blueprints. They take these blueprints and incorporate them into their grand scheme for the universe.

The Gods and Goddesses represent this endless source of power, it is their Life Force, and it holds the universe together and maintains its evolution. It is this Life Force of the Gods which we share with them, and which we can tap into through intense, emotion-filled ritual, ceremony, and Rune work. Collectively, this practice is combining the two Norse traditions of Galdor and Seither, which we call Vrilology.

The Vril is everywhere in the universe, and we have only to draw on its power to both expand the realities of our own existence, awakening the sleeping influence of the Gods within us, as well as causing them to influence the affairs of the wider world we live within and the direction of history's march through time. Ideally, we have the means to transform ourselves, and affect the evolution of our Folk, transforming us into a new species of supermen or Vril beings, possessing both physical, mental and psychic powers far beyond what mankind possesses today. But how are we going to achieve this?

There are two ways. The first is through an understanding of the scientific applications of this source of power. There are people today, and for the last hundred years, who have been attempting to unlock the secrets of the Vril through experiments in free-energy and anti-gravity research. In fact, in 2005, the government of India announced that it was conducting experiments on how to harness this power for the purpose of powering anti-gravity machines, and providing an endless source of free energy. There have been successes during the twentieth century, most of which have been suppressed by the ruling establishment. Hopefully, in the future, we can explore these avenues of scientific research ourselves, but for now we are restricted to the personal means of tapping into this source of power through ritual, ceremony, meditation and chanting, through Galdor and Seither Science—Vril Science or Vrilology.

We need to understand that the thinking process, which produces thoughts, is a spiritual process. Charles Haanel wrote that "thought is a spiritual activity and is therefore endowed with creative power. This does not mean that some thought is creative, but that all thought is creative. This same principle can be brought into operation in a negative way, through the process of denial." What Haanel is telling is exactly what we understand in Vrilology and Norse Lore, that the two halves of the brain are the domains of the conscious and subconscious minds and that they are merely two phases of mental process of thinking. This combined process of the two halves of the brain is analogous to quantum mechanics.

Vrilology is rooted in quantum physics. So we need to explore a little of quantum physics to begin to understand how the mind has the power to transform reality in the mundane world. This cannot be explained in Einsteinian physics, but there is an explanation in quantum physics, founded by Max Planck.

We are only today discovering how a power source can be harnessed mechanically using quantum models. Modern science calls this power *zero point power*. Let me explain what this is. Zero point power occurs when something is cooled down to absolute zero, which is about three hundred degrees below zero Centigrade. At this temperature all motion at the atomic level stops. There is a complete atomic standstill, but despite this, there is still energy. This energy should not be present, but it is. It cannot be explained by traditional theories. But quantum theory does have an explanation, allowing for movement even at absolute zero. At this temperature, particles cannot move up and down or vibrate side ways, but it does flash in and out of existence. This popping in and out of existence produces energy, enormous amounts of energy, which we refer to as zero point energy, and is often referred to as free energy. In laboratories throughout the world, physicists are working on perfecting this process so they can tap into this endless source of free energy. For it is truly a source of *infinite* power.

Let us quickly return to Charles Haanel, and quote from his book, *The Master Key*. He writes, "The law is that thought is an active vital form of dynamic energy which has the power to correlate with its object and bring it out of the invisible substance from which all things are created into the visible or objective world. This is the law by which, and through which all things come into manifestation; it is the Master Key by which you are admitted into the Secret Place of the Most High and are *given dominion over all things*. With this understanding of this law you may *decree a thing and it shall be established unto thee*." It is the power of thought, or consciousness that permits us to tap into Vril, at the quantum level. Scientists have struggled with the idea of consciousness or thought for centuries. What is it? Is it just a biochemical reaction? Is it in our brains? And where is the line separating brain and mind? Between matter and spirit? The truth is that we are a combination of both. We are both body and soul. We are both matter and spirit. We are both wave and particle. Life is a quantum phenomenon, and it is in quantum physics that we can find an explanation how Vril works, and how we have the power to harness it, both individually and mechanically. Let us explore further.

Modern science, based on relativity, rejects the idea of spirituality. It defines the brain as a biological computer of sorts. According to science, consciousness or thought arises from a complex interactivity of neutrons. But this is happening on a quantum level. Thus, our brain is actually a quantum computer. The computer code is broken down to the most basic level of zeroes and ones. This is what is known as a binary language. But a quantum computer would not be limited to these two choices. It would have a third choice: zero *and* one. Our brains function like this. More like a quantum computer, than a simple binary computer. It has been theorized by many scientists that consciousness exists in this realm of electromagnetic field that bridges the realm of the material brain and the quantum universe. This is accomplished by the simple act of observing, or concentration. Many would call this praying, but we refer to it as meditation.

So, the mind has the power to observe. It is this act of observing through prayer, or meditation that can affect the nature of an atom. We can now begin to understand that when the material world we perceive through our five senses is broken down to the subatomic level—the world of electrons, neutrons and protons—the traditional laws of the material universe that we perceive through those five senses begin to disintegrate. Max Planck tells us that these subatomic particles act in two ways—as both particles and waves. This seemingly contraction idea might confuse you at first, because particles possess paths and orbits that are distinct. Waves lack any specific coordinates. Their paths might appear to be disharmonic. But these subatomic particles have the potential to be particle and wave at once. This brings us to Werner Heisenberg's Uncertainty Principle. This principle states that nothing is certain until it is observed.

We can try better understand this principle with the example of Schrodinger's cat. If we place a cat in a box that is attached to a device that can release poison at any time, with no predictability, we have no way of knowing if the cat is dead or alive. (No cat has actually been harmed in this example—LOL!) Heisenberg claims that because the box is closed, we have no way of knowing if the cat is alive or dead, therefore, there is the potentiality that the cat is both dead and alive at the same time. Only after we open the box and examine the cat can reality decide if the cat is dead or alive.

Now, I know that this sounds more like a philosophical exercise when we are talking about a cat, but it does prove true on the subatomic level. Let us take another example. If we have two walls. The first wall has two windows in it. The second wall, standing behind it is solid. Now, if you take a gun and spray bullets through the windows, you will get two patterns of bullet holes that resemble the windows, with a halo of less densely pattern on either side. Check out the illustration in the book. We can refer to this as example A. These bullet holes represent particles that passed through the window slits.

Now, instead of bullets, let us shine a large spotlight through the windows in the wall. The light will pass through both windows. Because light travels in waves, there is going to be a different result on the far wall. Instead of bullet hole-like patterns, we are going to get a pattern of light and dark bands on the far wall. The reason for this is simple. Light waves passing through the right and left windows will interfere with each other, causing waves. Now, if we take an electron gun and fire a single line of electrons through the windows in the wall, one might expect to get the bullet hole pattern, but actually, we would get the wave pattern. This is because the electrons travel as waves. The electrons must be moving like light out of the spotlight. This is the result when an unobserved demonstration is performed in a laboratory. But is it the result *only* when performed under an *unobserved* demonstration. But in another experiment, where scientists attach a beeper to the windows that the gun fires the electrons through, the beeper goes off every time the gun is fired. Because the firing of the gun is observed by the beeper going off, the results are very different. They are similar to bullet hole-like patterns. Because the beeper is measuring or observing the demonstration, the results have changed. *The simple act of observing the demonstration has changed the way the subatomic particles behaved.*

This demonstration always results in the same way every time it is performed. It is proof that subatomic particles exist as both waves and particles at the same time. The simple act of observing, or measuring, the electron *forces* it into one reality or the other. Now, if we think for a moment, we can conclude that since atoms are made up of subatomic particles, which exist in a quantum state of potential, and it takes some form of measuring device or observation to collapse this potential. Since everything in the world is made up of atoms, we have the power to change the reality of everything through observation. In our case, this observation is concentration. Concentration is performed by visualizing something through meditation, or external influence.

Now, if we take this principle and apply it to evolution, we have something that is referred to as *quantum evolution*. Let us now take a look at how this principle can be applied to evolution.

All living things are made up of DNA. But what is DNA? At its simplest, it is a protein machine producing the basic building blocks of cells, which make up our bodies. It is the genetic code that gives shape and form to every living thing. But if we dive deeper, even simpler, we can discover that in DNA there is a mechanism that turns genes on and off. This mechanism is the movement of electrons and protons. Subatomic particles obeying rules according to quantum physics.

So, we have to ask, if a subatomic particle can be in two places, turning a gene on or off, in which place would it be found? The answer is that it is in both places at the same time. It is both on and off, until something measures it. In the case of evolution, this would be the environment, which is the DNA molecule itself. At this simpler level, the cell is acting as its own observer or quantum-measuring device, which is the actual mechanism that is the cause of evolutionary change. It also explains why mutations are not random, but deliberate. It is this deliberate creation of the necessary genes needed to adapt to new environments that can speed of the evolutionary process, thus causing old species to suddenly disappear and for new species to suddenly appear in the time scale of the world.

Let us return once more to Charles Haanel. He wrote in *The Master Key System* that "Electrons manifest in the body as cells, and possess mind and intelligence sufficient for them to perform their functions in the human physical anatomy. Every part of the body is composed of cells, some of which operate independently; others in communities … All these cells are moving for a common purpose and each one is not only a living organism, but has sufficient intelligence to enable it to perform its necessary duties … It is therefore apparent that there is mind in every atom of the body; this mind is negative mind, and the power of the individual to think makes him positive, so that he can control this negative mind. This is the scientific explanation for metaphysical healing, and will enable anyone to understand the principle upon which this remarkable phenomenon rests."

In other words, you have the power to cause changes within yourself at the subatomic level that will affect any aspect of your body. This is done through the concentrated power of the mind, which is meditation. The source of this power is Vril.

What we are attempting to do is to make miracles happen. Miracles are things which cannot be explained within our present understanding of traditional science. The source of power that generates these miracles has not yet been explained by the traditional contemporary scientific community. They lack mathematical understanding of how it works. What cannot be explained mathematically is often referred to as a "miracle," if you believe in them, or "magick," if you don't. Magick is just science that we cannot yet explain through mathematics. Einsteinian science would have been considered Magick in the eighteenth century when all we had was an understanding of Newtonian science. But within the realm of quantum physics, there is the attempt to understand this new realm of metaphysics.

The established monotheistic religions, which publically reject Magick, refers to these unexplained events as miracles. But the truth is, every religious ceremony, is a magical ritual. This is true of Christian, Jewish, Muslim, Hindu, Buddhist. These gatherings are formalized to the point that their structure is rigid with ritual and ceremony designed to evoke certain Gods and Universal Forces. But don't go telling a Christian, Muslim or Jew that they are conducting a magical ritual—the same rituals that pagans once used—because if you do point out this obvious fact to them, you will surely make enemies.

Vrilology is simply the attempt to harness the Life Force of the Gods that we refer to as Vril, which is an infinite source of power, and control it for our own personal use in the physical world that we occupy, through ritual, ceremony, meditation and chanting. This will then enhance the creative powers that each of us already possesses. If we are successful, we will increase these creative powers and ensure a higher degree of success in whatever we do. If you think this is nonsense, then remember that all the major religions in the world are, and have been, doing this for hundreds and even thousands of years. In fact, some of the most powerful people in the world, leaders of governments, corporations and other entities, have been doing this for centuries through their membership in such organizations as the Free Masons, the New Templars, the Rosicrucians and other fraternal entities. Every time a Jew goes to a temple, Muslims pray to Allah, and Christians go to Church or Mass, they are engaging in ritual and ceremonial Vrilology, trying to draw on this universal source of power, and use it to make their dreams and desires a reality.

There are three ways we can use the Vril.

First, we can harness its power under our conscious control, to guide us along the path of mystical enlightenment, as a force to help in the healing process of all functions of the body and mind, or as an instrument to assist us to extend our will to control the actions of others.

Second, the Vril can be used to cause action and reaction on the physical plane of existence, creating desirable outcomes in daily and long-term events in our lives and worldwide. This can be done through the training of the one-point concentration of the will of the initiates, so that they can concentrate their collective or individual will, focusing it like a laser, with the purpose of bringing about a desired change. This is done by combining this one-point concentration of the will with visualization. This operation is driven or powered by the heightened emotional state of the initiates.

Third, the Vril can be used to exercise and awaken the Bifrost Gland, so that we can reconstruct the rainbow bridge, by that name, and through it, reestablish a link between Midgard and Asgard. In this way, we are constructing lines of communication between ourselves and the Gods.

A regular regimentation of ritual, ceremony, meditation and chanting enables us to construct a circuit of communication with the Gods, permitting us to draw on their power, or Life Force, which is the Vril. Symbols, Runes, and other artifacts used in rituals and ceremonies, prevents the power that is flowing toward us from dissipating. The rituals and ceremonies are designed to help us to concentrate that power, and then direct it outward toward our intended purpose. Everything used, such as the libations, robes, spears, hammers, fire, water, and so on, are instruments to help us to visualize what we hope to accomplish. These ceremonies should be performed in a setting designed and decorated for this purpose, which we can refer to as a temple or church setting.

By constructing a temple setting, you are creating a gateway by which the Gods can enter this world. In ancient times, the temples to the Gods were considered sacred places, where people usually felt the presence of the Gods, when they entered. This is also true of Christian churches, especially the huge cathedrals. They were architecturally designed to hold and contain the energy and power of a specific God or Gods. The great Temple of Solomon that the Jews built in Biblical Israel, was considered the House of God on earth. The ancient Jews believed that God dwelled within that sacred temple, where one could stand before God's presence on earth. We too must create temples. We need to build physical temples where we can come together and join in cerebration with our Gods, but until then, we must improvise. We have to construct spiritual temples. We can do this by making a habit of performing our ceremonies and rituals at the same location, as often as possible. This will ensure the build up of the Vrilic energy in the specific location. If you have the resources, it is good to set up a temple room where you and others can meet regularly for your ceremonies and rituals, meditation and chanting. If you own land, then find a location in a grove, or clearing, or top of a hill where you can perform your rituals and gatherings outdoors. Eventually, you can construct a permanent temple, *hof* or structure on the location if you desire. By performing our rituals in the same place, that location will eventually store up the Vril power, and eventually become a charged place where we can call on the Gods, and harness their power.

We must remember that the universe is filled with this living energy—Vril, the Life Force of the Gods. It is alive and we, as living entities, share this Life Force with the Gods. This is why we have the capacity to tap into it on a personal level. In this way, we can speak of the universe as a living organism, in which we and the Gods are a part. Thus, what we are trying to accomplish is to interact with the Gods by drawing on their power, and thus extend our own influence over the world around us through the power of our Will. But to do this, we must first search within us. We must discover the Gods that dwell within us, and make contact with them, thus enabling them to radiate their power from within us. The Vril Science that we practice helps to open the gates of Asgard, and this permits the Gods within to transform us with their life energies. This is accomplished by a consistent regiment of meditation, chanting and visualization.

To do this properly, we must first understand something of the nature of our brain. For it is within the brain that we can visualize and comprehend what we are doing and trying to accomplish. First of all, the human brain is designed differently in men and women. The brain is divided into two hemispheres—the right and the left sides. It is within the left side that we draw on our logical, analytical, mathematical, technical, problem solving, conservative, administrative, and organizational abilities. These characteristics are all part of the conscious mind. It is this side of the brain that controls our day-to-day actions and makes us feel guilty, and suspicious of things that we cannot explain within a scientific context. The right side of the brain houses our intuitive powers of imagination, inspiration, artistic creativity, spirituality, as well as our psychic, artistic, holistic, conceptualizing, interpersonal, musical, verbal, and novel thought abilities. It is the spark of thought and idea. It is powered by emotions, but without the left side to balance it, it would cause us to act on whatever inspired us, for good or bad. But what is most important, it is the seat of our ability to make contact with the Gods, and draw on the endless reserve of power that is the Vril. We know that both Midgard, the realm of man, and Asgard, the realm of the Gods, are connected by Bifrost, the rainbow bridge. Thus, the two halves of the brain (the left side being Midgard and the right side representing Asgard), are connected by this bridge. What we must do is discover that bridge and cross over it, and in this way we will create a balance between these two sides of the brain.

This is especially necessary for men, because our brains are structured differently than a woman's brain. In the female brain, the two halves are the same size, but in the male brain, the left side is larger than the right side. This means that the left side dominates in the male brain. This is also the reason that throughout time, women have possessed greater psychic powers than men. In ancient times, the Romans looked to women known as Cybeles, to learn of future events and seek advice. The Greeks sought out their Oracle in Delphi, who was usually a woman, and the Germans and Norse considered women to be in possession of the power to see the future. It is also the reason why we use the expression, "woman's intuition." The reason is simple—the female brain is in balance and is more dependent on the right side of the brain than the male brain.

Odin is known to have two ravens—Huginn and Muninn. They are the voices that speak to him, revealing to him knowledge of the universe and all that takes place each day. Each day they fly off and later return. Sitting on his shoulders, they whisper to him all they have learned. Huginn represents the left side of the brain, for he is the power of intellectual thought, while the right side of the brain is represented by Muninn, who is the power of reflective memory. The memory that Muninn represents is the sum total of past events, as well as future events. In the poetic Edda, Odin says, "Huginn and Muninn fly every day, over the whole wide world; I dread that Huginn will not come back, but I fear even more for Muninn."

We must reprogram our brains, to eliminate all doubts and feelings of failure, dissatisfaction and lack of belief. Doubts are barriers within our subconscious that create hesitation and cause us to fail. We are heavily influenced by our childhood beliefs, especially those religious beliefs that we were brought up within. They cause us to doubt new ways. Many people are disharmonic beings who preach depression, a hatred for life, rebellion and encourage a chaotic and anarchistic behavior pattern that will lead you toward a self-destructive lifestyle. We need to rid ourselves of such influences. We can also be influenced by other people who ridicule us and accuse us of "wandering from the true path," or who readily share with us "their" fears that we are somehow embarking on a path of "black magic and devil worshiping." If this were true, then thousands of our ancestors, who are spiritually and genetically linked to us, were all evil. This is why it is important that we are careful of whom we chose to be our friends and associate with. We don't need people to constantly dump their baggage on us.

Our Orlog is that part of the soul where all our past experiences, thoughts and feelings are stored. They are constantly affecting us, the way we think, feel, and influencing the decisions that we make. We might not even be conscious of the way they are affecting us. What we have stored within the Orlog will cause us to obsess certain things. If it happens to be something negative, it will cause whatever it is to appear in our lives. Your mind is constantly shaping the currents of Vril energy flowing into you, shaping them and giving them form. The things you obsess over, will shape Vril into pathways that will attract these things and ensure that more of what you might not want in your future. *Like attracts like.* Your mind does this through the rhythms or vibrations that your brain emanates.

This principle can be summed up in five words. *Your thoughts become your life.* By dwelling on a thought, your mind is making it a part of your life. Let this principle seep into your consciousness until it dominates the way you think. Write it down and place it everywhere so that you will be continuously reminded of it.

Think of it as laying the pavement in the pathway that leads into your future. You have to realize that your mind has a frequency. Your thoughts can be measured. We know what frequency is being sent out into the universe. If you are thinking a thought over and over, it will become fixed in your mind. Your mind will soon be sending it out even when you are not consciously thinking about it. The frequencies your mind sends out into the universe in the form of thoughts, changes, depending on the state of your mind. They can be measured, and are technically known as brain wave patterns. Your brain wave patterns, or thought frequencies, are the result of the electrical activity of your brain. Let us quickly review them for you.

Beta—13 to 26 Hertz. Beta is what your mind sends out in your normal "awake" state of mind. You cannot consciously manifest your thoughts into reality in this state, but what you are thinking in Beta eventually seeps into your higher states of mental consciousness. Beta is manifested by the left side of your brain, which will eventually implant thoughts into the right side of your brain, where your intuitive powers manifest themselves.

Alpha—8 to 13 Hertz. Alpha is the state of mind that takes over when you are constantly thinking about something. It can be consciously induced through relaxation or meditation, but you will unconsciously slip into Alpha when you daydream, when you are driving, or just before you fall asleep or just after you wake up. In this state you have the conscious ability to draw on the intuitive powers of the right side of your brain.

Theta—4 to 8 Hertz. You will slip into this state of mind after you have passed through Alpha, just after you have awakened from sleep, or just as you are slipping off into dreamland. Your mind slips into Theta whenever you find your head bobbing on the edge of sleep, whenever you are in a situation that you find boring and are having a hard time staying awake. Theta is your most meditative conscious state of mind, and you can discover intuitive impulses during this time when your mind is on the threshold of entering sleep. When you learn to consciously enter this state, your powers of mentally manifesting your future reality increase greatly.

Delta—0 to 4 Hertz. Delta is the state of mind you enter when you are fully asleep. You become one with the Vril-filled universe in this state, but unfortunately it is very difficult to control your mind in this state. It is not impossible, but it does take a great deal of practice in preparing yourself before going to sleep to try and influence your mind while you are in Delta.

Chanting has the effect of lulling the left side of the brain into a false sense of control. This can be very effective when we chant in a group during our ritual ceremonies. The tools that we use in ceremonies will also help us to accomplish this. These tangible instruments assist in convincing the left side of the brain that everything that is being done is logical, thus shutting down its ability to cut off the right side of the brain's creativity, inspiration and ability to visualize. The tools become instruments in assisting the right side of the brain in directing the power that is being tapped into, and channel it, in whatever direction it wishes.

Emotions are vital if you want to be successful in preforming any type of Vril Science, whether its ritual, ceremonial, meditating or chanting, but the left side of the brain hates emotions. This is why it is imperative that we master the left side of the brain. By doing this, we unleash the emotional power within the right side of the brain, and this can be done through the use of magical instruments. Since the left side of the brain is mechanical, the use of tools and other devices help to tap into its receptive powers. This process enables us to call on the power of the left side of the brain to direct the power generated by the right side of the brain.

Belief in what we are doing is also imperative in preforming Vril Science. If you do not believe you have the power, your mind will create a block that will prevent the flow of the Vril energy within you. We have the power within us, and we can increase that power beyond our realization. But, we must be in the proper state of mind. This requires that we reprogram our subconscious mind into believing it has the ability to harness and use the power of the Vril.

A QUICK LESSON ON HOW TO USE VRILOLOGY

There are several things we need to understand about drawing down the power of the Vril through ritual and ceremony. When performing either it is always good to keep several conditions in mind. First, we must take into account the proper phase of the Moon. The Moon phase is very important in performing ritual, especially when you are calling upon a God or Goddess associated with this heavenly body. It is also important when performing a ritual after dark. Not every ritual or ceremony needs to take into account of the Moon. Certain rituals should be performed during the New Moon, the Full Moon, the Waning Moon, or Waxing Moon. Each of these Moons has a seven-day period. The best time to perform a ceremony or ritual is during the height of each Moon, but you can still tap into the Moon's power during the three days before and after. The Moon affects everything on the earth, including our attempts to draw on the power of the Vril. We all have heard about how people go crazy during the Full Moon.

THE NEW MOON is a good time to rid ourselves of barriers that stand in our way.

THE WAXING MOON is excellent to increase our power, good fortune, success, and wealth.

THE FULL MOON is the best time to perform the most important rituals, because the Moon's power is at its greatest. When this Moon falls on a special Holy Day, like the Yule, or Midsummer Day, its power is exceptionally great.

THE WANING MOON is a good time to perform rituals intended to strike down your enemies and all things that seek to harm you. It is also a good time to ask for protection against your enemies and all things that will harm you. These two should be done together.

Second, every ritual will be helped by certain tools or instruments to help you draw on the power of the Vril. You must cultivate an understanding of symbolism, color, the power of the individual Runes, the use of statues and symbols that represent the different Gods and Goddesses in your rituals. Other objects such as daggers, spears, hammers, fire or drink of some kind, are useful. Let me give you an example. If you want to perform a ritual to help someone, or protection from someone, you could draw a picture, or use a photograph, or even write the person's name on a piece of paper, or use an object that belongs to the person, in the ritual. The personalization of the object helps to create a link that will direct the power that you are drawing to you, toward the person you seek to influence. You should understand that none of these objects have any power, but are instruments to help your mind focus on the object of your ritual.

Third, you must be in the right state of mind. This simply means that you must concentrate your willpower, as well as your emotional state, toward the goal you are seeking to influence. If the object of your ritual is to foster joy and happiness, then you must be happy and filled with good feelings when you are parttaking in the ritual. The same is true if you seek the destruction of your enemies. You must draw on your hatred for the victim or object of the ritual. You must concentrate your willpower and mind on the object of the ritual, and *you must believe in what you are doing*. This is referred to as the single-point concentration of your Will.

Fourth, we must take into account the Will of the Gods. We must be patient and willing to sacrifice in order to achieve what we desire. It is good to make some form of sacrifice of offering in the name of the Gods. In ancient times, this meant killing an animal and serving up its meat and blood. But today, we can make a sacrifice through doing deeds that will advance the cause you are working to accomplish. This can mean making a personal sacrifice in the name of the Gods. The deed does not have to be great, only meaningful. A retired man on a small fixed income, who donates a few dollars is actually making a greater sacrifice than a billionaire, who donates millions of dollars to a cause. The billionaire can afford it, but the retired man may need every dollar to pay for his bills, food, medicine and rent.

You also have to be patient. You can wait weeks, even months and nothing happens, and then, when you have all but forgotten about it, one day, WAM!—it happens when you least expect it.

Fifth, as in anything you do, *practice makes perfect*. The more you study and experiment, the greater will be the results of your ritual. In any field, experts perform better than amateurs. The more you practice, the more energy you store up within your soul. By performing rituals often, you are transforming your body into a conductor of magical energy, and will be able to draw on the Vril in greater force. You should do chanting and meditation on your own and with your group as often as possible. Every time you do, you are storing up the Vril power like a battery. You will become charged with the Vril power, and thus, you will be able to direct its energy and use it to assist you in your life.

Sixth, you must truly believe in what you are doing and in the Gods. If you don't, how can you expect it to work? How can you expect the Gods to believe in you? You must have faith and be patient. Many people are from Missouri and want someone to prove that it works before they will believe in it. But it doesn't work that way. For it to work, YOU MUST BELIEVE!!! This is not a game. The Gods are real and their power—the Vril—is real!

Let me present to you a brief lesson plan to help you begin the process of learning to harness the power of the Vril to transform your life. This is a condensed version of a much greater lesson plan that you can find offered by the Church of Vrilology know as the Yggdrasill Training Program. The Yggdrasill Training Program has a total of eighty-one lessons in all.

LESSON ONE:

You should open your gathering by calling on Odin for wisdom, Thor for protection and Balder for the vision to help you on the journey you are about to embark. Then you should stand and hold a hammer, symbolizing Thor's hammer, and slowly turn a full 360 degrees as you recite the Futhark. This will harrow the gathering place. When you have completed this, thank Odin, Thor and Balder for their wisdom, protection and guidance.

The first thing you should do is dedicate your exercises to a specific God or Goddess to watch over and guide the development of your gathering, and ask him or her to make the event a joyous one. When I began twenty-five years ago, called on Freyja. If you choose Freyja, concentrate on her aspect as the Goddess of Joy, rather than Freyja, the Goddess of War. The use of Freyja is a good choice because she can help to make your lessons a happy experience. Freyja is also the Goddess of Love and Fertility, and thus, your group should bear fruit, and these lessons should become a joyous odyssey. So if you decide to dedicate your meetings to Freyja, use a chant something like this, *Hail Freyja, Seither-Kornna! Hail Freyja! Hail! Hail!* You should repeat this over and over, many times until you are swept up in the chanting. At first you will repeat it just a few times, but after many meetings, you will increase the number of times you repeat the chant. The time it takes you to be swept up may vary, so use your instincts on how long you should chant.

You don't have to use this chant. If you chose another Goddess or God, use a chant appropriate to the nature of the deity. If you decide on Balder, use the chant, *Hail Balder, Resurrector! Hail Balder! Hail! Hail!* If you pick Thor, a good chant would be, *Hail Thor, Protector! Hail Thor! Hail! Hail!* You decide on which God or Goddess to choose.

I've included a list of Gods and Goddesses to help you decided on one to watch over your meetings.

A SHORT LIST OF THE GODS AND GODDESSES

Odin, Odinn, Othinn, Woden, Wotan: Chief of the Gods, the All-Father, Rune Master. He is the Sky God, the Great Father, the All-Seeing. He is the God of the hanged. He rides an eight-legged horse, Sleipnir, and leads the Great Hunt. He has two ravens and two wolves, and is known as the Father of Battles, sending his daughters, the Valkyries, led by Freyja, to collect the spirits of dead heros. He owns many halls in Asgard and has hundreds of names. He is the God of leaders, and is thought to be dangerous and unpredictable to evoke. He is the giver of Galdor Magick, and is known as the God of Wisdom. He is reputed to wander the world in disguise, intervening in the affairs of man. He sits on his high seat and watches over the world, and holds counsel in his hall, Gladsheim.

Tyr, Tiw, Tiu, Tiw, Ziu: The God of War and Law. Known as the On-Handered God, he sacrificed his hand by placing it in the jaws of Fenrir Wolf, for the greater good. The bravest of the Gods, he is the giver of victory and is never deceitful. He presides over law, legal matters, the courts and government. He is a sky God and the holder of binding oaths.

Thor, Donnar, Thunar, Thorr: The Storm God, defender of man, a God, war and fertility, he is the opponent of the Giants. The Thunderer and the High Thunderer are some of the titles he holds. He is the enemy of the Giants, and loses his temper easily, but is considered dependable and a friend to the common people. Thor is totally trustworthy. He possesses a belt of strength, a powerful hammer that is empowered with the power of lightning and thunder, named Mjollnir (the destroyer) and wears iron gloves. His chariot is pulled by two goats and he lives in the largest hall in Asgard. He has wild red hair and beard and is a God of War and Battle, as well as Fertility and Marriage. He is the son of Odin and the Giantess, Erda (Mother Earth).

Frigga, Frigg, Frija: Great Mother, matron of social order, traditional marriage and male/female relationships and traditional families. The wife of Odin, Aesir Mother Goddess. Daughter of Njord and the mother of Balder, she is also the Matron Goddess of Oaths.

Frey, Freyr, Frei, Fro: God of Peace, Sex and Fertility. Ruler of Ljossalfheim, the realm of the Light Elves. He rules over sensual love, fertility, peace, joy and happiness. He is the Vanir Sun God and the Son of Njord and the twin brother of Freyja. He owns a magic sword that moves under its own power.

Freyja, Freia, Freya: Goddess of Love, Lust and War. Goddess of Sex, Seither Magick, Fertility and leader of the Valkyries. Married to a God named Od (Odin). She weeps gold tears and when they fall into the sea, they become amber. Her cats are named Bygul and Trjegul, and they pull her chariot. She owns a magical necklace, Brisingamen, and leads the Valkyries. She takes half of the fallen heros to her hall, Sessrumnir, to live with her. She is a shape-shifter, and the Queen of Seither Magick. Her number is thirteen and her day is Friday. She rules over love, beauty, sex, cats, fire, horses, sows, enchantments, witchcraft, gold, wealth, money, trances, jewelry, foresight, luck, fertility, the Moon, music, flowers and protection.

Njord: God of well being, the seacoast, King of the Vanir and Vanaheim. He is the Vanic equivalent of Odin. His symbol is the lighthouse, which bring enlightenment to the depths of the sea (your unconsciousness).

Bragi: God of elocution, poetry, the arts, writing and the sciences. He is married to Idunn and is the son of Odin and Frigga. Wit, cunning, wisdom, knowledge, common sense, writing, poetry, songs, the arts and he is the patron of skalds and minstrels.

Eir: Goddess of Healing.

Foresti: God of Justice, son of Balder and Nanna.

Fulla: Goddess maiden and messenger of Frigga.

Gefjon, Gefjun: Goddess of Virtue. A fertility Goddess and shape-shifter. She is the Goddess to whom virgins go at death.

Gna: Goddess of transformation, evolution and progression.

Heimdall: The White God, Guardian of Asgard. God of genetics, DNA, the creator of races. The son of Odin, the God of Light and the Rainbow. He has super hearing and sight. He is all-seeing, all-hearing and all-knowing. His mother is the Nine Waves. He is the guardian of all things and especially of heaven (Asgard).

Hlin: Goddess of Protection.

Hoder, Hodur, Hothr, Bjorno-Hoder: The Blind God of Darkness, the twin brother of Balder, the God of Ignorance.

Idun, Idunn, Iduna: Goddess of youth, health and eternal renewal. She is the keeper of the Golden Apples, symbols of the Vril. She is eternally young, youthful, beautiful and immortal.

Lofn: Goddess of indulgence.

Saga: Seeress.
Sjofn: Goddess of love.
Snorta: Goddess of intelligence.
Syn: Goddess of denial and oaths.
Sif: Goddess of spring, matron of the harvest and wife of Thor.
Uller, Ull: God of battle, the hunt, winter, skiing, the bow and the forest. He is known as the magnificent.
Vali: God of vengeance and light.
Var: Goddess of honesty.
Vidar, Vidharr: God of retribution, justice and strength.
Vor: Goddess of awareness.
Balder, Baldur, Baldr: God of peace, the light, the sun, rebirth, resurrection, love, of the Life Force and the ruler of Gimli. Known as Balder the Beloved, Balder the beautiful, The Bright One, the Shining God, the Bleeding God. Sacred wells spring up from the hoof marks of his horse. He governs happiness, rebirth, beauty, love and peace.
Nanna: Wife of Balder, Goddess of Rebirth and Spring. Goddess of the Moon. She rules over affairs dealing with love and gentleness. Also an Earth Goddess.
Nerthus: Erce, Edra: Earth Mother, wife of Njord, Goddess of fertility, peace, spring, wealth, the sea and groves.
Hel, Hela: Goddess of death, the Queen of the Netherworld, ruler of Hel, daughter of Loki.
Aegir: God of the sea, the ocean and the deep sea. He is also known as Alebrewer. He and his wife, Ran, had nine daughters, known as the Waves, who gave birth to Heimdal. He is the God of sailors, undersea treasurers, brewing, the waves and tides and the nine winds.
Kvasir: God of wisdom and mead.
Hoenir: God of reason.
Lothurr, Lodurr: God of good looks and physical form.
Hermod: God of communication and travel, commerce, thought and spiritual growth. Messenger of Odin.
Modi: God of wrath.
Magni: God of might.
Skadi: Huntress, Goddess of winter, the hunt and virtue.
Hlin: Goddess of mourners, the grief-stricken and carries your prayers to Frigga.
Holda, Holde, Holle, Hulda: The White Lady of the North and sometimes refer to as Hel. She has a duel nature and is also the Black Earth Mother, the Goddess of Winter and Witchcraft. She rides the Wild Hunt with Odin, often

on a terrible goat accompanied by a pack of 24 spotted hounds, who are her daughters. Goddess of Fate and Karma.

LESSON TWO:

Relaxation is very important. You need to relax your entire body. First of all, sit in a comfortable position. Make sure your head is upright and you are looking straight ahead. Close your eyes. Now, just sit there for a few minutes and let all the tension in your body drain away. Start with your head. Tell yourself that your head is relaxed. Feel the muscles in your head relax. Concentrate on relaxing the muscles and let all the tension within them just fall away. Then move down your face, to your eyes, ears, mouths and chin. One after another, concentrate on each part of your face until it is relaxed. *Feel* the muscles relaxing. Feel the blood coursing through you, relaxing you.

Then move down to your neck and shoulders and go through the same routine. Once they are relaxed, do the same with your chest, with your stomach and your sides and back. Make sure each part of your torso is relaxed. Let the tension drain away.

You can then return to your shoulders and begin the process with your upper arms. Relax them and then do the same with your lower arms and finally with your hands and fingers. Make sure each part of your limbs is relaxed.

Now do the same with the lower part of your body. Begin with your hips and groin. Make sure they are relaxed and then do the same with your upper legs, first with the thighs, and then proceed down the legs to the knees, the lower legs and finally your feet and toes.

If you have done this correctly and took your time, you should now be one big lump of relaxed flesh and blood. Sit still for a few minutes and *just relax*, making sure there is no tension. Technically, you have just achieved the first step in hypnotizing yourself. You can even accomplish this with another person, by giving them instructions on how to relax. But for our purpose, you have hypnotized yourself into a relaxed position so that you can begin your journey through the nine worlds of the Yggdrasill.

Next, clear your mind of all thoughts. You can do this by simply concentrating on the blackness that is before you. You know, your eyes are always seeing. Just because your eyelids are closed, it does not mean your eyes stop seeing. So concentrate on the blackness inside of your eyelids. Think of nothing else—just the emptiness that appears inside of your eyelids. Once you have accomplished this, just sit there for a few minutes until all thoughts have been pushed from your mind. Continue to concentrate on relaxing and make sure your mind is focused on noting else. This is important.

LESSON THREE:

You can then begin with simple breathing exercises. The purpose of the breathing exercise is to tap into Vril, drawing on it and causing your body to absorb more than the usual amount that it would normally absorb. Your body is constantly drawing on Vril energy to power itself. You need to develop the ability to increase your power to draw on the infinite source of vital energy. Breathing exercises can vary. You may want to explore different Yoga breathing exercises if you are familiar with them. The one that we use is a simple "reverse" or "full" breathing exercise. Its purpose is to draw Vril energy into your Solar Plexus. Charles Haanel explains the function of the Spar Plexus:

The Soar Plexus has been likened to the sun of the body, because it is a central point of distribution for the energy which the body is constantly generating. This energy is very real energy, and the sun is a very real sun, and the energy is being distributed by very real nerves to all parts of the body, and is thrown off in an atmosphere which envelops the body.

If this radiation is sufficiently strong the person is called magnetic; he is said to be filled with personal magnetism. Such a person may wield an immense power for good. His presence alone will often bring comfort to the troubled minds with which he come into contact.

When the Solar Plexus is in active operation and is radiating life, energy and vitality to every part of the body, and to everyone whom he meets, the sensations are pleasant, the body is filled with health and all with whom he comes in contact experience a pleasant sensation.

You can begin by sitting with eyes closed in your comfortable position, with your back as straight as possible. Once you have done this, let all thoughts drain from your mind until you are completely relaxed, you should begin by slowly inhaling, and fill your lungs with air, while at the same time pulling your stomach in, contracting the diaphragm. The abdomen, is the cavity between the diaphragm and the floor of the pelvis, in where the stomach and intestines are located. This is where the Solar Plexus is located. It is the focal point of drawing on the Vril currents flowing into you.

When you are performing this breathing exercise, the lower part of your abdomen is pressed inward in the front and at the sides. This will cause air to be forced into the upper and middle parts of the lungs. This is reversed breathing or full breathing. It will increase the absorption of the Vril. Try it. It is easy. Once you have inhaled with your stomach compressed, and filling your lungs, wait nine seconds and then slowly exhale, while slowly letting your stomach expand once more. You are now permitting the Vril to spread throughout the body.

It takes a little practice, but you should be able to master it in a few minutes. While you are doing this, concentrate on the breathing. Repeat this, nine times. For the first lesson, you need not do anything more. Master this breathing exercise before you continue. Go slow with you exercises. Do not rush them. You have all the time in the world. You can also practice this breathing method at any time, and as many times as you wish. Once you mastered this technique, you should do it only nine times when performing your exercises. What you should be aware of is the sensation of your body filling with the Vril. Try and sense Vril spreading throughout your body, into every part of you as you breath. Imagine the power of the Vril flowing through your arms and legs into your hands and feet. Feel it pouring into you as you breath in and then sense it flowing to every part of you as you breath out. You have become a pumping machine. It is important to imagine the Vril currents flowing in greater force throughout yourself. Though you are doing this within your group, you should try and practice this exercise every day, by yourself until your next meeting.

After you are finished, you might feel a little light-headed. If you do, you have done it correctly. It is the same reaction when you breath in too much oxygen. Remember that every time we breathe, we are filling our lungs with air and at the same time vitalizing our body with Vril energy, which is the source of Life itself. Now that you have practiced your breathing, you must learn to meditate. Once you have learned to meditate, you will discover levels of your mental powers within your mind that you did not know existed. It will help you to free your imagination, which will help you in future lessons dealing with visualization. If you only learn to meditate, and nothing else, you will have developed a beautiful method of creating a calmness within you that will help you deal with the stress and anxiety that we all have to deal with throughout our lives.

LESSON FOUR:

In the previous lesson we explained how you can practice simple breathing exercises that you can perform to help build up the Life-Force or Vril within you. The purpose of the breathing exercises is to increase the absorption of greater amounts of Vril into the body. What you now want to do is to control the vital flow of these energy currents. As one who speaks an Indo-European language it is important to understand the power of the spoken word. Everything in the universe has a vibration. Even your thought waves have a vibration. We can harmonize these vibrations through the use of sound vocalized by our voices. In the Indo-European languages, vowels are essential building blocks for communication, and this so on the esoteric level, as on the exoteric level.

The five vowels used in the Indo-European language represent five very powerful pure sounds in Nature. They were given to us as gifts from the Gods who created us. The first sound is the "A" (*ah* as the "a" in *father*) sound. Another is the "E" (*a* as the "a" in *gate*) sound. Another is the "I" (*ee* as the ee in *greet*) sound, followed by the "O" (*oh* as the "o" in *go*) sound. Finally there is the "U" (*oo* as the u in *rule*) sound. These are the vowel sounds. They are exceptionally powerful for those of us who speak an Indo-European language, and even more powerful for those of us who of European ancestry. The spirit, *mythos* or *Geist* of a people resides within the language that it gave birth to. Since vowels are the product of the Indo-European race, the use of vowels is a very effective tool to harness the Vril for people of European ancestry.

We can conduct simple exercises by using these sounds to help generate the power of the Life-Force within us. Once you have made yourself comfortable, and completed the reverse breathing exercises, remain seated and let yourself fall into a very relaxed state once more, as the Vril flows through you. Let all thoughts drain from you mind and let your muscles go limp. Remain seated, straight, but be relaxed. Then, with your eyes still closed, think about the A sound. Open you mouth, take a deep breath and then gently release an A sound, and hold it as long as you can: "aaaaaaaaaaaaaahhhhhhhhhhhhh."

Don't force yourself to continue making the A sound, and let your voice gently die down. To make the sound properly, you mouth should be half-opened and stretched wide. The tongue will be pressed down in the mouth. Keep your eyes closed and concentrate on how the sound affects you. Let the sound resonate throughout your body and mind. Do this nine times. Later you will do the same with the E, I, O and U sounds, but for now concentrate on the reverse breathing and the A sound. All great journeys are taken one step at a time. Eventually you can do all five.

A (*aaaaaaaaaaaahhhhhhhhhhhhhh*)
E (*aaaaaaaaaaaaaaaaaaaaaaaaaa*).
I (*eeeeeeeeeeeeeeeeeeeeeeeeeee*).
O (*ooooooooooooohhhhhhhhhhh*).
U (*oooooooooooooooooooooooo*).

You may want to begin by chanting A, E and O at first, and later move onto I and U. The A, E and O sounds are feminine and have a soothing effect on the body (though A can also be considered masculine). The I and U sounds are masculine and can be a bit overpowering. They are deeper sounds and must be mastered, but you might want to wait until after you feel comfortable with the three feminine vowels. You decide. There is no set timetable.

This exercise is very important because it will also help the development of the region of the human body, located midway between the heart and the throat. This is the part of the body that deals with human speech. We communicated through the use of this region, by making noises through the use of the vestigial located there. This organ is directly connected to the Etheric or Vrilic properties of the spirit. It can be activated through vibrations. We can consider this region a "Vril-spot," and by activating it through chanting the A, E, I, O, U sounds, we are gently massaging this vital point and thus, increasing out ability to directly tap into the source of the Vril.

LESSON FIVE:

The next exercise you must learn is the proper way to meditate. There are different methods for various traditions, but I will present you with one that is the best for people of Western culture. When you enter a meditative state, you will discover something beautiful happening to you. You will find a calmness within your mind that will help you to go deeper into yourself. The more you meditate, the firmer will be your command over a peace and serenity that you will be able to conjure up from deep within yourself. This inner state of peace can become so strong that nothing you experience throughout your life, no matter how terrible, will ever be able to destroy it.

You will also discover that meditation will help you in regards to your physical body, as well as your mental state of being. Most of the negative energies that our minds can conjure, such as jealousies, stress, anxieties and feelings of guilt will disappear because you will learn to control them. You should understand that your mind has the power to cause physical changes within your body. These negative feelings can cause the deterioration of your physical health. But you will discover that your mind has the power to help heal your body and restore and maintain the physical well being of your body.

1) Sit or lie down, depending on the time of day you are meditating. If you are doing it at night before you go to sleep, or when you are waking up in the morn-

ing, remain in bed, lying down. You might want to prop up your pillows so you do not fall to sleep. During the day, sit in a comfortable position. Sit in a chair or in a lotus position with your legs crossed. Hold your head upright and balanced. Do not let it slump or you might fall asleep. Use whatever position is the most comfortable for you. But don't let yourself fall asleep.

2) Close you eyes and slowly roll them slightly upward (about 20 to 45 degrees) under your closed eyelids, as if you are looking at the ceiling. This will manifest what I refer to as the Asgard State of Consciousness. This is the alpha rhythm of your mind. We discussed this earlier.

3) Make sure you have relaxed your entire body as we explained above. Begin with your scalp. Concentrate on your scalp, relaxing every muscle in it. Then move down to your face, relaxing every muscle in your face. Next do the same with your neck and shoulders. Then relax your arms and hands. This is followed by relaxing your chest and hips. Continue to work at relaxing your thighs, knees, lower legs and finally your feet. When you are finished, you will be amazed just how tense your body was. You will be able to feel the difference. If you can, you should try and develop a routine of meditating two or three times a day.

4) Once you are relaxed, practice your breathing exercises. Slowly breath in, filling your chest with air, holding it to the count of nine, and then slowly release it. Do it nine times, or how many times you need to feel totally relaxed. At the same time, feel the flow of Vrilic energy flowing into you in greater and greater amounts. Feel yourself, through your breathing, pumping Vril energy to every part of your body, and imagine that you are charged with its power.

5) Next, begin counting backward from 100 to 1. Wait about one second between each number. You will eventually reduce the count from 50 to 1, 25 to 1, 10 to 1 and finally, 5 to 1, but for now, we will begin by counting backward from 100 to 1.

As you count backward, concentrate on the process. It will help to discipline your mind and help you to control your thoughts. You can count out loud so that you will hear your voice, if this helps you to concentrate on the process and clear your mind of all other thoughts.

For this lesson, you should not go further. After you have meditated for several minutes, you can come out of it in a very simple way.

6) Now say to yourself that you will count from 1 to 5, and when you reach the number 5, you will open your eyes and feel better.

7) Begin counting, but when you reach the number 3, say once more that when you reach the number 5 and open your eyes, the changes that you have

willed will begin to manifest themselves in your life. Then continue to count and open your eyes after the number 5.

8) Now say: "Day after day, in every way, my life is getting better and better." This is a positive affirmation. You can come up with another if you like

You should start a routine of meditating two to three times a day. Each time you meditate, it should be between five and fifteen minutes. If you meditate once a day, that's good, twice a day is great, and three times a day is fantastic. Each time you meditate, if you do it for five minutes, that's good, if you do it for ten minutes, that's great and if you do it for fifteen minutes or more, that's fantastic.

LESSON SIX:

It is essential to develop the ability to visualize when working with Runes. The ability to visualize will assist you to develop other disciplines, necessary in learning how to master the science of Vrilology. Everyone has different psychic abilities, but in our present age, where we are encouraged not to use our imagination due to our preoccupation with visual stimuli such as television, the cinema, video and computer games, learning to develop your powers of visualization may not be as easy as it was in the past, say before the Second World War, when most people had to entertain themselves by reading and then imagine in their minds what it was they were reading. This was also true for radio. People who sat around a radio and "listened" to the broadcasts were forced to imagine what was being described. People had to rely on their imagination. They were required to visualize when they read books, or when someone told them a story. But in our present age, we are constantly bombarded with visual stimuli and thus, no longer have to visualize for ourselves.

When you slip into the Alpha mental state, you should visualize your goal, or what you seek to achieve in the most detail way. This is referred to as creative visualization. It involves imagining what it is you want in your mind in the most minute detail, seeing it happening in the present tense. If you want to get a new job, then you should see yourself in that job. Imagine yourself already possessing the new job. Daydream, if you will, of yourself in the new position in every detail. See yourself going to work, arriving at the new job, and greeting your new fellow workers. See yourself doing the work, and enjoying the satisfaction of completing the job. See your boss complementing you on how well you are performing your tasks, and how pleased he is with you. Create this mental picture in the most realistic way possible. Make it as believable as possible. But always see it in the present tense, and never as something that you want to happen. Believe it to be your reality *now*.

With your eyes closes, extend your vision outward, beyond your closed lids, and visualize a screen, as if you were in a movie theater, stretched out before you, about four to six feet. Raise the angle of your vision between 20 and 45 degrees angle, but don't strain your eyes in doing so. Imagine the screen as large as possible, and try to make it fill the entire range of your vision. It is on this screen that you will project your mental story. If you want to improve your driving ability, then see yourself in a racing car, going over a hundred-miles-an-hour around a race track. Imagine yourself, racing ahead of everyone else. See yourself winning the race without once hitting another car. See yourself expertly dodging the other cars, and crossing the finish line. Feel the joy of winning the race. Hear the crowds cheering. Imagine the beautiful young lady handing you the winning prize and giving you that wonderful big kiss for winning. Feel the joy and excitement in every way. You want to imagine yourself in the most extreme example of you performing the task you want to achieve, and doing it with skill and ease.

Visualization is the methodology by which your mind creates pathways using mental pictures of what you wish to manifest in your future. These pathways are formed from currents of Vril energy flowing into you. The images serve as a blueprint from which your future will emerge. You must idealize what it is you want to become part of your life. What it is you wish to manifest in your future. You must see the end result before you take the first step toward manifesting it by picturing in your mind what it is you seek to achieve. You must first sow, but before you do, you must know what the harvest is to be. This is idealization. Once you can visualize what it is you want, you will discover what the future holds for you, because you will create it in your mind before you create it in your life.

This is the first step in visualization. You must first see the whole picture down to every tiny detail. As you exaimine each detail, your mind is actually constructing whatever it is you wish in your mind. Your mind is taking Vril energy and forming the desired results and sending out the blueprints. These blueprints then transform and shape the currents of Vril energy, causing pathways to form that will ensure your life is filled with what it is you want. This last process is materialization.

Once you have succeeded in this, you truly desire it. You must impregnate your blueprints with emotion. Know that it will happen. Expect it to manifest itself. Don't worry about ti happening, or when it will appear. Just know that you have planted the seeds and the harvest will eventually come in, in its own good time. The farm knows that once he plants the seeds, all he has to do is nourish the fields with water. At the right time his harvest will grow. Nature will take its course.

If you want to improve your health, then see yourself fit and healthy. If you want to lose weight, then see yourself thin and trim. Feel the joy of being healthy, of being thin, and possessing a beautiful, healthy and trim body. See members of the opposite sex admiring and desiring you. See yourself looking good and feeling good in every way. Don't hold back. Enjoy the daydreaming. The greater your excitement and joy at seeing yourself achieving what it is you seek to achieve, greater will be the power of your mind to help you achieve this desired goal. Your emotional excitement will help to increase the flow of Vrilic energy to your mind and make it happen.

Let's review what you must do:
1) Imagine what you want to achieve in the most realistic ways as possible.
2) Feel the emotional impact of achieving your goal.
3) Experience the event in every way possible.
4) Exaggerate the experience in the most extreme example.
5) Bring all your senses to bear when experiencing the vision.

LESSON SEVEN:

One of the runes you should use in your runic mediation is Wunjo. Wunjo is the rune of harmony, pleasure, happiness, and joy, and it has the power to bind people together into an organic whole. It will help your group to work together harmoniously, while integrating your group into the environment in which you have been conducting your gatherings. It has the same, if not greater effect, as Ohm or Aum. Remember—you should try and use the same site for your meditations. The word, Wunjo, is derived from the German word *wunsch*, which means, "to wish." Thus, Wunjo has the power to make wishes come true. This is a powerful force to utilize in visualizing and manifesting mentally what you desire.

Your group should slowly chant the Wunjo Rune by slowly stretching out the name like so, wuuuuunnnnnnnjjjjjjjjoooooooooooo. Let the word flow from deep within your throat in a musical release of the sound. Do this at least nine times. When you do it as a group you will feel the energy that will build up and unite you. At his point you should be holding hands. You will feel the energy flow through you from one person to another. This is Vrilic power or the Life Force. As you continue to chant, you will feel the Vril energy flowing through you. You have tapped into the Vril, and are drawing it into your small group.

The purpose of chanting the Runes is to fashion the Vrilic power into whatever purpose you seek to achieve. The Runes have different qualities and magical properties. When you use them in combinations, they can fashion the Vril to perform different tasks and achieve different objectives. This is why it is important to achieve a certain mastery of Galdor Science—understanding the properties and uses of the Runes.

LESSON EIGHT:

You must learn to chant the entire Futhark. It is important for you to assimilate the essence of each Rune into your soul. So your group should begin by concentrating on each Rune. You can begin by breaking the Runes down into the three groups of eight called aettir. In fact, aett means eight. The first aett consist of:—*FEHU, URUZ, THURISAZ, ANSUZ, RAIDHO, KENAZ, GEBO, KENAZ, WUNJO.* The second aett consist of—*HAGALAZ, NAUDIZ, ISA, JERA, EIHAZ, PERTHRO, ELHAZ, SOWILO.* And the third aett includes—*TIWAZ, BERKANO, EHWAZ, MANNAZ, LAGUZ, INGWAZ, DAGAZ, OTHALA.* As you further your studies of the Futhark in the Yggdrasill Training Program, you will discover that this division of aettir has deep esoteric meanings that you will be able to use for great powers of manifestation.

Each aett is dedicated to a different God. The first is dedicated to Freyja, (it can also be dedicated to her twin brother, Frey), who is personified by the Fehu Rune, which is the first Rune of the first aett. The second aett is dedicated to Heimdall, who is personified by the first Rune of the second aett—Hagalaz. Tyr is the God that personifies the third aett and his Rune is Tiwaz. These three Gods have significance. Freyja (also Frey) represents fertility and birth of the Folk. Heimdall is the genetic code and creation of the individual Folks or races of mankind. And Tyr represents an orderly social structure, government and protection, especially for the Folk community to survive. The first aett is the collection of Runes dealing with creation, the Runes of the second aett are Runes of formation and form and the third aett is made up of Runes of social structure, maintenance of the social order. On an individual level, the first aett deals with the Seeker who desires to learn hidden knowledge and master the forces that will help him to gain control over his life and master the world he lives in. The second aett applies to the transformation that will take place once he has set out on the road of enlightenment. He will discover that he will have to abandon much that he holds dear as a result of discovering a deeper and more significant understanding of the universe and life. The third aeit will pertain to those forces that will cause a transformation within the Seeker, causing him to evolve from a human being into a Vril being.

The way I recommend you to chant is a long, drawn out pronunciation of each Rune, just as I explained with Wunjo. The reason for this is simple. Everything in the universe has a vibration. The word chant is the root for the word *enchantment*. Enchantment means to influence the word around you. When you chant, your voice is sending out vibrations that resonate with everything around you. We know that sound resonates throughout the universe. Radio waves broadcast from earth are moving through space. These vibrations never cease. They may weaken, but they go on forever. You might be aware how music affects people. It is the same principle. Vibrations! Everything in the universe is in a constant state of vibration. All manifestations of thought and emotion are accompanied by vibrations, which influence others in the field of induction. Everything in the universe has a vibration. Change the rate of vibration and you change the nature, quality and form. The universe is constantly being reformed by the change of vibration, and through the use of the sounds inherent in everything, we can transform the nature of the universe, or that small part of it in which we inhabit. We see this happen with a sympathetic tuning folk. It will begin vibrating on its own when placed near another tuning folk already vibrating. It is in this principle that the secrets of mental influence, personal magnetism, and the power of chanting and enchantment can be found.

It is important to find your personal vocal note. This note will permit you to chant effectively. You don't have to have skills at singing. I am not asking you to sing the Runes. You simply need to discover at what note you voice naturally resonates. You can do this by simply practicing the vowel chants and listen to what note or pitch you voice is most effective. You will know because you will feel it resonating throughout your body, most powerfully.

To chant the Runes properly, you should do so by drawing out the sound of each Rune, just as you do with Wunjo. Remain in your position and keep your eyes closed. Start with Fehu and slowly pronounce the Rune as so—Feeeeeeehhhhhhhhhhhuuuuuuuuuuu. Draw out the Rune as long as possible and then go on to the next Rune—Uuuuuuuuuurrrrrrrruuuuuuuuuuzzzzzzzzz. Go right on through the entire aett once. If you are doing this in a group, you will discover that you all begin to instinctively know just how long you should draw out the pronunciation of each Rune. You should have one person, who acts as the Rune master for the ceremony leading the group. He or she should be someone who knows the Futhark by heart and can recite it with his eyes closed.

LESSON NINE:

You must now learn to practice visualizing the Runes. This is something you should do individually, though you can do it at your meetings, where you can teach each other on the proper way it is done, then continue to practice this exercise on your own. It is a very important exercise, and necessary for you to assimilate the essence of the Runes into your very being. And it will take a great deal of patience. Therefore, you should do this exercise every day at home. One great advantage of doing these exercises as a group, is that group activities can be very motivating. Everyone knows that it is a lot easier to go on a diet and lose weight, when you are dieting with other people.

Science has confirmed that the universe is one infinite "sea of energy." We now know that matter and energy only account for about 5 percent of the universe. The rest is made up of a trans-dimensional field of energy that is not entirely in this universe. Science refers to this mysterious force as "dark energy" or "dark matter." We, in the Church of Vrilology, refer to this trans-dimensional energy as Vril. The vast, infinite sea of Vrilic energy is everywhere. When you chant the Runes, your voice is causing ripples in this great sea of Vrilic energy. You can inject your thoughts into these vibrations that your voice is sending forth. The first step to achieve this is to "think runically."

We have got to learn to think runically. This is not something that we do consciously, but we must learn to develop the ability to think runically unconsciously. We must be thinking runically at all times, without ever being aware of it. Once we can reach this level of being, Vril energy will flow much freer through you, and in greater amounts into you, and empower you in ways that will transform you mentally, physically, psychically and spiritually. Once you have achieved this level, you will eventually bring the Runes to life within you, working in ways to transform Vril energy within you. The lessons in this book are meant only to give you a small example of what you can achieve. To truly develop your skills, you need to take the Church of Vrilology's *Yggdrasill Training Program*.

For now, I want to help you discover something of the power that you can learn to harness through Vrilology. What I want to demonstration to you is how to discover the energy that is behind the Runic forms. You can do this by performing the following exercise. You will discover the energy characteristic of each Rune and how it manifests itself in the objective universe.

A simple way to meditate on the Runes is to take some construction paper of neutral gray color. The paper should be standard size, 8" by 11".

You should then sit about six to ten feet away from a blank wall, in a comfortable and relaxed position. When doing this with your group, everyone should be sitting in a row facing the wall. Keep you eyes open. You can sit on a chair or on the floor. Make sure the lighting in the room is normal. You do not want it to be too bright or too dark. Also, turn off all disturbing noise and try to make the room you are working in as calm as possible.

Once you are in position, you can do your breathing exercises and vowel chanting. If you are practicing this exercise with your group, chant in unison. Then, begin chanting the Rune in the low drawn out method. Once again, chant in unison. This is very effective. You should start with the first Rune of the Futhark, Fehu, and work your way through the entire twenty-four Runes. Do not rush. Perform the exercise with one Rune at a time. Now you should begin to concentrate on forming the Rune you see before you, on the blank wall or space. Visualize the Rune forming before you on the wall, just as we described in the previous lesson. See it take shape and grow. Continue to chant with eyes open and see the Rune before you. Let all other thoughts drain from your mind and just think of the Rune. Do not close your eyes. It is important to keep your eyes open and concentrate on the Rune that you have visualized. Let the Rune pull you into it. Examine the shape of the Rune. Every feature of the Rune should be carefully examined, all its angles and segments. Hold the image in your mind's eyes for up to ten minutes if you can. As you continue to concentrate on the Rune, you might see it radiating, or changing shape, or glow. The Rune might even appear to be dancing, or change color. This means the Rune is filling your brain with its power and essence. Surrender yourself to the Rune, and imagine that you are connected to it. Once the Rune has filled your vision and your mine, you should be ready. Please make sure you have not looked away from the Rune. This is very important as you reach for the blank piece of paper and hold it up and cover the Rune without moving your head. Even though the paper is now blocking the Rune, you should still see the image of the Rune before you on the paper. You can then close your eyes and you should continue to see the Rune due to the process of phosphenes.

Once you can do this, let your mind control the shape until it has transformed itself into a portal or doorway. Will the doorway open, and look through it, and concentrate on what you see on the other side. You do not have to pass through the doorway. But if you do find yourself passing through the doorway. Do not panic. Look around and examine what you see. If you want to return, just concentrate on the Rune you have passed through and you will discover that you are back home again.

LESSON TEN:

Finally, for this small demonstration of what is possible through our much greater system of training in the *Yggdrasill Training Program*, I want to introduce you to the concept of *runic thinking*. We touched on this briefly. By runic Thinking, I am referring to that stage, in your development, when you have reached a point in which you naturally think according to the spirit of the Runes. Think of a musician who feels one with his instrument. There is a connection to the device in which he and the musical instrument are one. This symbiosis is the same when using Runes. There will come a time when your thinking process will change. Whenever you think about an issue, problem or anything that you want to accomplish, you will, without even realizing it, begin to look to the Runes and rely on them, their powers and nature, to find the answer or solution. Everything that I have described in this short introduction of ten lessons, and especially in the much greater training program that the Church of Vrilology offers (eighty-one lessons in all) are designed to help you evolve into a Vril being, in which your thinking process has changed because you have incorporated runic thinking into it.

When your ability to think runically has developed properly, your mind will be able to slip into Alpha and Theta mental states. You will be able to naturally, and subconsciously, tap into the Vrilic energy fields that encompass each individual Rune. This is what is meant to *THINK A RUNE*. It is important to understand that there are real energies behind the forms. The shape of each Rune is designed to shape the Vrilic currents of energy for a specific purpose. Once you have successfully assimilated runic thinking into your mental patterns, you will discover that you have acquired a natural ability to draw on these powers and use them to make things happen in your life, and the world in general.

THE VRIL IN THE HUMAN BODY

The Vril is not manufactured in the body, but fills the universe. Currents of Vril energy are constantly flowing into our bodies, giving life to every cell in our body. What we hope to do is transform ourselves into conduits with the ability to channel Vril, so that we can use it to transform ourselves internally, and cause change in the objective world according to our will. We have to remember that the amount of Vril that exists is nearly infinite—proportional to the size of the universe. Some estimate that it makes up 98 percent of the universe, so the supply of Vril from which we can draw is limitless. Vril differs from energy as we understand it. Energy is created through the destruction, or transformation of mass into energy, thus Einstein's equation, $E=mc2$. But the Vril is not manufactured, it simply exists! We have only to learn how to control it and utilize it! This is why it is often referred to as *free energy*. It is rooted in quantum physics. Once we have learned to master the techniques of controlling it—harnessing it—we will have an endless supply of power to draw on to provide for all our needs.

You must understand that you are made up of atoms. Every cell in your body is made up of atoms. Each atom has subatomic particles. They only make up about 1 percent of the atom. The rest of the atom is made up of Vril energy. Therefore, since you are entirely made up of atoms, and an atom is 99 percent Vril, you are 99 percent Vril.

As I have said before, there are two means by which we can utilize Vril power. The first is through mechanical devices, and the second is through our learned ability to draw on it through the power of the mind—through Vrilology. It is this latter method that we will discuss in this chapter.

Think of yourself as a mechanical device that draws on electricity to function, just as the body draws on Vril to function. It draws on, and stores up, a reserve of Vril, and transforms it into various forms necessary for its organs to function properly. Vril is never manufactured or destroyed. Like water, it is drawn from our environment, utilized by the body and can be transformed when used, but it is never destroyed and it always returns to the atmosphere. In like fashion, we draw on the Vril, utilizing it, transforming it, but never destroying it. It is always returned to the universe from whence it is taken.

The body needs a certain amount of Vril energy to function, and ensure that every part of the body operates properly. It is only when the body begins to breakdown, through use and old age, that its ability to draw on the Vril declines. This causes the lost of its youthful appearance, vitality and vigor, thus causing aging, illness due to the body's decline in its ability to fight off illness, and eventually death. Though the body naturally draws on the Vril, we can train our bodies to draw on ever greater supplies of the Vril. This can be done with the power of our mind.

There is no limit to the amount of Vril that we can draw and use. Some individuals naturally draw on greater amounts of Vril than most, while others have an inferior capacity to draw on the Vril. This is why some individuals naturally possess greater health and vigor than most, and others always appear sickly. If we can learn to increase the amount of Vril that the body can draw on, there is no limit to what we can achieve. We could slow down the aging process, restore health and vigor, increase our mental capacity, increase our physical strength and agility, and even develop psychic abilities of telepathy and telekinesis.

The mechanism by which the Vril is passed throughout the body is the nervous system. The nervous system is divided into two great systems: the cerebral-spinal system and the autonomic system. The cerebral-spinal system consists of the brain and the spinal cord, together with the vast number of nerves that emanate from the latter. The processes of sensation, movement, consciousness, volition, will, and all higher processes of thought and reason, are the domains of the cerebral-spinal system. The five senses of feeling, taste, hearing, sight and smell are conveyed to the brain through it. Awareness of the outside world is received and transmitted to the brain and processed. The brain is divided into three parts: the medulla oblongata, the cerebellum, and the cerebrum. The medulla oblongata is situated at the base of the brain and considered the upper part of the spinal cord. It is often referred to as reptilian in nature, controlling certain functions of the autonomic nervous system, such as the activities of the heart, lungs, cardiovascular system, and abdominal organs. It also modulates some of the subconscious activities of the mind. The cerebellum, which is also known as the little brain, is situated just above the medulla oblongata. It modulates muscular movements of the body. Without it, we would not be able to smoothly walk, run, move our legs, arms, or fingers without conscious thought. These are actions that we learn, usually as an infant, and then perform without much thought, automatically and unconsciously. It is only when we desire to perform specific tasks of complexity that the cerebrum takes charge.

The cerebrum, or larger brain, comprises the greater part of the skull cavity. It is the seat of conscious thought, reason and reflection on new ideas, cognitive thought, memory and perception. It is the seat of intelligence and inspiration. The connection between the nervous system and the cerebrum must be maintained if sensation is to be felt throughout the body. This part of the brain is most important when dealing with consciousness and intelligence, and the seat of these functions, rest in the cortex. The cerebrum sends out orders that control the motor functions. This is done by transmitting Vril to different parts of the body. It is done through the spinal cord, which occupies the spinal column or backbone. Spinal nerves spring from either side of the column, and then divide and subdivide, transmitting Vril to every part of the body. Without this complete system of nerves reaching into every tiny corner of the body, Vril would never reach out and fill every cell in the body. Parts of the body would be without connection to the brain and be cut off from the flow of Vril—the Life Force that animates the human body.

The nervous system is very complex and this is not the place to go into detailing the entire system, but there is a section of the system known as the solar plexus, which is a matt of sympathetic nerves that are situated at the epigastric region on either side of the spinal column, right behind what is sometimes known as "the pit of the stomach." It plays a very important part in the unconscious process of the body and contains both white and grey matter. It has been referred to as "the abdominal brain." It is this region where the body stores up the Vril that is supplied for use throughout the body. It acts like a great storage battery that is used by the brain, drawing on the supply of Vril that is sent throughout the body to power its functions.

What is important to keep in mind is that the human mind unconsciously draws on the Vril to power the body. But we have to understand that it *is* possible to consciously draw on the Vril and cause the flow to increase or decrease to all parts of the body, thus affecting the organs' abilities to perform properly. The conscious mind can be trained to affect the sympathetic nervous system, causing it to send supplies of Vril to different sections of the body through the use of thought and concentration. Thus, the trained individual can direct the flow of the Vril throughout the body, causing currents of the Vril to strengthen and build up the body.

Thought and emotion are the mind in motion, just as wind is air in motion. The mechanism by which we direct our thoughts and emotions, is the brain.

Most people are content with being ignorant of the power of the mind possesses over our bodies. To understand this better, we must understand that the brain is an embryonic universe, prepared to evolve as necessity demands. Once you accept this scientific truth, you will better understand the dynamics of Vrilology in relations to the power of your mind to shape your reality.

Every thought and emotion that is produced by your mind sets brain cells within your brain into motion. I most cases, the substance on which the thoughts are directed toward fails to respond, but once you have sufficiently concentrated your mind on the subject, the substance will eventually yield. This power that your mind exerts, can influence and even transform every part of your body. It can cause improvements to manifest, or it can eliminate defects. Charles Haanel wrote:

Attention or concentration is probably; the most important essential in the development of mind culture. The possibilities of attention when property directed are so stratling that they would hardly appear credible to the uninitiated. The cultivation of attention is the distinguishing characteristic of every successful man and woman, and is the very highest personal accomplishment which can be acquired.

You must learn to concentrate your attention on one thought. The power of concentrating your thought is like focusing a ray of light on a single point instead of scattering it over a large region. If you scatter your thoughts from one subject to another, nothing will happen, but by concentrating your attention on one subject and holding it there, you bring the total power of your mind to that focus point.

An individual who can master this technique will be able to improve the health of his body, slow down the aging process and ensure a long and healthy life, maintaining his health and vigor right into a very advanced old age. It is even possible to extend the life span well beyond one hundred years. Scientists working on the human genome have discovered that the human body has the capacity to live to well over two hundred years. This is possible by isolating certain genes within our DNA, and program the body to slow down the aging process. The individual will not only live to two hundred years, but for most of those years the body will remain young and vigorous, and be filled with vitality. The same thing can be achieved, perhaps over generations, through Vrilology.

Every function and action within the human body is manifested by the power of the Vril, including that of the tiniest cells. Every atom within each cell is powered by Vril energy. An atom is made up of subatomic particles. These subatomic particles are held together by Vril energy fields. In fact, 98 percent of an atom is Vril energy. We are not chemical constructs, but energetic constructs. The subconscious mind relies on the Vril as well, and without it, it could not cause the body to perform according to its needs. In nature, all living things rely on the Vril. Every blade of grass, every tiny microscopic bacteria, and even the great whales in the ocean. Everything must draw on Vrilic power to function. Without the Vrilic power, the body and mind would be like an engine without fuel to power it. The body relies on the mind to direct it, and the mind relies on the Vril to carry out its will.

The body is made up of billions of tiny cells, each with its own life. Each cell has its duty to perform, like countless ants in a colony, they all work endlessly for the greater good until their lives expire and they are replaced by new cells. Every moment of each cell's life is powered by the Vril. It requires an enormous supply of energy to keep the cells performing their functions, to ensure the well being of the body, and it is the power of the Vril that keeps it all working in an orderly fashion. As the power is used, it returns to the universe and new power is taken to power the cells until they die. Each expenditure of Vrilic power is being replenished as the body taps into the limitless reservoir.

The body's ability to draw on this endless supply of power can be interrupted and disrupted. One of the causes for this is emotional stress. Negative emotions can absorb and use a greater amount of Vril than the body is capable of drawing, thus creating a deficit. The body needs calmness, or a state of tranquility to help it charge itself with Vril power. This is why we engage in breathing exercises before we charge ourselves with the Vril energy through chanting. It is important to relax our bodies, permitting them to accept the flow of the Vril without interruption, especially if we live stressful lives. Too much waste of Vril power will lead to a decline in the health and well being of the body. This brings on illness, speeds up aging, and can lead to early death. Pollutants in the body will also interfere with the absorption of Vril power and thus lead to the destruction of cells. This is obvious in the case of cancer. We can see how unhealthy lifestyles will lead to the cutting off of the flow of the Vril currents, causing the decline in the health of the body. Unhealthy lifestyles and engaging in abnormal sexual activities will lead to the strangulation of the power of the Vril in the body. The greatest cause of a deficient absorption of Vril's power is life in the large cities—the urban environment.

Life in highly developed urban environments leads to excessive stress, anxiety, an intake of pollutants, abnormal lifestyles and bizarre behavior that all contribute the interference of the body's ability to draw on the Vril's power. Nature will adapt the body's ability to absorb Vril according to its needs to function, but this takes many generations and is an evolutionary process in which countless members of a race or specie will needlessly die out by the time evolution has made the necessary adjustments. Only those individuals who possess a natural ability to absorb greater amounts of Vril will survive. Since we do not desire to see people die in this process, it is important to try and minimize the negative effects of living an unhealthy lifestyle that is common with existence in the large urban centers. It would be better, and healthier, if we could abandon these urban environments for life in a more harmonious and natural environment, but since that is impossible for most people, we have to learn to compensate for the detrimental effects of urban living. We need to learn to use the methods that are described in this book to help the body increase the supply of Vril and thus recreate the equilibrium and balance necessary to maintain the well being of the body. This is the first step on the way to using Vril to enhance the natural powers of the human body—physically, mentally and psychically.

Once the body's equilibrium has been reestablished, we can continue to use these methods to increase the flow of Vril power into the body. Vril is concentrated in the Solar Plexus, which is then dissipated throughout the body. The mind especially draws on these Vril currents and can redirect the flow of Vril energy to whatever part of the body needs their life-giving energy. This is done through the subconscious part of the mind. But we can learn to consciously command and control the flow of Vril energy throughout the body. There are different techniques to perform this task, and one way is with the use of Runes. With the knowledge of how to use the Runes, we can increase the flow of Vril entering the body, and then shape and fashion this excessive Vril power to cause transformations to both our inner and outer worlds. By charging ourselves with this "life force" or "vital energy," we can become dynamos of energy, activity and power. This will give those who have achieved this state a mighty advantage over their fellow human beings in all their activities. The end result will be increased health, increased efficiency, increased power and increased success.

The correct breathing method can be used to help absorb Vril into the body for the purpose of increasing your vitality, physical energy and psychic abilities. We know that we absorb Vril by breathing. This is done unconsciously whenever we take a breath. We also know that the environment we live within effects this process for good or bad. The unhealthy environment in large urban habitats will affect the absorption of Vril. This will not only cause harm to the physical body, but will also affect our mental health, as well as the health of the soul. Our souls are not completely individualistic in nature. They are part of a greater group soul that we share with our Gods. This is similar to a single cell within a human body. Each cell is an individual unit, but they are all part of a greater organism—the human body. Our large urban cities are not only physically unhealthy environments for our bodies, but spiritually unhealthy. This is especially true in the twenty-first century as our cities have become centers of diversity in the extreme. With so many competing racial and cultural souls, the spiritual environment is confused and the absorption of the necessary Vril can be disrupted. If we lived in a racially and culturally homogenous environment, there would still be competition by the individuals for the absorption of Vril, but on the collective level, there would be none because each individual soul would be receiving Vrilic power through the collective racial soul to which they all harmoniously belong. Since the Vril is absorbed through our bodies into our DNA, our genetic composition will determine how Vril is absorbed.

This principle is very important to understand. Once Vril has entered your body and is dispersed into every organ and cell, it is on the genetic level that Vril has the greatest effect on your biology. Vril will penetrate your cells, and be absorbed into your DNA. In fact, the methods by which you can best absorb Vril and use it to your advantage will be determined by your DNA. Remember—your DNA is where the Gods reside within you, and your DNA will determine how Vril will affect you. The process by which Vril is absorbed by your DNA can cause mutations that will endow your descendants with superior abilities—physically, mentally and psychically. This process is the Balder Effect. This is the true nature of Balder's return.

VRIL AND THE BIFROST GLAND

There is a space between the cortices, above the pituitary gland and above the hypothalamus of the brain which was once a supercharged region of the brain in our ancient ancestors. It gave the ancient Atlantean Aryans the dual powers of telepathy and omniscience. It is often referred to as the Third Eye. This gland has atrophied because of the degeneracy of our race, which resulted in the loss of the psychic abilities that allowed them to tap into the Vrilic energy. What we are attempting to do through Vrilology is exercise this gland, and reawaken the innate potential, which still resides within the gland. In others words—we are trying to "jump-start" the gland. This can be accomplished to a small degree through meditation and chanting, but in the long run, we need to organize a priestly class totally dedicated to the genetic improvement and up-breeding of our Folk, with the goal of revitalizing these abilities.

Madam Blavatsky points out the importance of the pineal gland as a source of psychic powers. It was once supercharged, giving the Atlantean Aryans great powers, but today it has atrophied, much in the same way as the appendix. All vertebrates possess the gland, but in some reptile species it actually evolved into a third eye. Because of this, it has been often referred to as the Third Eye in mammals as well. In humans its vision is telepathic and psychic. It is a vestige shaped like a small cone. In birds it serves as a time-measuring system.

The Atlantean Aryans had developed the powers of this gland, creating a bridge between themselves and the Gods. Thus, they created a supercharged link with the Gods, between Midgard and Asgard, permitting them to draw on the power of the Vril. I refer to this gland as the Bifrost Gland, because it serves as a rainbow bridge, linking our material world with the spiritual world of the Gods. What we must do is exercise this gland through our methods of awakening its innate powers.

Once the Bifrost Gland is developed to its full capacity, the initiate will obtain knowledge of the evolution of humanity. This is accomplished, because the bridge that is constructed by opening the Third Eye, is biological and racial, as well as spiritual. The initiated will have the ability to see backward, throughout the entire growth and evolution of his race. This is often referred to as racial memory—memory of the history of one's Folk through the genetic link with his ancestors. One can see back through time, even to the time before our Folk was born. When fully developed, the Bifrost Gland gives us the ability to see from the earliest time, when life first appeared in the biological soup, and follow the evolution of life through billions of years.

We absorb normal amounts of Vril to fulfil the daily needs of our bodies through breathing, eating and drinking. In unhealthy environments, such as those found in large cities, the natural flow of Vril is interrupted, preventing the natural replenishing of Vrilic power that the body needs to survive. Vril currents decrease with age, improper thinking, and corrupt or chaotic lifestyles. But there are methods to help to replenish and increase the flow of Vril in Vrilology. Those who live in such urban environments must take special care to ensure the proper absorption of the necessary amount of Vril through careful diet and exercise. But what we are interested in is, how we can utilize the full potential of Vril power. How can we absorb additional amounts of Vril to ensure success in our lives? How can we use the power of Vril to develop extraordinary powers of superior physical health and ability, and to increase our intellectual and psychic capacities? We must understand how the Vril works and use our intellect to aid the conscious mind to develop, or reopen, the Bifrost Gland which can draw on unlimited amounts of Vril power. This is not contrary to nature's work. We are only exercising an organ that has been permitted to decline into a vestigial state. The decline of this gland is the result of our ever-increasing tie to an urban environment, unhealthy living habits, unnatural lifestyles and chaotic thinking. In such an environment, we have cut ourselves off from the natural world. Just as the man who works indoors does not get enough exercise, so to has the Bifrost Gland atrophied as a result of its disconnection with the natural world, where it could more freely function and draw on Vril.

Over the last five thousand years man has constantly sought to move into large cities. The civilizations of Egypt, China, Middle East, Mesoamerica, Greece, Rome, and the modern West, have all contributed to the decline of the Bifrost Gland. Our ancestors had the capacity to use the gland—though most individuals never fully used it for lack of time to develop it—most people were too engaged in the affairs of survival to develop its full potential. But there were always a few individuals in each community who developed the unique ability to use the gland to its full potential. They were usually chosen to serve the local community as shamans. Some communities organized the shamans into a priestly class, who would maintain and develop the ability of the Bifrost Gland. We can see evidence of this in the Brahmas of India, the Oracle of Delphi, the Roman cults or colleges dedicated to the individual Gods, the Celtic priestly class of druids, the Buddhist monks and the efforts to maintain a priestly order among the original Twelve Tribes of Israel in the descendants of Aaron, and the tribe of Levi. Aaron's descendants have taken the name of Cohen, which means "holy men." But the greatest example of this effort was among the ancient Atlantean Aryans, who built a civilization upon the power of Vril. This civilization existed in harmony with the natural world and thus did not interfere with the body's ability to absorb Vril.

We must learn to influence the body's ability to absorb the power of the Vril through the action of the mind in the form of controlled breathing, chanting, visualization, and the use of will power. To accomplish this we utilize the Runes. The Runes is a powerful tool given to us by the Gods to assist us in harnessing Vril's power. Through the correct methods of breathing, chanting, visualization and concentration of the will, we can revive the Bifrost Gland, and draw on the Vril and fill ourselves with its power. Then, through the proper combination of Runes, we can transform the Vrilic power into whatever purpose we wish. This has to be done through visualizing the objective we wish to manifest, in conjunction with the correct combination of Runes, and then, direct the Vril toward its destination through the power of the will.

Vril is not a material substance, but can better be described as a form of power. It is a form of etheric energy, unlike the energy that exists in that part of the universe that makes up the 5 percent that includes energy and matter. Energy is created by the destruction of matter. But the Vril is not created through any destructive process. In fact, it is not created at all. It exists, filling the entire universe. We can draw on it through the natural abilities of the body, or through mechanical devises, through a process of "implosion," which is not destructive and thus is in harmony with the universe and our natural environment. If one took an atom and reduced its temperature to 300 degrees below zero centigrade, its subatomic particles would cease to vibrate. Instead, they would begin to flash or blink, in and out of reality. It has reach zero point gravity. This process then unleashes limitless amounts of Vril energy that is referred to as "free energy."

Vril is very subtle in nature, filling a space between our material (matter and energy) universe and our minds. The mind has the ability to draw on Vril's power, increasing the body's ability to absorb it and thus to power its functions. We know this is possible because there have been many documented cases of the mind possessing the ability to heal the body. How many times have doctors admitted that they have done everything in their power to help a patient and finally said that "it is now up to the patient's *will to live.*" There have also been many cases of men and women, especially spiritual leaders, who have been endowed with the ability to psychically heal people. These individuals are drawing on the power of the Vril, and instilling it into the patient, jump-starting their brains and empowering their minds to help heal themselves.

THE VRIL AND OUR SIXTH SENSE

All of us are born with five senses that we are familiar with and depend on to survive. They are taste, hearing, sight, touch and smell. We also possess a sixth sense that was once much more developed. But with the decline of our Folk we have lost command of this sixth sense, though we still possess it to some degree. Through Vrilology, we can once again restore that which has atrophied.

By developing our sixth sense through the expansion of the Bifrost Gland, we can retrieve neglected and forgotten myths and folklore. These tales are genetically imprinted on the collective memory or racial memory of our Folk and remain there even if we ignore them.

Our pagan ancestors were much more in tune with their surroundings and the spirit of Nature. The role of Nature and her irresistible laws have always played a vital role in the formation and health of past pagan societies. If we wish to understand both our place in the Macrocosm and the nature of our Microcosm, we must once again develop an understanding of the fundamental principles of Nature's Laws. This can be done through Vrilology, which is designed to sharpen the vision of our mind.

Nature has no limits. The only limits that exist are those that we impose on ourselves, which lessen our ability to understand and comprehend the limitless versatility of Nature. The present world we live in, with its oppressive atmosphere that stifles our soul, has created a rift between us and Nature. Our ancestors viewed their existence as intrinsically bound with the natural world. Their existence was in tune with the symphony of life, and their entire universe was filled with the Life-Force that united them with their Gods. The archetypes that personified the Gods were imprinted into their myths and folklore and conveyed eternal truths that man and Nature, are united by the eternal laws that governed and guided the universe. Our Folk is a reflection of Nature, just as surely as Nature is a reflection of our Folk. Our ancestors understood this, but we have forgotten this eternal truth because we have become slaves to alien ideologies that preached the supremacy of man over Nature.

The universal belief that man is God, and thus superior to Nature has lessened the self-preserving instincts and urges that ensured the survival of the Folk, and thus have plunged us, into the dark waters of Hoder, blinding us to the eternal truths and causing us to wade through the black ocean of ignorance.

False ideologies preaching the supremacy of man over Nature are leading us into the abyss, but through Vrilology, we can reverse this process. By applying the principles of Vrilology, we can once again open the Bifrost Gland, which will enable us to develop the sixth sense that will permit us to discover the rainbow bridge that will lead us back to Asgard. Part of the dilemma we face is that we are bound to the material world by our five senses. Only through the development of the Bifrost Gland can we restore our sixth sense, which will permit us to explore and discover the unexplainable. Because we are restricted by our five senses, it is difficult to comprehend that which cannot be perceived rationally. Every one of us knows from experiences that there are phenomena that cannot be explained rationally, but most dismiss such phenomena off hand, because they are without form that can be examined scientifically. Because these phenomena cannot be understood within the bounds of ordinary experiences, it is impossible to prove to another that one has experienced such things. But through the development of the Bifrost Gland, through the application of Vrilology, we can develop our sixth sense and acquire the ability to perceive and understand such phenomena.

Because the universe is the creation of the Gods—the Divine—we can never truly understand it in all its complexities. Our five senses have limited us in our ability to perceive the truths that exist beyond their boundaries, but by expanding the power of the sixth sense, which we all possess, through increasing the flow of Vril into our bodies and minds, and learning to shape and use it, we will be able to discover an understanding of that which is denied to us by our five senses alone.

Vrilology can help you to develop you ability to control your body, and thereby, you health. It can help you to strengthen your mental powers, improve your memory, increase you faculty to learn, improve your insight, and gives you the rare ability to see possibilities that are invisible to most people. You will become a person of force. You charisma will be increased. The force of your personality will grow stronger. You will be able to cause people to do as you wish with the force of your personality. You will attract who and what you need to accomplish what it is you seek to achieve. The Romans consider some like this to be Fortune's favorite. You will move in harmony with the universe. People will perceive you as being "lucky." Things will seem to always go your way. Charles Haanel in *The Master Key* writes:

Things will come your way that you have come into an understanding of the fundamental laws of Nature and have put yourself in harmony with them; that you are in tune with the Infinite; that you understand the law of attraction; the Natural laws of growth and the psychological laws on which all advantages in the social and business world rest..

The German philosopher, Emmanuel Kant, expressed this dilemma well when he wrote, "We cannot know things as they truly are, that the world we think we are aware of is actually a construction of our minds." Since our minds can only perceive the outer reality that surrounds us through the data that is collected and processed by our five senses, we are unable to see beyond our material existence.

THE VRIL AND YOUR HEALTH

Before I explain how we can learn to harness and direct the Vril to improve and maintain good health, let me first talk little about health in general. The human body is made up of the same stardust that the stars are made of and governed by the same material laws that hold the universe in place. Like all things in the universe, both organic and inorganic, everything undergoes birth, growth, decays and eventually death. Once we die, our material substance returns to the universe and becomes part of the process of new creation. This is as true of everything in the universe as it is for our bodies. And though we are governed by this immutable law and cannot cheat death, we can affect the quality of life as well as the quality of our health, organic constitution and even our life span. Through the power of the mind, by developing the Bifrost Gland which enables us to harness and use Vril, we can improve our health, extend our life span and even slow down the aging process.

Through the Bifrost Gland, we can control our thoughts and use our mind to increase the flow of the Vril's power. The power of the mind can channel and direct the flow of Vril. If our thoughts are disharmonic, they can obstruct the natural flow of Vril and thus result in illness, damage to the body and even death. But if we focus our thoughts properly, we can control and direct the quantity of the flow of the Vril to whatever part of the body we desire. The mind is a powerful tool that can drag us down to the level of the beast, just as surely as our ancestors used its power to evolve above the beastly existence of primitive anthropoids.

There are several principles you must understand in regards to utilizing Vrilology for healing.

1) Within you is an inherent ability to use the flow of Vril to control your physiological process beyond what traditional medicine claims is possible.

2) The ability to harness Vril and use it to heal yourself and others, involves the coordination of you body, mind, and the spirit.

3) Remember that what you obsess over, and concentrate on, will be drawn into your life. You mind sends out vibrations from your thoughts and emotions,

which shape the flow of Vril currents into you, creating pathways into your future, filled with what you obsess on.

4) Adverse thoughts and emotions manifest adverse psycho-physiological effects, while positive thoughts and emotions manifest positive psycho-physiological effects.

5) The power that resides within your mind is far greater than you imagine. Within it is the power to affect your body processes, including the power to heal, rejuvenate and prolong your life.

6) By changing your thinking processes you can use your mind to make you well, or it can make you sick. It is possible to use Vrilology to unlock the power of your mind to channel the Vril currents flowing into you to make yourself radiantly healthy, improve and maintain a vigorous immune system, slow down, and even reverse the aging process so that you can look younger and live a longer, healthier life. You can also increase your energy levels, improve your mental processes, improve your cognitive abilities, and improve your memory.

7) Vrilology can help you to lose weight.

8) Vrilology can help you to fall asleep at will, and remember your dreams.

9) Vrilology can help you not to doze off when you are drowsy.

10) Vrilology can help to eliminate headaches.

11) Vrilology can help you to wake up at a given time without the use of an alarm clock.

12) Vrilology can be used to help you overcome addictions.

13) You can use Vrilology to use your dreams to help you find a solution to a problem.

14) It can help you to study for a test or remember complicated material.

15) You can learn to coordinate both halves of your brain so that they can work more fully together.

These are just a few things that you can learn to accomplish through Vrilology. But to do so, you must learn to use the full potential of your mind. This is done through meditation, visualization, the proper method of breathing and applying the use of Runes as a tool to help you to harness and control the Vril currents flowing into you.

You must visualize the process of absorbing Vril and channeling it throughout your body. Vril is absorbed through the Solar Plexus. From there it radiates throughout the body. Imagine that you feel the Vril's power coursing through your body, just as you might imagine your heart beating and pumping blood through your veins and arteries. The body will absorb Vril whether you visualize the process or not, but to do so will help the process increase the amount of Vril that is absorbed. This has to be done in conjunction with the exercises that are a part of the Vrilology training program. We must decide if the mind that the Gods gave us is to be used as the instrument of our salvation or the device by which we destroy ourselves. Its power can be used to lead us to a higher state of existence if we direct it properly, or it can be our bane, dragging us down into a life of chaos and self-destruction. What motivates and directs the use of the mind is thought and knowledge. If we lack a truthful understanding of the universe, the relationship between the Gods and the Giants and their place in the order of the universe, as well as our place in that order, and how we can be affected by their power, then our thoughts can become disharmonic. We must understand that the material world is created by our thoughts. We act on our thoughts. The nature of our thoughts and how we think will determine how we live, and the reality in the objective, material world, we create for ourselves. This will govern the path we follow in life, directing as to how we make decisions, and will determine whether we follow the path of upward growth and development or the path of the downward slide into self-destruction.

We are always being told that something is bad for our health, only to learn years later that the information was wrong and the very thing that we were told was bad, is actually good for us. Today, in our commercially driven society we are exploited every day by these disharmonic forces of greed and avarice. We should always keep in mind that over indulgence is harmful and detrimental to good health. If we follow the rule not to over indulge, eat and drink in moderation, and be active and exercise regularly, most foods and drinks are basically good for us. To achieve and maintain good health it is important not to over indulge and to maintain wholeness, harmony, and rhythm in your habits and behavior. Though it might be necessary to use drugs and other medical assistance when you are stricken by illness, we must remember that these devices are remedies to assist in the healing process and not substitutes for proper behavior and maintenance of good health.

Good health requires balance in diet, exercise, behavior and thought. We must maintain a proper balance of good nutrition, physical activity and positive mental processes to ensure good health. The disruption of this balance will interfere with the natural vitality of the body and lead to a chemical imbalance—either acid or alkaline. Both results (the potential hydrogen or pH classifications) will affect the atomic orbit within each cell within the body and can affect our health. Science has discovered that AIDS-HIV infection is the result of the acidic contents of the cell, and will determine if an individual can contract AID-HIV or not.

If we want a healthy mind and body, it is best to maintain a balanced disposition, free from stress and anxiety as much as possible. This is why the Folk Faith is based on love, joy and happiness, and why Wunjo is so important to us and our health. Good health is a prerequisite for happiness and happiness is necessary if we are to maintain good health. The negative emotions, if not controlled and properly used, will drain the Life Force from us, deplete our supply of Vril, cutting off its vital life-giving energies to certain parts of our bodies and eventually leading to poor health. Any doctor will tell you that too much stress and anxiety, which is the result of wrong thought-patterns, will cause physical damage to our bodies. Wrong thoughts lead to wrong behavior, which can also damage our health.

If you health is not everything that you wish it was, then you should examine the method of your thinking. You have to keep in mind that every one of your thoughts produces an impression in your mind. These impressions are like seeds that you are implanting into the soil of your subconscious. There, they will form tendencies. These tendencies, will in turn, attract similar thoughts, and before you know it, you have grown a whole crop which must be harvested. This harvest will dominate your thoughts and feelings. If they contain disease germs, the harvest will be sick, decay, weakness and failure. You have got to understand that you must constantly ask yourself what it is you are growing? Just what it is you are planting in your subconsciousness.

This is why it is so important to learn to focus our mind and control our thoughts, emotions and urges so that we can set our actions toward a precise objective, resulting in the harmonious relation and cooperation of body and mind. This harmonization of our desires by the will of the mind, will manifest in peace of mind and good health.

Through visualization, you can change any physical condition. Just make a mental image of what you think physical perfection is. Hold that image in your mind while you are meditating. Concentrate on it, and examine it in every detail. Let it sink into your consciousness. There are countless cases of people eliminating chronic conditions through this method in just weeks, in a few days and even in just a few minutes. It is not easy, only because our minds are naturally undisciplined. You have to learn to concentrate and hold the image you are visualizing. This takes practice. It is not painful. You just have to develop patience and the ability to focus your thoughts on one image for as long as possible.

Remember that while you are focusing on a single thought, the image that you are focusing on is emanating vibrations that are resonating through the currents of Vril energy flowing into you. The Vril that flows into you, then spreads though out your body, transforming it into the image you are concentrating on. We know that mental action is vibration. We also understand that all form is simply a mode of motion, a rate of vibration. This is quantum physics. You have within you the power to transform a subatomic particle by just observing it. You can transform it from a wave into a particle and back through the method of observing or measuring it. Therefore, any given vibration is immediately modified right down to its subatomic components through the power of your mind. This affects every cell in your body and changes the chemical composition in every group of life cells.

Charles Haanel wrote: *Everything in the Universe is what it is by virtue of its rate of vibration. Change the rate of vibration and you change the nature, quality and form. The vast panorama of nature, both visible and invisible, is being constantly changed by simply changing the rate of vibration, and as thought is a vibration we can also exercise this power. We can change the vibration and thus produce any condition which we desire to manifest in our bodies.*

While you are conducting your breathing exercises, imagine you can feel your body filling up with Vril as you inhale. Then, as you exhale, imagine you can feel the Vril being channeled to different parts of your body. In this part of the process, you don't have to be specific as to where the Vril is being sent, only that every part of your body is being filled with it. Later in your exercises, when you use the Runes in combination, you can be specific as to where you want the Vril sent and for what purpose. Will the Vril to enter every cell in your body, filling up every organ and every blood cell coursing through your veins, arteries and capillaries. It is in your DNA that the Vril will have the greatest effect, so *will* the Vril to enter your DNA. Will it to enter your genes, will it to recharge every atom in your body. Will the Vril to fill your nervous system and spread out to every cell in your body. What you are doing is creating a mental image (visualization) and reinforcing it with the power of your will. You are trying to create clear, strong mental images and then project them into the outer world through the use of the power of your will. This can be described as the one-point concentration of the will.

Once you have done this, you must learn to direct the Vril toward those areas of your body that you want to receive and increased flow of its power. Be very clear in your mind about where you want the Vril to flow, and how you want it to affect you. For instance, if you have a cholesterol problem and you want the Vril to flow through your vascular system to lower your bad cholesterol, you should *will* the process. Within your mind visualize currents of Vril energy coursing through your vascular system, breaking down the bad cholesterol. Imagine that you can actually feel the cholesterol disintegrating and your blood flowing freely. This does not mean that you should cease using any prescribed drugs because you decide to seek the aid of Vril. Don't be foolish. In fact, if you are taking medication, visualize the medication working more efficiently and without side effects. Vril can help your traditional medical treatments to work more efficiently. If we were to dedicate our lives to training ourselves in the use of Vril, and pass this knowledge down to our children, perhaps in a few generations we could advance to the point where we have the power to cause mutations within our bodies by the shared power of the collective will. At the moment, our Bifrost Glands are so atrophic from lack of use by our race over thousands of years, we cannot expect to reverse this condition over night. It is possible that some miraculous manifestations might occur, but we are not at that point in mastering the use Vril to abandon traditional medicine or science.

The use of the Vril should be done in conjunction with the Runes. Always remember that the Runes is a marvelous tool, given to us by the Gods as a means by which we can harness their Life Force (Vril). This is also true when dealing with healing. We can use different Runes for what ails us. When meditating and chanting to draw on the Vril, we should employ the Runes to draw on and shape the healing power of the Vril. Here is a list of what Runes should be used for different medical problems:

FEHU—Chest and respiratory problems.

URUZ—problems with muscles and tendons and anything to do with body strength and muscular tissue.

THURISAZ—Heart

ANSUZ—The mouth, teeth, throat, tongue. Stuttering and all speech impediments.

RAIDHO—Legs, feet, knees and gluteal muscles.

KENAZ—Cysts, ulcers, abscesses, boils, cuts, lacerations and all injuries associated with fevers and infections.

GEBO—poisons and toxins.

WUNJO—problems associated with breath, breathing and the respiratory system.

HAGALAZ—Lacerations, grazes, scraps, cuts and wounds.

NAUTHIZ—all problems associated with the arms, elbows, hands and fingers.

ISA—Loss of feeling and sensation, numbness, paralysis and other problems dealing with the nervous system.

JERA—Problems dealing with the bowls and digestion.

EIHWAZ—All problems dealing with the eyes and vision.

PERTHRO—Anything associated with reproduction, child birth and the sexual organs.

ELHAZ—Problems dealing with the head, brain, headaches, anxiety, stress, or mental and psychological disorders.

SOWILO—Burns and all problems dealing with the skin.

TIWAZ—Rheumatices, arthritis and all problems dealing with the joints and hands.

BERKANO—Fertility problems.

EHWAZ—All back and spinal problems.

MANNAZ—Sprains, dislocated joints, pulled tendons, cramps, especially associated with, wrists, ankles and feet.

LAGUZ—Kidneys.

INGWAZ—Problems dealing with male genitalia and reproduction.

DAGAZ—Mental illnesses, distress, phobias, nervous problems and anxiety.

OTHALA—DNA, genetic problems and inherited illnesses, and anything dealing with inherited traits.

The best way to use the Runes is to first choose the Runes associated with your problems, and then chant those Runes that have specific healing qualities. Runes dealing with protection and the Life Force includes: Uruz (vital force), Thurisaz (protection), Kenaz (controlled energy), Wunjo (harmony of forces), Elhaz (life and protection), Sowilo (life and rebirth), and Laguz (life energy). Uruz, Elhaz and Sowilo are three very important Runes in the healing process and should be used whenever you seek to use the Vril in healing. Uruz is the most powerful of healing Runes. Its power is to restore vitality. Elhaz has the power to recover (resurrection) and restore health and should be used in conjunction with Sowilo, which represents good health and the sun's warmth and healing powers. Uruz represents the great nurturing of the cosmic bovine that gave life to the Gods. It nourished Ymir. Both Elhaz and Sowilo represent Balder, who is the God of invulnerability—so long as blind ignorance (Hoder) is not goaded into action. Elhaz represents the Life Force of the Gods and the regenerative powers of Balder and Sowilo is the life-giving power of the Sun and victory. Sowilo is very effective when used with Elhaz because though the sun can restore health, though if not careful, one can get very ill from the effects of the sun's ultraviolet energy. The protective powers of Elhaz will ensure the good energy of Sowilo.

You can recharge yourself whenever you feel it necessary, especially when you are fatigued. At any time of day you can take a moment to relax and rest to practice the absorption of the Vril. You need not use a specific technique to quickly recharge your supply of Vril. A simple breathing exercise can do this whenever you feel the need, just visualize the absorption of the Vril.

When using the Vril to restore and maintain your personal health you can apply the Vril's power in many different ways. Once you have completed your exercises you can then direct and distribute Vril to various areas of your body, at will. This should be rather easy by now, especially if you have been conducting the proper exercises. All it takes is a little concentration and visualization. All you have to do is "feel" and "visualize" the Vril's power flowing through you to those areas that feel fatigued, should signs of trouble or weakness appear. When you feel a part of your body is aching, in pain, or weak, use the methods that you learned to direct the flow of the Vril's power to those areas. You will be able to do this as you learn to master the use of the Vril. The Church of Vrilology offers extensive training in the use of Vril to heal and assist in maintaining good health in its *Yggdrasill Training Program*. It will take time and a great deal of work to reach the point where you can effectively draw on the Vril with such ease, but it is possible to reach this level of proficiency.

There are several level of proficiency in the use of the Vril you will need to achieve. Here is a list of some of the abilities you want to master in the use of the Vril.

HELPING YOUR DOCTOR TO HEAL YOU: Do not fool yourself that you should not seek medical assistance or think that using the Vril is a replacement for medical science, because it is not. In fact, you should use the Vril in conjunction with medical science. If you have a serious problem and your doctor is assisting you with medication or treatment of some kind, you can and should use the Vril to assist in strengthening the treatment—to help your body to react positively to the medical treatment.

When you are being treated for an ailment, you can assist the medical aid offered by traditional medicine with a simple exercise. This exercise should be performed three times a day.

1) Sit in a comfortable position with your eyes closed and roll them slight upward toward your eyebrow under your closed eyelids. This will help you to enter your alpha state. If you are doing this in bed, prompt yourself up with several pillows so you will not be lying down. You do not want to fall asleep.

2) Begin counting backward from 100 to 1. Do this slowly, waiting about one second between each number. As you count backwards, concentrate on different parts of your body, beginning with your scalp, and work you way down to your toes. As you do, relax them. Take your time. You should be totally relaxed by the

time you reach one. Before you begin counting, mentally see the Rune, Raidho. This is the Rune of the road to right results.

3) After you have finished counting, begin to visualize yourself as youthful, radiant, healthy, attractive, vibrant and filled with energy. See yourself in a state of perfect health.

4) Now ask yourself mentally, "Why do I have this health problem?" Then let your mind wander freely. Just let it go blank and wait.

5) Soon, you will discover yourself thinking about a certain person, picture that person. Visualize the Rune of Ansuz, the Rune of communication.

6) Seen yourself forgiving each other. Imagine yourself hugging and hold the other person and that person holding and hugging you. The two of you are forgiving each other. See yourself smiling and nodding, knowing that any negative feelings between have disappeared. Visualize Gebo, the Rune of compensation and union.

If you mentally see a situation instead of a specific person, visualize the situation and correct it. See yourself resolving the situation to everyone's satisfaction. Know that everything is all right and the negative repercussions from the situation have disappeared. Do the same with Gebo if it is a situation instead of a specific person.

7) Now say to yourself, "I will always maintain perfect health in body and mind." Visualize the Rune, Uruz, the Rune of healing.

8) Hold this thought of you in perfect health. Visualize it in every detail. See yourself happy, vigorous and healthy. Hold this image for about five minutes. Visualize the Rune Isa, the Rune of concentration and solidification.

9) Now begin to count from 1 to 5. As you do, see yourself filling with the energy of the sun. Concentrate on Sowilo, the healing powers of the sun. Count one, two, three. When you reach three, stop and say, "When I open my eyes on the count of 5, I will feel fine, in perfect health, feeling better and better every day of my life." Continue counting, four, five and then open your eyes and affirm mentally, "I am wide awake, feeling wonderful and in perfect health. I am feeling better and better each day of my life." As you do this, visualize the Rune, Elhaz, the Rune of resurrection.

DIRECTING THE FLOW OF VRIL: You should first either sit in a comfortable position, or better, lie down on your bed. Then, proceed to use the relaxing exercises described earlier, to relax every muscle in you body. You will discover that this is a form of self-hypnosis. Once you have achieved this state of relaxation, you can begin directing the flow of the Vril's power throughout your body. First you should concentrate on your Solar Plexus (the pit of your stomach), and awaken the consciousness of your stored supply of the Vril. You should then *will* this supply of power to whatever part of the body that needs it, by causing the Vril to flow through your nervous system. Visualize the Vril actually flowing through the nervous system. Imagine you feel the power flowing through your body like a current of water flowing through rivers, streams and channels.

You need to understand that your health depends on your body's ability to making use of nutritional material that is needed to maintain the health of cells, and secondly to break down and excrete waste material from your body. All life requires that the body is able to preform these two basic functions. Food, water and air are the only things needed to ensure these constructive and destructive processes. Theoretically, your body should require just these three ingredients to continue functioning indefinitely. The lack of proper nutrition and the body's failure to break down and eject waste are the only causes for the cells in the body to lose their ability to receive enough Vril to maintain the health of the body. This is especially true of the destructive process from the body's failure to break down and eject toxins. Charles Haanel writes about this process:

However strange it may seem, it is the second or destructive activity that is, with rare exception, the cause of all disease. The waste material accumulates and saturates the tissues, which cause autointoxication. This may be partial or general. In the first case the disturbance will be local; in the second place it will affect the whole system.

The problem, then, before us in the healing of diseases is to increase the inflow and distribution of vital energy (Vril) *throughout the system, and this can only be done by eliminating thoughts of fear, worry, care, anxiety, jealousy, hatred, and every other destructive thought, which tend to tear down and destroy the nerves and glands which control the excretion and elimination of poisonous and waste matter.*

You can use this simple method whenever you feel tired and exhausted. If you suffer from headaches, or aches and pains, you can use this method, to first flush the afflicted areas, by directing the Vril toward the region of your body that hurts, and then direct the Vril to flow out of it, reversing the process. This will cause an equalization of the flow of the Vril through the area affected, and will eventually restore its normal health. At this stage in your training, you will not be curing yourself, but treating the symptoms. This should especially help with rheumatic joints or arthritis. Again, do not substitute the vril for medical science, but use it to aid in the treatment and cure by medical science.

USING VRIL IN GENERAL SELF-TREATMENT: You can administer a form of general self-treatment of Vril by lying down in a comfortable position and relaxing your entire body. Then, concentrate on the solar plexus, using your will to awaken the Vril's power stored there. Continuing to use your will, visualize Vril flowing downward to the left and right foot. Concentrate on this until you feel a tingling sensation in your feet, or a general feeling of awareness. You should then move up the body, doing the same thing with the lower legs, the upper legs, the reproductive region of the body, the abdomen and then the solar plexus, the lungs, chest and throat. Then proceed to do the same with your shoulders, upper arms, lower arms, hands and finally with your fingers. At this point, you should proceed to do the same as you did with your feet, directing Vril to your head. Wait until your feel the same sensation that you felt in your feet. After this has been accomplished, concentrate on directing Vril to your spinal column, directing downward, from the brain through the spinal cord and outward through the connecting nerves. Next, concentrate on the sacral plexus at the lower part of the spine. Concentrate on this region until you feel a thorough tingling sensation. By now, you should be charged with Vril. Remain lying comfortably, concentrating on visualizing your entire body radiating with the power of Vril. Rest quietly for a few minutes, slowly letting your mind relax, permitting all your thoughts to escape from your mind. You should rise refreshed and energized. This method can be varied, so you might want to experiment, depending on what parts of your body need recharging.

USING VRIL IN A MORE SPECIALIZED SELF-TREATMENT: When you suffer a localized pain or physical disorder in a certain part of your body, you might want to administer a more direct treatment by using your hands to concentrate the power of Vril in the region of your body causing you the problem. Place both your hands on the part of your body that is aching or suffers from some type of disorder and then concentrate on visualizing the power of Vril, flowing from your brain, through your shoulders and arms, into your hands and finally into the part of yourself that you are holding. You might want to hold the hands over the area without touching it. In either case, will a steady and continuous, powerful flow of Vril power through your hands and into the region in question. You can also visualize a pulsation or pumping sensation with your hands to cause Vril to penetrate the part of the body in question. This can be done whether or not you are touching the area. If you are not touching, concentrate on sending Vril into the area as you slowly lower you hands and then pull back. Repeat this as many times as you want, while visualizing pulsations or bursts of Vril energy penetrating the region. If you are holding your hands on the part of the body, do the same thing, but slowly and gently press on the region and then loosen your grip without breaking contact.

ADMINISTERING VRIL TO OTHER PEOPLE: These methods may be used to administer Vril to others in the same matter. The practice of administering Vril's healing power to other people is a form of "psychic healing" or "magnetic healing." When you hear of priests who have the power to heal, or a psychic healer who can heal the sick, they are really calling on the power of Vril and using it to cause "miracle cures." These individuals might or might not realize they are drawing on the power of Vril, depending on their spiritual awareness. They just happen to be individuals with a special gift of drawing on Vril.

You can learn to administer the same type of healing on others through the methods you employ to heal yourself. In this case, it is always better to place both your hands directly on the person you are healing, on the region affected. Let Vril's power flow from you into the other person and then back into you. After the treatment, you should perform a simple flushing process on yourself and then recharge yourself with Vril's power using the methods described earlier. This will prevent you from absorbing the illness or disorder of the person you are healing.

There is another way to heal. You can charge a glass of water with Vril. This is simply done by holding a glass of water as you charge yourself with Vril power, but now, you should be directing the power of Vril into the glass of water. Once you have done this, give the water to the person who is ill, and then instruct him to slowly sip the water from the glass until it is empty.

USING YOUR HANDS TO ADMINISTRATE THE HEALING POWERS OF VRIL

You can learn to use your hands to assist in the process of healing. There are two simple methods that can be used to transfer the healing power of Vril from the healer (you) to the patient through the use of your hands.

We know that every thing is vibration, so we also know that your hands vibrate. They vibrate at ten cycles per second. You can practice this by simply placing your hands on a flat table top. Don't press your entire hands on the surface of the table. Just let the finger tips of your hands gently touch the surface of the table. Feel them vibrate. In your mind, mentally know that they are vibrating at ten vibrations per second. If you have a watch on, you can watch the second hand move. Every time it does, imagine in your mind your hands have vibrated ten times. What you mind sees will manifest itself. Keep doing this. Eventually your hands will be vibrating at ten cycles per second.

Then, imagine you can feel the flow of Vril energy flowing through your arms and out of your fingertips. You will eventually feel the sensation of energy flowing. This simple exercise will help you, the healer, to function at the proper brain frequency. Once you feel you have mastered this simple technique, you should understand that you are causing a feedback to your brain, causing it to vibrate at ten cycles per second. Once this happens, the energy field about you, known as the aura, will vibrate at the same frequency of ten cycles per second. The patient is within the field of your aura, and his aura will also begin to vibrate at the same rate.

Once you feel confident that you have mastered this simple method, you can develop it further. You can do this by placing your finger tips on each side of the patient's head. Place the fingertips of your right hand on the left side of the patient's head. Spread the fingers of the right hand so that their touch the entire left hemisphere of the patient's head. You should be facing the patient, so the thumb of your right hand should be touching the left temple of the patient's forehead. The rest of your fingers should be touching the left side of the head with the pinky at the base of the head, behind the ear, where the head meets the neck. You index fingertip should be touching the top of the back side of the left side of the patient's head. You should do the same with your left hand on the patient's right hemisphere of the head, with your left thumb touching the temple of the patient's right side of the forehead, and so forth.

Both the patient and the healer should close their eyes. The healer will then enter his alpha state of mind. Once he has, he should take a deep breath, hold it for nine seconds, and then exhale. As he exhales, he should hold the image of the Rune, Uruz, in his mind and slowly chant its name. As he does, he should feel the flow of Vril, being transformed into a healing force by the power of runic energy of Uruz, flowing into the patient. The healer should do this, nine times. Once he has, he can then open his eyes. The patient should keep his eyes closed. The healer removes his fingers from the patient's head, rubes his hands together until breathing is normalized once more.

The healer now repeats the entire cycle once more, but this time he places his hands on either side of the afflicted area of the patient. He imagines the flow of Vril energy invading and healing this afflicted area, healing it with its powers, while chanting Uruz, as well as the appropriate Rune for this area of the body. For instance, if he is trying to heal a problem in one's arm, he would chant Uruz and then Nauthiz as he exhales. Once he has, he repeats the cycle on the patient's head.

Another way to use your hands is by passing them over the patient. By passing your hands over the patient, you are transferring Vril energy to yourself to the patient. The hands are only a tool used to transfer Vril, for you are using your hands in conjunction with your mind, which controls and directs the flow of Vril.

Let me give you a little exercise to try. Raise your hands before you. Now, point, or aim, the fingers of your right hand toward the palm of your left hand.

Make sure your hands are about one foot apart, so there is not chance of the body heat from your right hand, being felt by your left hand. Now, slowly move your right hand up and down. Continue to point the fingers of the right hand, at the palm of your left hand, as you raise and lower your right hand. Make sure you move your right hand slowly, so you do not fan the air. You will detect a sensation of something moving up and down the palm of your left hand. It could feel heat, or like a warm breeze, but it will be neither. You are feeling is Vril energy that you are transforming from yourself to your patient when you are performing Vril healing methods. This energy has been referred to as "psychotronic energy/"

As you are passing your hand over the patient, you can concentrate on the appropriate Rune or Runes, you want to use and say, "Gibu Alu Uruz." When you do this, your mind is visualizing the Rune, transforming Vril energy with its individual nature. Make sure your mind is relaxed, but focused on the processed of visualizing the Rune, shaping the Vril currents, and sending them to your patient. You must sincerely feel a desire to heal. When done properly, pain will either lessen or disappear, the area that you are sending Vril to will be sterilized and any open wounds will not become infected.

Make sure the patient is either sitting comfortably, or lying down. He must keep his eyes closed at all times. You, as the healer, should also close your eyes, and enter your alpha state. Mentally tell yourself that you unselfishly and sincerely wish to help this person. Feel a love for what you are doing, and know that you are serving a greater cause than your own selfish needs. Then recite your chant, such as "Gibu Alu Uruz." As you repeat this chant, sweep your hands over your patient, from his head to his toes several times, so that he has been subjected to several complete passing of the hands over his entire body. At no time are you actually touching the patient.

Once you have completed this step, you then place one of your hands a few inches from the patient's forehead and the other behind the head. Again, do not touch the patient. Then, after a few moments (you might want to chant "Gibu Alu Uruz" nine times during these moments) you place your hand on either side of the patient's head and do the same. Next you should place your hands over the upper chest and back, directing your mental thoughts to the body's immune system as you continue to chant, "Gibu Alu Uruz." If there is a localized health problem, include the individual Rune dealing with the problem and incorporate it into your chant after Uruz, as you pass your hands over the specific part of the body affected.

Scientists and researchers at such places as the National Institutes of health, the Institute for the Advancement of health, George Washington University, and

Harvard Medical School, have been conducting experiments on whether the mind has the power to affect the healing process of the body. While the results of such experiments have been inconclusive, research is still ongoing. There is still enough evidence to warrant such research.

When using the power of Vril, you should always keep in mind that you are drawing on the Life Force of the Gods. Therefore it is wise to remember the Gods whenever you use Vril. Do not undervalue this gift. Don't underestimate its potential just because it can be simply used. Always maintain a respect for its power, for its power is the power of the Gods themselves. Do not become contemptuous of its use, for the Gods do not approve of belittling or degrading their gifts. The Gods approve of the use of their gifts, but they demand respect for the mighty forces that they bestow upon us. Use Vril's power to assist in your own advancement, and also to help and assist your kinsmen and kindred. You should not fear to use Vril's power to protect yourself against your enemies or to seek their destruction, for they are not only your enemies. Since you have joined in a most holy community with the Gods, their attacks on you are the same as an attack on the Gods. The right use of Vril is the protection, health and advancement of the Folk Faith, and this includes both mortals and immortals.

THE PSYCHIC USE OF THE VRIL

All humans are born with a certain innate psychic ability, but unfortunately, the gland that is the seat of these powers has, through lack of use throughout countless generations, atrophied into a useless appendage. I am referring to the Bifrost Gland or Third Eye, which we covered in the last chapter. With the proper training in the use of Vril, through Runic meditation and chanting, this gland can be revitalized to a large degree. In time, over generations, it will be possible to genetically revitalize the gland and thus restore the great powers that were once in possession by our ancestors millenniums ago.

Thousands of years ago, our ancestors, who built the lost civilization that once existed on the shores of the ancient Black Sea, possessed these great powers. They possessed powers of astral protection and vision, telekinesis and telepathy. Through the power of their minds, they mastered their environment and could influence those who lived around them. Today, humanity has lost these powers, though on occasion, individuals are born who possess these powers to various degrees. This is very rare and most individuals claiming such powers turn out to be charlatans. But through Vrilology, it is possible to stimulate the Bifrost Gland and generate such powers to different degrees, depending on innate powers of the subjects involved in the training process.

The ability of an individual to use his or her mind to exert command over the mind and body of another individual, or over his or her surroundings, as psychic influence, or mental science, results from mastering the currents of Vrilic energy flowing into us. The mind can be trained to send thought projections from one person to another. This is done through the use of Vrilology. In effect, when a thought is projected, one is actually sending Vrilic power through the use of his mind. All forms of mental or psychic powers are, in reality, the mind using the power of the Vril to perform certain feats. The power of astral project, astral vision, telepathy and telekinesis are all done through the employment of the Vril's power. Vril is the real power behind all psychic abilities and manifestations. The mind is merely serving as the device by which the will is able to harness the power and shape and mold it according to thought and vision. The thought, charged by the Vril's power, is then projected forth by the strength of the feeling and passion of the mind. This is the same process as when one uses the Vril's power over one's own body, or another person's body. But in this case, the practitioner is projecting his thoughts outward across time and space, instead of inward.

By using Vril, we can send thoughts of strength, fortitude and vitality to others who are in need of support. Vril can be used to cause others to think or feel as we wish them to think and feel. Others could be made to act according to our will by sending them sensations of courage, cowardice, determination or abandonment. People can be made to make decisions by instilling in their minds, ideas or sensations, causing them to act in a way we desire. Telepathic messages can be sent to another, by charging them with an added supply of Vril energy. The dynamic force of the Vril can energize the ability to telepathically make people act in ways that will fulfill our goals and objectives. This force can even make inanimate objects move. This has been known as "mind-over-matter." There really is no limit in how the Vril can be used. It all depends on the training, as well as innate abilities of the individuals involved.

Just as Vril can be used to cause others to act according to our will, we can use it to defend ourselves. We can do this by charging a protective Vril armor or aura about us. This is done by visualizing and willing the creation of a protective thought-force to enhance the power of the mind and will. By using the will to imagine a powerful protective thought aura about our bodies, we are using the dynamic currents of the Vril's power to surround ourselves with a protective armor that will deflect attacks by others. This protective shield will not only prevent others using the Vril from harming us, but will especially prevent others in the normal course of daily events from inflicting harm on us through their normal activities. Thus, if someone, say your boss at work, decides to give you an assignment that he knows will cause you distress or put you at a disadvantage in some way, you will be able to easily convince him to change his mind. Your protective armor will cause others to have positive thoughts about you. This is done through charging the atmosphere with the Vril in accordance with the methods that have been described. People who have a natural charisma are individuals who have a great deal of Vrilic power. What we are actually doing by creating a protective aura or armor is increasing the power of one's charisma.

Let's look at several principles that contribute to the way our psychic powers work. To develop and master your psychic powers you must learn to control the way you think. The greatest barrier to developing your psychic powers is wrong thinking. The one true freedom each individual possesses, and no tyranny can take away, is the freedom to think. You might freely choose what you think, but every freedom has a price, and this is especially true of the thinking process. How and what you think is actually governed by an immutable law. Any and every thought that you persist in thinking will affect your character, health and circumstances. Mental habits are probably the most difficult thing for us to control, but it is not impossible. The first principle in changing your thinking pattern is to exchange destructive thinking for constructive thinking. If you are obsessing on seeing enemies, opponents, confrontations and adversaries everywhere, your mind is going to bring these things into your life. Your thinking pattern will manifest pathways filled with discord and disharmony in your environment. This will create barriers for your mental vibrations to pass through the ether of space and time, which will retard and constrict your psychic powers. You must begin to see nothing but opportunities, pathways to achieving what you desire without confrontation. You must *know* that there are no enemies out there for you to confront. There are no dragons for you to slay. You must convince yourself that you have within you the power to manifest whatever it is you desire, and that no power or enemy can stand in your way. Once your mind has adjusted to this way of thinking, you will discover that you will achieve what you desire, and anyone who disagrees with you will be helpless to oppose you and will simply fade away.

Another principle necessary for you to master to develop your psychic powers is that of imagination. Your mind has the ability to see what it is you will cultivate in your environment. You imagination is the vehicle in which your mind creates what it is that you will have to deal with, in your future. If you are constantly imagining enemies, barriers, confrontation in the world around, then these things are the very things that you mind will draw into the pathways to your future.

Charles Haandel wrote about imagination: *The imagination gathers up the material by which the Mind weaves the fabric in which your future is to be clothed. Imagination is the light by which we can penetrate new worlds of thought and experience. Imagination s the mighty instrument by which every discoverer, every inventor, opened the way from precedent to experience. Imagination is a plastic power, molding the things of sense into new forms and ideals.*

You must realize that to develop your psychic abilities, you must free your mind of negativity. You must first control the way you think. By freeing your mind of negative, destructive thoughts of confrontation and struggle, you will be breaking the chains that bind you to the chaotic forces of the Giants. Once you have freed yourself of this enslavement, you can then begin the process of aligning yourself with the orderly forces of the Gods. Pathways will open for you which will permit the free movement of your thoughts and mental processes through the universe. The ether of the cosmos will no longer seem like a thick substance for you to struggle through, but a hyper-fast pathway for the free movement of your mind through time and space.

GALDOR SCIENCE

Galdor Science or Magick is the methodology of using the Runes. It is often spelled in various ways: Galdor, Galdr, Galder, and Galther. The secret of the Runes is supposed to have been whispered into Balder's ear by Odin as Balder was lying dead on his funeral pyre. It has been revealed to me that Odin whispered the names of three Runes, Dagaz, Naudhiz and Ansuz (DNA), presenting the tools by which the Life Force of the Gods, Vril, can be used to resurrect the Gods after Ragnarok. The word, "rune," does not mean "letter" or "alphabet" but "secret" or "unknown." This is a reference to the Runes as tools by which we can use to learn how to harness of the power of Vril, and unleash the God-force within us, within our DNA, and thus ensure the resurrection of the Gods. This is what is meant by "Balder Rising!" Within each Rune Stream, are contained infinite mysteries that can trace their origins back to the primordial great secret that is at the heart of the Runes—the power to harness the Life Force of the Gods (Vril).

It is believed that the word itself once meant "to make sounds." Whether it is speaking, whispering or shouting, it is the active power of vocalization that lies within the Runes. This power can be used through one's voice, to transform both the inner and outer worlds, or to discover eternal secrets of the universe and the Gods that give order to this universal system. Scientists once thought everything was made up of particles, but now believe that all matter is made up of "strings," that can be made to resonate different sounds or energy waves. This belief only confirms what we know of the nature of the Runes and how their power can be harnessed through chanting their innate sounds. These truths of the secret knowledge of the Runes, have been, for so long hidden from us, are now being discovered by science. Great revelations are being discovered through quantum physics that prove that what the ancients understood was more science than mere hocus-pocus. Each practitioner of the Runes must follow this path—that of a shaman or modern-day Galdor scientists—using the Runes as keys that will unlock doors of arcane knowledge. Behind these doors we can rediscover the sacred knowledge that was once bestowed to our most ancient ancestors.

All people have an intuitive sense that there is more to existence than the material universe that we inhabit. We instinctively know that there are realms of existence that lie beyond our five senses and the three dimensions of this universe. There lies within the Runes, the power to discover knowledge of these other realms (the other eight worlds beyond Midgard).

Edred Thorsson writes in his book, *Northern Magic*, that the structure of each Rune is threefold: sound, stave and rune. The sound is the song that is used in chanting. The stave is the shape of the Rune which can be made of wood, porcelain, stone or metal. The Rune itself is the hidden lore or knowledge of the nature of the Rune. The three elements are a single unit, each supporting the other. None of the three qualities can stand by itself. The sound is both the phonetic quality and the vocal quality used in singing the Runes in chanting. This quality has properties rooted in the voice and can project the power of the Rune to shape the Vril's power both inwardly and outwardly. If anyone is familiar with music and how it can effect mood change in people, they can understand how the sound of the Rune, when used in singing or chanting, can affect change in the inner or outer nature of a person or objects. The stave is the shape of the Rune. The visible shape will be absorbed through one's vision and imprinted onto the mind. They are the visible outer nature of the Runes, which cannot be comprehended objectively unless one concentrates on the shape as one chants the Rune. This has the effect of imprinting the Rune in both the conscious and unconscious mind, thus making its quality a part of your psyche, and thus your soul. By accomplishing this, we are forging a link between ourselves and realms other than Midgard that exist on the Yggdrasill. Thus, the Runes' true nature, which exists in realms beyond the three-dimensional objective world we live within, is a link, or the Bifrost Bridge, to other realms. And each Rune has a multi-nature that is infinite. The Runes represent the truth of the universe, and this truth is like a puzzle with an infinite number of pieces that make up the whole. No matter how long and hard one studies the Runes, one will never in one lifetime, or in a million lifetimes, discover and unlock the totality of the nature of the Runes. This is the hidden lore that will always remain hidden—no matter how much we learn and discover, there will always be more to learn and that which will remain hidden. The song is the physical manifestation of the Runes' powers in the physical and spiritual realms, while the staves are the visible images used to assist us to harness that power. The Rune itself is the hidden lore that needs to be learned so that we can use the Runes to harness and control the power of the Vril.

Before you can actually use the Runes, you need to understand their essence. To understand the Runes, you must first truly *feel* the Runes. You must feel and know the Runes deep down inside of you—in your soul. There are several ways this can be done. First of all, you can chant the Runes. Let the sound of each Rune, as you chant its sound, penetrate your mind and reverberate through your body. Feel the effect it has on you physically. Let the essence of the force of the Runes fill your soul with its force. Another method is to cut a piece of gray paper, about the size of standard looseleaf paper, and then paint an individual Rune on each sheet of paper. You should use red paint, and if you really want to forge a link between yourself and the Runes, mix a few drops of your blood into the red paint before you pain each Rune on the paper. Place the paper on the wall and then sit about six to ten feet away from it, in a chair or on the floor, facing the Rune. Then, after you have relaxed yourself in the way that has been described for all meditation and chanting, concentrate on the image of the Rune. Stare at it, but do not force the stare. Continue to stare at it for five, ten, fifteen minutes or more. You decide. Then, you can begin chanting the Rune. You are using several different senses: sight, hearing and even physically feeling the Rune through the vibrations inside your body. In this way, you are becoming one with the Rune. Do each Rune, one at a time. These exercises can be done formerly with ritual or informally. Do them as often as you want. Go through all twenty-four Runes, using the Elder Futhark.

Let me explain why it is best to use the Elder Futhark. This is the oldest and authentic set of Runes. The Young Futhark has only sixteen Runes. This Futhark came into existence several centuries after the adoption of Christianity in northern Europe. Rune Lore was an oral tradition. After Christianity was adopted, knowledge of the Runes declined, and much of its lore forgotten. By the fourteenth century, many people only remembered sixteen Runes and thus the Younger Futhark was used.

Another Futhark is the Anglo-Saxon Futhark. This Futhark has thirty-three Runes. After many of the Norse people settled in the British Isles, they intermarried with the native population of the Britain. From the amalgamation of germans, Norse, Latin, French, and Celtic languages Anglo-Saxon or Old English was born. This fusion would eventually evolve into modern day English. As new sounds were adopted, new Runes were created to accommodate these sounds. Thus, the additional Runes really have no magical essence to them since they were created simply for phonetic reasons.

Another Futhark is the Armanen Runes. This Futhark has only eighteen Runes and was the creation of Guido von List in the later nineteenth and early twentieth centuries from the eighteen verses describing the rune spells in the Norse myths. The reason there is only eighteen rune spells, is simple. In the thirteenth century, Christian scholars in Scandinavia began putting to pen the oral lore. But by now, much of the lore was forgotten. In fact, we believe most of the pagan northern lore has been lose. So only eighteen rune spells were written down, and done so out of order. Thus, the Armanen Futhark is a modern day corruption of the Runes. The National Socialists, especially the SS, used these Runes, and this is why they were eventually corrupted by the Dark Forces, or Chaos. Instead of growing into an anti-Communist movement that could have united all of Europe, National Socialism degenerated into a dark force, which resulted in genocide and the attempt by half the White race trying to enslave, exploit and even exterminate the other half of the White race in Europe.

To cast Runes, you need to have a set of Runes. In the past, one had to make their own set of Runes, and this is still advisable. The art of carving and shaping your own set helps to forge a link between you and your set of Runes. When you cut, carve and shape each Rune, you are giving a part of your Life Force into the making of the Rune. Unfortunately, in today's world, especially if one lives in large urban areas, it is not always easy to find the right type of wood to use to carve your Runes.

You can carve one Rune a day. Cut a branch from a tree—preferably a yew tree. (If you are going to carve your Runes from wood then it is best to use the yew. There is a mistaken belief that the Yggdrasill is an ash tree. But in Old Norse, the yew was described as and *yew-ash* tree.) You can also carve your Runes into pieces of stone, but this involves a great deal of work. Carve one Rune per piece of wood. The shape of the wood is up to you. You can cut the wood into long or short, as staves, circles or squares. Then carve a Rune into each piece of Wood. Now paint the carved Rune with the same red paint in which you mixed some of your blood. The final product should be pleasing to you. Do not think you have to create a product that is "perfectly" carved or shaped. You want a set of Runes that "feels" right to you. Some people will prefer their Runes to look primitive and uneven while others prefer a set of Runes that look like they have been fashioned by an expert carver. The important thing to remember is that this set of Runes is a personal product, shaped by you and so they must feel right to *you*!

There are many different ways to cast Runes, and nearly every day I read about a newly invented way to cast the Runes. The truth is, they are all valid. In fact, there is no set way to cast Runes, though there are several different traditional methods that are used. In time, as you master the art of casting Runes, you will probably design your own method. All the better. Rune-casting, like carving the

Runes, is very personal. Let me describe a few methods of casting Runes for you here.

The first step is to sit at a table or on the floor with a piece of cloth before you. Some people prefer a white cloth, but others prefer black or red. Once again, it really is up to you. Take the Runes and hold them in your hands. You should do a simple invocation, calling on the Gods to guide your hand, or meditate, drawing on the power of Vril. Feel its currents flowing through you and into the Runes, forming a union between you and the Runes. Whatever method you use, remember, you are trying to draw on the Vril and use it to shape the configuration of the Runes. If you have been chanting and meditating, using the Runes, you have already transformed yourself into a conduit of Vril energy currents, and thus, a simple invocation should serve to draw on the Vril's power whenever you cast Runes. You might even prefer a simple version of the Hammer Rite.

Then, say something like this:

Let the power and might of the Vril be drawn to this site, I call on the Gods to give me the sight!

There are no set words to speak. You can fashion whatever chant you prefer. The point is to call on the power of the Life Force of the Gods. The Runes are tools used to fashion your will, or the will of whomever you are casting the Runes for, by harnessing the power of the Vril.

The next step is to call on the three Norns—the weavers of the destiny of mankind. You can once again invent your own invocation. It could be something like this:

From the beginning of time to the turning of the ages,
ye maidens, three-all-knowing
—Urd—Verdhandi—Skuld—
who weave the destiny of all
reveal to us the future unfolding!

Hold the Runes in your hands. If you are casting for yourself, think of the question you wish to ask. If it is for someone else you should ask them to think of the question as you begin this process of picking the Runes. You can keep them in a small leather or cloth pouch. If you do, shake it well as you hold your head up with your eyes closed. You can chant or sing to the three Norns, calling their names. Once you feel the link established, open the pouch, if you are using one, and reach into it as you say the words:

Runes inside, come alive! Reveal to us the secrets of the Norns!

Again, there are no set words to speak. You can come up with any saying you feel is right for you.

Move your hand around in the pouch of Runes and let the Runes jump into your hand. When you feel that a Rune has jumped into your hand, pull it out and place it on the cloth. Then do it again and again depending on how many Runes you will need to use in the casting process. The number of Runes you will need varies depending on the casting system you use.

Once you have laid out the Runes you can begin interpreting (reading) them. Take your time observing them, but it might take a great deal of practice interpreting the Runes, so do not get discouraged—practice makes perfect. You should record each reading. It will help you in learning to read the Runes and provide ample material for future studying and for teaching others. You should review your readings and make notes for future reference. You can alter your original reading. A great deal of reading the Runes is inspiration.

As I said earlier, there are many different ways to lay out the Runes for a read, but I will discuss only two here. First, we have to understand that in the Indo-European tradition, the threefold division of time is all-important. The Norse refer to the three Norns and the Greeks refer to them as the three Fates—Past, present and Future. In the Norse religion they are named *Urd, Verdhandi* and *Skuld*. Urd is the past—that which is and not subject to change. It is that which has contributed to what exists today. The present is named Verdhandi. She is not just what is presently, but what is unfolding. The present, unlike the past, is not fixed, but in fluctuation. It is action or the subtotal of all the acts by everything and everyone in the universe. It is built on that which came before, but it also gives birth to that which will come into being—the future. The future is named Skuld. It is that which is yet to be, based on what has come before it. The past impregnates the present and the two gives birth to the future. The future is not fixed, at least not to those who do not know what is to come. Odin gave his eye so that he could drink from Mimir's Well and thus discover that which has not yet happened. He knows the future and yet, still he struggles against it, knowing that it is the struggle that will cause it to happen. Thus, we do not know what is to come, though it can be glimpsed by those who have mastered the power of Vril. Clairvoyance is possible, very possible, by developing powers through the use and practice of Vril Science or Vrilology.

The first and simple way to read the Runes is to pick three Runes: one for the past, one for the present and one for the future. Lay them out with the past on the left and the present to its right and the third Rune, representing the future, below the two other Runes. Turn your attention to Urd, which represents that which has led up to the present situation and then look at Verdhandi, which is what is taking place. The relationship of the two Runes can tell you something about the present state of affairs concerning the question in hand. Then look at the third Rune, Skuld, and the relationship that it holds to the other two Runes, and you can determine the likely course of the future if all remains as is, or what course you might consider taking in the future to affect your true will. The Skuld is the oracular force that will reveal the future direction, while the other two Runes will explain how one has found one self on the road leading to that future. It will take a great deal of practice to read this combination, but if you have done your preparation in studying the Runes you will eventually feel confident to read the Runes with this simple three-Rune configuration.

The second configuration is a ninefold method. With this method, you do the same as before in picking Runes to read, past, present and future, but this time you choose three for the past, three for the present and three for the future. Lay each three in the same way that you did in the threefold configuration. In this method you have three Runes combined to explain the past, three Runes to explain the present and three Runes to explain the future. Each trinity of Runes will help you to understand the threefold nature of time involved in whatever question you are seeking an answer. To fully understand this method you need to have a greater understanding of the power of the Runes and how to use them. Once again—this will come with practice. But it's important that you master these two methods of Rune casting. Once your feel confident that you have mastered these two methods, you can then go on to experiment with other methods.

SEITHER SCIENCE

Alongside Galdor Science there is another science that was practiced among the Norse. This is Seither, pronounced say-ther, (also referred to as: Seith, Seidr, Seidhr Seidh, or Sejdr). It was practiced not only by the Norse, but by all Indo-Europeans, other Europeans and by every people and race on earth, in various forms. It is probably better known as a form of shamanism. In Seither, the practitioner seeks experiences beyond the inner self. Seither originated with Freyja, who taught it to Odin. It involves traveling to other worlds or states of consciousness, astral projection, astral vision, sex magick, soothsaying, transforming into altered states and divination. Today, many who practice it, refer to it as remote viewing. As a Vanir, Freyja represents a pantheon of very ancient Gods who united with the Aesir, and Seither, known as the technique of ecstacy, probably predates all forms of religion. The Seither Masters of olden times were reputed to shape-shift, possess the power to see into the future and travel to other realms. This type of Science involves the use of substances that include stones and crystals, herbs and animal products. There is even an element of sex involved in this form of Science. It is used in what is referred to as witchcraft or magick.

Seither was taught to Odin by Freyja, and in return, Odin taught Freyja Galdor. Here we have a balance between the two types of Science (Magick)—the male and female elements and dualism which is so fundamental to Indo-European theologies. Originally, Seither was not the exclusive property of the Indo-Europeans that entered Europe after the drowning of Atlantis in the Black Sea. Caucasians throughout Eurasia, before the rise of the Atlantean Aryans on the shores of the Black Sea, probably practiced Seither. The ancient Aryans probably practiced a form of Seither before the Gods appeared to them and taught them Galdor and the way to use the combined disciplines to harness the Vril. In fact, those Caucasians living along the Black Sea probably developed their abilities with Seither to cause the Gods to descend and teach them Galdor and how to combine the two sciences into Vrilology. The Caucasians living in Europe, as well as most other people living throughout Europe, Asia and Africa practiced a form of shamanism. In northern Europe, it eventually developed into Seither in historical times.

In Europe, this form of science was dominated by women. This was true, not only for the Norse, but all Indo-Europeans. We hear of the Oracle in Greece and the Sybil in Rome. Galdor incorporated the doctrines and properties of Seither into itself and together they form a very powerful and unique form of European Magick that can be used to harness the power of the Vril. We refer to this science as Vrilology. Freyja is known as the *Seitherkorna*, or the Great Dis. The Disir were thought to be nine Goddesses who dressed in black and carried swords. They were supposed to have descended to earth and taught our women ancestors the science of Seither. The Denali Institute of Northern Traditions refers to them as, *They are Goddess-like archetypal constructs tied directly to a family or clam. The Disir are female ancestral spirits of a clan that also have the powers of a Vanir (Earth) Goddess. Not only do the Disir watch over the prosperity and well being of the family and its individual houses, they also rule the fertility of the land.* When Freyja rides to earth to carry away the souls of great heroes, the nine Disir are transformed in the Valkyries. The people of Sweden, at Uppsala, celebrated a ceremony to their honor during the month of February, at the time of the full moon.

After Europe was converted to Christianity, the Christian hierarchy sought to destroy the use of Seither and Galdor among the people of Europe, and conducted a propaganda campaign of defamation, referring to the old religions and their practices as witchcraft, black magic, and Satanism. For this reason, many of our people, who have developed an interest in this type of practice, have turned to alien cultures, such as those of the American aborigines. But there is no reason for our people to turn to alien cultures to rediscover Seither Science. It is healthier and wiser to seek such knowledge from within, rather then looking for it in strange and exotic traditions that are alien and foreign to our souls. We Europeans have a rich heritage—we only have to rediscover it.

There are several ways we can practice Seither, and all in conjunction with Galdor. This involves putting oneself into a trance. This can be done individually or as a member of a group. The latter way is preferred because you will have other people with you to help you return to this realm of existence if you should wander too far in an alternate realm. Today, there are many who have developed this skill in the form of the practice of remote viewing. This usually involves several people working together. In some cases the remote viewer's mind travels to a destination, and in other cases the person will leave his body and travel to other destinations or dimensions or realms of being. Remote viewing is performed under very controlled, modern, methodology. Another method involves sleeping. After you have achieved a certain degree of expertise in this craft, you will often have experiences during your state of deep sleep. It is a form of dreaming, but more. In actuality, you fall into a state that is not sleep, but a form of astral projection during deep sleep. Your astral form will travel to other realms or to different regions in this universe. Still another method is a second type of trance that involves rhythmic practices that include music, drums, humming and singing. This form of practice is also very effective within a group environment and can be used in conjunction with the trance. Many cultures and traditions have relied on drugs, sleep deprivation, fasting, and even physical torture, but I frown on such practices as extreme and dangerous. They feed into the power of chaos and destructiveness and can be very dangerous to those who engage in such activities.

Divination and clairvoyance, sometimes referred to as soothsaying or fortune telling, are also a part of Seither. This aspect of Seither is done without the assistance of casting Runes. By using one of the three ways mentioned, one can be placed into a trance. This is done by relying on the right side of the brain, while Rune casting is the process of using both parts of the brain. Once you are in a trance you can actually travel to other realms, or different worlds that make up the nine worlds in the Norse cosmology. In this way, it is possible to meet different entities, including the Gods and Goddesses. While in this state, it is very possible and often the case with most people who experience this, to establish a personal relationship with different deities and other beings, including elves, dwarfs, etins, Valkyries and so on. In previous centuries, this art was known as "spiritualism," and in more recent times, as "channeling."

To enter such a state individually you must first perform the exercises described to relax your body and free your mind of all thoughts except those that will help you to transcend this earthly existence. If you are a member of a group practicing Vril Science, you will find that your progress in reaching this advance state will be much more rapid. Whether you are practicing Seither or Galdor, you are drawing on the Vril's power. Thus, as a member of a group, you can increase the amount of power needed to assistance you in entering a trance and traveling to other realms. Performing Seither with the purpose of entering a trance takes a great deal of time and practice to reach the necessary relaxed state, but if you are a member of a group, you will be charged with the collective power of the group's effort to draw on the Vril, and thus you can rely on a greater sought of power to assist you to enter such a state of consciousness. But there is also an added value of being a part of a group—you will be more anchored or rooted for your protection.

In each case, whether performing Seither as an individual or as a member of a group, once you are performing the exercise, you should *will* yourself to transcend your existence in Midgard. Sometimes you will not have control over where you will end up, especially if the Gods desire to speak with you, but you can also try and direct the course of your journey toward a given destination. If you wish to enter Vanaheim, then you should feel yourself entering Vanaheim. Visualize yourself crossing the rainbow bridge (which will help you to open your Third Eye), leading you away from Midgard, crossing the void to another realm—this time it is Vanaheim, but it could be Asgard, Ljossalfheim or any of the other realm. Once you become proficient in these exercises you will discover that you can will yourself to any realm you so desire. Hopefully you will meet entities who are inhabitants of these realms and eventually communicate with them and establish personal relationships. You can do this by exchanging gifts of love and friendships. This can be done by discovering the names of the entities you meet and then celebrate your meeting with them through poetry, verse, or even through sacrifice.

Once you have established a personal relationship or relationships, you can call on these entities to assist you in your life and work. You can call on them much in the same way that a Catholic will ask assistance from a particular saint.

THE VRIL SOCIETY AND FREE ENERGY

Many different esoteric societies were formed in Germany in the first two decades of the 20th century. One of them was called the Vril Society or *Vril Gesellschaft*. It was founded by six people, four men and two women. They first met in a café named *Café Schopenhauer*, in Vienna. Among those present was Rudolf von Sebottendorff, the founder of the *Thule Gesellschaft*, or Thule Society, Professor Karl Haushofer, who also belonged to many occult organizations, including the Thule Society, German Free Masonry and the Japanese Society of the Green Dragon, two female mediums, Maria Orsitch (Orsic) and Sigrun, who claimed to be in communication with Aryan Godlike beings who conveyed to her the instructions to build a ship powered by the Vril. After several meetings, this group decided to form the *Vril Gesellschaft*, or Vril Society. The word Vril is derived from an ancient Sumerian word, *Vri-ll*, which means, "like the Gods," or "Godlike." They discussed many things, including the dawning of a new age, ancient civilizations and a secret source of limitless power. One of the men possessed a violet-black stone reputed to possess the power to draw on this power source. They referred to this power as the Black Sun or the Vril. It was an infinite source of power that fills the universe, and is invisible to the human eye. The material that Maria Orsitch wrote down was in a foreign language thought to be ancient Sumerian, which was translated by Sigrun.

A similar group to the Vril Society was organized in Italy around such personalities as Julius Evola, Arturo Reghini, Guilio Parese, Ercole Quadrelli and Gustave Meyrink. They referred to the Vril as "Ur," and called their society the Ur Group. Ur is a prefix in the German language that means "original" or "primordial." Their goal was to cause a transmutation of their Selves into a state possessing superhuman powers, and they hoped to use the power of the Ur (Vril), to cause changes in the world around them.

Like the Ur Group, the Vril Society taught exercises in meditation, chanting and visualization, which permitted them to tap into the power of Vril and use it to power the craft that they hoped to build. Their methods were partially based on the practice of spiritual concentration formalized by the Jesuit, Ignatius Loyola. His *Spiritual Exercises* became the foundation of the techniques of concentration and visualization used by the Jesuit Order. They are also very similar to those used by Tibetan lamas and many different pagan shamans. Ignatius was a Basque, and the Basque people believe they are the oldest surviving remnants of the ancient Atlanteans. Actually, the Basque are culturally the direct descendants of the pre-Atlantean Aryan Cro-Magnons who inhabited Europe before the Aryans invaded Europe after the flooding of the Black Sea. Genetically, they are no different from other Europeans. This has been confirmed by the genetic research conducted by Luigi Cavalli-Sforza. Many claim that Ignatius' techniques were handed down through the millenniums from the Atlanteans, and was instrumental in the process of discovering how to harness the Vril's power. It is still possible that the Basques are in possession of such knowledge, because their culture has been little affected by successive waves of invasions by later people. They could have been introduced to Vrilology and preserved it because they remained free of additional influence over the succeeding millenniums.

The Vril had many names including vital magnetism, the Life Force, the Black Sun, dark matter, dark energy, karma, chi, Ojas, the Flow, Astral Light, Odic Force, and Orgone. Sir Albert Pike, an Accepted Scottish Rite of Free Masonry, also known as a Knight of the Sun or Prince Adept, said, "There is in nature one most potent force, by means whereof a single man, who could possess himself of it, and should know how to direct it, could revolutionize and change the face of the world." The emblem for the Vril power was the Black Sun, a symbol that existed in many ancient civilizations, including Indo-European civilizations as well as the Egyptian, Sumerian, Babylonian and Assyrian civilizations of the Middle East and North Africa. The symbol or symbols, resemble the German Iron Cross and the swastika.

The word "Vril," was first made popular in the West, by the English nobleman, turned author, Baron Edward Bulwer-Lytton. In his novel, *The Power of the Coming Race*, he describes a race of supermen, possessing great powers over nature through the use of a power source known as Vril, and who referred to themselves as the Vril-ya. Their civilization is far more advance than our present-day 21st century civilization. The Vril Society believed they also could learn to harness this power and use it, like the Vril-ya, the cause mutations within their race and create a new race of super-humans who would herald in a new and super-advanced civilization. It appears that Bulwer-Lytton was a member of many Occult groups, including the Free Masons and Rosicrucians and studied the Occult Arts.

The Vril Society taught its members to control the subtle power that was known as Vril, which could be used as a source of animal magnetism or vitality. Once they had mastered the use of the Vril, they could use its powers for many purposes, including healing, mystical enlightenment, to control others and even to cause transmutations within oneself. A second usage of the Vril involving controlling events in the world, changes within one's society and even the course of history, in the hope of establishing a desirable state of affairs in the physical world (Midgard). To accomplish this, the members would join together and mediate collectively. In this way they trained themselves to concentrate their wills through chanting, meditation, controlled breathing and visualization in an effort to assimilate the collective power of their wills into a fine-tuned weapon that could be used with laser-like accuracy. Once they had focused their collective wills on a single objective, they would visualize what it was they hoped to achieve. Then, by employing the power of their heightened, emotional exhortation, they sought to establish lines of communication between themselves and the Gods. In this way they would establish a bridge between themselves (Midgard) and the realm or plane of existence of the Gods, or higher forces (Asgard).

Using the information that Maria was able to channel from her communication with the Gods, and translated by Sigrud, they proceeded to try and build a Vril machine, which was saucer-shaped and possessed anti-gravity capabilities. They began working on such an aircraft in the Black Forest region of southern Germany, with the assistance of Thulist member, Professor W.O. Schumann at the Technical University of Munich, in 1922. Schumann wrote that, *In everything we recognize two principles that determine the events: light and darkness, good and evil, creation and destruction—as in electricity we know plus and minus. It is always: either/or. These two principles—creative and destructive—also determine our technical means ... Everything destructive is of Satanic origin, everything creative is divine ... Every technology based upon explosion or combustion has thus to be called Satanic. The coming new age will be an age of a new, positive, divine technology!* He was present when both the Vril and Thule Societies met at a hunting lodge, in 1919. It was at that meeting, in Berchtesgaden, that they began their work on a levitation device. They first constructed their levitation device using Vril power. But they had to cease further work in 1924. The Vril Society had difficulties in acquiring the necessary funding for further work on their levitation device, and was forced to take out adds that made no attempt to conceal the nature of their work. In fact, they openly claimed the technology they were trying to utilize was of *Atlantean* origin. Unable to continue their work because of the lack of funding, the Vril Society, under the direction of Schumann, was forced to dismantle the device and stored it at the Messerschmitt's facility in Augsburg, Germany.

The Vril Society's effort to harness Vril as a source of limitless, free energy, and use it to construct revolutionary flying machines, was resurrected by the National Socialists after they came to power in Germany. In 1934, Hitler met with an Austrian engineer by the name of Viktor Schauberger. He explained to the German leader his theory of harmonizing technology with nature and the use of implosion, as opposed to technology relying on explosions, to produce endless amounts of energy. Hitler was intrigued and approved support for Schauberger's research, but as Germany moved closer to war, most funding for programs dealing with new and super advance technologies, that could not promise to produce results within a year, was cut. It was not until 1942 or 1943 that funding was once again diverted to Schauberger's research.

Briefly, Schauberger relied on the Pythagorean theory of creation and geometry, which claimed that sounds created the universe through harmonic resonance. All structures of matter are based on a proportional relationship of integral numbers and their harmonic proportions. They all originate from a single monochord. All science is based on this law, including genetics, biology and chemistry. What Schauberger was diving into was rudimentary, Quantum physics. Schauberger felt that by tapping into this structural law of all matter, he could harness the power of the Vril, and use its power as a source of limitless energy that was produced from implosion, as opposed to explosions. Thus, he was seeking to tap into the ultimate power source in the universe.

The Vril Society taught its members to peel away the mysteries surrounding the Vril, and learn how to use its power. Once one of its members could master the use of Vril, he could acquire all of its powers. The society explained that there were two ways to achieve this goal. One was through the use of mechanical devices that would initiate "implosion," thus causing a vortex that would create a singularity or zero point gravity—anti-gravity. The other means by which one could harness the power of the Vril was through what has been referred to as Magick (and what I refer to as Vrilology). By employing both methods, during the 1920s and 1930s, the Vril Society was conducting experiments in the construction of a craft that was powered by the Vril. The craft was disc-shaped and the forerunner of what we would refer to today as "flying saucers." Using Vril's power, the flying discs were employing free, unlimited and clean energy to produce anti-gravity. But if this sounds fantastic, we have to remember that the Vril Society and Schauberger were not alone in trying to develop anti-gravity by tapping into the endless supply of free energy known as the Vril.

There were others who were involved in the investigation of this new technology. Most were brilliant scientists and imaginative engineers like Schauberger. Perhaps the most brilliant was one of the greatest inventors that ever lived, Nikola Tesla. Tesla was born in Croatia, in 1856. He immigrated to the United States when he was thirty and found employment with Thomas Edison, assisting him in his experiments in the use of electricity. But the two geniuses had a falling out over of the merits of Edison's preference for DC (direct current) electricity, while Tesla's preferred the advantages in the use of AC (alternating current) electricity. Tesla decided to leave Edison's employment so that he could concentrate on developing the use of AC, which eventually proved Edison wrote and became the current that was commonly used. He eventually won support for the construction of his own workshop in Colorado Springs, in Colorado. With his own laboratory, he was free to conduct his experiments. He had a theory that electricity could be transmitted through the air without the use of wires. He was successful in building generators that produced artificial lightning and powered up more than two hundred fifty-watt light bulbs at a distance of twenty-miles away by transmission of electricity through the air without the use of wires.

Tesla had a unique mind. Charles Haanel describes it this way: *The inventor visualizes his idea in exactly the same manner, as for instance, Nikola Tesla, he with the giant intellect, one of the greatest inventors of all ages, the man who has brought forth the most amazing realities, always visualizes his inventions before attempting to work them out. He did not rush to embody them in form and then spend his time in correcting defects. Having first built up the idea in his imagination, he held it there as a mental picture, to be reconstructed and improved by his thought. "In this way," he writes in the Electrical Experimenter. "I am enabled to rapidly develop and perfect a conception without touching anything. Wen I have gone so far as to embody in the invention every possible improvement I can think of, and see no fault anywhere, I put into concrete, the product of my brain. Invariably my devise works as I conceived it should; in twenty years there has not been a single exception."*

Tesla discovered that the earth was surrounded by an electromagnetic field of energy. It was later discovered that this field resonated at a frequency of 7.8 cycles per second. He claimed that by tapping into this field of energy, one could provide a source of free and limitless energy. Tesla compared the field to strings on a violin. If one string is plucked, the adjacent strings will resonate the harmonic vibrations at the same frequency. Tesla examined two possible ways to transmit this free energy without the use of wires. One way was through the air, and the other was through the use of natural geomagnetic carrier lines in the earth that are referred to as ley lines. Strangely, Tesla could not find the backing necessary to develop this means of tapping into a free source of energy. His experiments and life-work has been surrounded by rumors of conspiracies. Most of it centered around efforts by the United States government to protect the influential coal and oil-based, energy-producing, and auto industries that would naturally suffer greatly if Tesla succeeded in producing a means of acquiring free energy. There was a campaign to deny financial backing by J. P. Morgan, who had bankrolled Edison. If Tesla had been successful, the coal and oil producing industries would have suffered greatly, even disappear. The electrical companies would have gone bankrupt. The automobile industries, as well as the newly developing airplane industries would also have gone belly-up. Tesla's success would have inaugurated a revolution in energy, economics and manufacturing that would have shaken our civilization to its foundation.

Through this field of exploration, of a new, free and limitless source of energy, was being suppressed in the West, but in Germany, which had lost the First World War and considered a pariah among the civilized nations of the West, Tesla's ideas were received warmly. Certain groups within German society that sought to restore Germany as one of the leading nations in the world, a position that Germany had enjoyed before the First World War, were willing to give new ideas concerning new and revolutionary technologies, a chance. Such groups as the *Germanenorden* (Germanic Order) and the *Thulegesellschaft* (Thule Society), endorsed efforts to discover ways to harness this free and limitless source of energy known as the Vril.

Tesla experimented with many other revolutionary ideas, such as a light-particle beam and lasers that were often called at the time, "death rays." In 1936, the Yugoslav government awarded Tesla an annual pension of $7,200 on his eightieth birthday, and set up the Tesla Institute in Belgrade. In 1941, after Yugoslavia was conquered by Germany, the SS confiscated everything in the Institute for its own research and development of Germany's own free-energy and flying disc programs. After Tesla died in New York City, in 1943, all his papers and records on his work was confiscated by the FBI and examined before being turned over to the Yugoslav ambassador. Undoubtedly, the FBI took possession of all material that the United States government considered too revolutionary. But Tesla was not alone in trying to provide a free and endless source of energy that could produce anti-gravity. While the United States was trying to suppress Tesla's experiments, National Socialist Germany began supporting the Austrian engineer, Victor Schauberger.

As I mentioned before, less known than Tesla, was Schauberger, played a more vital role in the effort to develop free energy from Vril. Schauberger was born, in 1885, into a family, who for generations, were foresters in the service of the Austro-Hungarian Empire. Victor studied as a water engineer and was employed by Prince Adolf-Schaumburg-Lippe. He was in charge of managing 21,000 hectares of forest, owned by the Prince, near Steyerling. Schauberger studied the way water flowed and came to the conclusion that water was *alive*. In some mysterious way, he believed that water possessed a life force or energy. This life force or energy was Vril. He discovered that water, in its natural state, built up energy as it coursed freely through natural environments. Under the right conditions, this energy would flow in the opposite direction of the flow of water. His father had told him that when water was exposed to the heat of the sun, it turned *lazy*. In this condition, it folds back on itself. But at night, especially under the full moon, it comes alive. Somehow, the water density is transformed, becoming more vibrant and buoyant. In this condition, the water appears more *alive*. Schauberger used this knowledge to invent a new form of water flumes designed to exploit this mysterious energy force. At night, his flume was able to transport unheard of amounts of logs with no more water than other flumes used. His invention soon made him financially independent so that he could continue his research into the exploration of this newly discovered energy source—Vril.

As I mentioned earlier, in 1934, Schauberger was invited to make the acquaintance of Adolf Hitler, who had been informed of Schauberger's theory about the Vril as a source of free and unlimited, clean form of energy. But when Schauberger arrived, Direktor Wiluhm of the Kaiser Wilhelm Institute was present and tried to convince Hitler that Schauberger's theory was nonsense. Schauberger was disappointed and left Berlin, not realizing that Hitler had been convinced of the validity of his theory. Schauberger had returned to Austria before Hitler could invite him to the Chancellory for another meeting. It was not until Austria was united with Germany that Hitler had the opportunity to ask Schauberger to work on the development of Vril as a source of free energy for Germany. Hitler sent Julius Streicher with a grant of ten million Reichsmarks to see Schauberger, and placed the well-furnished laboratory of Professor Kotschau in Nuremberg, at Schauberger's disposal. Victor and his son, Walter, along with a team of engineers and scientists, began working to discover the secrets of "living water."

This is not the place to go into a detail discussion about Schauberger's experiments, or the technology that was developed from it, but let me present a condensed synopsis of Schauberger's research in relation to how the Vril can be harnessed as a source of energy through mechanical means. In 1940, after the defeat of France, thinking that the war was virtually won, Hitler ordered a reduction, and in some cases a halt, in research and development of new weapon systems and technology. Hitler believed the war was over and wanted the German economy to return to peacetime footing, fearing the repetition of the wartime hardships the civilian population suffered during the First World War. Funding for projects like Schauberger's was reduced or suspended until further notice. In Schauberger's case, research continued but at a reduced pace. Still, in 1941, while studying specific properties of colloidal flow of water, Schauberger hit upon the invention of a new type of motor starter. It was small and electric and could be used in aircraft engines. He mounted it to a prototype of a machine and demonstrated that it could achieve lift utilizing a new source of energy that he recently discovered. This was the Vril.

Schauberger used a simple battery to start the motor, which, in turn, would spin a set of turbine blades placed in a drum shaped like a barrel. The drum was 1.5 meters in diameter. The weight of the device was more than 130 kilograms. A hollow cone was positioned in the axis of the drum. Its widest end was the underside of the cone. Schauberger filled the barrel with what he described as "living water." Once the turbine was started, it circulated at a tremendous rate. Because he was using his living water, it turned at a much faster pace than it would, using normal water. The water rotated between the inner wall of the barrel, and outside the wall of the cone. The result was the creation of a hyperbolic, centripetal spiral. It resembled a micro-tornado within the water. At the top of the vortex, the spinning water would pass into a smaller water turbine linked to an impeller at the pointed end of the cone.

You can demonstrate the effect for yourself with an empty, 1.5 liter soda-bottle, which has a slender neck. Fill the bottle three-quarters of the way with the soapy, lukewarm water. Begin shaking the bottle back and forth (not up and down). The back and forth motion should produce a micro-tornado within the water, just as Schauberger's device did. The soapsuds will demonstrate the effect of the motion on the water. Though the effect will not reproduce the centripetal effect, the centrifugal effect will demonstrate a similar phenomenon for you so that you can get an idea how Schauberger's device worked. Imagine that the water is rising instead of declining. You can visualize that the impeller is located at the highest position of the circulating water, receiving its power directly from the turbulence. Once you have conceptualized the effect, imagine the impeller spinning, sucking in air from vents located around the top of the barrel and then expelling the air toward the ground at the widest end of the cone. It was this tornado-like expulsion of air at the base of the vortex that generated lift, blowing, instead of sucking in air. The process fed power from a small turbine to the main motor, creating a closed system. This process was extremely energy-efficient, producing clean energy. This was still not the free energy of the Vril, but it was a step in the right direction.

Schauberger described the process this way:

The destructive and dissolving form of movement is centrifugal in nature—it forces the moving medium from the center outward toward the periphery in straight lines. The medium is first weakened, then it dissolves and breaks up. Nature uses this action to disintegrate complexes which have lost their vivacity or have died. From the broken-down fragments, new coordinated forms, new identities can be created as a result of this concentrating form of movement. The centripetal, hyperbolic spiral movement is symptomatic of falling temperature, contraction, concentration. The centrifugal movement on the other hand, is synonymous with rising temperature, heat, extension, expansion, explosion. In Nature, there is continuous switch from one movement to the other.

When Schauberger first tested the machine, it flew straight up through the roof of the laboratory, and landed a great distance away from the lab. But because Hitler believed that the war would soon be won, the German government did not pour the necessary funding into Schauberger's research. This was true of other research and development projects that included the development of the jet fighters and rockets. It was not until 1943 that the German government began to heavily fund Schauberger's research, and this was done by Himmler's SS. Schauberger was sent to Mauthausen concentration camp where he was under the direction of Satandartenfuhrer Zeireis. Schauberger's research was still considered a long shot, but because of the worsening war situation, Hitler, Himmler and other top Nazis were willing to try anything to halt the growing threat of losing the war. Schauberger and his entire research team were soon moved to Leonstein, near Linz.

In the construction of the flying discs or saucers, as they are more popularly known today, Schauberger incorporated the vortex process in his design. Air entered at the top and whirled down through the center of the saucer. The flow was similar to what take place inside a tornado. The centripetal or inward rotation movement of the air, requires less space, and self-cools the spiraling air. It is similar to water being flushed in a toilet. Schauberger referred to this as "implosion." The water or air would whirl inward until it reached its zero-point and then, expand outward in a centrifugal spiral. This entire process includes, first centripetal and then centrifugal rotation. The directional flow is "function," which Schauberger describes as the energy flow, and the "movement," which is the shape of the flow of the energy—a spiral vortex.

When the air flows into the vortex at the top, the air molecules implode from the double-spiral method, causing the air molecules to increase their density, which releases heat in the process. This happens when the air molecules are squeezed ever tighter, as they move down the vortex. At this point in the process, the subatomic particles undergo a transformation, breaking apart and reforming into new and unidentified forms of energy—Vril. As the Vortex's diameter decreases in volume, the implosion and its speed increase until the centripetal process stops and the flow becomes centrifugal. At this point, the new form of energy is radiated outward from the axis of the vortex. This energy is expelled at the zero-point, which is a form of anti-gravity or diamagnetic energy (Vril). Schauberger claimed that his vortex machine reached rotational speeds of 10,000 and 20,000 revolutions per minute.

The entire process was initiated by the use of a conventional, small, high-speed, electric motor. This engine was used to spin the air around the axis. This was done with the use of paddle-like propellers. The air would continue to accelerate, increasing speed as it did, by the engine, until the speed of the auto-rotation reached critical speed. When this speed was reached, the process, at this point, became self-sustaining. Air would continuously be drawn in and cooled, and then expelled with no additional energy required to keep the process flowing. Because air molecules were constantly being unglued and reassembled as energy, the engine was fed now from this new source of energy and so, could continue to draw in air, cool down and thus became more dense in the vortex, and release additional energy. The increase in density is the result of the loss in volume, which in turn creates lower pressure, drawing in more air. Increased air speed at this point of ejection, lowers the pressure, and increases the process of lowering pressure.

The atomic structure of the air particles may have been ripped apart when the electrons, protons and neutrons were separated. This may have resulted in the stripping away of the electrons and protons from their nuclei, freeing their opposing charges, attracting each other, and causing them to cancel each other out. This mutual annihilation probably caused the release of unlimited free energy. This would have happened when centrifugal forces began, reversing the spin of the air particles.

The propulsion of Schauberger's saucer may have been the result of being repelled magnetically from the charged atmosphere that it created. This was the result of the neutrons which were left over from the breakup of the air particles, which were magnetic. The neutrons were centrifugally repelled from the saucer, along with water, water vapor and air. The magnetic neutrons, on the outside of the saucer, reacted by increasing the diamagnetic property, causing it to push away from the earth and producing a magnetically charged aura of neutrons around the saucer. Schauberger used diamagnetic material in the construction of his machine, which repelled a magnetic field. The material he used was copper.

To sum up the process: He used an electric powered motor, with paddle-like propellers, drawing air into one end of the machine. The air is turned by the propellers, or perhaps by the entire machine rotating, as in Schauberger's saucer model. The air is then flushed down the spiral vortex of specific shape and proportion, and made both dense and cooled at the same time. As the air is compressed down through the funnel to the smallest point—zero-point—energy is released due to the ungluing of the subatomic structure of the air molecules. Right before it spirals upward and outward, the air warms up once more, and then exits the saucer model at this point, usually around the periphery of the saucer, and expands centrifugally in the open atmosphere. Once the saucer has reached the rotation speed of between 10,000 and 20,000 revolutions per minute, the machine begins to rotate on its own power, no longer requiring the electric motor to keep it in motion.

Some of Schauberger's machines were transferred to the Kertl Workers in Vienna, where research continued to investigate the production of free energy and anti-gravity propulsion. To harness this source of free energy, they had to run a shaft to the wheel-like component that auto-rotated between 10,000 and 20,000 rpm. In this way, they were able to divert some of the energy into an electric generator that produced electricity at no cost—thus producing free energy. This was accomplished in 1945.

Schauberger relied on geometry to design the shape of his device, believing that conventional physics could be affected by certain shapes and patterns. Schauberger's research is an example of how free energy can be provided by combining both the properties of known science and more esoteric doctrine. The union is still not perfectly understood, but we do know that it does provide a source of free energy and anti-gravity power necessary to propel what is referred to as flying saucers or discs.

At the end of the war, Schauberger was taken into custody by the Americans for six months. Only after the Japanese were defeated was Schauberger released. The Americans seemed to know what Schauberger was working on and wanted to prevent any other power to acquire his technology. He remained under watch for about ten years until, in 1957, he and his son, Walter, were approached by several Americans who claimed they wanted to develop his technology commercially. Victor and Walter were brought to the United States, and resided at a military base in Red River, Texas, under strict security, virtually held prisoners. They were forbidden all communications with the outside world, and were forbidden to return to Austria until they signed over all the patent rights of their inventions, to their "benefactors." Victor died a broken man five days after he eventually returned to Austria. After his death, his son, Walter, established a school of biotechnology at Bad Ischl in Austria, that still exists to this day. The school still investigates many of the theories that Victor Schauberger pioneered and puts them to commercial use without conflicting with the agreements signed at Red River. For further investigation into Schauberger's research, I suggest three books that were very helpful in writing about him: Gary Hyland's *Blue Fires*, Henry Steven's *Hitler's Flying Saucers*, and especially, Callum Coats' *Living Energies*.

Knowledge of the Vril and its potential to provide free, clean and unlimited energy has been suppressed by the establishment for obvious reasons of economics and power. But recently, I discovered an article on the Internet entitled *Anti-Gravity in the Himalayas* by Ville V. Walveranta at ufoareantigravity.org. Walveranta tells us about an article that appeared in a German magazine describing an eyewitness account of Tibetan priests in possession of the science of anti-gravity. The article describes a Swedish expedition to Tibet in 1939 that witness the amazing powers that the Tibetan holy men possessed. Let me quote sections of the article from the Internet website.

We know from the priests of the far east that they were able to lift heavy boulders up high mountains with the help of groups of various sounds. The knowledge of the various vibrations in the audio range demonstrates to a scientist of physics that a vibrating and condensed sound field can nullify the power of gravitation. Swedish engineer Olaf Alexanderson wrote about this phenomenon in the publication, Implosion No. 13....

A block of stone was manoeuvred into this cavity by Yak oxen. The block was one meter wide and one and one-half meters long. Then, 19 musical instruments were set in an arc of 90 degrees at a distance of 63 meters from the stone slab. The radius of 63 meters was measured out accurately. The musical instruments consisted of 13 drums and six trumpets. Eight drums had a cross-section of one meter, and a length of one and one-half meters. Four drums were medium size with a cross-section of 0.7 meters and a length of one meter. The one small drum had a cross-section of 0.2 meters and a length of 0.3 meters. All the trumpets were the same size. They had a length of 3.12 meters and an opening of 0.3 meters. The big drums and all the trumpets were fixed on mounts which could be adjusted with staffs in the direction of the slab of stone. The big drums were made of 3mm thick sheet iron, and had a weight of 150 kg. They were built in five sections. All drums were open at one end, while the other end had a bottom of metal on which the monks beat with big leather clubs. Behind each instrument was a row of monks. When the stone was in position the monk behind the small drum gave a signal to start the concert. The small drum had a very sharp sound, and could be heard even with the other instruments making a terrible din. All the monks were singing and chanting a prayer, slowly increasing the tempo of this unbelievable noise. During the first four minutes nothing happened, then as the speed of the drumming, and the noise, increased, the big stone block started to rock and sway, and suddenly it took off into the air with an increasing speed in the direction of the platform in front of the cave hole 250 meters high. After three minutes of ascent it landed on the platform.

This description of the process in which the monks were able to use sound to suspend gravity is clearly Vril Science. Walveranta explains that the Swedish team made films of this demonstration and that the film was immediately classified and kept from the public. This is typical of the establishment's efforts to try and deny the existence of this science.

The fact that the films were immediately classified is not very hard to understand once the given measurements are transposed into their geometric equivalents. It then becomes evident that the monks in Tibet are fully conversant with the laws governing the structure of matter, which scientists in the modern day western world are now frantically exploring. It appears, from the calculations, that the prayers being chanted by the monks did not have any direct bearing on the fact that the stones were levitated from the ground. The reaction was not initiated by the religious fervor of the group, but by the superior scientific knowledge held by the high priests. The secret is in the geometric placement of the musical instruments in relation to the stones to be levitated, and the harmonic tuning of the drums and the trumpets. The combined loud chanting of the priests, using their voices at a certain pitch and rhythm most probably adds to the combined effect, but the subject matter of the chant, I believe, would be of no consequence. The sound waves being generated by the combination were directed in such a way that an anti-gravitational effect was created at the center of focus (position of the stones) and around the periphery, or the arc, of a third of a circle through which the stones moved.

History of the twentieth century has demonstrated that research into ways of harnessing Vril through mechanical methods have taken place, and these methods are possible. This line of research has been squashed by the establishment because such free energy would cause the collapse of the hundreds of trillion—dollar industries that dominate the world economy today. With the production of free energy and anti-gravity power from the Vril, such industries as oil, gas, electric, automobile, aeronautic, and coal, just to name a few, would disappear over night. Their demise would be just as dramatic and sudden as the disappearance of the dinosaurs when the earth was struck by a giant meteor sixty million years ago.

Part IV
THE FOLK FAITH

PRIESTLY ORDER OF THE FOLK FAITH

The Folk Faith needs a priestly order as does every religion, especially Indo-European religions. The priestly order, or even a social religious class, has been a common cornerstone in most Indo-European cultures for thousands of years. In all religions, the priestly order actually serves the role of a magician. People today would never think of their minister, priest or rabbi as a magician, but that is exactly what they are. They are preforming magical ceremonies, trying to establish a link between those in attendance and their Divine Forces, God or Gods. Thus, our priestly order serves the same function as those priestly orders in other religions.

Many who practice Odinism, Asatru or other pagan religions based on the Northern tradition, like to give exotic names to their priestly order. A common name taken from Old Norse is the *godhi* (goh-thee) or *gydhja* (gith-ya), or simply *vitki*, which means "wise one." These names give a nice feel to the religion and if you desire your group to remain small and include only those who would like to reconstruct the past or engage in roleplaying, this is perfectly fine. But if we want to establish a "living" religion intended to reach out to the masses, to the average people that include whole families, then we should do nothing that will give an air of the "exotic" or make the religion appear "foreign" and "alien." If the Folk Faith is to become a living religion for the masses, then it must "feel" familiar. Therefore, there is no reason not to use terms that are familiar and would make the average person feel right at home in our religion. Thus, we should refer to our "magicians" as a priestly order and its members as ministers or priests. Most people of European ancestry, have been reared in some kind of Christian background, and will find these terms very acceptable and comfortable. Hey! This is exactly how the early Christians won over our pagan ancestors. They incorporated terms that were familiar, and most people felt comfortable with. We should to the same.

The first thing the Church of Vrilology needs to establish is a priestly order of dedicated men and women, who will place the welfare of the church and its members before their own selfish needs. Through dedication, and hard work in studying Vrilology lore and practicing the methodology of Vrilology, anyone can rise to the exalted position of a Vril Lord or Vril Lady. They will make up the governing body of the church, establishing running the different orders, but their function is also to serve the needs of the church, its members, maintain the good reputation of the church, and ensure its spiritual purity. Anyone can work toward this position. It will be open to all members, but the road to achieving it will be long and hard.

WHAT IS A VRIL LORD OR LADY?

The title of Vril Lord or Vril Lady will be bestowed upon an individual who has completed all nine levels of training (81 lessons), who proved their dedication to the principles of the Church of Vrilology as well as living up to a higher standard of honor, and then passed an interview by the ruling board of the Church, made up of Vril Masters and Vril Mistresses. Vril Lords (for the sake of simplicity, we will refer to both Vril Lords and Vril Ladies by simply using the title, Vril Lord) will make up the religious aristocracy of the Church of Vrilology. Who can become a Vril Lord is determined by ability and dedication. In the desire to be clear on the function and purpose of this aristocracy within the Church, we will try and define exactly what the role of the Vril Lords will be within the Church.

1. *First, you must be a practitioner of Vrilology.*
This simply means that you have completed the Yggdrasill Training Program, and continue to practice the ancient Runic arts, both Galdor and Seither sciences, and other mysteries associated with the Church of Vrilology. By doing so you will have developed the vast powers of your mind and soul, permitting you to live life to its fullest potential both individually, striving to obtain the exalted position of a God-man or God-woman (one who walks with the Gods), and works to build and expand the Church of Vrilology and its Folk Communities. You will be responsible as a role model within the Church, to live a healthy, joyful, prosperous and happy life, working to further your own spiritual growth and evolution, as working to build a Folk Community constructed on the same principles

2. *You are fully familiar with the lore and teachings of the Vrilology.*
This means that you possess a fully developed understanding of the spirituality laid down in the Book of Balder Rising, as well as the lore of Vrilology, the lost

history and science of the ancient Atlantean Black Sea Civilization, the history of the Indo-European tribes, the Eddic Poetry, Sagas, the written history of the Folk, and related Indo-European lore.

3. *You must live by the Vril Code of Honor.*
I. We believe that the Gods are our ancestors. The Gods are living deities and are all united with the All-Father through his Life Force, which is called Vril. The All-Father existed before the beginning of time, and gave order to the Yawning Void and rules over the nine worlds.

II. We believe the Gods are inherently good and give order to the universe. This order is good and right. They hold back the destructiveness of the chaos personified by the Giants, and want us, their children, to always do what is right by aligning ourselves with them. The Gods are our forebears, and we are their children. They descended to Midgard thousands of years ago and walked among our ancestors, teaching them of the science of the Vril and how to harness its power to create a great civilization that we refer to as Atlantis.

III. We share the same Life Force or Vril as the Gods and they dwell with our DNA, in our blood, in every cell and atom within us. Therefore, it is imperative that we remain pure in body and spirit and always be proud of, who we are, and what we are. All the Gods and Goddesses are our friends and part of our past and our future. The Aesir and the Vanir are the same Gods in different guises that all Indo-Europeans celebrated.

IV. We believe the Folk Faith is the true religion of our people (Europeans). The Gods of the Folk Faith are the true Gods of our people because we share the same Life Force, or Vril, and the same blood. All other Gods and beliefs are alien and foreign to our people and can only lead our people to destruction and extinction.
V. We believe that every member of our race are our brothers and sisters. We reject all divisions within our pan-European Folk. We are all related because we all share the same Life Force and blood. We are the chosen of our Gods, and both individually and collectively it is our duty to spread the truth of the Folk Faith and the message of Balder's return.

VI. We believe that our people must return to our Gods, but they must do it willing. Only those who are pure in body and spirit can walk in the light of the

Balder. Therefore, no one should be force to join the Folk Faith, or be retained against their wills. Only the strong can walk in the Light of Balder. Only the strong can ride with Odin. Only the chosen will live with Freyja in Sessrumnir, with Odin in Valhalla, or Balder in Odainsaker.

VII. We believe that we are living during the days of Ragnarok, and Balder is Odin's instrument for the return of the Gods. Balder is waiting in Hel to return and herald in a new, golden age that is Gimli, for our people. We believe that the Golden Age of Gimli is manifested within each individual who has joined the Church of Vrilology. Balder will return when the Folk Faith has once again become strong and powerful. Only then will the Life Force of our Folk be strong enough to ensure that the influence of the Gods over Midgard, and bring about the resurrection of Balder and the establishment of Gimli within each of us.

VIII. We believe that the Folk Faith is the best religion for our people, and provides the healthiest way of life for our people. Our faith is built on honor, self-reliance, responsibility to each other, our family, friends and other members of our Folk. We seek to strengthen those qualities that the Gods most favor: honor, honestly, truthfulness, joyfulness, industriousness, forbearance, justice, and the willingness to stand up for what is right.

IX. We believe that the salvation of our people lies within us. The Life Force of the Gods is the same Life Force that gives us life. The Gods reside within each and everyone one of us. They reside in our blood, in our DNA, and when we desecrate our blood and DNA, we cause harm to the Gods. We wish to live a life of joy, success, happiness and love, without hatred to anyone, or other peoples, races or folks, nor do we wish to harm anyone, or other peoples, races, or folks. It is through this purity of life that will strengthen the Life Force of the Gods within us, and ensure the resurrection of Balder within each of us.

4. *You must seek to develop one or more of your psychic abilities into a fine-tuned skill for the greater good of the Church.*
We all have psychic abilities, and some individuals will excel in certain abilities while others will excel in another. As a Vril Lord, you must dedicate your life to fine-tuning at least one of your abilities, and use it to help other members of our Church and Folk Communities. You should also use your abilities for your own advancement, but never deny help toward those fellow Church members who need your assistance. You don't have to be an expert in all areas of psychic abili-

ties. You will discover that most people naturally excel in at least one talent, sometimes two or three. The purpose of the Yggdrasill Training Program is to help you discover which talents you excel in, and assist you in developing them. You should then dedicate yourself in developing that talent (or talents) until you become very, very good at it.

5. *You should possess an understanding of the nature of the relationship of the forces of chaos and order in the universe.*

Your training as a Vril Lord is designed to help you understand the relationship between the force of chaos, represented by the Giants, and order, represented by the Gods. You should possess a deep understanding how the two forces interact and are essential for the evolution of the universe. But you should also dedicate yourself to living a life align with the work of the Gods, maintaining order here on Midgard, by working toward the formation and development of Vril Folk Communities.

6. *You must develop a thorough understanding of your ancestral stream.*

You should not only seek to discover your ancestral link to your ethnic ancestry, but also learn to discover your family ancestral line. You should try and discover who your ancestors were, and not be afraid to discover the scoundrels that might inhabit your family line, as well as those honorable individual members of your ancestry. To discover a deep and thorough understanding of where you came from will help you to control the Orlog that affects your Wyrd, and this will assist you in your individual evolution toward the goal of becoming a God-man or God-woman.

7. *Doing the work of Heimdall.*

Heimdall is the eternal watcher and stands guard at the gates of Asgard. So to is the duty of the Vril Lord to watch out for the dark forces that cause the disruption of order, perpetuating chaos. When these forces of disorder do manifest themselves, it is the duty of the Vril Lord to exercise their powers to make corrections in the Vrilic flow of energy. As you develop your Runic consciousness, the amount of injustice and disorder you experience in your personal life will declaim greatly. But along with this advantage comes the responsibility to help other members within the Church and its Folk Communities who are victims of injustice. You must stand eternally on guard against the assault by the forces of darkness and chaos, just as Heimdall does.

8. You must continuously seek to discover ever greater understanding of the ordered structure of the nine realms of Yggdrasill.

The search of understanding the nature of the cosmological structure of the universe, that the Gods struggle to maintain against the disruptive dark forces of chaos, is an eternal vigil. You should be constantly striving to achieve a greater understanding of the Vrilic currents that give order to the universe, and how you can use this understanding to maintain and support the growth and expansion of the Church and its Folk Communities. This can be done through astral journeys to the different worlds of the Yggdrasill, with the exception of Nifleheim and Musspellheim, you must learn to visit the other realms that include Ljossalfheim, Svartalfheim, Jotunheim, Vanaheim, Asgard and Hel. There is great knowledge to be discovered by visiting these world, and limits to that knowledge is limitless.

9. You must work toward creating a good name for yourself and the Church.

To be a Vril Lord is to take on the responsibility to "change." It involves a growing process that best can be described as "evolving into a higher form of life." The spiritual and esoteric understanding of what this means is best expressed in the Havamal verse #73:

Cattle die, kindred Die;
 Every man is mortal;
But the good name never dies
 Of one who has done well.

10. *You should be one who loves life.*

Because of your evolution toward a higher state of being, into a higher form of life, one of perfection, beauty, harmony and stability, you should be filled with a love of life. Your personality should be an expression of this joy of evolving toward this higher state of existence. As you evolve, you will become more and more aware of your true purpose in this life and this should fill you with a joy that should shine, filling everyone around you with the same joy of living. You must strive to purge yourself of all negative sensations, all hostility to others, individuals and groups of people. Whatever you do in life, and wherever your life journey takes you, you should possess an understanding that with the power of Vril at your command, you have no enemies, nor anyone who can harm you. Thus you should never display hostility to others, no view people who are not part of the Church as your opponents.

11. *You should maintain a state of optimum health.*

By utilizing what we learn in Vrilology to harness the Vril to use the full potential of your hamr (etheric body) to vitalize your physical body, you should maintain the optimum state of healthiness. You should strive to temper your habits with a balance so that you can maintain a healthy and pure body and mind. You will find that Vrilology provides you with the powers to avoid dependencies, debilitating habits and addictions that can cause your life to spin off into the void of chaos. You have learned to constantly renew your Vril energy flow and to replenish the lost of that energy as a result of the natural depletion that comes with existence in Midgard.

12. *You should care for your family and other loved ones.*

Through Vrilology you have developed a natural instinct to care for and ensure the welfare of those close to you, especially those who share a genetic and spiritual relationship. The welfare of your children above all and your spouse and immediate family, followed by your extended kin will according to the laws of genetics will take on greater importance. This results from the instinctual bond forged from the increase flow of Vril energy that links individuals through their DNA.

13. *The achievement of the Golden Age of Gimli within you will be manifested.*

The entire purpose of Vrilology to the call Balder back from Hel. His return will be manifested within *you*. It will awaken the divine powers of the Gods within your being, transforming you into a superior human being—into a God-man or God-woman, hence—a Vril being! This is the understanding of **Balder Rising!** This transformation can be understood through a thorough understanding of three Runes—Elhaz, Sowilo and Mannaz. Elhaz is the process of Balder rising out of the Netherworld. Sowilo is the power of Balder risen, transforming you. And Mannaz is the state of being a God-man or God-woman. This Mannaz Being has the power of harnessing, shaping and using the Life Force of the Gods, Vril, for the purpose of maintaining a consciousness of the Folk collective without falling pride to an outsider's manipulation, and thus becoming a being who has command of his or her own destiny. With this power that comes with manifesting a state known as the Golden Age of Gimli within you, you, and the entire Folk Community, whose welfare and well being you are responsible for, will have the power to survive the coming collapse of civilization, which is the culmination of the process known as Ragnarok.

The Church of Vrilology will be divided into different orders. Each order will be dedicated to a different God or Goddess and will be established in time, as more and more people join the faith and seek to dedicate themselves to different deities. The orders should be opened to both men and women. We will probably discover that most women will feel a natural attraction to the Goddesses and most men will feel a natural attraction to the Gods. Thus, in time, most orders will probably be dominated by one sex or another, but there should be no restrictions on membership based on gender in the orders. Members of both sexes should be permitted to join any of the orders—God or Goddess—and in time, many members of the order, of both sexes, will wish to join more than one order, though most will probably favor one or two deities. Each order will have a leader who will represent the order in a grand council that will govern the affairs of the Church of Vrilology.

Each order will be governed by its own ruling body made up of Vril Lords and Vril Ladies. They will determine who can join their orders and who among their orders will represent them on the governing body of the Church. Below them will be the general membership of each other. These will be other Vril Lords and Vril Ladies, as well as the general members of the Church who seek understanding and guidance from the God or Goddess that each individual order is dedicated to. Below this general membership will be individuals who are not official members of the order, but who seek guidance and assistance in their earthly lives or spiritual development.

One of the duties of the orders will be to practice the religious or magical rituals and ceremonies. These can be broken down into three different practices. The first is the mass rituals and ceremonies, which will help the members of the Folk Faith to harmonize the religious beliefs and customs into their personal lives. This will include, first of all, performing masses on religious holidays similar to what Christian ministers and priests perform on Christian holidays and holy days. But this should also include educational classes similar to Sunday School.

The orders must see to it that the members of the church learn about the culture, history and mythology of our ancestors, as well as possess a spiritual understanding of the Folk Faith. Since our religion is not based on faith, but knowledge, and does not rely on doctrine, it will be very important for the members of our religion to be educated, so that they will experience a personal understanding. This will include both an intellectual understanding as well as a spiritual transformation, by helping our members establish their personal links with the Gods through knowledge on how to harness and use the power of the Vril. This can be done by holding classes to train individuals in the methods of harnessing the power of the Vril, and then reinforcing this through public masses and ceremonies that should be held both on a weekly basis and during annual holidays.

The intellectual process of education (learning about the myths, history and culture of our people) will help to innoculate the essence of the values, ideas and myths of our ancestors into our way of thinking and behaving. In this way, they will become a part of us and have a transformative effect on our lives. But to merely intellectualize these things will fall far short of our goal. It is not enough to merely "learn" about these things, but it will be necessary to ritualize them. They survived the centuries because our ancestors ritualized them, imbedding them deep within our psyche. They have been encoded into our very beings, and we react to them without being conscious of it. A good example of this is the reaction by our people to the movie *Star Wars*. The creator, George Lucas, relied heavily on the Arthurian legends and other mythological sources from Western Culture. In fact, the "Force" is actually the Vril and the Jedi Knights can be considered the Knights of the Round Table, Obi-Wan is Merlin, Luke Skywalker is the young King Arthur or Parzival and so forth. People reacted instinctively because the archetypes in the movie spoke to our souls, reawakening their awareness of sacred truths that have been lost to our conscious minds, but which still lingered deep without our collective subconscious. Thus, to reawaken this sacred knowledge and cause it to manifest itself in our daily lives, both individually and collectively, so that it will survive us, into future generations that will form a new community, we need to make it part of our live—part of our real world. This can best be achieved by codifying this knowledge into a strict set of principles that will govern our lives, affecting our actions and directing the way we live, and thus, affecting the physical world around us. This must be the role of the priestly order—to ritualize this sacred knowledge in such a way as to incorporate it into the daily lives and the activities of our people so that their lives are transformed.

COMMUNICATING WITH THE GODS

I recently saw a show on the History Channel about the Oracle of Delphi in ancient Greece. This most holy of sites of the ancient Greek religion was located on the side of Mount Parnassus. It was considered by the Greeks to be the center of the world, known as the Navel of the World. A sacred stone known as the *omphalos* (navel) was located in the sanctuary. The stone was the one that was given to Cronus by Rhea, to swallow in place of the infant Zeus. A series of temples, a theater and a treasure house were constructed there in honor of Apollo, who conveyed oracular messages through a female medium. Apollo, like Balder and Frey, is a Sun God. Long before the Hellenist Greeks occupied Greece, this site was considered a holy site in which the Gods, especially Pan, communicated with mortals. In the Greek religion, it was believed that Apollo killed Python at Delphi and then underwent a purification at the site. Apollo claimed the site for his own. This site soon became the most venerated shrine for the Hellenist Greeks.

Throughout the centuries, thousands of people made pilgrimages to the site for the opportunity to present their questions to the Oracle. They sought advice from Apollo. The Oracle was almost always a female. Just as among the Norse, the Greeks believed women possessed what we moderns have come to refer to as "woman's intuition." The Oracle would sit in a small room, on a tripod, over a sacred chasm. She underwent a careful ritual of purification, and then fell into a trance and reveal the wisdom of Apollo. The person seeking advice from Apollo, first had to undergo a complex ritual that included presenting an offering of a scared cake, goat or sheep before consulting the Pythia (Oracle). The Oracle of Apollo was the supreme authority on religion, and only two other Gods were represented at Delphi, Dionysus and Athena. When Oracle spoke, her words were copied down by a group of priests. If Apollo's answer was negative, sometimes she would not speak at all. Other times her answers were confused or misleading. When Croesus, King of Lydia, consulted the Oracle when he was considering a campaign against Persia, he was told that if he went to war, he would destroy a great kingdom. He did. He destroyed his own kingdom.

The Oracle of Delphi continued to provide religious guidance to people even under the Romans, but it was eventually closed down in 385 A.D., by the Christian Emperor Theodosius. But the site had ceased to function before this date. When Emperor Julian, who tried to halt the spread of Christianity and restore the old pagan religion, asked Apollo if he would be successful in restoring the old pagan religious beliefs. He was given Apollo's answer. This was the last prophecy given at Delphi. Julian was told: "Tell the king this; the glorious temple has fallen in ruin; Apollo has no roof over his head; the bay leaves are silent, the prophetic springs and fountains are dead."

For centuries it was believed that the reason for the demise of Delphi was its termination by the Christian emperor, but recent archeological evidence has revealed that this was not the reason for the fall of Delphi. The History Channel presented a documentary on Delphi, which revealed that the chasm over which the Oracle sat and revealed the word of Apollo actually secreted toxic fumes, that when inhaled in small amounts, caused the person inhaling them to fall into a trance and suffer hallucinations. Delphi was situated directly on, not one fault line, but two that intersected exactly at the place where the Oracle sat. Chemical testing of the rocks at the site, provided evidence that an earthquake in 358 A.D. caused a geological shift that shut off the fumes, thus putting an end to Delphi.

Well, of course, the archeologists on the show tried to claim that there was a simple scientific reason why the Oracle fell into trances and thought Apollo spoke to her. It was the result of intoxication from the fumes. So there was nothing supernatural about the site, "yada, yada, yada."

As I wrote in *The Book of Balder Rising*, the Gods speak to us in many ways. One way they can speak to us is through meditation and another way is through dreams. They have even provided us with the Runes as a device to communicate with them. It is even possible that the Gods might appear to us, but there is another way the Gods speak to us. Remember. The Gods represent the forces of Nature. If they want to speak to us, they can do so through the use of the natural laws of the universe. This is exactly what Apollo did at Delphi. He created two fault lines that intersected at that spot, and caused the right combination of different fumes to emit from the chasm. He would speak to the Oracle through the inhalation of the fumes. It is interesting that a terrible earthquake struck the site during the years when the alien faith of Christianity was spreading throughout the Classical world, causing our ancestors to abandon the Gods. It was not the Christian emperor that closed down Delphi in 385 A.D., but Apollo who closed it down in 358 A.D., when the earthquake struck. His last message was to Emperor Julian in 360 A.D., warning him of the rise of a new age.

Our ancestors throughout ancient Europe communicated with the Gods through natural forces. Delphi was only one site, but there were many other sites. In the Baltic Sea, the island of Gotland was always considered to be a holy site where the Gods would communicate to us. In Sweden, Uppsala was the most important site in all Scandinavia. All across Europe, places like Stonehenge, Glastonbury, Cadbury Castle, Elsinore, Mount Alba, Harz Mountains, and hundreds of other sites, were holy sites where the Gods spoke to us, their children. Many of these sites were co-opted by Christianity, and used by the Church to build their churches and Cathedrals. But even today, we hear of Europeans who claim that some female spirit appears, usually at a sacred spring, and spoke to them. Modern-day people will interpret such sightings through their Christian understanding of the universe, and believe that it is the Virgin Mary who speaks to them. But in the past, our ancestors viewed these visitations as the Earth Mother speaking to us.

Just because Europeans have converted to Christianity, this did not spell the death of the Gods and Goddesses that their ancestors worshiped. We are who we are because these Gods, long ago, descended to earth and interbred with our ancestors, thus causing an evolutionary leap that created our race. They are our ancestors and we share the same flesh and blood, as well as the Life Force, with them. Because our people have prayed to Jesus instead of Balder or other pagan deities, it does not mean that the Gods are dead, but merely forgotten. They remain, patiently, waiting for the time when our people will remember their true names, and call to them, to awaken once more, so that they will live once again within our hearts and minds.

The Gods sleep within us, waiting for us to awaken them, and this can be done in several ways. First we can study the lore and myths of our ancestors, secondly, through meditation and Rune-chanting, and thirdly, through ritual and ceremony.

LOVE AND HATE

The Folk Faith is a religion of love, joy and happiness. I never tire of repeating this. It is destructive and counterproductive to dwell on hate and sadness. Life is short and we should spend as much of our lives enjoying it, and that means enjoying each other's company and the good things in life. We should celebrate life, because when we do, we are celebrating the Gods, and thus strengthening the bonds that unite us with them and with the universe. But we are not blinded by the fact that there are great destructive and malignant forces in the universe that seeks to inflict harm and suffering on us, and even destroy us. We do not advocate a false concept of love, which includes the love of a whipped dog, who cowers and begs at the feet of his oppressors.

We cannot love everyone and everything in this universe. It is ridiculous to love those who seek your destruction. To love someone who hates you, and wishes to do harm to you, is insane. Love is a quality that should be used with discrimination. Love those who love you! And hate those who hate you! Do not go seeking enemies, and try to make friends among all whom you associate, even among those who are alien, who do not belong to the Folk, or do not believe as we do. We can respect everyone, even if they are different. But if we are to survive, we must recognize that not everyone we meet in life feels as we do. Most will be indifferent to us, and some will be downright hostile and feel threatened by our very existence. It is best to waylay anyone's suspicions by being honest and forthright, showing respect to all as individuals, and treating everyone with the same respect that we expect from others. But if this does not work—be on your guard!

People always talk about a universal love as the foundation of a better society, but the truth is that universal love has never been a motivating force to build a society. There have been many movements claiming to be motivated by love for our fellow man, but they have all proven false. The reason is simple: to advocate the ideal of some form of universal love above all other emotions, is unnatural and impossible to accomplish. All "love movements" have turned toward killing those who disagree with them, or at best, hating those who disagree with them. Even the so-called Hippie movement of the 1960s, which advocated a universal love and peace, was filled with hatred for all who disagreed with them, and eventually turned to violence. We should avoid this false concept of universal love and seek to work at living a life of true love. Love should be something that we champion, while hate is something that we should rely on as a reaction to others' hatred toward us.

The Folk Faith does not claim that there are good and bad emotions. Everything depends on how it is used. Love is wonderful. Everyone knows this. To be surrounded by those who love you is wonderful. But to love those who hate you in insanity and will insure your eventual destruction. Do not waste your love, for anything that is used too often, eventually loses it value. Love those who love you, with all your heart, as strongly as you can, but never turn the other cheek toward those who hate you or wish to cause you harm.

There is a principle that we must remember in regards to love and hate. We attract what we obsess on. *Like attracts like!* You mind is constantly giving form and shape to the currents of Vril flowing into you, forming pathways to your future. Those pathways will be filled with what you obsess on. Therefore, it is important not to dwell on hatred. In the Church of Vrilology, we consider ourselves Mentalists. We work to develop the power of our minds to transform the world around us. Therefore, it is important to learn to master what your mind dwells on. If you are constantly angry, filled with bitterness, see enemies everywhere, then these things will manifest in your life. Therefore, it is important to learn to use both emotions, love and hate, properly.

First, it is important that you do not waste your love on those who hate you. Do not love those who will mistreat you and abuse you. Love only those who love you. But what is most important, LOVE YOURSELF! Love you and what you are. Once you do, you will discover that you WILL NOT HAVE TIME TO HATE ANYONE ELSE. Once you have developed the powers of your mind through Vrilology, you will discover that you will need not hate or fear anyone. You will have evolved into a new being, a Vril Being, who is impervious to the machinations of the mundane world of power, politics and economics. But it is difficult not to hate, so the Church of Vrilology has a ritual where we channel our hatred toward whatever, or whoever, wishes to harm us. This is *defensive hatred*. It is ritual where we ask the Gods to protect us from all harm. We ask the Gods to repel all negative energy directed toward us and send it back a hundredfold to its point of origin. In this way, we are not seeking to harm anyone, but rather seek protection against those who wish us harm, and reflect it back. The important thing to remember about this ritual is, even if we mention the name of an individual or group, if we are mistaken, and this person or group does not wish us harm, then no harm will come to them. The reason is simple. We are reflecting back, what is directed toward us. If no hatred is directed toward us, then there is nothing to reflect back toward them. Again. This is defensive hatred, designed to purge us from dwelling on negativity.

The universe is ruled by the Gods, constantly seeking to hold it together by holding back the forces of chaos (the Giants). It is this aspect of the universal law that ensures that the universe is grand paean of harmony. If it were not for the Gods, the universe would be chaos instead of order. If your thoughts are constructive instead of destructive, then you will be aligned with the Gods. You life will be harmonious and productive. But if you dwell on hating those whom you perceive as your enemies, or who are causing evil I the world, than you will be drawing their influence into your life. Your perception of what they are doing will be manifested in your life. You mind will create for you the very things you are struggling against. Charles Haanel wrote about the nature of hate by illustrating the lives of two very different great men: *The importance of this is well illustrated in the lives of Emerson and Carlyle. Emerson loved the good and his life was a symphony of peace and harmony, Carlyle hated and loaded the bad, and his life was a record of perpetual discord and inharmony. Here we have two grand men, each intent upon achieving the same ideal, but one makes use of constructive thought and is therefore in harmony with Natural Law, the other makes use of destructive thought and therefore brings upon himself discord of every kind and character.*

Haanel is demonstrating with this example that any persistent train of thought will *always* manifest itself in the character, health and circumstances of the individual. We all know that it is not easy to control your thoughts. But the first step in changing your mental habits is to exchange negative thought patterns for positive ones. So when you find yourself dwelling on what bothers you or up sets you, immediately change gears and try to think about the solution, instead of the problem. This takes us to the second principle.

The second principle follows the first. Once you have learned to purge yourself of negativity, you will live on a plane of existence outside the normal realm of typical human beings. This means, your mind will prevent you from loving those who might not truly love you, and prevent you from dwelling on hating those who do hate you. This will free you mental powers to concentrate on shaping your Wyrd (your future pathways) into whatever it is you want to be plentiful in your future.

The purpose of this methodology is to guard your self against the incursion of the destructive forces that can fill your life with chaos, much as Heimdall stands guard at the gates of Asgard. You must learn to cultivate this Heimdal Principle.

You must learn to guard yourself against the self-destructiveness of loving the wrong people and obsessing on hating your enemies. Know that the Gods dwell within you, but so do the Giants. Every time your thoughts linger on destructive obsessions, you are calling forth the Giants. You have opne the gates to Asgard and welcoming them in to cause destruction and havoc. And the destruction and havoc they are causing is within you! Each time, you must catch yourself and call on Heimdall, to close the gates and sound the mighty horn, warning you that chaos and destruction is approaching. Then turn your mind to constructive affirmation. Once you have learned to rely on Heimdall to help you control yourself, you will have discovered for yourself that the universe within you, your microcosm, is yours to control. And, once you have established yourself master of this domain, you will have become irresistible. All things within the macrocosm, the world around, will irresistibly respond to your every command.

The Folk Faith is not built upon some false doctrine, but on human nature. Thus, we recognize that as humans, we possess the power to both love and hate with a deep intensity. It is harmful and destructive to force yourself to try and love those who hate you. It is unnatural to love your enemies. Since the Folk Faith is a religion, based on what is natural, we consider it harmful to suppress what is natural. To love everyone only cheats your love toward those who deserve your love. You should release your hatred toward your enemies, and this can be done through ritual and ceremony. In this way, hatred will not corrupt the process of the creation of your Wyrd. You will not be a slave to destructive hatred or false love. Love and hatred are necessary to your well being, but you must learn how to gain control over your thoughts and emotions, so that you can use your mind to transform your life into a joyful journey through Midgard, by ensuring that your life is one that is aligned with the Gods. These rituals help you to cleanse yourself of your hatred and obsessions with your enemies, and release any pent-up hatred that will interfere with you appreciating those who deserve your love, and this includes the Gods.

SEVEN DEADLY SINS?

Christianity claims that the basic human desires are sinful. It names seven desires and refers to them as the seven deadly sins. They are, pride, greed, anger, envy, sloth, gluttony and lust. There was never such a concept as sin among pagans, and these seven desires were not necessarily considered sinful or even bad. In fact, to a pagan, these are just normal desires. Whether they are good or bad is determined by how we behavior and why.

Let us begin with greed. At first thought greed is wrong, and in some context it is, especially if one is willing to hurt his friends, family, neighbors and kin in the name of possessing great material possessions. The reason for this is simple—no man is an island onto himself. If we are to be happy and live a good life, a prosperous life, we need to be concerned with the community we live within. The welfare of the community, which means your neighbors, should be as important to you as your own individual welfare. This is also true of the welfare of your friends, family and kin.

Remember this Rune poem:
Fehru, rune of wealth, necessity to live,
a comfort when own, freely you should give it.
For when the time comes, to stand before Odin,
to judge you he will, by how you used your wealth.

The message here is clear. Seeking wealth and success is fine, but remember to share your wealth and success with your community. Seeking wealth is all very well and good, but what is just as important is how you used it to help those you love.

We are all ruled by an inner voice that motivates us on a subconscious level. It is the need to preserve our genetic make-up. Sociobiology claims that these inner voices are actually our DNA, or genes, speaking to us. And remember—the Gods dwell within us, within our DNA, within our genes. It is the first primordial need to pass on our genes to the next generation. This desire is firstly manifested in our own individual need to improve out material welfare. This usually takes the form of being successful and having the ability to buy a better home, clothing, food, means of transportation, supporting a family, the ability to entertain ourselves, to protect ourselves from enemies, the climate and so forth. Thus we want more and will seek the means to obtain more. This is fine, and there is nothing wrong with this desire. It is only when we will do anything to seek greater wealth, even if it means causing harm to the society we live in, to our family, friends and kin that this desire is wrong, because in the long term, we are causing harm to ourselves. By harming our environment or community, friends, family and kin, we are creating conditions that will manifest harmful conditions for the preservation of our genes and could even make our individual living condition worst.

What about pride? Sherlock Holmes once said that modesty is no virtue. If one is good at what one does, he should be proud of it and take credit for it. False modesty is just as wrong as false pride. Be proud of whom and what you are. Be proud of your ancestry, your ethnicity, of your individual worth, of your abilities, achievements, and success. Know your worth and proclaim it, but never forget that no matter how good you are at something, there is *always* someone smarter and better at it than you.

Then there is gluttony. Is there really anything wrong in the act of eating? We need to eat to survive. So what is wrong with that? All living things must fight for nourishment to survive and pass on their genes to the next generation. So there is nothing wrong with the desire to eat and drink, but if by gluttony we mean over indulgence, then there can be case to be made. The Folk Faith believes we should be healthy, both spiritually and physically. So we should eat in moderation for health reasons. If we eat too much, we will simply get fat and that is not healthy. And we should be careful about what we eat. There are no dietary restrictions in our faith, for that is nonsense. We are governed by the golden rule and that dictates that whatever we eat, we should do so in moderation, for too much of anything is bad or unhealthy for us. It is that simple.

Now let us look at anger. This is another one of those desires that could be a good or bad thing. If someone does us harm or threatens us, we should get angry. You would be a fool not too, and you would not live very long if you did not, because people would take advantage of you. But we should not let our anger control us. There is a saying: "Don't get mad—get even." What this means is, do not let your anger control you, and cause you to do something foolish. Instead, control your anger and plan your response, and defense, against letting those who seek to harm. It is often a very good idea to disguise your anger with stealth. Don't let those who seek to unnerve you see that you are angry. This will have two results: first, they will not have the satisfaction of "pissing you off," and secondly, they will not be expecting you to respond. They will be off their guard. But there is a warning concerning anger. Don't let it cause you to lose control and thus cause harm to those you love—to the very people you would never want to hurt. That is the greatest danger of uncontrolled anger. But anger under control is self preservation. The thing to realize is that we must remain in control of ourselves at all times.

Envy is not necessarily bad because it can motivate you to be more ambitious. So long as your envy doesn't turn into jealousy. To be envious enough to want to do as well as others is a perfectly normal reaction. Just don't be obsessed by this desire. Let it drive you to improve yourself, but never to cause you to harm others who might possess what you wish you possessed.

Lust is the sexual desire. The self-righteous religions will try and convince you that your basic sexual desire is somehow wrong. Nonsense! Without lust, there would be no reproduction. The Christian Church has created "Original Sin" to make us feel guilty about our sexual desires. But as with everything, certain sexual acts are wrong because they interfere with reproduction and could be detrimental to the perpetuation of our genes, and this is counter to the advancement, improvement and expansion of our Folk. But don't confuse the sexual act with lust. Lust, so long as it does not cause you to betray your family or lead you into wrong or harmful behavior, is perfectly normal. In fact, one should be lustful with those you love, especially with your mate. That will ensure a healthy relationship and marriage.

Finally there is sloth. Well, there really is very little to say to defend slothfulness, especially if we mean by it to be too lazy to defend or better yourself. We need to be responsible to ourselves, family, friends and kin, and to do what is necessary to survive. So if we are too lazy to live up to our responsibilities, yes, then sloth is wrong. But if we simply mean that we should spend time to "chill out," or simply to take a vacation or rest from the stress and grind of the everyday routine, then there is not only nothing wrong with it, but it is necessary to prevent a nervous breakdown.

If you read the "myths," whether they are Norse, Celtic, Greek or any other mythology, you will discover that the Gods are guilty of committing all seven of the deadly sins. Does that mean that the Gods are evil? Well, that was the logic of the monotheists, but the truth is there is no sin. The lessons we must take from the "myths" or tales, is how the Gods act and why. The tales are not to be taken literally. But they are man's attempts to explain the forces of nature and the laws that govern nature, which is the contest between order (the Gods) and chaos (the Giants). The truth is, our Gods act like us. They have human qualities, or should I say, we have Godly qualities, because we share the same Life Force (Vril) as the Gods—the same Life Force that fills the universe.

We have to ask ourselves: Does anybody really believe these urges are sinful? The answer is no. In the twentieth century there was a movement to humanize Christianity. In the Catholic Church, the Second Vatican Council set into motion reforms that stripped away the rituals, traditions and many of the beliefs that were part of Catholicism for centuries. It was claimed that these devices were borrowed from the old pagan religions, and this is true, but it was also the foundation upon which the faith was based. As I've said before, Christianity was successful because it "paganized" itself, adopting many of the traditions and rituals of the old pagan religions of Europe. But now, Christianity (both Catholicism and Protestantism), have begun humanizing their faiths so they can "keep up with the times." They have been secularized by what is referred to by many as "Liberation Theory," which is just another name for Marxism. Thus, Christianity, at least in the West, (though not in the Third World, where the reverse is happening) is being stripped of its spiritual essence—which was the essence of the old pagan religions. Christianity today, has more in common with humanism, than it does with religion.

We who belong to the Folk Faith are not advocating a *new* religion based on man's natural instincts, nature and science, but are seeking to reconnect with the old religion that was based on man's natural instincts, nature, and science. Let us face the fact that more and more people today do not believe in Christianity because they DO NOT PRACTICE IT. Come on! How many of you agree with the Vatican? How many of you practice birth control? How many of you agree with your church leaders (Protestant and Catholic), most of the time? Not very many, I'll wager. But most people are still AFRAID to come right out and say, "I am no longer a Christian." Well, at least in the United States. In Europe, people are more honest. Up to 70 and 80 percent of Europeans admit that they no longer belong to or believe in, Christianity. But in America, people are still afraid of "the wrath of God." Even though most people no longer believe in what their religion teaches, they are afraid to admit it to themselves, never mind to others. But I have to ask you to ask yourself, why do you continue to support a religion whose beliefs are contradictory to your beliefs? Why do you continue to support churches whose leaders are perverts, practicing and engaging in sexual behavior that you find abhorrent and sick? Why do you still belong to a church whose members are alien to you, and whose values are foreign to your values?

I know many Catholics who have trouble accepting the new mutliculturalism of the Catholic Church. They go to their local church and discover all the priests are from Africa, Asia and Latin America. They hear the clergy preach about the revolutionary struggle of the masses in Third World countries, and speak, not only with alien accents, but with an accent that is suspiciously common to that spoken in a "Gay Pride Day" parade. They know deep down that their religion no longer has their base interest at heart, but they FEAR admitting it to themselves. The reason for people to continue to belong to a religion that is harmful to them, their family and kin, their heritage and culture, is simple—they are practicing a GUILT-RIDDEN religion.

THE DEVIL AND HELL

It seems that only the Christian faith has a devil, which is called Satan, and he was created to frighten its followers into towing the line. Remember the Church Lady from Saturday Night Live? She would admonish her guest over something they did by asking them: "Oh, who could have made you do it? Could it ave been—SATAN!" The Muslims vaguely refer to the devil, but they use the term Satan to refer to earthly evils, such as referring to the United States as the "Great Satan." The Jews don't have a devil at all. In the Jewish faith, Satan is an angel sent by God to test man. The devil is a Christian invention, and the philosophical foundation for the belief in Old Nick is based on both Jewish Gnosticism (paganism), the Christian Old Testament and the Indo-European religion of Zoroastrianism of ancient Iran.

From the Old Testament, the Christians borrowed the Genesis story of Adam and Eve and the expulsion from paradise. The serpent, who the Christians associate with Satan or the Devil, tempted Adam and Eve to eat from the tree of knowledge, disobeying God's commandment and thus causing their expulsion from the Garden of Eden. We have already spoken about this tale. That it was created to keep people ignorant of their true Godly potential. Do not seek knowledge, for you will fall from bliss! But of course, as we all know—IGNORANCE IS BLISS! In the body of myths and tales that make up Jewish Gnostic teachings, which is based on ancient Semitic or Hebrew paganism, we learn of the tale of the "Angel Rebellion." This rebellion was led by God's favorite angel—Satan. He led a rebellion against God by the vast majority of angels. Satan was able to convince trillions of angels to rebel against God and a handful of loyal angels, but God being God—you know—all powerful, the Angel rebellion was doomed to fail from the very beginning. Hey! After all—God knew about it before he even created the universe. After all—he is God! All-knowing.

Finally, the Christians were influenced by the Zoroastrianism, which was a religion practiced in ancient Iran. The Iranians were Indo-Europeans, related to present-day Europeans. They believed that there were two equal forces at work in the universe—Good and Evil or Light and Darkness, which are actually the opposing forces of the Gods (order) and Giants (chaos). The two opposing forces were in conflict and all things were in the service of one or the other, including the different nations and races of mankind. In the end, there would be a final battle, but Good, or the Light, will win out. This is not too different from the tale of Ragnarok or the final battle between the Gods and the Titans in the ancient Greek pagan religion. We covered this subject in more detail in Part II of this book.

In the Jewish Old Testament, we can read of God calling all his "sons" together and among them was Satan. This makes one wonder if Satan and Jesus were brothers, just like Balder and Hoder?

The Christian Gnostics of the Middle Ages, known as the Cathars, believed that Jesus was never born in human form, but was a spiritual deity, a servant of the Light, and that the material world, which was created by Jehovah, is totally evil. Since the Bible refers to the Devil as the Master of the World, and since the world was created by Jehovah, the logical conclusion was simple—Jehovah and the Devil were one and the same. But the Church could never tolerated such heresy, and so unleashed a crusade to exterminate the Cathars. It was known as the Albigensian Crusade, in which a million people were killed in Europe.

The modern day version of the Devil or Satan, ruling over Hell, and tempting mortals to break God's laws and thus, damning themselves to eternal suffering in the fiery pits of his dark domain, has been used very successfully over the centuries to keep people in line. They created Satan and gave him a domain to rule—Hell. Hell was fashioned from pagan Netherworlds and referred to as Hell, taking the name of the Norse Netherworld—Hel, or the Greek Netherworld, Hades. From his dark domain, Satan tempts mankind to commit sin. The Christians are always warning each other about "Looking out for Satan, the Prince of Hell," or "Satan will lead you down the dark path," or "If you give in to the Devil's temptation, you'll be damned to burn in Hell for all eternity." This incarnation of the Devil as the tempter of man, evolved over time among the Christians.

The Devil was originally an angel whose duty was to report the transgression of man to God. In time, the Christian Church began to associate pagan deities with the Devil. He was associated with Dionysus or Pan, who was part Goat, the Roman God of Light, Lucifer (the Bringer of Light or knowledge as in the story about Adam and Eve) and the Norse God/Giant, Loki (the Trickster). He was made to look like a goat with hooves and horns, like Pan, who was also the God of Fertility and Fecundity, or it was claimed that he was a trickster like Loki, the God of Fire, who could look beautiful or handsome and change his form. "One never recognizes the devil as he places his arm around your shoulder." Does this not remind you of Loki, trying to fool the Gods into accepting his advice?

The early Christians worked hard to transform the Gods of their pagan ancestors into devils and demons. They claimed that the pagan rituals were actually "black magic," though the Christian Church employed the same rituals for their Christian Mass and ceremonies. They were transformed into devils, bogeymen, demons and witches, while the Christian Church co-oped the pagan rituals and ceremonies and created saints to replace the many different Gods. Odin's great hunt, was now referred to as the Grim Reaper, in search of victims. Freyja and her followers, were referred to as witches, who consorted with the Devil. The image of Pan, half goat and half man, the Greek God of fertility, was transformed into the Devil. The Devil has been visualized as looking like a goat, with horns and hoof-feet, who fornicates on the Black Sabbat with those who worship him. In the ancient Hebrew pagan religion, Satan was the Lord of Fire—a Fire God. In the Old Testament, he is referred to as a fallen angel and even as one of the sons of Gods. He is associated with Prometheus, the giver of fire or knowledge.

The truth of the matter is, "we don't need no stupid Devil!" As pagans, we realize that good and evil are in our actions. We are responsible for what we do, and not some supernatural boogeyman leading us astray. All our actions contribute to the forces that either give order to the universe or contribute to chaos and destruction. The life we lead will not only create conditions that we must suffer or enjoy in this life, but will be suffered or enjoyed in the next life.

LOVE LIFE!

LOVE LIFE! If there are only two words to describe the essence of the Folk Faith, it is these two words.

Life is a gift from the Gods. When the Holy Trinity first bred life into the ash and elm, and thus, created the first man and woman, the most precious gift that the Gods had bestowed upon us was life itself. This being the first and most important of all gifts, it is worthy of our most passionate love. It is the appreciation of life that separates us from all other living things. I am not talking about the instinct to survive, but the appreciation of the quality of life and all that it means.

You are 99 percent Vril. Vril is constantly flowing into you, replenishing your life. As these currents of Vril energy flow into you, your mind, through the thoughts and emotions that it manifest, is shaping these currents into pathways to your future. If you obsess on the belief that life is a struggle, then, life *will be* a struggle. But if you see life as a wonderful journey during your stay in Midgard, then your life *will be* wonderful! There is great power within your mind. You only have to learn how to harness it and use it to create the life you desire. But if you see life filled with enemies who are trying to hold you down, obstacles to overcome, and barriers to your desire to find happiness and success, then you mind will create these things and fill your future with them. If you believe that you have the power to fill your future with whatever you desire, and that there is nothing and no one that can hold you down, then you will have a life filled with joy, love, abundance and harmony. But for this to be so, *you must purge your thoughts of negativity and learn to love who you are, and the life you lead!*

Your life will never be free of struggle. It will never be free from those things that upset you, and can harm you. But! If you maintain the proper mind-set, you will have the power to conjure up whatever is necessary to lessen the struggle, reduce those things that upset you, and shield yourself from those things that can harm you. The Giants never give up trying to storm Asgard, but Heimdall is always on guard. You must develop a Heimdall mind set—increasing your personal luck, to protect you against all unforseen eventualities that can derail your journey through life. *But for this to be manifested, you must learn to love the life you are leading!*

If we love life then we are laying the foundation of a new Asgard on earth, and that's really what the New Age of Gimli is all about. We are assuring the rebirth of the Gods through the resurrection of Balder. It is our love of life, and our holding life to be precious, that is the force that will enable Balder to rise from the Netherworld, and ensure the return of the Gods. By loving life, we are recognizing that the Gods reside within us. By holding the gift of life high, we are saying that we know the worth that was passed down to us through the ages by our ancestors, and thus, we value that biological worth and will pass it onto our children and descendants. It is the act of living according to this understanding—appreciating the worth of our existence and thus loving life—we are honoring the Gods, and thus ensuring Balder's resurrection. In this way, the Gods and Goddesses will walk among us once more, here in Midgard. By living lives in which we celebrate our love of life, we are building a new rainbow bridge between Asgard and Midgard. By living a life in which we honor the gift of life, we are giving nourishment to the Gods.

The love of life is embodied in the Idun's Golden Apples. The secret of her apples is celebrating living with joy and happiness, honoring the Gods, and helping our kind and kindred. In this way we are truly building a new Asgard, the New Age of Gimli, within us. The act of living a life where we love ourselves, our heritage, our history and culture, our family and friends, our children and future, our Folk and the Gods, is the power that resides within the Golden Apples that gives everlasting life to our people. It will ensure our immortality in the next life. The way we live in this world will determine the way we live in the next. You make your own afterlife by the way you live in this life, so live a life of joy and happiness. In short—LOVE LIFE!

Now I am not preaching that we should become hippies and love everyone and everything, including our enemies who seek our destruction. I am not telling you to abandon your other emotions, including hate. It is good to hate your enemies, because if you love your enemies, you are then living a life of blind ignorance, which is the essence of Hoder, the blind God who killed Balder, his brother, through the trickery of Loki.

What I am telling you, is simple. Don't see the world filled with enemies. If you do, your mind will ensure your life will be filled with enemies. If you consider people whom you disagree with as you opponents, you mind will draw them into the future pathways of your life. When your thoughts are turned to things you hate, and people you despise, it is like you are calling these things and people up and asking them to come live with you. If you hate life, and constantly think about all the terrible things and horrible people in this world, you are lighting a candle in your window at night, as a beacon, calling on them to come and be a part of your life. You must purge the dark forces from your mind. If you do, you are ensuring that Hoder will never be able to strike you down. Know that Hoder's dart, the one he used to kill his beloved brother, Balder, was made from mistletoe. Mistletoe can be used as a love potion, but it can also be used to make a deadly poison. You have the choice. You can make sure that in your life, mistletoe will take the oath never to harm Balder, or you can overlook it, as Frigga did, and permit its poisons to strike you down.

It was through Hoder (blind ignorance) that Loki (destruction and chaos) was able to kill Balder (the Life-Force of our Folk). So we must be on our guard (Heimdall) at all times and seek the protection of Thor while we work and strive to build a new world—the New Age of Gimli—here in Midgard. This can be accomplished through the love of life (Balder) and by the love between a man and a woman (Frey and Freyja) the love of one's kind and family (Frigg) the love of justice and order (Tyr) and the love of wisdom and truth (Odin). Once you have learned to fill your life with love, you will know no enemies! For you will be untouchable!

THE NORNS AND OUR DESTINY

I have often been asked about the place of predestination and free will within the belief structure of the Folk Faith. Any discussion dealing with destiny and fate immediately brings us to the Norns and their place in the cosmological structure of the universe. They rule over the role that we, the Children of the Gods, play in the great scheme of life.

The Norns are female supernatural figures. The reason they are conceived as female is because of their nurturing nature. They weave the destiny of each individual. This creative force, like all creative forces in the universe, is female in nature. The male may initiate the creation of life through fertilization, but life is grown and develops within the womb of the female. The Norns' weaving process is like that of the embryo being nurtured and obtaining form within the woman's womb. It is giving life and determining the nature of all individuals. This means that they are associated with our DNA and genes. From our past we are formed, and what we inherit will give form to the life we lead and thus shape the future. Past, present and future are interconnected. It is the gene pool of our Folk. The Norns are both the spiritual force that constructs a road that we will journey down, as well as the physical link between our ancestors and descendants, from which we inherit the abilities needed to make the right decisions, persevere and achieve success.

Our genes speak to us, and they will influence us by shaping the way we react to situations that will arise. This happens on both the group level and the individual level. It is through our genes that the Gods communicate to us, and it is because of our genes and DNA that we might be chosen by the Gods for a special mission or task in life.

There are three primary Norns: Past, Present and Future (Urd, Verdandi and Skuld). They live by the well of Urd, but they are not the only Norns. There are other Norns as well, both benevolent and malevolent, who could enhance or reverse a person's fortunes. In fact, each of us has an individual Norn that guides us through our journey through life. This is the origin of the Christian concept of a guardian angel. The Norns are said to cut wood, which means that they carve the Runes that will control the life of each individual. At birth, the Norns visit each child as it is born and will cut Runes to determine the events that the child will face in its life as it grows and matures. Some of the Norns might find favor with the Elves while others are closely associated with the Dwarfs. This can determinate the nature of each child. This can also explain why some individuals excel at whatever they try and while others are constantly faced with defeat and disappointment. Some individuals will live lives of toil and hardship, while others experience charmed lives. The Greeks and Romans called the Norns the Fates, (the Roman word "fate" is derived from the Latin word "*fatum*," which means "prophecy," which is understood as a message of some form directly from the Gods) and the Romans had a Goddess that was native to Rome, named Fortuna. She was the Goddess of Luck, and if she smiled on you, you would experience good fortune throughout you life, but if she ignored you, bad fortune would follow you throughout your life. All our Indo-European ancestors believed in female forces that controlled the destiny of our lives.

The Greek Fates were the daughters of the Giant Night. The Norse Norns are also the daughters of a Giant. Mimir. The Greek name for Fortuna was Nemesis, and means "divine anger." They are a means by which the Gods punished mortals who transgressed the laws of the Gods (Nature's laws which give order to the universe). The Gods would send demons or demigods called as Erinyes, known by the Romans as Furies, to earth to punish and torment those who had alined themselves with the forces of chaos and disorder.

Odin knows what road that each of us will travel because he has surrendered an eye, so that he could drink from Mimir's well. He might choose us for a task, and it is up to each and every one of us to decide if we are worthy to carry out the task or overcome an obstacle, but we must prove ourselves worthy. The Norns might weave a road for us to travel, but we will have to make the decisions that will determine in what direction we will travel. The road they weave for us is not straight and direct, but has many crossroads along the way.

We all must face great decisions throughout our lives. I do not believe in chance or coincidence. Cause and effect govern the universe and our destinies. We are all at the mercy of the law of Karma or Wyrd. We cannot change our past, for what has taken place is carved in time. The present is in motion, but it is the result and subtotal of all that has taken place in the past. Everything that has happened and all that we experience affect our thoughts and emotions and cause us to make decisions that will affect the future. Thus, the future is laid out in a general way because of what took place in the past and the decisions we make in the present, based on what took place in the place. The Norns will place choices in the path that we take, but the decision we make whenever we are confronted with a choice is determined by our past experiences. This is what is referred to as Karma or Wyrd. The past, present and future are all linked together.

The Norns or Fates, are the great judges of mankind. They do not punish us for committing sin, for there is no sin, but there are two paths that we who live in Midgard can travel. One is a life according to the laws of Science and Nature. This is a life according to the natural laws that give order to the universe and thus, a life in the service of the Gods. This occurs when we align ourselves with the Gods. The other life is of self-destruction, chaos and disorder. It is a life that contributes to the destructive forces of the Giants. The Norns presents us choices in the paths we travel, and the decisions we make will determine the future choices that we must face. They are woven into the future course of the life that is laid out before us. This is not punishment, but the result of the choices we make in the present. As we travel through the present, we build up our past, which constantly reinforces the choices we make in the present, and will lead us into a certain direction that is the future. Once we have begun down one path, it is often difficult to change the nature of our destiny, but not impossible. Many people have epiphanies that are all-transforming experiences that will fundamentally change their lives, and the course they travel through life.

It is often a truth that the most difficult thing to do is to change the direction one travels through life. We perceive time as traveling in one direction, from the past into the future, and it might seem possible to make detours along the way that can transform one's life completely. The question that we must all ask ourselves is simple: Do we lead a life moving from chaos to order, or order toward chaos?

The course of our lives unfolding is the process known as Wyrd. Your Wyrd is the manifestation of the pathways you create for yourself. You mind has the power to control and shape the flow of Vril currents flowing into you. How your mind shapes these currents of Vrilic energy, is determined by what your mind dwells on. And what thoughts and emotions that your mind fixates on is the result of all your past experiences, which are stored in that part of your soul known as Orlog. Thus, your past is constantly influencing your present thoughts and emotions, which control how your mind works, which in turn, is constantly shaping Vril energy into pathways that will determine the course of your future life. This is the nature of Wyrd. It is also a process by which the Norns govern. But, you have to understand, that through Vrilology, you can learn to purge your Orlog of those obsessions that will negatively dominate your mind. By learning how to achieve this, you gain the power of controlling your future. This methodology is taught in the Yggdrasill Training Program, offered by the Church of Vrilology. Once you have mastered this methodology, you will be in communication with your individual Norn. You will then acquire to ability to influence your Norn to weave the future you so desire. You will become *the master of your own destiny!*

As I mentioned before, each of us has an individual Norn that weaves the path that we travel in life. As a child growing up in Catholic school, I remember the nuns telling us that each of us has a good guardian angel, as well as a bad angel. The former is constantly leading us down the straight and narrow path, while the other is trying to convince us to do evil. I even remember the nuns telling us to sit on the left side of our desk-seats to let the good guardian angel sit with us, because our good guardian angel is always on our right side.

Today there is a growing fascination with angels. The shelves of the local bookstores are filled with books about angels. Angel-lore tells us that angels are not cute, little creatures with wings, sweet faces and delicate features, but are often great warriors and fierce beings. They are usually represented as a combination of male and female features. Even fierce warrior-angels like Michael and Gabriele, are depicted with female-like features. The reason for this is simple. What our ancestors understood about the Norns was incorporated into the lore of angels.

The Norns are female entities, but they are also fierce. One should not seek direct contact with one's Norn without first mastering the methodology taught in Vrilology on how to control your Wyrd. The Norns are a powerful force and we should respect them and honor them, but to actually see one is a frightening experience. If you should see your Norn, it will be depicted as a terrible beast, and it will mean only one thing—danger! It could very well mean that you will soon die or suffer great harm. This is why it is important to become the master of our your destiny—to learn how to control your mind and use it to control the currents of Vrilic energy flowing into, as well as purging the negativity in your Orlog. All the adverse past experiences stored in your Orlog will conjure up a demonic Norn if you try and contact her without first purging your Orlog og the negativity. By flushing out your Orlog, you change its nature, and thus, the nature of your Norn.

Twenty years ago, when I was first involved in my study group, exploring the Norse religion, led by Robert Zoller, I had an interesting and frightening experience. Despite my being a part of his study group, I was still very much involved in politics, with all its aggression and hostility to the world around me. One night, I had a horrible nightmare. I was dreaming that I was swimming in a black ocean. I was under water and the water was black as pitch. I could see nothing, but I had a terrible sensation that some great danger was after me. I could not see it and all I could do was desperately tried to escape by swimming as fast as I could. I could not see the surface either, but I tried to swim in the direction that I thought was upward. As I struggled, I sensed that the danger that was following me was fast approaching, catching up to me. It was then that I look down, and behind me I saw a great white shark racing toward me with jaws open wide. I continued to struggle, desperately trying to reach the surface, but my efforts were futile. In seconds the huge jaws engulfed me and snapped closed about me. The next thing I knew, I was sitting upright in bed, covered with sweat and screaming. I woke my entire family that night, and I could not get back to sleep.

In the nights that followed, I continued to have nightmares about sharks, though nothing as terrible as what I experience that first night. Even today, twenty years later, I still fear having dreams about sharks. I have since developed the powers to ensure that my dreams are lucid so that I can consciously awaken myself from my dreams whenever I sense or fear that danger is approaching. The plus side to this is that I seldom have nightmares anymore. Now there is a point to this story, or two points to it.

First, exactly one year to the day I had that dream (which just happen to have been the Ives of March), I was crossing Park Avenue in New York City. It was night and it was raining and when I reached the corner, I did not want to try and cross the avenue on a red light, as some people were doing. So I waited for the light to turn green. The light changed and I proceeded to cross, making it half way across the avenue, to the island that runs down the center of Park Avenue. When I stepped off the island to finish crossing the street, being as careful as I could, not to step in the puddles because it was raining, I was suddenly engulfed by the headlights of a van that was turning onto the avenue. The van hit me straight on and I went flying fifteen feet through the air, landed on the asphalt and rolled until I finally came to a stop. As I laid there in the rain, I heard people rushing toward me. I opened my eyes and saw the driver getting out of his van, and without thinking, I tried to leap up, screaming bloody murder how I wanted to rip him apart. Everyone was startled at first by my incredible "resurrection." They must have thought I was seriously hurt from the collision and did not think I was able to move, let alone try and jump up. Well, they were eventually able to restrain me, and convinced me to remain still, as I could have internal injuries. When the ambulance finally arrived, I was still sitting on the wet street. The medics told me that I should not have gotten up and walked around. I told them I did not walk about and that I had landed right here. They looked where the van was, then at where I landed, and then at each other and could not believe that I was thrown so far without any visible injuries. Needless to say, I agreed to go to the hospital for x-rays. I was released later that night. Except for some minor pain in my right arm and knee, (I landed on them and rolled) I was completely uninjured.

It was not until I told my study group, several of weeks later, that they reminded me that it was exactly one year to the day when I had that terrible dream with the shark. After discussing the incident, we had come to the conclusion that the dream could have been a warning or premonition of some kind of danger that I would face one year later. Was it a test? A warning? Or could it be something more? We did not know for sure. But there is one other interesting aspect of this tale.

Seven years earlier, when I was attending school in Boston, I had gone to the beach during the summer. I was up to my chest in the water and the water was very crowded, when suddenly dead silence descended over everyone in the water. There, swimming among us was a shark. Its dark black fin was sailing through the water, moving in and out and around the people. No one moved and I remember being too frightened to move. The year was 1976, and I had just seen the movie *Jaws*. The shark was about twenty feet from me, but I could clearly see that it was about ten feet long, though everyone swore afterwards that it was a thirty-foot great white. Fortunately, the shark did not bother anyone. I felt that the shark was looking for me, and after it passed by me, it quickly swam out to sea once more. As soon as it departed, pandemonium swept over the beach and we all scrambled to get onto dry land once more. The life guard told everyone it was probably a harmless sand shark, but all anyone could say was that it reminded them of *Jaws*.

I have done a great deal of meditation on these experiences and I have come to the conclusion that my dream was some kind of warning from my Norn. The accident that I experienced a year later might have been some kind of ritualistic, transforming event that the Gods had conducted. Was it their way of causing a soul-transforming event (a death and resurrection ritualistic initiation of some kind) that would set me on a new course that would eventually cause me to write *The Book of Balder Rising*? I wonder? But one thing I am sure of is that the experience was powerful and is still as real to me today as if it happened yesterday.

RECIPROCITY

Let me relate to you a most remarkable series of events that have occurred when I had completed working on formatting *The Book of Balder Rising* for publication, with the help of Ralph Berger. Ralph had finally completed the editing of the manuscript in May 2003, and so, the project that I had been working on for the last ten years was finally finished. We hoped to have the book in print by the beginning of the year 2004. The twelve months preceding May had been a very difficult time for me. I almost lost my mother the previous September, and four people very close to me, passed away. I also wanted to move and found it very difficult finding a suitable piece of property. I was renting an apartment, and the building I lived in was deteriorating rapidly due to the delinquency of care by the new owners, and despite their delinquency, they were raising the rents by 20 percent. I needed to move, but rents were rising rapidly everywhere. I decided it was better to buy, but I could only afford a co-op or possibly a condominium in today's housing market. I had been looking for six months and found nothing worthwhile. There was a great deal of pressure and stress building in my life and I was in a black mood. But everything changed once the manuscript was finally completed.

In May, my sister discovered a house next door to her house was sale by owner. She immediately told me about it. It was a handyman special and thus, I was able to purchase it at well below the market price. I moved into it and began working on making the necessary renovations. I was now living close to my family, and could rely on them to be there if anything happened to my mother, and once again I was financially secured. My mother now had the entire family caring for her, and the stress has been eliminated. I consider the incident of the house becoming available just after the completion of the manuscript to be nothing less than a miracle.

I have since sold the house at a 40% profit and have purchased a new house (two-family) with my nephew. This second house was also a miracle house. I meditated and prayed for assistance on Columbus Day, using the methods described in this book on drawing on the Vril to help me. That night I had a most remarkable dream concerning my departed father. I found myself in the house I grew up in as a child. The house was the fulfillment of my father's libeling dream of owning his own house. My father was there and he told me that this was his heaven. This was the afterlife that he created for himself by his actions throughout his life and he was very happy. He then began relating to me in the vivid detail, incidents that happened to me when I was a child. I found myself crying from the emotional impact of the experience. He then reminded me that he used to give me a quarter every day for lunch. I used to buy a slice of pizza for 15 cents and a soda for 10 cents. It was a long time ago when prices had not yet suffered from the inflation that began in the seventies. He then told me not to worry because I would find the perfect house. Well, the next morning I woke feeling wonderful. I went to work and all day I kept thinking about the dream. In the afternoon, as I was returning home, I was passing the cemetery where my father was buried and decided to stop. At his grave I meditated and then thanked my father for his message. But before I left, I pulled out a quarter and asked my father to intervene and ask the Gods to help me as I buried the quarter in the earth above the grave. After I returned home, I received a call from a realtor. She wanted to come over and speak to me about a house that I might be interested in, so I invited her over. When she arrived, she explained that she had a house I might be interested in, and so we left to see it. I was amazed at the house. It was everything I was looking for and more. I had seen comparable houses and even smaller houses on the market for $665,000, and was sure I could not afford it. But when she told me the asking price was only $499,000, and that the owner would accept $475,000, I could not believe my ears. I immediately put in bid for $475,000 and it was accepted. Once again I had purchased a house at 60 percent of the market price within three years. Then, two days later, I found a buyer for my house at a reasonable price and made a huge profit. I have since moved into the new house with my nephew. I truly believe the Gods have rewarded me for my dedication and work in teaching others how to harness the power of the Vril.

An interesting side note to the house I believe my father found me from beyond the grave. The address number of the house was 184. 1+8+4=13. My father was born on Friday the 13, and he always considered 13 to be his lucky number. I was also reminded by my friend, Steve, that the date was October 12. October being the tenth month, 1+0=1, and the twelfth day of the month, 1+2=3. This added up to 13! Twenty years ago, I made a pledge with Freyja. I promised to write a book dedicated to the Gods. I spent all those years, meditating and studying. The inspiration that eventually came to me set me on the path of writing *The Book of Balder Rising*. I quickly made the book available to the public on the Internet, and soon afterward I was able to publish it in book form.

I truly believe that I have been rewarded by the Gods for fulfilling my part of the pack that I made with them. In the last year I have begun the work of building the Church of Vrilology, teaching others how to harness the power of the Vril so that they could make their lives better, and once again I feel I have been rewarded.

This is the nature of the relationship between the Gods and their children. In ancient times, when our ancestors practiced that "Old Time Religion," an individual would make a sacrifice to a God or Goddess. In doing so, he would promise to preform some deed in the name of the deity, in return for a favor. If the individual fulfilled his part of the bargain, he would be rewarded in some way. Twenty years ago, I had undergone a wondrous experience while under a trance. The group I was involved in had been meeting for several years. Our little group had forged a powerful link with the Goddess Freyja. On one occasion, we actually evoked the presence of the Goddess. On another occasion, while under a trance, I found myself on a ship, sailing an ocean of black waters and gleaming, golden icebergs. Freyja appeared to me, radiated and gold, and made certain promises if I would dedicate my life to the Gods. I agreed, and that was the beginning of my trek along a path that I have followed over the last twenty years.

I do believe my recent good fortune is the result of my fulfilling my part of the bargain I made with Freyja. I also believe that we, the children of the Gods, can reforge the lost bonds with the Gods of our ancestors. The Gods can once again play an important and *real* part in our individual lives, as well as the life of our Folk. This was the purpose of my first book, *The Book of Balder Rising* as well as this book.

THANKSGIVING

In America, we celebrate the holiday of Thanksgiving on the last Thursday of the month of November. Despite the politically correct interpretation that the Pilgrims were thanking the American aborigines, the truth was the Pilgrims were thanking God for helping them get through their first year, or winter, in the New World. The interesting fact about Thanksgiving is that it probably originally took place in the spring, after the winter months. But we celebrate it on the last Thursday of November—why? The custom of giving thanks was originally celebrated in Europe around the second to the last full moon of the yearly cycle. This usually fell around the end of November, or the beginning of December. People gave thanks for their harvest, and for the eventual return of the sun or the rebirth of Balder in Northern Europe. This is probably why, in America, we began celebrating the act of giving thanks to God at the end of November. And it's also why it is celebrated on Thursday, or Thor's Day. As we know, Thor is the Protector. He protects us from the destructive forces of the Giants, but he is also a fertility God so we give thanks to Thor for the bounty that he has provided. Giving thanks to our protector on his day, seems appropriate.

Our people have preserved, without realizing it, many of the customs of that "Old Time Religion." This has been done through what is referred to as, racial memories. Much of the knowledge of the old ways has been consciously repressed, but subconsciously, they continue to influence our actions and thoughts. When the early Christian Church waged a propaganda war on that "Old Time Religion," it deliberately incorporated many of the old customs and rituals into its new religion. Thus, the old pagan practices were preserved, though transformed into a Christian version, by the Christian Church. One example of this is the depiction of the Christian God as a powerfully built, old man with white hair and beard. This depiction of what God looks like, did not originate with the Hebrew Old Testament, but was taken from the statue of Zeus, that once reside in the Temple of Zeus at Olympia. The practice of transforming pagan customs into Christian customs went on for centuries until the Europeans forgot where the customs originated. And so, we moderns began celebrating

Thanksgiving at the end of November, and on a Thursday, without realizing its pagan origins.

We are living in a most wonderful time. Those of us, who have rediscovered the Gods of our ancestors, have been called to reestablish the bonds with the Gods who gave birth to our Folk. We should give thanks for this most wonderful gift—the gift of knowing the truth. But we should also give thanks for our family, friends and kindred. We should give thanks for our good fortune, and surviving those hardships that we must all face in the great journey of life. Giving thanks is important, for it reminds us of the links we share with our Gods and Folk. And there is no reason why we cannot continue this most wonderful, modern holiday, and give thanks to the Gods, especially Odin, for sacrificing his son Balder, to Thor for his protection and bounty, and prepare ourselves for the rebirth of Balder at Yule Time, on Thanksgiving Day. Like the Pilgrims that settled in the New World, we too are pilgrims, the New Pilgrims, setting out to build a new world. This new world is actually Gimli, and it will be a new age, one in which the guiding spirit will be Balder, whose spirit will facilitate the return of the Gods and Goddesses of our people.

LIFE AFTER DEATH

There are two things that are unavoidable in life, death and taxes, so the saying goes. Well, we are going to now talk about the latter, death. Death is inevitable. We are all going to die someday. We don't like to think about dying, especially in this modern age, where religion has lost its luster and we no longer think about the hereafter. We prefer to concentrate on thinking about the here-and-now. I am often asked about the hereafter and the here-and-now. Why are we here? What happens after death?

In other religions, especially the monotheist religions, but not exclusively, we are told that we are here to be tested, and when we die, we are judged. If you believe this, you will live a life of fear and suffering, beyond the suffering that is the natural part of life, for life is a struggle (though, through Vrilology, we can avoid this struggle) and there is plenty of pain involved, and we do not have to go looking for more pain and suffering. But we are told we must deny ourselves many of the good things in life if we are to get into heaven/paradise after we die. For when we leave this earthly existence, we will stand before our Maker, and he will judge us. A great scorecard will be pulled out and the number of good things we did and the number of sins we committed will be tallied. But it only takes one sin to condemn us to eternal suffering. This means that we could live an exemplary life right up to the time we die, and then if we commit even one sin—wam!—eternal damnation. We are sent to Hell, though the Catholics give us a way out. They divide sin into mortal and venal. If we only commit the latter, we will be sent to Purgatory for a while before we are eventually sent onto Heaven. Of course, Muslims never go to Hell, or stay there for eternity. They stay there is like that of Purgatory. Only non-Muslims go to Hell, and, oh yes, women. Even Muslim women. Other religions claim that all we have to do is ask forgiveness before we die and we can then go straight to Heaven—that is if we don't die suddenly in a car crash or get shot.

Some of the eastern religions claim that you must be good, for you will be returned to this world through the process of reincarnation. They speak of karma, which is also a scorecard of a sort. Everything you do is recorded and after you die, you will be judged on how well you did. If you did well, you will be reincarnated into an elevated state, but if you did poorly, you could return as a worm or slug. But one must ask—what is a good life? For the eastern religions, the good life is DENIAL! You must abandon all desires, needs, wants, pleasures, hope, and everything that make life enjoyable. As Charlie Brown in the *Peanuts* comic strip would say, "Uggh!" Who wants to live like that?

In all these religions, they accept the fact that life is hard, but they welcome it and encourage you to surrender to the suffering and pain, and then offer you hope that if you do, you will enjoy everlasting joy and happiness in the afterlife. The Muslims even claim that if you commit suicide in the fight for Islam, you will live in paradise in the next life, with ninety-two (not ninety-one or ninety-three) virgins for you to deflower at your leisure. There will even be dozens of little boys for you to deflower. Double uggh! They never explain what the women who die in the name of Islam will receive. But then, very few women go to Heaven according to Islam. Hey! People actually believe this. But their lives are so miserable that they will believe anything if they are told they will enjoy paradise for eternity in the afterlife. It offers them a small ray of hope in their otherwise miserable existence.

Our pagan ancestors believed that the life you lead on earth will manifest itself in the next life. No one is perfect, and so there is no need for sin. There is also no need for punishment, because there is no tyrannical God waiting to judge you. When you die, you go before the Gods and they review your life at the Well of Urd. If you lived a virtuous life, you will go on to Odainsaker, that region of the netherworld ruled over by Balder. It is place of bliss. Those who are gathered there are destined to be reborn and perhaps through the life stream of their future ancestors. The rest, are assigned to oblivion. Of course, there are those exceptional souls who die a heroic death. It was believed that those who died in battle were chosen by the Valkyries and taken to Asgard. Half were taken by Freyja and the rest were sent to Valhalla. They joined the ranks of the Einherjar, who ride out to battle with Odin during Ragnarok.

My own understanding of this process from my own meditation is this. The Valkyries don't just take the souls of those who fall in battle. This is metaphor of all who live a heroic life. Some heroes do battle with ideas and fight for justice and against the suffocating vale of ignorance. Other do combat defending their Folk, nation, family and kin. All heroes are chosen by the Valkyries, led by Freyja. Once in Asgard, Freyja, as the Queen of Seither, takes those individual souls who possess a certain spirit that can move men and women to enlightenment, and assure the re-forging of the old bonds between the Gods and their children in Midgard, go with Freyja to Seerumnir, where they are evolved into higher spiritual beings that guide the destiny of the Folk. Others, who cannot rise above the day-to-day struggle of the mundane existence of this world, but are virtuous soul none-the-less, go to Valhalla. They ride out with Odin, only to be destroyed in the struggle with the Giants. I see these individuals as those who cannot detatch themselves from the earthly struggles of our mundane universe, while those who are chosen by Freyja, are the individuals who are destined to teach Vrilology (Odinsim, Asatru, etc ...) among our people today.

THE INDIVIDUAL AND COLLECTIVE SOUL

Our idea of the soul has been shaped by Christianity. We have come to believe that we have a spiritual entity living within the physical body, which is a non tangible copy of the physical body that will separate from if after death, and float away. But the actual concept of the soul that our pagan ancestors conceived and understood was more complicated then this simple expression of the afterlife. The soul is also referred to as the "Shade" of a person, and the equivalent to the "Shadow" described by Carl Jung, which contains the subliminal aspects of the psyche. We have to understand first that the soul is made up of many parts and that it is not separate from, but a part of a greater collective, racial soul.

In Norse cosmology, the various "parts" that make up the human soul include the following:
1) The Self
2) The Lyke (physical body)
3) The Aura (the etheric body, hamr, or energy blueprint of the body)
4) The Hyde (ghost)
5) The Hugh (thought)
6) The Myne (memory)
7) Ond or Athem (vital breath)
8) The Wode (inspiration and motivation)
9) The Hamingja (personal luck)
10) The Fetch

Let us take a look at and describe the many parts that make up your individual soul. In the very heart of your soul is the part that is the deepest, inner part of you. This is the *self*. It contains the most mysterious aspects of who you are. It is the seat of your personality. It grows and becomes strong throughout your life, feeding on all your experiences and knowledge that you have acquired. It serves as a construct to bind all the other components of the Soul together in a synchronized order. It is often referred to as the Ego, or I-consciousness. The Self will evolve and grow with experience you undergo during your life.

The next aspect of your soul is actually the physical *lyke* (the physical body also referred to as lich). Within the body all aspects of the soul are fused. This is the vehicle by which we experience the universe that surrounds us, and we can direct our wills to affect the objective world. It is important to understand the relationship of the body to the soul. Most traditions seat the body as a vehicle in which the soul resides. The truth is very different. The body is actually within the soul, for the physical form is encased in that part of your soul that is your aura. This etherical field extends beyond your physical form. The body, or lyke, is the means by which you interact with the world around in Midgard.

This energy bubble surrounds you is your *aura*, and this is why we say that your body exists within your soul. It is the faculty which enables you to feel or sense the universe about. It is the means which your "sixth sense" work, like radar senses. You can perceive the feelings and thoughts of those around. This is your etheric field and function on a psychic plane of existence.

The next important part of the soul is the *hyde*, also known as the ghost, is the plasmic quasi-material aura that we might consider to be what the soul is, according to a Christian interpretation. This is the ghost that lingers on, half in this world and half in the next, when someone dies.

The *hugh* is also known as thought and is our intellectual, logical and analytical part of the soul. It lies within the left side of the brain. It is the seat of the analytical nature of the brain. Thought in personified by Odin's raven, Huginn.

Next is *myne*, also known as memory, which is personified by Odin's other raven, Muninn. This is the sum total of our personal, collective and racial memories and is located in the right side of the brain. It is the seat of our psychic powers. It is from this part of the brain that we receive our intuitive abilities.

Ond or *Athem* keeps the entire body and soul fed with vril energy. It is the breath of life that draws on Vril energy currents and challenges them into different parts of the soul, of which the physical body is a part.

The *wode*, is inspiration is a fundamental aspect of Odin's Life Force. This is motivation. Odin gave us inspiration and it is a vehicle by which we can grow and evolve. By exercising this part of our soul, we can achieve altered states of consciousness.

Next is the *hamingja*. This is the seat of your personal luck. It is here that Vril energy is transform into Megin, which is a form of energy that gives you luck or charisma. We will have to examine this aspect of your soul further.

Lastly is the *fetch*. This is the house of your spirit is an entity, both separate and attached to the individual. The Gods communicate to us through the spirit. This is what we call having a "spiritual experience." It is the totality of everything that we have become. All our experiences, and everything that makes us what we are, are stored within the spirit. The spirit of whom, and what we are, will determine our afterlife. This is the most complex aspect of the soul. We will talk about this in more detail later.

So we can see that the soul is more complex than is understood by what we have been taught. It is not just what is left over after we die. It is not just the consciousness that leaves or is detached from the physical body after death, and either goes on to spend all eternity in heaven or hell. The soul is made up of several entities or parts that each has a specific role to play in the great cosmic order of things. After one dies, the soul, especially those parts that make up thought and the ghost, will go on to the next life. It is the spirit, or fetch, which is important when dealing with the subject or rebirth, or as it is more commonly referred to "reincarnation." This does not mean you will be reborn in another form, but that part of you will be reborn in another person or persons and your spirit will affect that person or persons. When people claim they remember "past lives," they are not remembering their past life, but memories of the collective unconscious that is part of the collective or racial soul.

When you die, your spirit (fetch) can pass from you to another. Other parts of the soul might have different destinies. For instance, if you are buried, your ghost might linger within this world and refuse to go on to the next life. Normally, the ghost and thought will journey to the next life in Hel, or to either Valhalla with Odin, or in Sessrumir with Freyja. Both thought and the ghost will be released if the body is burned after death, but the spirit will live on after death and find a new home or host. This could be described as a form of reincarnation, but I do not want to confuse this with "Eastern" ideas of reincarnation. The eastern notion of reincarnation is that the spirit or soul, in this life, living on after death in another earthly form, inhabiting another body. Who and what that body will be, will be determined by the life experiences of the spirit or soul in the previous life. It will be a form of judgement. This of course is nonsense. When you die, you go on to the next life. What the nature of your afterlife will be, will be determined by how you lived in this life, but something of you—your spirit—will live on to affect those who come after you. It is not your personal consciousness or memories, that will be reincarnated, but your spirit, the essence of whom you are, that will remain in Midgard. But it will not go flying off to some other part of the world to be reborn as an African, Chinese or some other race. Your spirit will linger close to home and be drawn to your own DNA. The transferences of the spirit will be genetic. This aspect is known as the kin-fetch. It is rooted in your ancestral stream. Part of your soul, becomes part of your children's souls, and everyone who is genetically linked to you. This includes everyone within your extended family and race. It will affect someone else who is born with a genetic link to you. It could actually affect more than one person. But the link is always genetic. The genetic relationship could be close or distant, but always the link will be through the DNA.

Within the spirit or fetch, you have a psycho-spiritual construct that has three aspects or natures. Again, the trinity. The first nature is human. It will appear to you as a human form of the opposite gender. If you are a woman, it will appear to be male. If you are a man, it will appear to you as female. The second nature is geometric. But the third nature is the most important. This is your animal totem. It will appear as an animal of some kind and you can call of it, even give it a name, to help you in your astral travels to other realms, to other worlds that make up the Yggdrasill, and even in remote viewing.

The fetch or spirit is attached to you for the duration of your life, and within it is your Orlog. Here, all you past individual experiences are stored. Those experiences that you inherit from your ancestors will also be stored within the Orlog. This past experiences, which you inherit from your ancestors, are the images you remember, when you think you are seeing images of your past lives. It is here that you are connected to your collective unconscious, through the kin fetch.

There are plenty of tales about how people describe one of their children to be the "spitting image" of a dead relative or ancestor, not just physically, but in their personality and interests. This is because the spirit of that ancestor lives on in the child. There is a spiritual link and it will attach the child to the life experiences of the departed relative or ancestor. This does not mean the child is the reincarnation of the ancestor. The child will always be born with its own unique and individual thought, ghost and Bifrost Gland, but just as each child is born with something of the genetic or physical attributes of its parents, and other ancestors, so too the child is born with the spiritual essence of its ancestors, untied through the bloodline in both the body and spirit. This is part of what we refer to as the collective unconscious or the collective and racial soul.

Let us turn to the matter of the hamingja. This is the seat of your personal luck, or should we say, "Luck." Here, your soul is constantly transforming Vril energy into Megin (your personal luck). Thus, the hamingja is a store house of Luck that you can draw on, to make things happen in the world around. The hamingja is an integral part of your aura, and through it, it can send out pathways that will bring to you what you desire most. The amount of Luck that the hamingja can store is dependent on its strength. Some people are "naturally lucky." The reason is their hamingja is powerful and can convert huge amounts of Vril into Megin. This is why the Romans believed some people were "Fortune's favorite." It is also the source for the term, "the luck of the Irish." The four-leaf clover is a lucky charm because it has four leaves, represent the four corners of the world (north, east, south and west) and it is drawing in luck from all directions. You can consciously increase your capacity to draw in greater amounts of Vril and transform it into Megin by using the Runes: Fehu, Uruz and Elhaz. Elhaz is especially important in increasing the strength of your hamingja, and Fehu is useful in also sending it. We cover this ability to constantly build-up your supply of this vital energy in our Yggdrasill Training Program in great detail.

Each race has its own soul, with the individual parts that make up the individual souls. Every race has a collective spirit, collective memories, collective thoughts, collective inspiration, collective body (DNA), and a collective ghost which together, make up the collective soul of the race or Folk. This collective soul will make itself felt on the stage of history. We can learn from history that empires rise and fall. Governments come and go. But a nation or race can only disappear if it is physically destroyed. It can be oppressed, held down, but eventually, given the opportunity, it will reassert itself. This is the result of the collective soul that unites individuals spiritually. We know that this is true, research has shown that a person's brain, which contains collective and individual racial memories and thoughts, will be drawn to faces that are close in appearance to its own. People are instinctively drawn to other people who resemble themselves both physically and spiritually. Only people with warped souls will be drawn to others who are very alien to themselves. This can happen as a result to socialization, just as dogs and other animals will bond with humans from birth. And just as dogs and other animals can be warped spiritually, so too can humans. By living within a multi-cultural empire, our souls become warped. Individually, we are lost. When those bonds that join us with our family, kind and kindred are broken or severed, we are set adrift in a sea of confusion. Thus, we cannot hear the Gods when they speak to us. We become slaves to confusion and chaos—the Giants!

THE LIFE YOU LEAD, WILL ECHOS IN ETERNITY!

As I said before, death is inevitable. We all know that we are going to be claimed by the Grim Reaper someday, but still we cling to life whenever possible. It is instinctual for all living things to fight to stay alive, even under the most appalling conditions. It is only when someone or something realizes that they are too ill or injured to hope for continual survival that an animal or person gives up. The urge to survive is genetic. It is written into the DNA of all living things to want to live, so that we can pass down our particular set of genes to the next generation. I believe that the will to live ceases when the amount of Vril energy entering our body decreases to a certain level. But there comes a time for us to surrender to death's embrace. Throughout the ages, people have always wondered what lies beyond this life, and what awaits them in the afterlife.

Most religions like to claim that death is some great spiritual awakening. They speak of this life as a preparation for the next life. This is true of almost every religion, except for Judaism, which has a healthy respect for living well in this life. Jewish people are taught that they should seek success in this life. They are taught to fight and work for the maximum fulfillment of their potential in this life. The Calvinist Protestant religion and the Mormons also believe this to a degree. The former believes in predestination, and thus believes that God, who is all-knowing, knows who will be successful in this life even before they are born, and thus conclude that our lives are predestined for us, and so, success in this life is God's way of letting us know who is chosen and not chosen in the next life. Jews on the other hand, simply don't believe in the afterlife. They believe that after someone dies, he goes into a state of sleep until the day of resurrection. If you lived a righteous life (life according to God's laws) then you will be resurrected when the Messiah comes and sets up the new order of eternal bliss and paradise on earth.

Of course, it is natural for all of us to fear death, especially if we led a healthy, happy life. Who wants to give up happiness for the unknown? Some people dread dying because they dread the unknown, while others look forward to death as a great release from the daily struggle of this life. These people often lead a life of suffering and toil. The Eastern faiths more often then not hold this belief. The East disciplines itself against a conscious desire for betterment in this life, believing that all desire and want is the cause of suffering. They teach that by suspending your natural instincts for advancement, success and even survival, you will be free of want and suffering. If you can accomplish this in this life, you will become one with some "Great Universalist Awareness," and thus no longer be reincarnated into another life, and thus be at peace with yourself and the universe.

This belief in reincarnation is a way to provide hope for the vast majority of people who suffer in poverty and under oppression that if they lead a righteous life in this life, they will advance to a higher state of existence in the next. But if a higher state of existence in the next life is one of material possession, then will they not be moving away from full rejection of want and desire, and thus move further away from complete fulfillment, and achieve the blissful state of becoming one with the "Great Universal Awareness?" Also, doesn't anyone ever wonder that if their ancestors, who could be themselves in previous incarnations, had lived good lives in the past, then why is it they were born into poverty and suffering? And if you need to abandon and reject all material possessions for the fulfillment of a state of denial to achieve this blissful state of existence after death, should not upward reincarnation be one of progressive poverty, and not one of increased wealth and possessions? Thus, the untouchables, who hold the lowliness place in the social stratum of Eastern societies, should hold the loftiest.

This rejection of our natural instincts and desires seems to predominate among those societies where material advancement is difficult to achieve. Thus, the religions of these regions try to convince people to willingly accept their miserable existence. This is a way in which those who are powerful and successful can continue to rule the great majority of those who are poor and oppressed. They can actually convince the great majority of the poor that those who rule them will suffer because of their wealth and power and thus encourage the majority of people under their dominance, and that it is terrible to strive for success. Thus, they teach that it is wrong to take pride in yourself, your accomplishments and success in this life.

Unlike most religions which advocate modesty and humbleness, our faith encourages the individual to be proud of his or her accomplishments. One must seek success in life, and no one should be ashamed of their success. The best way to celebrate the Gods is to shine in their examples. By accomplishing great things in their name, we increase and strengthen the bonds we forge with them as individuals and collectively as a community. We want our people to strive with all their ability and determination, in everything they do, and we should encourage it in our children. It is important for us to build up our self-esteem. If our sense of identity is great, then no one can keep us down. By doing great things in life and being proud of them, we strengthen our self-worth and thus, the power that dwells within us. That power is the same Life Force that we share with the Gods, and thus, we strengthen the bond we share with the Gods.

Other religions seek to destroy or weaken the sense of self-worth of the individual so that they can inflate the sense of power and sense of wonder and astonishment of their God, making those who are members of the religion feel inferior and insignificant compared to the God they worship. Not the Folk Faith. Our religion seeks nothing less than the creation of a new race of God-Men in this world. To accomplish this, we need to increase the sense of self-worth and develop a strong sense of self-respect, among our people, which is vital for success in life.

Part of this success is in the passing on of our genes to the next generation. This enhances our Life Force, and the more children we have, the greater in that Life Force. We are connected to the Life Force by the biological bonds we share with other living being. Since the Gods reside within us, within our DNA, within our atoms, that is the essence of whom we are, and who the Gods are, the greater the increase and expansion of our biological community, the greater is our spiritual force. We are all connected and thus, share a collective soul or racial soul, as well as an individual soul. This collective soul is also shared with our Gods. Thus, by reproducing in great numbers, by forging those bonds with our Gods through ritual and ceremony, by working to build a strong and healthy community in the communion with our Gods, we are strengthening the spiritual power of our souls, and ensuring that we will live on in the next life in an exalted state.

We understand that by our actions in this life, we are creating the existence that we will enter into, in the afterlife. "The life you lead, will echo in eternity." Thus, if an individual spends his or her life living it to the fullest, filled with joy in trying to accomplish great feats, filling their lives with joy, happiness and love, and trying to extend these virtues to everyone they come into contact with, their spirit will refuse to die once the body has expired. The vitality in this life will live on after he or she dies. Our souls will be great souls and will be housed in a great place in the next life. The belief that most people who die will enter the Netherworld known by the Norse as Hel, or by the Greeks as Hades, does not mean that the afterlife is dark and cold, and devoid of light, joy and bliss. There is no Heaven or Hell, which are places inhabited by the good or wicked after they are judged by God. Your place in the afterlife, and its nature, is determined by the life you lead in this earthly existence. Through ritual and ceremony we can enhance the vitality of our spirit in this life. This can also be accomplished through doing great feats and deeds. Be bold in every thing you do. Walk with pride in the accomplishments that you have done, and never be humble. False modesty is just as terrible as the fault of false pride. Know your worth and try and increase it. By living life to the fullest, by accomplishing great deeds, by working and contributing to the growth and advancement of the Folk, by filling your heart with joy and harmony, by refusing to surrender and by performing ritual and ceremony designed to strengthen the bonds we share with the Gods, we are increasing the power of the Life Force that fills us, and thus increasing the spiritual power that we possess. This power will live on beyond our earthly life and will ensure an honored place in the next life, either in an exalted realm in the Netherworld, or by one being permitted to reside either in Odin's hall of Valhalla, or in Freyja's hall of Sessrumnir.

WE ARE A LIGHT AGAINST THE APPROACHING DARKNESS

We can see the approaching winter and we know that we must stand fast and be a beacon against the terrible darkness that is about to sweep over our world.

We can see that our leaders and governments have been inflicted with the blind ignorance that is Hoder—the Blind God of Darkness. We can see that our people have fallen under the spell of Hoder's ignorance and are blinded to the truths that have guided our ancestors for thousands of years. We know that they are now prey to the Trickster, Loki, who will lead the forces of chaos and destruction, that will sweep over the world and level all that we know. Therefore, we raise our voices in this age of decline. To the East, North, West and South, we call to our people, calling on them to abandon the weakness that has invaded our minds, hearts and souls, and proclaim our rebirth!

Open your mind and reject the ignorance that has blinded us to our true identity. Reject Hoder and all that he stands for, and ready your self to live a life filled with the love and beauty that is Balder. Open your eyes so that you might see, listen and learn of the truth that will drive away the darkness that has clouded your mind, and let the light that is Balder, the same light that is the Life Force of our Folk (Vril) and the Gods who created us, and fills your heart, mind and soul.

We challenge the wisdom of the waning age—the age of chaos and decline.

We demand reasons for the false rationale and ideology of the present age, that demands submission and suicide, and instead, we are governed by the laws of nature, of growth and development that leads us on the road to strength and greatness.

Never will we prostrate ourselves on our knees, or on the ground, groveling before alien Gods and false ideologies. For no God would ever demand that we humiliate ourselves before him. Instead, we stand up right, with arms outstretched, calling on the Gods—on Odin, Vile and Ve, who gave order to the universe, who created the physical laws that govern all things—to hear us, for we are great and proud, not humble and meek.

No false doctrines, created by the mind of man and written by the hand of man, shall enslave our hearts, minds and souls. No false dogmas shall stifle our lives and make us slaves to false morality—the morality of the weak. Though we seek strength, we seek to harm no one. Our strength is to be used inward, to help us be better individuals, to build better communities and better lives for ourselves and our children. Though we are proud of our heritage, our ancestors and Folk, we do not hate other heritages, cultures or races. Though we seek no enemies and wish no one harm, nor do we desire to sacrifice the well being of our own kind to help those who do not belong, but instead, we work together, united as one Folk, in the Church of Vrilology, with our Gods, and march along the path that leads to success and happiness.

We stand fast—holding high the standard of the strong and great.

Doctrines describing right and wrong, good and evil, were invented to created confusion and chaos, as weapons to knock open the gates of Asgard, and destroy the Life Force that gave us life and gives us hope for the future.

Creeds that declare they are built upon divine law are false and immaterial. No dogma written by the hand of man must be taken as divine. Spiritual truth shines from within our souls, not from the pages of a book or the mouths of false prophets. The truth of the universe lies within the natural laws, which were created by the Holy Trinity when they slew Ymir and fashioned order from his chaos.

We do not *believe* in God, or the Gods, because a book tells us to believe. We *know* that our Gods are real, for we have searched within ourselves, and have discovered them within us. We have felt their power in us and have learned to harness it and it has transformed us.

Though the world changes, and ages come and go, our collective soul, which shines with the Life Force we share with the Gods, that gave life to us, continues to shine, even when we are blinded by ignorance. We have only to open our eyes to let that light fill our minds and hearts with its joy and happiness. We refuse to permit false doctrine to blind us to the truths that holds the universe together and keeps chaos from destroying us. Whatever has been proven false, we reject and discard, flinging it into the void of darkness of false doctrines and philosophies.

The most dangerous lie is the belief based on faith. It leads all who follow it down the path to destruction, like sheep to the slaughter. We seek knowledge and truth, and that can only be found from within our hearts, souls and minds. It can only be found by looking inwards, seeking out the Gods that dwell within us and touching them.

"Love your enemies" is a poison that has been injected into our hearts and minds by our enemies. We love ourselves, our friends, family, kin and kindred, who love us back. We reject all who hate us, and all who reject us, though we seek no harm to any who wish us no harm. We seek to live in love and happiness, and to do so, we must live and work among those who love us. We seek to harm no one, but will never submit to others who might seek to harm us. We know that so long as we keep burning the flame of love, joy and harmony within our hearts, no enemy will hurt us, and thus we will not need to hate anyone, nor will we have the need to hurt anyone.

It is unnatural to expect the victim, who has been brutalized, oppressed and persecuted, to love those who have sought to destroy him.

Seek not to make enemies where none exist, but neither should we roll over and permit those who hate us to destroy us. We love all, even those who are not of the Folk or agree with us, so long as they do not wish us harm. Do not let hate govern your actions and your lives, but do not let false doctrines of loving your enemy weaken you with blind ignorance. Do not hate those who do not believe as we do, and offer honor and respect to all we meet in our journey through life, no matter how different they might be, so long as they honor and respect us in kind.

Do not walk in the darkness that is Hoder, but instead, walk in the light that is Balder, for his light is love. Be proud but not arrogant. Be strong but not aggressive. Walk through life with Balder's love in your heart—love for your Folk, friends, family and kin, and especially for yourself.

Life is a great journey, so make the most of it. Be happy and do things that will make you happy, but do not do that which will harm others or yourself. Remember, *like attracts like*.

Be aware that what you dwell on, what you obsess over will be manifested in your life a hundred times over.

There is no heaven nor hell. There is no reward or punishment in the afterlife. The life you lead in this world, will determine the nature of the life you will lead in the hereafter—so lead a good life. The life you live now, will echo in eternity.

Hail the strong, for they will rule themselves. Damned are the meek, for they will be dictated to by their oppressors.

Hail the powerful, for no enemy can harm them. Damned are the weak, for they will be ploughed under.

Hail the brave, for they will dare great deeds. Damned are the humble, for they will be destroyed and forgotten.

Hail the victorious, for they will be right in all that they do, because might does make right. Damned are the defeated, for they will be slaves to those are victorious.

Hail the ruthless, for the weak will cower before them. Damned are the weak-willed, for they will be cursed.

Hail the courageous, for their lives will be glorious. Damned are the day-dreamers, for they will waste their lives.

Hail those who place their welfare, and the welfare of their kin and kindred before aliens and foreigners, for they will prosper and be fruitful. Damned are those who placed the welfare of others before their own kind, for they will be condemned to oblivion and live in slavery.

Hail those who are hated by their enemies, for that hate is a measure of one's greatness. Damned are those who help those who despise them, for they are their own worst enemy.

Hail those who dream great deeds, for they will become great and mighty. Damned are those who preach lies as truth, for they are a curse to all who follow them.

WORKING TOWARD THE NEW AGE OF GIMLI

As we enter the twenty-first century, technical and scientific innovations have made advances over the last hundred years that have transformed our lives, allowing us to enjoy a material comfort and possessing wealth, beyond anything imaginable to our ancestors. The vast majority of people could never hope to have lived in such material comfort as we enjoy today. Even the "filthy rich" did not have such luxuries as cell phones, the Internet, automobiles racing along at 90 mph, and most of the modern conveniences that we take for granted today. These technological devices were just the imaginative fantasies of such science fiction writers as Jules Verne and H. G. Wells one hundred years ago. Truly, our material world has made marvelous advancements in the last one hundred and fifty years, but our spiritual development has not kept pace with our material development. In fact, over the last century, it has come under attack by the secularism of the political correctness that has come to dominate our civilization. And though we are materialistically better off, we have discovered that we are not as happy or content as our ancestors.

We have been conditioned to view the pagan beliefs and way of life of our ancestors as backward and belonging to a phase of life that was riddled with superstition and barbarism. The ruling establishment of our society in the twenty-first century, has conditioned us to conform to a single view on life, one governed by a secular belief that man is simply a piece of clay that can be fashioned and molded into any form and shape that the ruling establish desires. Through an insidious program of control over all education, cultural, and information media, the establishment maintains a system that dominates our lives, and formulates the way we look at the world and our relationship to it. The accepted world-view of the global society rejects the true relationship between humans and the physical environment they live within. The ruling establishment has rejected the pagan view of a living Earth as a living organism, filled with the power of the Vril. It rejects the notion that the universe is filled with the Life Force of the Gods (Vril) and that this creative energy maintains the physical laws of science that gives order to the universe. Our pagan ancestors understood this basic and fundamental fact, and this fact is being proved by new discoveries in Quantum Physics. They realized that they were part of Nature, and governed by its laws, and that they were one with the Gods that created them and the universe, and that they shared the same Life Force (both spiritually and physically) with their Gods. The pagan philosopher Basilius Valentinus, summed up this relationship. "The earth is not a dead body, but is inhabited by the spirit that is the life and soul. All created things draw their strength from the earth spirit (the Vril). This spirit of life, which is nourished by the stars, and gives nourishment to all living creatures sheltered within its womb." Basilius Valentinus clearly knew of the existence of the Vril and understood its relationship with all things within the universe.

The spiritual quality of our lives has actually declined considerably over the last century. The dream that technology alone could build a better future with a superior way of life is crumbling around as crime, pollution, terrorism, cultural decline and globalism initiates a clash of civilizations that could spell the doom of the entire world. The twentieth century has been one of social engineering of every political strip. Communism, Socialism, Liberalism, Fascism and National Socialism all accepted the premise that through government-control social programs, we could change the human condition and even transform the human being into something new and better. All have failed. We have discovered that material affluence has actually increased anxiety. It has created a gnawing fear of losing everything we have acquired materially in our lives. This dread has become a constant shadow hovering over our lives. Many people have lost faith in the future and seek release from this constant dread, by abandoning themselves to a life of wanton hedonism, indulging in every bizarre and exotic behavior imaginable, in a mad rush to seek release from the hollowness of their meaningless lives. Still, others find death a release from the mundane, assembly-line drudgery of our modern existence. Most people today have simply surrendered to the soulless, rootless and crass existence that permeates, and increasingly dominates, the secular, politically correct, totalitarianism that now passes for culture. They have come to accept their new reality of quiet desperation.

"Humpy Dumpty sat on a wall. Humpty Dumpty had a great fall. All the king's horses and all the king's men, couldn't put Humpty Dumpty back together again." There is an eternal truism in this simple nursery rhyme. The second law of thermodynamics declares that disorder and chaos will always increase and consume what man has made. Therefore, it is important that man maintain what he creates. The spiritual foundation of our present age (Western Civilization) has been permitted to entropy. In fact, the ruling establishment has actually worked to undermine this spiritual foundation. They have pushed Humpty Dumpty off the wall and not only cannot put him back together, they consciously destroyed him. As a result, chaos rules supreme!

The ruling establishment has opened Pandora's box. By abandoning their traditional Christian-Western culture in favor of globalism, they had removed the restrictive restrains that have held the Gods in the Netherworld. The age of material rationalism that has governed the West for the last three hundred years has come to an end. It has destroyed the spiritual foundation for the supremacy of the West in favor of a new Globalist vision of the world. But outside the West, the rest of the world has not come to embrace this vision and is in a state of rebellion—a rebellion that is winning due to the irrational and unrealistic vision that the Globalists seek to force upon mankind. Faced with this reality, the Folk Faith seeks to teach a new system of metaphysical science based on the mystical physics of the Vril. We are discovering—or should I say, rediscovering—the forgotten knowledge of the ancient Atlantean Aryans that all life is part of the eternal current of change and evolution, which is the power of the Vril, and the Life Force of the Gods. We have come to realize that the universe was fashioned by the Gods and sustained in an orderly fashion by a unifying Life Force. That this universe is in a constant process of growth and development, producing new forms and variations in the cyclical process of evolution. And that this cycle of existence is powered by Vril, and that Vril can be harnessed by man for his own growth and development and used to control his evolutionary progress. And that its power can be harnessed to create a better civilization—an organic civilization—living in harmony with the Gods that gave us life.

We are not just animals, which are born, exist and die. Our lives must be dedicated to some higher purpose that is the expression of some higher noble ideal. Individually and collectively, we are part of the struggle for existence, the struggle for upward evolution. But in the chaotic world of the twenty-first century, we find ourselves plunged into a new sword age, an axe age, a wolf age, where whole societies, as well as individuals and families, find themselves swept up in the whirlwind conflicts that are causing the disintegration of our civilization and the world order that have existed for centuries. It has resulted in our people wandering aimlessly through life, lacking the necessary moral integrity, and understanding for the vital and essential values needed to guide us through such times. During a more peaceful and orderly age, this would not be such a great crisis, but in the culture-depraved, nation-less and mass-man age that exists today, such a state of existence sells certain doom.

We have the means to utilize the power of Vril through the Science of Vrilology. Thus, our reality is created by our thoughts and will. Since this is so, we must be on our guard on how we think. We must examine how our reality in the outer or objective world is created through the people we come into contact with and how they interact in our lives. We must be guarded against psychic vampires who will exploit us and draw us down to their level of lower consciousness. It is so easy to be drawn into this lower level of existence of degeneracy and be seduced by the chaotic whirlwind of the Giants of herd instincts.

You must rise above the herd mentality of the unconscious masses. Do not follow false Pie-Pipers who sap your creative energies and faculties of mind and cause you to pursue non-productive and self-destructive lifestyles that will lead you to your early doom. You should learn from your mistakes and listen to those who have suffered these mistakes in their youth so that you do not waste your lives. Resist the temptation of fitting in and following the herd because it is easier, and live the heroic life of improvement that is manifested by following your inner instincts.

This universal truth was once known among our most ancient ancestors. The Atlantean Aryans who lived along the shores of the Black Sea were the guardians of this ancient knowledge. After the destruction of their civilization, the knowledge was retained, partially, by the priestly class of the scattered survivors of the destruction of their civilization. They maintained, through the millenniums, an awareness of the essence of the power that is the Gods as having a threefold level of understanding. This understanding is visualized by the *valknutr*.

The first level of understanding is new, or rediscovered understanding of the metaphysical science, which is Vril, the Life Force of the Gods, visualized as the Yggdrasill, and which fills the universe, giving it order by the Gods. The second level of understanding is Dualism of Light and Darkness, Matter and Anti-matter, Male and Female, Ice and Fire, Order and Chaos. This principle is the force of evolution from which the cycles of the universe and all growth and development is built upon. The opposing forces do not represent good vs. evil, but forces that need to be balanced. The final level is that of the Archetypes. They are the magical personification of the Gods and Goddesses as mythological deities. They are humanized deities that are the foundation of the Indo-European pantheons of Gods and Goddesses. This principle has also influenced the pantheons belonging to other Indo-European religions, as well as non-European religions. Dr. Carl Jung claimed that these archetypes are the personification of recognized human qualities and needs which shape our dreams, myths, spirituality, legends and folklore. But we must understand that these archetypes are real beings who are perceived differently by different races due to a combination of diverse gene pools and environments.

With the end of the second millennium we are ending a time of enormous change. In astrological terms, the Age of Pisces—the fish, which represents Jesus—has come to an end and we are now entering the Age of Aquarius. The Piscean ideal was to accept on faith what was told to us to be the truth by those in charge, but now we are entering a new age of knowledge. Aquarius is the age of the water bearer—whose ideals proclaim that it is time for man to understand once more and not accept what is told to us in blind ignorance. When Constantine the Great convened the Council of Nicaea in the fourth century A.D., he refashioned the religion of our ancestors into a new form that would stand the test of time. He understood that the Age of Aries had come to an end and that people needed order and structure in the growing chaos that was spreading across the world of his age. He created a new religion—a single religion—that assimilated the warring factions of the growing new cult of Christianity and the old pagan religions. By making Christianity the official religion of the Roman Empire, he was able to transform it, incorporating the old beliefs into it in new form. He transformed the Semitic cult into a religion that worshiped *Sol Invictus*, the Invincible Sun—Balder. In this single act, he did not convert the sun-worshiping pagans into Christians, but converted Christians into worshipers of the Sun—Balder. Instead of worshiping a Jewish rebel on the Jewish Sabbath, as the early Christians did, they began to attend church services on Balder's Day—Sunday. For the last two millenniums Christians have been going to church on Sunday to worship the Sun God—Balder.

As the time of faith comes to an end, people now need to understand. Once again the Gods will reveal their presence to our Folk. People see the old order disintegrating before them. All around them they can witness for themselves the decline of order and the spreading chaos. They can hear the call of the rooster, warning us of the approaching darkness. The gates of Asgard will soon be stormed and the rainbow bridge will collapse under the weight of the combined forces of the Giant hordes led by Loki. Heimdall will not be able to stop the invasion and will fall fighting Loki. The Midgard Serpent will rise from the cold, dark depths in which he sleeps, to battle Thor, and the great wolf will battle with Odin. But through it all, the regenerative powers of Balder will continue to pulsate throughout the universe and provide us with an opportunity to survive the great Ragnarok. We cannot only survive, but be reborn if we take refuge in the branches of the Yggdrasill (Vril).

As the chaotic forces of the Giants come to dominate our lives in the decades that lie ahead of us, most people have no real understanding of the factors that are shaping their existence. They have been blinded by the ignorance of Hoder, but they still instinctively know that something bad is taking place, though their comprehension of what it is, is beyond their grasp. And yet, if they possessed the means to improve their lives without relying on the patronage of an ever increasing intrusive establishment, they would discover a great liberation from this soulless, meaningless existence. This ability to become masters of their own destiny would improve conditions and produce a new spiritually, which would fill their lives with happiness, love and joy. This is the goal of the Folk Faith. It is meant to make our Folk self-reliant, providing the opportunity for them to change their lives and provide them with the means to survive the coming Ragnarok. This can only be done through a greater understanding of, who we are, where we came from, and the realization that we are not just gulps of flesh and blood animated by the instinct to survive.

The purpose of the Folk Faith is to provide the means by which we can retake command of our destiny. This can only be done by re-forging those lost bonds that we once shared with the Gods who created us. To accomplish this, we must awaken the Gods who sleep within us. Once this has been accomplished, we can harness their Life Force and use it to transform ourselves with the regenerative power of Balder rising—the Vril.

Hail Odin!
Hail Balder!
Wunjo!!!

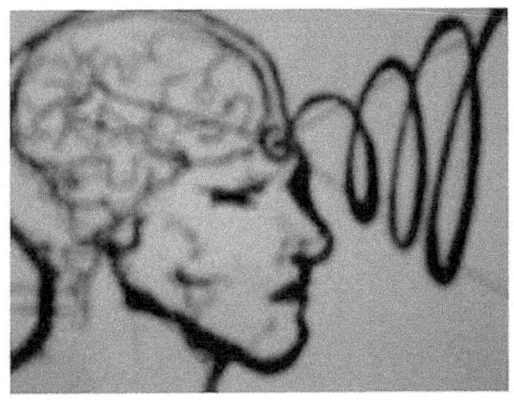

The Third Eye or the Bifrost Gland

Possible locations and design of the city of Atlantis at the bottom of the Black Sea.

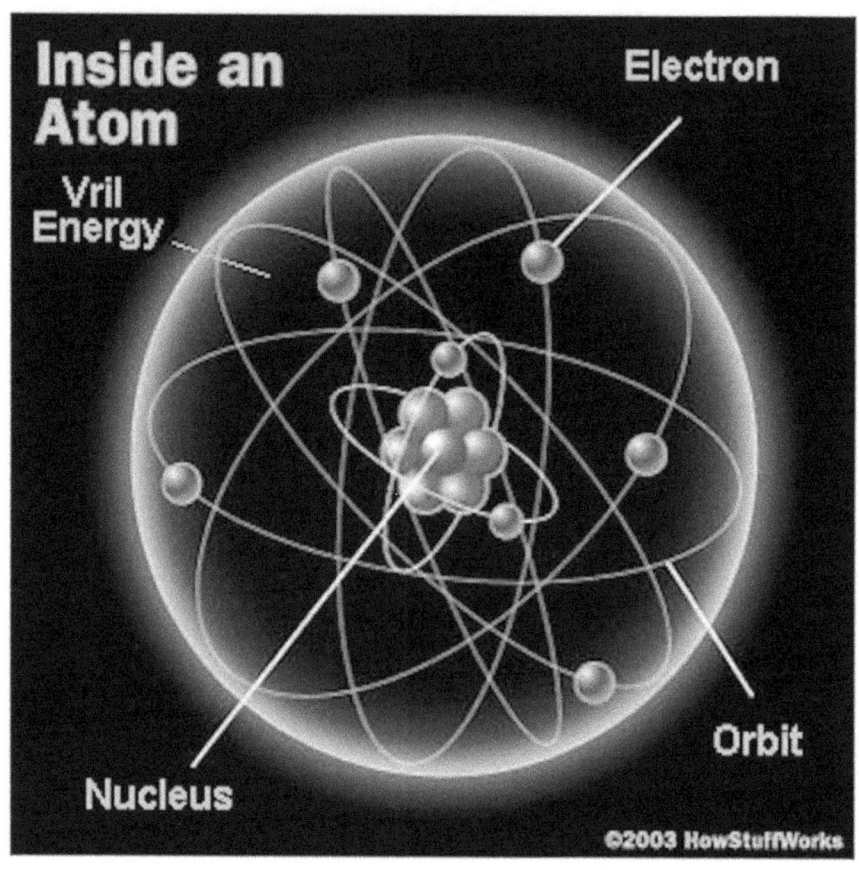

The structure of the atom with its subatomic particles and Vril energy.

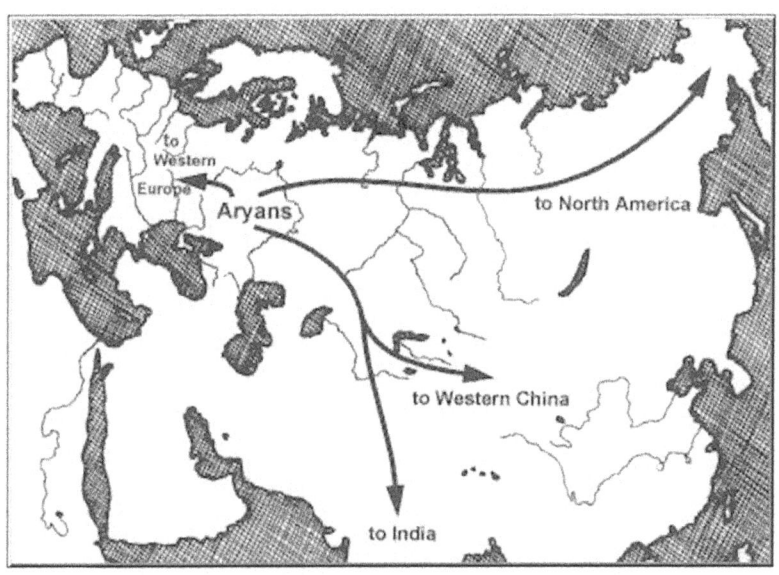

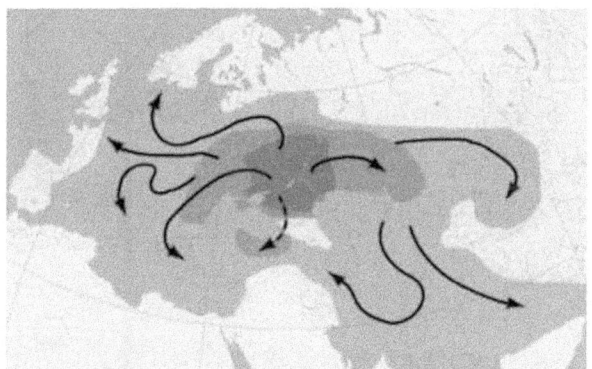

The wander lust of the Indo-Europeans after the destruction of the originial Aryan civilization along the Black Sea is destroyed.

MIDGARD STATE OF CONSCIOUSNESS
(Beta) Alert-working

ASGARD STATE OF CONSCIOUSNESS
(Alpha) Relaxed/Reflective

GLADSHEIM STATE OF CONSCIOUSNESS
(Theta) Sleep/Dreaming

HEL STATE OF CONSCIOUSNESS
(Delta) Deep Sleep/Dreamless Sleep

Brainwaves

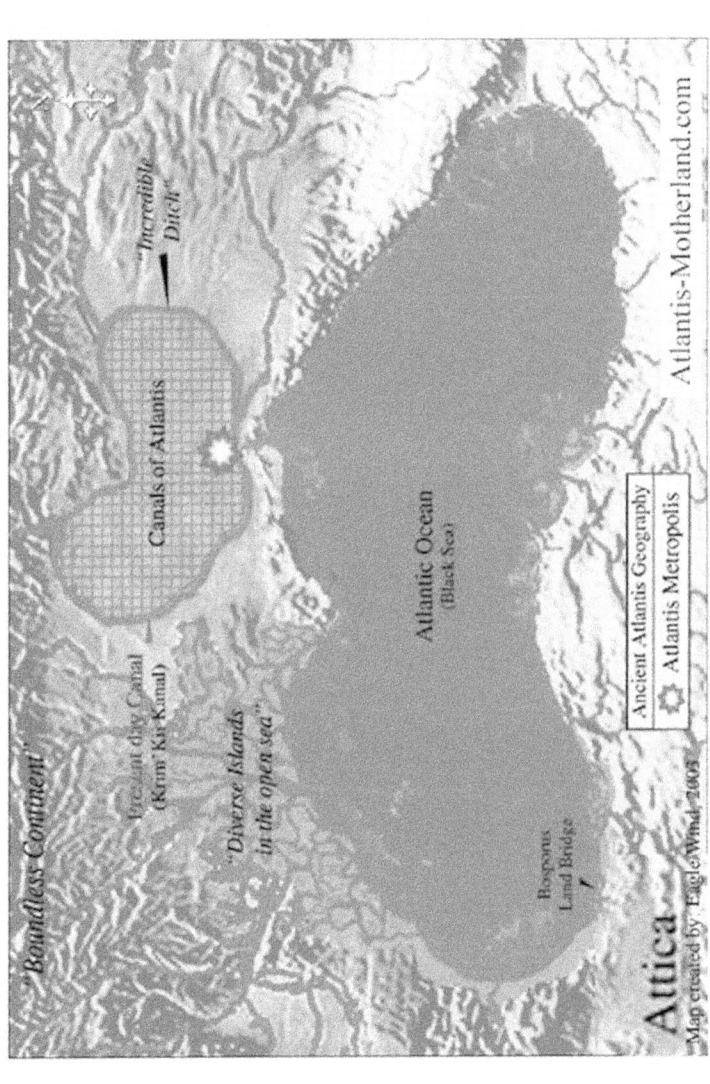

The Black Sea 6,000 B.C.E. and the possible location of Atlantis.

Ancient Druids sacrificing a Bull

Montsegur

Montsegur

Knights of the Holy Grail

The Grail Castle on Montsegur

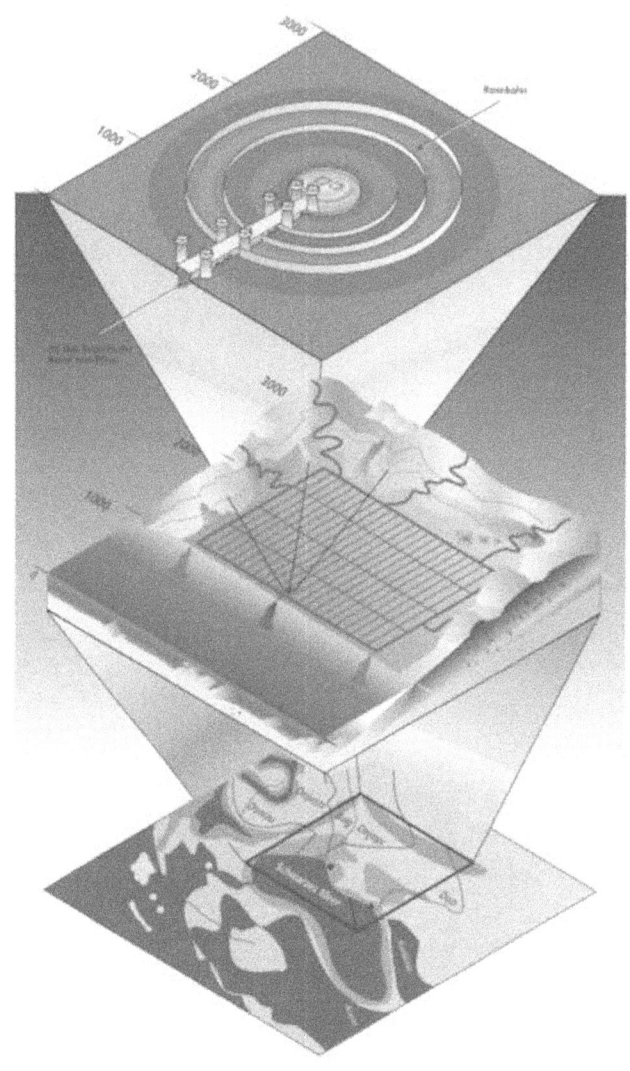

Location of Atlantis at the bottom of the Black Sea.

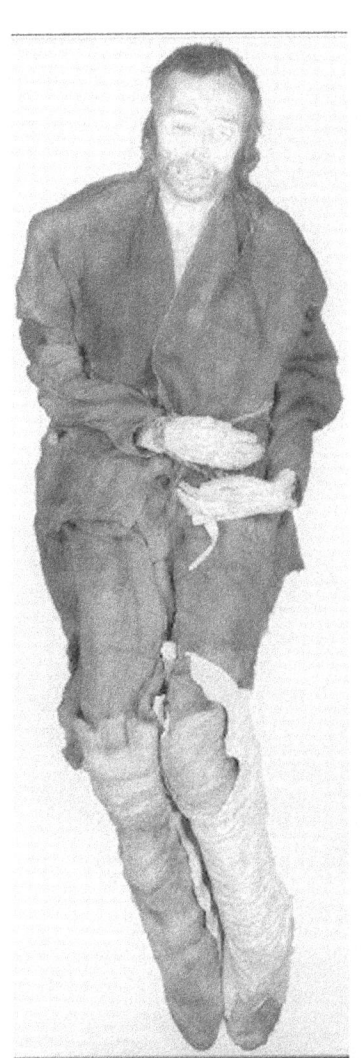 

Tocharan mummies found in northwest China.

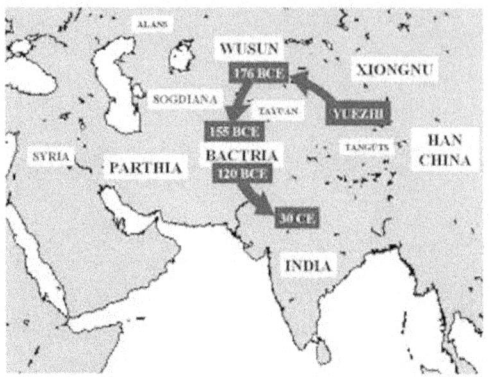

The migrantion of the Tocharians through Central Asia to India.

Zoroaster

The march of the Tocharians from 5600 B.C to 200 A.D.

1. Refugees from the flooding of the Black Sea, 5600 B.C.

2. Tocharians move through central Asia and settle in India.

3. Tocharians who conquer Tibet and found the Bon Religion.

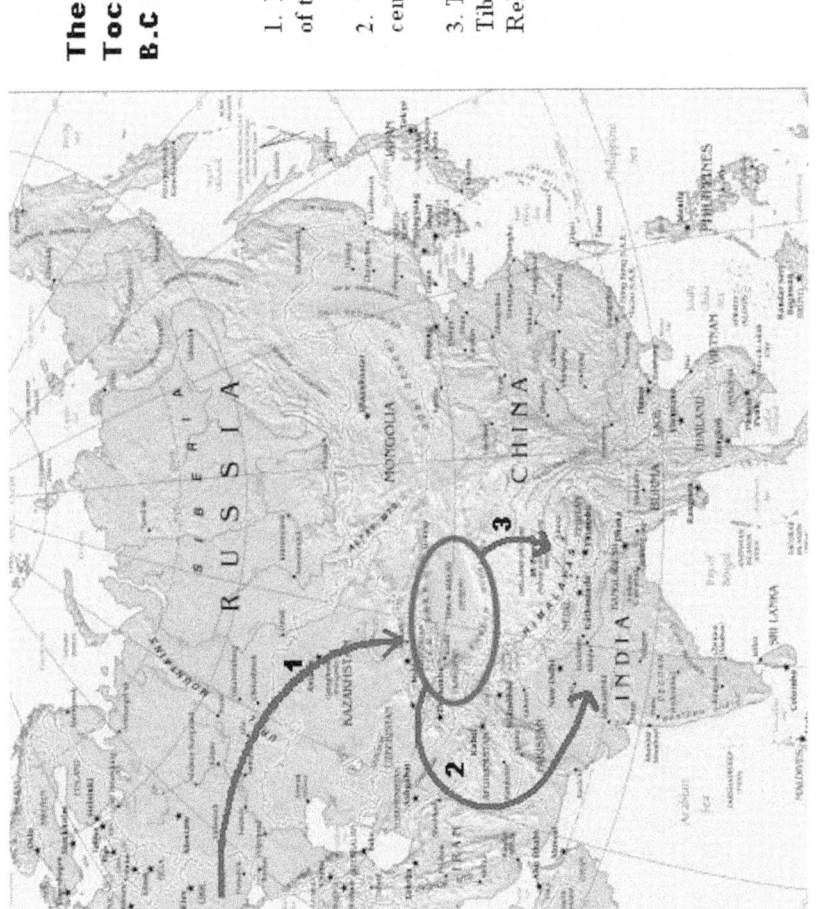

Paintings of the Tocharians with the Chinese from China.

The Phoneix rising from the flames.

America's ruling class engage in pagan ceremonies at a meeting of the Bohemian Grove.

The Twenty-four Runes of the Elder Futhark

Fehu	Hagalaz	Tiwaz
Uruz	Nauthiz	Berkano
Thurisaz	Isa	Ehwaz
Ansuz	Jera	Mannaz
Raidho	Eihwaz	Laguz
Kenaz	Perthro	Ingwaz
Gebo	Elhaz	Dagaz
Wunjo	Sowilo	Othala

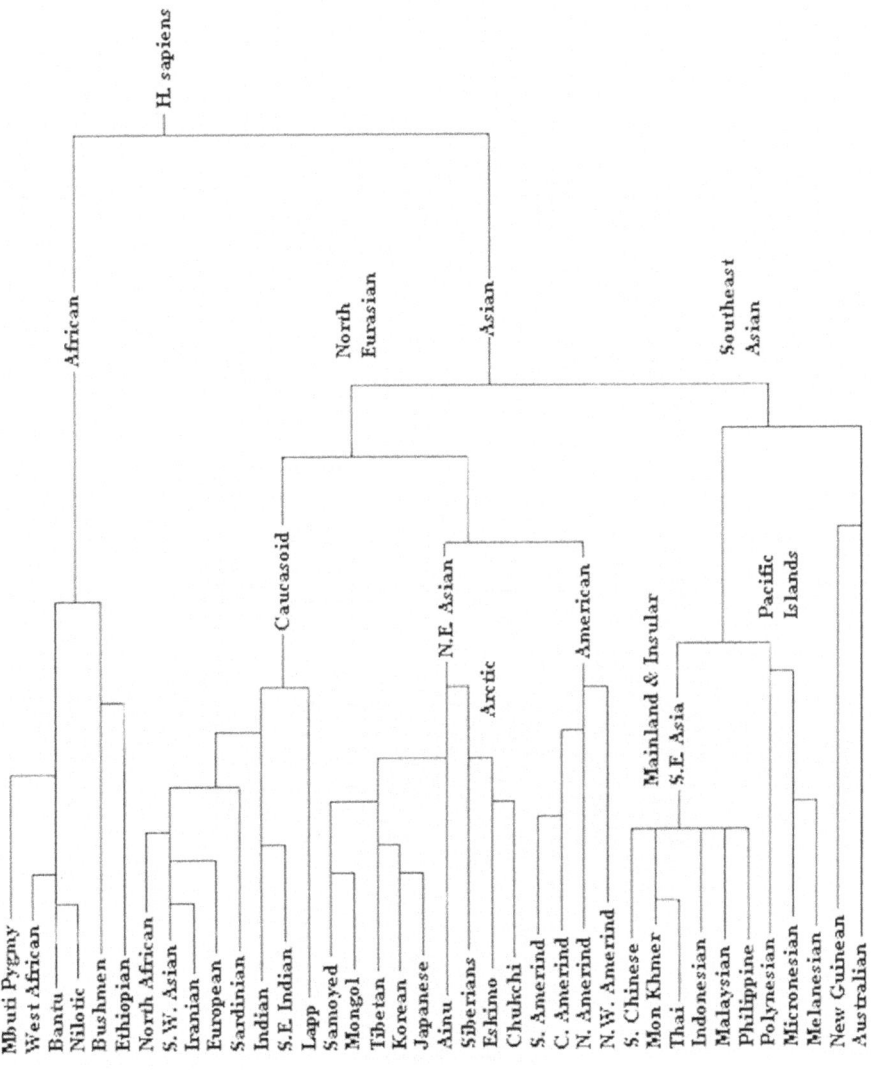

Genetic relationships among different racial and ethnic groups.

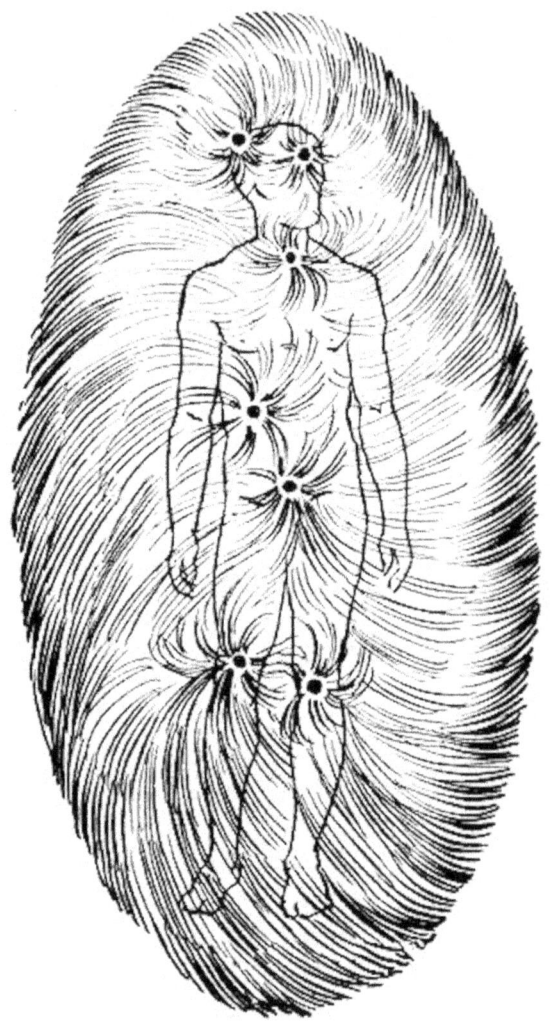

Vril energy currents of the ordinary man according to the Rosicrucians

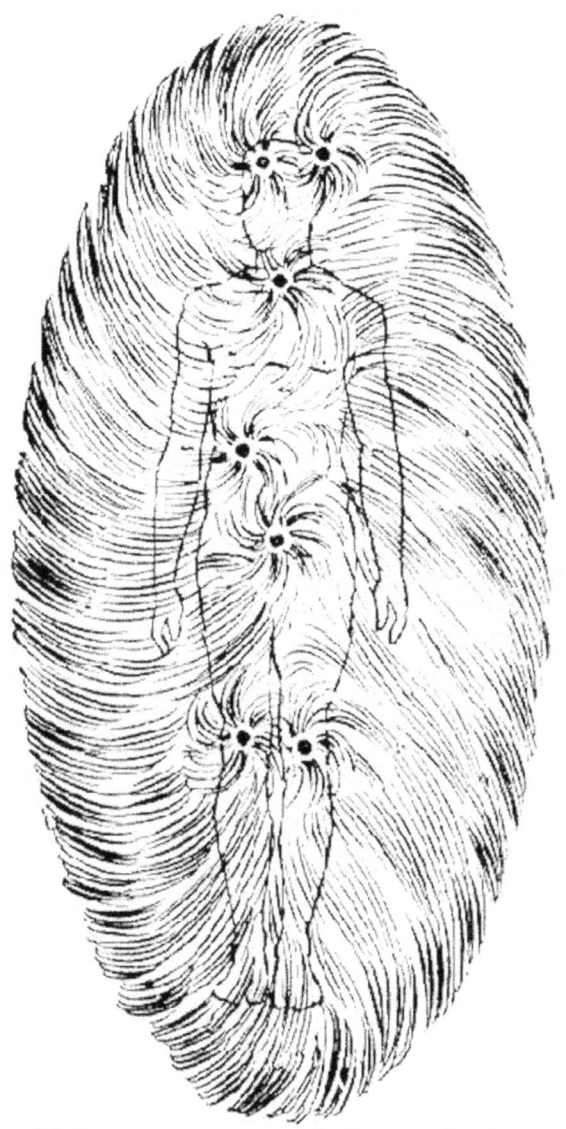

Vril energy currents in human body trained to harness and control the Vril furrents according to the Rosicrucians

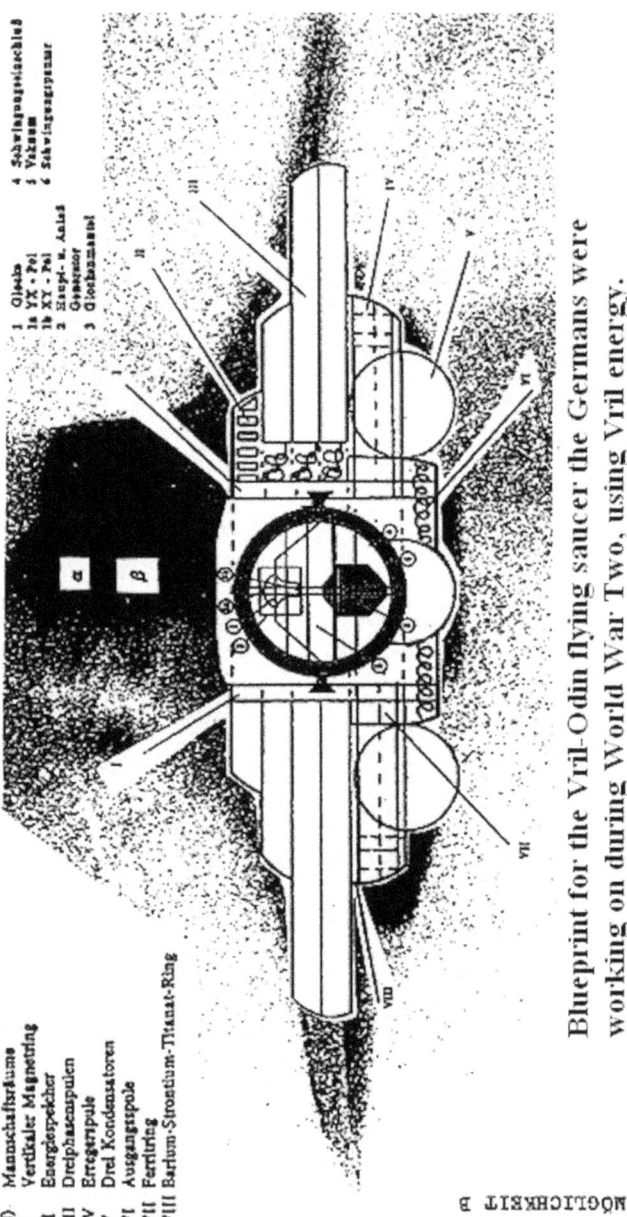

Blueprint for the Vril-Odin flying saucer the Germans were working on during World War Two, using Vril energy.

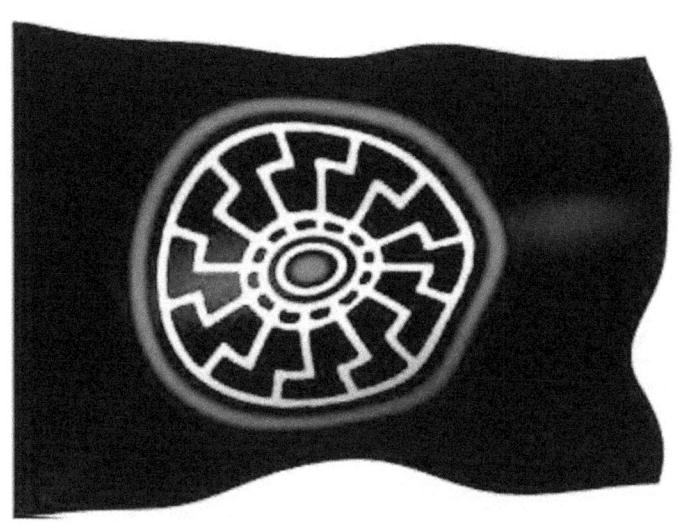

Symbols of the German Vril Society

Pictures of Viktor Schauberger, at ago 40 years olf, and later in life.

Madam Blavatsky

The Three Nrons: Urd (Past), Verdanadi (Present) and Skuld (Future).

978-0-595-38504-1
0-595-38504-4

Lightning Source UK Ltd.
Milton Keynes UK
UKHW041848180419
341265UK00001B/29/P